Psychology at the Threshold:
Selected Papers from the Proceedings of the International Conference at University of California, Santa Barbara, 2000

Edited by
Dennis Patrick Slattery, Ph.D.
Lionel Corbett, M.D.

Pacifica Graduate Institute Publications
Pacifica Graduate Institute

This volume is dedicated to all of our students, colleagues and friends who have mustered the requisite courage and curiosity to step across the threshold of what they know, to entertain the unknown.

Hermes bore himself over many waves.
But when he arrived at the island that was far away,
He stepped from the violetlike ocean onto the dry land,
And went on till he came to the great cave wherein the nymph
Of the fair braids was dwelling. (Homer's Odyssey, 5.55-58)

An archetype standing for change itself, he [Hermes] pops up whenever change is imminent.
(Ginette Paris' Pagan Grace, 1991, p. 110)

Whereas Hermes permeates the whole world because of his possibility of making
connections... He is the connection-maker and he is the Messenger of the Gods. (Lopez-
Pedraza's Hermes and His Children, 1977, p. 8)

Hermes is closely related to door hinges and therefore to the entrance, but also to a middle
point, to the socket, about which revolves the most decisive issue, namely the alternation life-
death-life. (Kerenyi's Hermes Guide of Souls: The Mythologem, 1976, p.84)

Cover: Image supplied by the Art Renewal Center artrenewal.org: "Psyche Entering Cupid's Garden" by John William Waterhouse

Library of Congress Cataloguing-in-Publication Data

Psychology at the threshold / edited by Dennis Patrick Slattery and Lionel Corbett.
Includes bibliographical references and index.
ISBN: 0-9723966-0-8 (pbk)

1. Psychology—theory and praxis. 2. Psychology and culture. 3. Psychology and history, mythology.

Pacifica Graduate Institute
249 Lambert Road
Carpinteria, California 93013
www.pacifica.edu

Table of Contents

Preface: Stepping Across the Threshold by Stephen Aizenstat, Ph.D.

This volume of selected papers from the international conference, Psychology at the Threshold 2000, held at the University of California, Santa Barbara, represents only a sampling of presentations that seek to imagine psyche into the future while remembering her past. In these pages, a diverse body of voices gathers to imagine psychology as an active participant in the culture, society and environment of the 21st. century.

Sponsored by Pacifica Graduate Institute, supported by various organizations that believe in the mission of the school, and organized under the visionary leadership of James Hillman, this conference, and the papers that emanated from it had a simple goal in mind: to challenge the presenters to offer their freshest images, ideas and approaches to describing, narrating and revisioning the complex relationship of Psyche and world. These papers extend and deepen the discipline of depth psychology, which has been informed by a long lineage of women and men who looked and listened with a metaphoric, poetic and imaginal sensibility to the subtleties of human experience. While pausing at the Threshold of another millennium, conference presenters and participants collectively honored, embraced and remembered the great traditions of mythology, literature and world religions all under the rubric of depth psychology. We are in the unique position of holding the tension between the push from 100 years of depth and archetypal psychological traditions and Psyche's pull toward the future; in such a movement we experience the generative impulse that is breaking through psychic reality in the present.

Jung himself returned often to the idea and the impulse of the Threshold as a key archetypal image as well as a profound psychological space. For example, he guides us into this terrain in writing that "not without justice we connect consciousness, by analogy, with the sense functions, from the physiology of which the whole idea of 'threshold' is derived" (CW 8, par. 367). Thresholds create a confluence between the senses, between the sensate world and psyche as well as establish the connective boundary between sensations, stimuli and consciousness wherein certain impulses gather enough energy to become "capable of crossing the threshold, that is, of becoming perceptions" (CW 9,ii, par. 3).

This volume then pulls diverse voices together in order to contribute back into the field of contemporary applied psychology as well as to the culture an archetypal perspective that promotes and assists new ideas and images to cross the Threshold into a fuller consciousness. As an institution, Pacifica senses its unique role in the field to protect and sustain the lineage of archetypal, imaginal psychology and to coax the field forward by listening to the new emerging voices and to honor what lingers importantly and profoundly on the margins.

We recall for a moment Pacifica's motto: Animae mundi colendae gratia, wherein the verb, colendae, derived from the Latin colere, began as a verb used in agriculture to designate 'to cultivate the fields.' Through time it metamorphosed into the verb used in connection with the work of those who tended the temples. The word itself draws our attention to a Threshold crossed from nature to culture to the gods and goddesses that guard a city. This idea of guardianship is at the heart not only of Pacifica but of our collective continued work with Psyche and the world. Cultivation of ideas and images draws us toward new Thresholds that consolidate new ideas in a rubric that continues the spirit of tilling both earth and Psyche wherein both are mutually and continually seeded.

Since I seem to have found myself in the natural order here, I am reminded of Walt Whitman's wonderful short poem, "A Farm Picture," that amplifies this Threshold archetype:

> Through the ample open door of the peaceful country barn,
>
> A sunlit pasture filled with cattle and horses feeding,
>
> And haze and vista, and the far horizon fading away.

Psychology at the Threshold extends Whitman's poetic image of seeing through. His poem is a simple and profound witness to the power of Thresholds as ways of seeing anew by means of seeing through. Thresholds are corridors of seeing and avenues for imagining; Thresholds are frames of reference, with no guarantee that all that is envisioned is fully clear or ever exhausted in its meaning. On the contrary, new Thresholds may at first offer hazy vistas and a "far horizon fading away." But the ground has been recognized; something new is on the horizon of consciousness, some novel seeing is promised as first one and then another image gathers itself with enough psychic force to cross the Threshold into consciousness.

This conference and these papers as witnesses to many new ideas and images crossing over the Threshold into awareness once again reinforces the power of the poetic Psyche as it seeks analogies in the world in order to foster new ways of seeing and new methods for actively engaging the world. We at Pacifica Graduate Institute like to think that such imaginal activity is at the heart of our enterprise. The diversity of arguments, images and ideas that unfold in these pages, after our friend, colleague and leader, James Hillman, has with the finesse and elegance that are his benchmarks, indeed set the table for the banquet that followed in those memorable days of August-September, 2000, is a fitting tribute to the banquet that you, readers, may be able to choose from in order to relish a few select courses.

I want to end with some of James' words as a fitting beginning to lifting one foot, then the other, across the Threshold into a new millennium:

Below the historical psyche and the movement of time lies the timeless psyche of archetypal urges. To sort out the receding from the oncoming, the dying from the living and to honor the dead without succumbing to their numbing power, all the while trying to discern the soul's moving images within the passing parade --such are the tasks of psychology at the Threshold. In what ways may the knowledge gained in the last hundred years bear upon the next? What viable seeds can be culled from old husks?

So we gather the tribe under the metaphor of a rural farming image, dispense the menu, lift our glasses and welcome all who enter these pages into the feast, one whose own promises of continued Threshold crossing remain alive on every page. Such is our hope, if not our promise. Buon appetit!

ACKNOWLEDGEMENTS

We express our gratitude to the following individuals and groups for assisting in making this volume a reality:

* Pacifica Graduate Institute and to its president, Stephen Aizenstat, for supporting the publication of this volume.

* James Hillman for initiating the conference, Psychology at the Threshold for the Fall, 2000.

* The presenters and panelists who spoke, sang, danced, recited, performed magic and jigged a jog, and then prepared their presentations for publication.

* The presenters who submitted papers that were ultimately not included because of space limits.

* The participants who entered freely and generously into the mayhem, the methods and the musings of all that presented itself.

* All of our students who join us in classes, seminars, conferences and gatherings, and who are willing to encourage, challenge and extend our own work.

* Nina Falls, our able and indispensable assistant who gathered, organized, and pieced together what appeared at times an unwieldy mosaic. She helped immensely to create a coherent text.

* The University of California, Santa Barbara, for their gracious hosting, fine food, beautiful campus facilities that sit on the cusp of the Pacific ocean. It was a perfect setting for a conference on Psychology at the Threshold.

* The human imagination's courage to cross thresholds, push back borders, slip under doorways, crawl up and over walls, dip below fences in order to see what has only begun to be revealed in psyche's meanderings to know itself and the world in this century.

* All who read these provocative essays and are inspired, provoked, incited to respond to them, and to carry these ideas forward.

*Let all of these figures and forms continue to emerge "out of the cradle, endlessly rocking."

Dennis Patrick Slattery, Ph.D.

Lionel Corbett, M.D.

Laying the Table[1] by James Hillman, Ph.D.

First, a toast to the spirits present in this place during these days and nights. May you not be too offended; may you even be pleased.

Second, a toast of welcome to each of you who has found your way here. Thank you for coming. You, participants, audience, attendees -- such denigrating words -- are the stuff, the matrix of whatever happens here in the coming days. *You* are the conference; we speakers are your guests. Your intelligence and good will, and your tenacity, will very much determine the echo of these days in other places and later times.

I shall take advantage of this official welcome to express my unofficial joy to be with so many personal friends and close colleagues. We meet here and there, off and on, but now all in one place for a weekend summit -- and with no problems to solve, no decisions to take. So welcome and hello Luigi Zoja from Italy, and Gustavo Barcellos and Roberto Gambini from Brazil, and Kalichi from Ireland -- how good of you to come. Hello Peter Bishop from Australia, Enrique Pardo from Paris and Allan Guggenbuhl from Zurich, and my dear friend Kazuhiko Higuchi from Japan. Welcome, from England, Noel Cobb and Richard Olivier, Mark Kidel, Alan Bleakley and Sonu Shamdasani. And heartfelt welcome to friend and superb critic Wolfgang Giegerich from Germany.

Through many years I have relied upon the thinking minds and good hearts of reliable friends -- David Miller, Ginette Paris, Mary Watkins, Ed Casey, Paul Kugler, Coleman Barks, Dennis Slattery, Stan Marlan, Robert Sardello. I call them on the phone to find things out; they send me notes and clippings, and laughs. Thank the Gods we can all be here together.

We are especially honored by the presence of Dan Kemmis, Ted Roszak and Andre Codrescu for the perceptive originality which has taken psychology's intuitions into the public arena. We are further most honored by the presence of Sharon Olds whose precise poetic insights have enriched psychology. I have used -- or misused -- her poems to teach psychology for many years. And last, but never, never least, a big and loving welcome to my companions in arms, inspirers and challengers, Michael Meade and Robert Bly who led me into their remarkable invention of men's retreats.

A special welcome in behalf of everyone here to Thomas Kapacinscas whose initiative launched the notorious Notre Dame Conference in 1992 -- the background to this unique and complex phenomenon: deliberative festival, consortium of scholars, public forum, sideshow, artsy party, family reunion, professional convention, picnic, weekend bash, celebration, feast, *eranos*.

Finally I draw your attention to what is emerging from Pacifica Graduate Institute: the presentations by faculty, alumni and graduate students, showing the ever-widening directions of an archetypal psychology's flourishing imagination.

*   *   *

During the final months of the twentieth century the modernized world went though a preparatory ritual. The presence of the unpredictable, the invisible loomed. We called this presence WY-TOO-KAY, and devoted immense concentration and tedious labor to the minutiae of prevention. Imagination focused on what could go wrong; catastrophe, apocalypse.

The fact that nothing happened, that the evening and morning of the new millennium dawned and passed as usual into another day, another year, another century, without incident affirmed to the intelligentsia of science, business, government and academia that we could rely on reason and human will. The defeat of WY-TOO-KAY reconfirmed the triumph of the Western mind. It was not at the end of its tether (H.G. Wells). Apocalyptic catastrophe was merely a myth.

Could we snatch some defeat from the jaws of this victory? Could we draw another, different lesson from that midnight anxiety, the preparatory rituals, the countdown of last winter's night?

We might have learned how inextricably interdependent is the world for its daily existence; that the machinery to which we have delivered our life-support systems can suffer massive breakdown; that we must devote more and more of our lifetimes to servicing systems we neither control nor even understand, yet on which we depend. For without these systems we are left isolated in tall buildings, cold dark houses, tangled in directionless traffic; food, water and shelter depending on the kindness of strangers, reduced overnight to that condition Hobbes (<u>Leviathan 1</u>, 13) described: "solitary, poore, nasty, brutish, and short."

We might also have learned that signal moments of the calendar must be heeded. For the calendar is a divine, perhaps divining, instrument opening to mythical powers whose movements it attempts to record in numbers. The schedule book and weekly agenda cannot keep out the Gods. Holidays, Holy Days, even the day's very names remind of their presence all week long. Their breakthrough or break-in is always possible, and rituals acknowledging them always necessary. We have been closer to the recognition of the power of myth during the last frantic days of 1999 than in the triumphal ignorance of January 2000.

We have come together from many parts, drawn by a program whose title states clearly that the millennium is still in mind. Y2K is still in the air. But the catastrophe averted is not the monster slain, and it is in the presence of the monster and the terror of helplessness it evokes that the archetypal psyche recovers its great myths of creation, of survival, and of a heroically founded civilization.

The questions we address here are placed in this calendar period. We are "after the catastroph," a phrase I take from the patron of these meetings, C.G. Jung. With what questions does psychology engage now; are its foundations adequate to that dreaded midnight? What revision must psychology undergo in practice and thought when catastrophe is kept in mind as the cradle from which this century's psychology emerges?

The maladies and issues psychologists presume to be today's currency -- family, relationship, spirituality, diversity, violence, gender, consumerism, addiction, community -- are remnants of the last phase of the last century. The language in which we encase our cases belongs to a time that already seems strangely distant: conscious and unconscious, projection and integration, ego and self, feminine and masculine, opposites and wholeness, development and regression, transference and counter-transference -- how professional and technical they strike the ear, how tired and jaded and worn away with over use, and how very far from carrying any of the menace of the monster or an adequate response to the power it can constellate.

Something grander is needed, foundations of vision and value that offer universal validity, else so-called depth psychology will be dibbling around in the topsoil of our personal gardens while Y2K is shifting the tectonic plates on which our private plots rest. Psychology is called by the monster to reach beyond itself, its techniques, its models of thought, its language, especially its language, so as to realize itself as a defender of civilization, adventurer of culture and advocate of soul. Depth psychology after all arose at a high point of central Europe's culture, its practitioners highly civilized, and its name proclaims it the psyche's thoughtful advocate.

Robert Sardello, Wolfgang Giegerich and Mary Watkins -- to name but three of those here -- have already seen the narrow paucity of psychology's self-conception: its obsession with subjectivity. Each has made a major turn: Sardello to differentiated spirit; Giegerich to relentless thinking; Watkins to societal oppression. I share with them a common discomfort that ignites into passion. We would release the imprisoned psyche from confinement in its own definition.

To the question, what is psychology after the catastrophe, my response is to go back, as did the Renaissance, before even Y2K, back to the catastrophe that calls itself modem psychology. I stumbled towards this move backwards, this jailbreak, in the Terry Lectures, by "suggesting a poetic basis of mind and a psychology that starts neither in the physiology of the brain, the structure Df languaLye. the organization of society, nor the analysis of behavior. . .". (Revisioning Psychology, 1975, p. xviii)

Were we now to dream this suggestion onward, we might come to altogether other grounds for psychology that are more true to the soul's desires and the culture's wants than the piddling sentimentalities of mental health, relieved relationships, self development or even heightened conscious.

Since time is short and there is much before us, allow me a puer flight from responsible elaboration. Instead, lets cut to the chase.

I propose three universals for founding psychology after the catastrophe: Justice, Beauty, Destiny. They more accurately qualify the "poetic basis of mind."

I am not turning to science for foundations. I am not seeking principles of explanation, but of value. Explanations like complexity, evolutionary genetics, microcomputer physics give cold comfort. Nor are these three alternatives for or fungible with familiar trinities like body, soul and spirit; black, white and red; faith, hope and charity; the good, the beautiful and the true or one. Justice, Beauty and Destiny offer universals of archetypal strength, that is, they are recurrent in time and ubiquitous in place, cross or trans-cultural, immensely fecund; they muster emotive and symbolic expression, and are instantly recognizable in daily affairs. They are universals on which cultured communities and human dignity rely and aim to further. Without them, existence becomes Hobbesian -- nasty and brutish. With them, psyche finds itself in a moral, aesthetic and intentional cosmos, and psychology becomes the study of the ways any phenomenon, including human being, measures its place in the world.

The very words -- Justice, Beauty, Destiny -- inspire. They evoke ideals that can neither be defined nor achieved, yet which bespeak yearnings of life-sustaining motivation power. Even as ideals, Justice, Beauty and Destiny offer practical touchstones for assessing the behavior of any phenomenon: where does it belong, fit; what is it, what qualities is it showing; what is it attempting to fulfill? And, we recognize their presence first in the usual way -- by pathologizings: the fury at injustice, the recoil from ugliness and the despair of aimlessness.

My empirical source for these fundamentals is suffering, that perennial source of depth psychology. No matter the ontologies offered for grounding the field in physics, in evolution, in spiritualities, its actual starting point is complaint, disorder, suffering. As Freud sought the ground of suffering in archetypal principles -- Eros and Thanatos -- beyond the personal case, so suffering can find poetic understanding in the *poiesis* of tragedy. Tragedy is an old word for the slouching beast, Y2K, what Yeats foresaw as "anarchy," "the blood-dimmed tide," "darkness drops again." [The Second Coming] Our feeling reflects tragedy, not energy; not the psycho-dynamics of opposites, the psychodramatics of struggle, the tragic heroic-comedy of the soul's life on earth. To live with the perpetual nihilism of the slouching beast always at the threshold, there must be some justice, some beauty, some sense of destiny.

The wound to humanistic hubris inflicted by Nietzsche, Marx, Darwin and Freud cannot be repaired by even the best of wounded healers until the wound be led back to the universality of tragedy, intimated by Y2K as the self-inflicted destruction of civilization owing to the flaw of its hubris.

An idea of Justice has hardly been important to psychology which has proceeded as if Justice could be ignored. Yet, Justice is the ruling principle of society, perhaps of the natural world as well, formulated as natural law. The Greeks considered Justice *(Themis)* foundational. She was a great earth Goddess like Gaia whom Zeus too had to obey. She lies in the roots of the polis, the city, making structural cohesion possible, giving each its rightful place, allowing it to belong, yet not overstep its bounds. Ostracism, banishment, exclusion for transgressions -- have long been punishments based on Justice's cohesive inclusion.

Inherent in society and making society possible and inherently necessary to individual survival in society, so Justice is inherent in the individual person, perhaps in all creatures maintaining their claims to mutually dependent existence. Justice lies so deep, feels so innate, it works like an instinct. Transgressions spring quick to the eye; injustice stinks and its wounds long fester. A sense of Justice comes with the newest soul. The smallest child cries: "That's not fair!"

Psychology has come upon justice indirectly. Empowerment, entitlement, victimization -- these miss the archetypal dimension that revalues these feelings as ethical and political claims. When Justice is foundational then injustice becomes a primary syndrome, a diagnostic category perhaps, and a primary focus of therapy. The justification of one's life becomes more significant than its individualized meaning. The pursuit of Justice leads psychology toward moral and political philosophy.

And to aesthetics: *le mot juste.* Justice insists on the right use of language, the right gesture, rhythm that bespeak the psyche's basic poetic requirements. Of all injustices psychology ought rectify, foremost is getting its words to fit the case, and the case is always the soul. Getting things right -- that is where ethics and aesthetics converge, which now leads us to Beauty.

"Divine enhancement of the earthly world," that Neo-platonic idea of Beauty overwhelms with its beautiful simplicity! Divine enhancement -- that's what strikes the heart, stops us up, catches our breath, calls us, and can shine forth from suddenly anything, anywhere, anytime. No wonder the Greek word *kalos* also bears the meaning of "call." Beauty calls: we fall in love, we buy the painting, the restless search to know thyself falls away as knowledge gives over to perception and appreciation.

Besides its calling power that draws into the world, making it desirable and waking our love for it, besides the pleasure and vitality it affords, Beauty offers one advantage as a psychological foundation: it can't be literalized. As Destiny literalized becomes determinism and Justice, legalism, so Beauty literalized becomes aestheticism, either programized or formalized or symbolized or kitsch. As an a priori, Beauty remains sheer enhancement of things, not a thing itself and therefore ideal, visionary, wholly immanent. First principles must remain prior in every sense so that they can stand as priorities of value toward which culture tries to move and for which the soul yearns.

This longing for Beauty, its effects so deeply transformative, its universality in the presentation of nature and in human culture of body, of food, of place and tools, to say nothing of the arts whose calling is to bring that immanent enhancement to sensible perception -- what could be more fundamental? Incredible that psychologies of depth and their therapies remain so insulated from these everyday facts. At least psychology's anesthesia makes one thing clear: we need to cross the threshold out of a deadbeat psychology.

A lack of Beauty as everyday fact, as clinical condition, was also described by the Neo-platonists: "Let the soul fall in with the Ugly," said Plotinus, "and at once it shrinks within itself, denies the thing, turns away from it, out of tune, resenting it." [1.6.2] Don't tell me an archetypal psychology is not clinical!

About destiny there is scarce to say: is it not simply the mythical sense of life: We are both chained to and carried by forces we pretend to understand. Their power emerges in our awareness as Necessity, *Ananke*. And this archetypal necessity translates into a sense of personal destiny, moments of feeling necessary. Something is meant, something is wanted, something is living alongside my life, nudging, urging, sometimes grabbing the wheel and setting another course.

Unless a sense of destiny is built into the foundations of psychology, it becomes essentially anemic, lacking *poiesis*, that envisioning force to engage the despair, the drifting loneliness and panic that psychology is called on to encounter. Without an idea of Destiny, psychology fails its own destiny.

The study of these forces we pretend to understand, this process of investigation is what makes psychology's activity interminable. It is an activity of observation which brings the breadth of mythical powers into the small world of the little people who whisper in the grass. Notice, listen, appreciate: something is always speaking. Observation becomes a daily practice of observances.

As a psychology founded upon Justice becomes ethical and political, and because founded in Beauty must then be sensate and aesthetic, so Destiny requires psychology to be observant, that is, religious and animistic.

I suggest that these three archetypal ideas can transport psychology across the threshold by affording a vision to uphold the psyche in the face of catastrophe -- whether environmental, technological, or holocaustal. As more cultural ideas than purely psychological ones, they prevent psychology from isolating itself as a specialist's discipline or a professional practice. As the soul belongs to no province of inquiry, the ideas on which psychology rests may not be provincial. That has been the thrust of an archetypal psychology from the start. Depth psychology, after all, is only one manifestation of culture -- late, minor, and mainly Western, wealthy and white. So our base must find itself in culture's principles, and culture attempts always to articulate its destiny by creating beauty and maintaining justice.

We in this room this morning are witnesses to this extended foundation. You have always known in your hearts that suffering is never more mollified and the menace of breakdown better endured than when ugliness and injustice can be averted, when there is a glimpse of beauty, some justice in the offing, and when destiny gives a blow of tragedy, the value is of importance.

I have been trying in these condensed minutes to lay the table for this threshold conference as an "adventure in ideas" for a value-based psychology, ideas that might possibly serve to urge psychology into the peculiar terrain with its peaks and vales of a yet unknown century.

[1]Editors' note: This chapter is the verbatim text of James Hillman's remarks that opened the Psychology at the Threshold conference August 2000.

Thresholds: Between Word and Image

Each of the five essays that comprise this section dedicate all or part of its exploration to the nature of language and the play of image by addressing one or both of these elements in relation to one another from a depth psychological or mythic perspective.

Robert Romanyshyn's "The Tears of God: Grief as an Opening to the Divine" remembers the sudden and unexpected death of his wife and the transformation of his own life that such a devastating event fostered in him. Such a loss brings him to reflect with a lyric nuance on the presence and nature of grief as an opening into both love and a realization of the divine within such intense pain.

JoAnne Stroud reflects on the French philosopher, Gaston Bachelard's book, Earth: Images of Will and Repose. Her study reveals where Bachelard and C.G. Jung converge and diverge in their respective beliefs in the power and primacy of the image. What emerges in her study is a confluence of psychology, psychoanalysis and poetry. Her essay moves back into some of Bachelard's earlier work and forward into this newly-translated one.

"The Wildlife of Words" by Joseph Coppin explores further his interest in how metaphor creates a living reality in language; he sees how words have a life and death of their own and that language, in order to stay solvent and organic, must allow words the movement of their natural lives and inevitable deaths.

Barbara Annan's "Khidr, the Mysterious Stranger: The Mythopoetic Encounter with the Other" continues an exploration of language, beginning with a poem by Mary Oliver and then on to the origins of al-Khidr, "the green one." She reveals his history as a psychopomp, an archetypal form in both eastern and western culture by showing his presence from a depth psychological perspective.

Remaining within the arena of a specific mythology, Dennis Patrick Slattery revisions Ovid's myth in "Narcissus, Echo and Irony's Resonance" by imagining Echo as the presence of irony which, if made into a companion and not rejected, saves self-reflection from turning into self-fixation, the latter being the result of losing one's sense of the ironic.

The Tears of God: Grief as an Opening to the Divine by Robert D. Romanyshyn, Ph.D.

Between Two Heartbeats

On July 1,1992 my wife, to whom I had been married for twenty-five years, died. She said, "Oh, my God," and fell to the floor. Her death was sudden, and unexpected. It came without warning and with no mercy. It came with a swift, terrible, and utter finality. A brief fifteen minutes before her death, I had approached her as she stood at the kitchen sink. I had placed my hands on her shoulders, and she turned and smiled. In that turning, in the arc of that space opened up by her gesture, I had said these words: "You are so beautiful."

When she died, my life shattered like a pane of fragile glass. In a single moment, in the space between two heartbeats, everything that I ever was, and everything that I wanted to be, was erased. In the interval between the moment just before her death and the moment just after it, a black hole opened in my soul and sucked into it the past that we had made together and the future we were dreaming.

There are, I believe, no maps for the journey into the grieving process, no programs of the mind which can allow one to escape, or even short-circuit, the double death which happens when a lover dies. Shortly after my wife's death, I dreamed I was at a party. My wife was there, clothed in a radiant garment of green, a green which itself pulsated with life. She was alive, mixing with our friends, and it was I who was dead. In the dream, I was sitting in the corner of the room, and I was invisible. I was there, but no one could see or was seeing me.

The Gift of Grief

Reflecting on the death of a woman whom he loved, the German poet Rainer Maria Rilke asks, "Who talks of victory?" "To endure," he adds, "is all." (Hendry, 1983)

To endure! But, of course, that is so difficult because the work of grieving is not something, which is under one's control. Our minds might think that it is, but from the deeper layers of the soul the grieving process is a matter of *its* seasons and rhythms. To endure is to let yourself become one of those elemental forces of the soul where psyche is part of nature. There were occasions, then, when in the winter depths of mourning, I felt a harmonic connection between the weary pulses of the blood flowing through my veins and the green sap

of a winter tree slowly coursing through sleepy stem and tired leaf.

> *A beech tree in the garden of a house in a small village on the northern coast of Devon, England. A cold November morning. The tree is bare, but its empty brown branches design a stark mosaic against the bleak winter sky. The morning light is weak, pale, and drained of any color; the gray sky, burdened with heavy clouds, only intensifies the sharp outlines of the twigs and branches, the arms of the tree with delicate fingers at rest in winter repose. The simple elegance of this lone tree against the washed out sky arrests my eye; a plain mosaic of black and white, a visible haiku, a poetry of form, the animate geometry of nature. In looking at this tree I long to be a painter, recalling how Cezanne once said that all he ever wanted to do was to capture one moment of the world's being. This mosaic is just such a moment.*
>
> *But I am no painter, and besides even the great Cezanne painted Mt. Saint Victoire some eighty-six times trying to capture that one moment. What was it that the poet Rilke said of Orpheus? Raise no monument to him? Yes, but let it be the rose, he said, which in its blooming is already fading. Eruptions of the world's being, always in moments when one is not looking for anything but is open and already near dreaming, need first and perhaps only our witnessing. Later, when we have been sufficiently penetrated, a word, or a color on canvas, or a note on a flute, might be made.*
>
> *So I sink back into myself in front of this tree, gather myself against the morning chill, hunch my shoulders, and feel myself becoming increasingly still and silent, as if, in the presence of this great being, the tempo of my own life is slowing down, resonating in harmony with the reduced rhythms of the tree, blood and sap flowing at the same languid pace, the difference between them fading, a boundary being crossed, now erased, as if the two juices are mingling together, as if one flow is now circulating between us. It is a moment of possession, and I know that I could become inert, like a stone, or fall into the winter sleep of this tree. I could release to these ancient rhythms, and I want to, to let go of wakeful consciousness and become only an element, a part of all this wintry slumber, content only to wait, to sleep, to dream. This vegetable siren is waiting for me. It welcomes a surrender with that infinite patience which has marked its rooted endurance to this place where, for how long now? it has welcomed winter snows and dreamed its winter dreams. One moment, exactly this moment, now becomes an eternity, and between each beat of the heart, eons can pass. I have been here before. I have been here forever, blanketed in winter snows, cousin to this tree, kin to this patient sentinel waiting my return.(Romanyshyn,1999)*

To endure grief is to lose one's mind. It is to risk oneself into those moments of oblivion

where consciousness slips away and you descend into the winter landscapes of the soul in

sorrow. In this dark place where night is longer than day, where the soul in grief, following its

natural rhythms, slumbers, you discover that you are kin to the tree and its barren branches, to

the leaf and its withered edges, to the rose which in its blooming has already begun to fade.

Snatched from this world, abducted into the underworld, mind is unhinged by grief,

and guided by soul it is taken into those wintry regions where it becomes (you become) something less than you ever were, or even believed yourself capable of ever becoming: a bud of sorrow nestling a seed whose dumb, vegetative tropism offers no promise, no guarantee that it will ever blossom into life again.

Poets, I believe, have always known these natural landscapes of the soul, and lovers, too, know it, because love follows the cycles of the natural world, those moments of bright sunlight and the dark moon, those seasons of high hope and shattered promise, those tides of expansion, when one becomes two and the heart of each lover increases because of its capacity to love and be loved, and contraction, when love is lost and the heart becomes a stone. Poets and lovers know these forces of the soul, because they know that life is about loss, and that love is the bride of death.

The ancient story of Orpheus and Eurydice poignantly presents this marriage of love and death. It is a story told by Ovid, the Roman poet, in his Metamorphosis, and it has been re-told many times. Of all the variations, however, I am drawn to the way in which Rilke re-tells the tale in his poem "Orpheus. Eurydice. Hermes." In his poem he recounts the tale from the point of view of Eurydice, emphasizing how in her death she has already passed beyond rescue. Not even one such as Orpheus, whose songs were so sweet that they had the power to tame the elements, to bend the willow, shame the brook, and even make the wind envious of his songs. Not even one such as he could bring his beloved Eurydice back from those dark places of death beyond the grave. Not even he who, by the lament in his songs, had won the gods favor and was granted permission to lead Eurydice back into life, provided that he not look back as he and Eurydice traveled that upward path from the wintry realm of death into life. Not even he could deny death's claim on love.

At the last moment Orpheus faltered, unsure that she was following, and in that turning he lost her again, this time forever. And yet for Rilke it is not because of that turning or not that alone. For in telling us what Orpheus saw in that backwards glance, Rilke lets us in on a deeper truth about love and death. In one simple line we know that in the arms of death Eurydice had already become a force of the natural world, something less, and more, than what her human self had been.

"She was no longer that woman with blue eyes

who once had echoed through the poet's songs,
no longer the wide couch's scent and island
and that man's property no longer.

She was already loosened like long hair
poured out like fallen rain,
shared like a limitless supply.

She was already root."

Root! Elemental, like rain, or wild, loosened hair, the beloved in death had fallen away from this life, had had all ties with this world severed. Orpheus, in grief over his loss, had traveled there, to that far winter country of the soul, to retrieve her, to escort her back into life. But only he returned. She had already become something else, and by that so did he. As they traveled the path, Orpheus in the lead, sensing his way in the dark night of the soul in grief, Eurydice was being escorted by Hermes, the god between the worlds. Underscoring what he has already said, how she had become root, Rilke describes that moment when Orpheus turns:

And when, abruptly,
the god put out his hand to stop he, saying,
with sorrow in his voice: He has turned around-,
she could not understand, and softly answered
Who? (Rilke, 1989)

Who? Whom do we become when the one who was loved has died? And them? Whom do they become in the arms of death?

The Soul in Grief is a story in response to these questions, an account of a journey into those wild, dark, winter landscapes of the soul in sorrow and mourning, and the account of a miracle. That from a well-ripened sadness there would blossom new life and love is a miracle like the green leaf of the tree that has awakened from its winter sleep. Do we really ever have a right to expect that the world will become green again? Do we even have the right just before the dawn, when the world in its silent turning is still seduced by the dark night, to expect that the morning will come and that the world, once again, will be flooded with light and the song of birds? No! These are miracles in the heart of the ordinary, and when grief plunges us into those places where the soul touches nature, where mind does become root, the miracle of new life and love from loss can happen. Certainly, that I found in the very center of sadness green life and starlight, dust and dreams, orphans and angels, and the radiance of the sacred spread throughout the ordinary was not an achievement of my will. It was not even a testament to any kind of courage. It was, and remains, a gift, a gift of grace, a miracle.

But, perhaps, it is too unsettling to call grief a gift. In the early season of loss, it feels nothing at all like that. And even later, when some ripening of sorrow has occurred, there is still no guarantee that one's life will become green again. But I can only tell my story as it happened, be a witness for love, loss, grief and transformation. I can tell the tale of this journey into the land of grief. But I cannot draw a map of this journey, because there are no maps for miracles.

So, when I write how in the season of melancholy which follows the long winter of mourning, I could find she who had died in the dying of the light at the close of day, or in the rising of the sun at dawn, or in the rain, or in the seasons, in the changing of the leaves and the falling of the snow; when I write of these moments and proclaim that she who has died is now present in them, that her absence has been transformed and is not now so total, that she now belongs to the rhythm of all life, that she is present everywhere, and that all these signs bring me a strange kind of solace and a peace I would never had expected, I am only one voice for this irrational, mindless claim that grief can be a gift.

In the end, all I know is what I have been given. On the other side of grief, my life is less ruled by fear, at least in my best moments. I know too that in my best moments, my life is more expansive in its openness to a kinship with Nature that reaches to the Stars. In these moments, I am also more aware and present to the Sacred in the ordinary, to the small miracle of a spider's web, for example, which suspended in moonlight becomes a galaxy of stars. In such moments, I also feel more attuned to the presence of something which is Divine and which seems to draw me towards itself, like a Beloved, as if all creation is a loving act of gathering back into itself the pilgrims that we are, Orphans on the journey home. Imagine that: Grief as homework! Perhaps that is the greatest gift of all, the way in which love in the face of loss seasons us for the journey home.

The Orphan

In Jung's essay, "Flying Saucers: A Modern Myth," there is a woodcut entitled "The Spiritual Pilgrim Discovering Another World."(1964) Commenting on it, he states that the pilgrim is on a "pelerinage de l'ame," a soul journey which gives him a glimpse of the other world, the heavenly realm of the Divine. Although Jung does not say so, it is important, I think, to note that the pilgrim is rooted in this world as he glimpses the other world of the gods. It is also relevant to note that his vision is a piercing of a veil that distinguishes this world and the other one. The divine is here now, around us, like a curtain or a mist, and the journey toward it is a journey of transformation wherein the pilgrim's way of knowing the world and being in it is radically changed. In other words, the soul journey of the pilgrim is not so much a change in place as it is a shift in attitude, a transformation of consciousness.

Grief is or can be the beginning of such a journey. At the moment of my wife's death, I saw her subtle form pass beyond a veil. In that moment I tried to reach my hand across a space which in material terms was a matter of inches. But I failed because the space between our worlds was now a qualitative difference and not a quantitative measure. In an instant between two heartbeats, she had already slipped beyond that veil. To find her again would require that soul journey of the pilgrim through this world.

What I never expected, however, is that the journey to find her would become an alchemical process of self transformation in which my longing and search for her, like that of Orpheus for Eurydice, or like that for any lover who has lost a beloved, would, of necessity, require a dissolution of all that I had been and ever planned to be, a dissolution of the past we had shared and the future we were dreaming, and a discovery of that self whom, perhaps, I once was but had lost or forgotten. What I never expected is that the journey of the soul in grief, which began with personal loss, would be enfolded within the larger, collective story of the pilgrim whom we all are, the pilgrim in search of home.

At the edge of sorrow, at the extreme limits of my grief, in that first season of the soul in loss when I drifted through the world as a ghost, the Orphan came. In the night's thick darkness, while sitting on the edge of a pier, I felt for the first time since my wife's death several months earlier touched by something outside of me. In this moment I was moved by the simple presence of the encompassing world, and for the first time tears dropped from my eyes. The stone, which had replaced my heart, was being dissolved in these tears, but I did not know for whom I was weeping. It seemed to me that in that moment I was crying for something beyond my own sorrow. It felt at that moment as if my grief over my personal loss was bleeding into a larger sorrow, mixing with "a grief older than mine, a sadness at the very heart of things," a melancholy at the core of creation. Writing of this moment much later, I said, "the ocean itself seemed like the tears of the world, mingling with my own, forging a bond of kinship rooted in sorrow." In that moment, in the very darkest hour of the world's night and the night of the soul, I felt "witnessed by the world, seen in my sorrow, no longer completely alone." The miracle of that occasion was that in the midst of that black darkness, I heard these words spoken to me out of the night itself: "We are all so far from home."

At the abyss I met the Orphan and I understood in my heart, perhaps for the first time, that indeed we all are far from home, and that in the depths of our personal sorrows lies the ancient grief of our shared homelessness. Without the presence of the Orphan, I know that I would not have been able to endure the season of mourning, when the soul in grief descends into the elements and dies into its winter sleep. The Orphan's presence at the edges of grief and in the far winter country of mourning was a kind of animal faith that there was something on the other side of loss and sorrow. Not a promise, but a force, like the tropism of the vegetable world which turns the flower toward the morning sun, the Orphan's presence was a figure of natural grace, of nature's grace and its patient and enduring wisdom.

The soul, unlike the mind, lives in paradox, and the Orphan, the homeless one, is paradoxically the one who knows the way home. In the presence of the Orphan, I am reminded how deeply etched the image of home is in the soul, and how wide is its expanse. There were times when in his/her presence, I felt how my grief was the bond which deeply connected me to the earth and to the animals, to the angels and to the stars. Without the Orphan I never could have known that within grief's stony heart lay the radiance of a star. Nor could I have ever come to know that the Orphan is the other face of the Angel. Like the Orphan who stands at the abyss, I have come to realize that the Angel waits at the edges of the world. At the edge, the Angel waits to escort us beyond the privacy of our own personal sorrows into a realm of connection, which I can only poorly describe as a sense of cosmological joy where the soul is held by forces beyond the human realm.

There is something ecstatic about these moments, something completely wild and unexpected in relation to grief, something that pulls from the heart slowly awakening from its winter sleep in an ejaculation of song, a lament which rises to the heights of joy. Rilke's <u>Duino Elegies</u> is an example of this voice of lament, which begins in sorrow and ends, for the moment, in a burst of praise. So too are the love poems of Rumi. Beethoven's ninth symphony, his "Ode to Joy," composed when he was already deaf, is another example of the heart attuned to those other voices, the angelic hosts, the music of the spheres. What is true, I think, in each of them is the abundant presence of love. In the final analysis what the Orphan-Angel has given to me is the realization that we grieve because we have dared the risks of loving, and that we can love again because we have taken the time to grieve.

That spirit of love, I now believe, is a cosmological force that unites the Divine and human as two lovers. But who or what is that Divine, holy Presence who calls us home? I have no rational or reasonable answer to this question. I have only those experiences of the journey, especially of those moments in the season of melancholy following the long winter of mourning after the initial storms of grief have passed. Each of these moments had for me a numinous quality, as if each of them was a glimpse of the holy face of God in the world. The 18th century visionary-poet William Blake once said that "All the World is Holy," and each of these epiphanies did seem to confirm his inspiration. Each of them did seem to part that veil between the sacred and the profane to give a brief vision of the world's divine radiance.

Now, almost a year since this journey has come to a close with the final words of thanks written in the text, I wonder about that holy splendor of the world, and I question who that God is who seems to draw us home with the force of a love which permeates all creation from stones to stars, from its darkest depths in the soil of the earth to its heavenly heights. Who are you, I wonder, and in longing I am led to new places. First I will offer a brief description of one of those numinous moments, and then I will close with a few remarks in response to my question.

It was a dark winter day when I made a visit to the Central Park Zoo in New York City. I have always been drawn to zoos in moments of melancholy, pulled by a loneliness that beckons me toward the animal. Winter days, particularly in midweek, have always been the best moments for zoo visits, as they afford solitude and private time with the animal.

On this occasion I was going to see the gorillas. Standing in front of the cage of a large silverback male, I keenly felt the presence of the bars between us. The gorilla was sitting in the front corner of his cage, and I could see him only in profile. On occasion, however, (as gorillas will do with zoo visitors) he would turn his head for a quick glance in my direction. His deeply set dark black eyes seemed like pools of time, and in those few brief moments of exchange I felt dizzy, as if I could swim through his eyes into another world. But the gorilla would just as quickly look away and the spell would be broken. The cage was so small, especially for so large an animal, and I wondered how he could bear it. His lethargy was inescapable, and I thought of the many hours of boredom he must daily endure, wondering, too, if I was reading my own sense of melancholy through him. But I had also been with animals in the wild, and the difference in behavior, in gesture, and in that imaginal space between us was pronounced. Caught up in these reveries, I had absentmindedly withdrawn an orange from my pocket and was tossing it in the air. The gorilla turned and began to watch me. Without thinking I tossed the orange through the bars to him, momentarily oblivious to the prohibition against feeding the animals. The toss of the orange through the bars covered a distance of only a few feet in real space and took perhaps only a second in real time. But the gesture, and what unexpectedly followed, bridged an ocean of time and space.

One would have expected the gorilla to take the orange and retreat to a far corner of the cage to eat it. But this gorilla did not. Instead, he tossed it through the bars back to me, I caught it, and in my astonishment, I tossed it to him again. We continued like this for perhaps three exchanges, until this ribbon between us, this embrace of a game, was broken by the sound of a voice from the far end of the corridor. "Don't feed the animals!" When I turned toward the voice, the gorilla turned away. He moved to the far end of the cage. He kept the orange.

I left the zoo and walked out into the city. The cold, dark, winter aftedness I felt at having left the gorilla inside. I was different, changed by that encounter and even lonelier in the midst of the crowded city. The gorilla had suspended his appetite for a moment. For the sake of an encounter, he had bridged an immense gap between our worlds. In his gesture of tossing the orange back to me, he had reached out his hand across emptiness so vast as to be beyond measure. Together we had built a tremulous bridge of gestures, and for a brief time we stood on opposite sides of that bridge, connected in a way that seemed to acknowledge in each other a lost kinship. Even to this day, I know that I'll never forget the eyes of my winter companion on that day of long ago. He had greeted me, and as strange as it might sound, I felt so grateful for that recognition. But I also felt how far I had come, and I knew with a deep feeling of sadness that we would remain forever more on opposite sides of this bridge, and that at the best moments of my life, I would be able only to stop and linger and turn around to see, once again, what was left behind. I knew that, and I knew, too, that what I saw in his eyes before the spell was broken was his sadness for me. (Romanyshyn, 1999)

There is an acute sense of longing in this example, a hunger for something once known but now lost and forgotten, a bond of compassionate kinship steeped in my desire to be known by this other, and a sadness at the gulf which separates us. This encounter, and others like it, awakens a melancholic chord in the soul. Through this mood of melancholy, which cracks the ordinary frame of my world, the Orphan slips in and signals by his/her presence a moment of breakdown, through which something else breaks through, something un-expected, something which seems extraordinary, a moment which in the root sense of the word is awe-ful, a moment which fills me with awe because something sacred, holy, numinous seems to be present, even in this brief glance from those black eyes which seem to say "I miss you, I remember you, I long for you."

But whose voice is it in these moments of simple, ordinary grace? Whose appeal is being spoken here? Can it be that the invisible presence of the divine enters the visible world in these moments which interrupt us, make us pause, enters through the cracks in creation, including, and perhaps especially so, in our moments of breakdown and loss? Is it possible that in these moments we are witnesses to how the divine presence of the world yearns for us as much as we yearn for it? Does God long for us as much as we do for Him/Her?

I am persuaded that grief opens us to the divine presence in the world and that the Orphan who appears in our moments of loss and sorrow is the mirror that reflects back to us our own God-face and the face of God. I am also persuaded that the face which God reveals in these moments is also one of longing and compassion, of loss and sorrow. In this respect, grief might be the bond that unites the human and the divine, the visible order of the created world and the invisible order of the creator. In this regard, the God who calls us home might be a god of sadness and tears whose sorrow yokes him to us who also grieve.

The Pathetic God

A God who weeps and in that weeping draws near to us, as we, in our sorrows, long for and go in search for Him/Her! This is not a God of power, an almighty God. Nor is it an ethical God, the guardian of the moral law. No! This God who weeps is a pathetic God, a term which the great Islamic scholar Henry Corbin takes from the Jewish scholar Abraham Heschel and develops within the context of Sufi mysticism.

It is well beyond the scope of this paper to enter with any depth into this topic. Two points, however, can be made. First, the root of pathetic in *pathos* unites in one family pathetic with passion as a hunger or desire for the other, and with com-passion as an attunement with the other, and with sym-pathy as a conversion or turning toward the other who calls us. It is a tropism, like that which I mentioned earlier, wherein the natural elements of the soul in grief seem to follow the rhythms of nature, those same heliotropic forces, for example, which turn the flower toward the sun, and which the Neoplatonist philosopher Proculus perceived as the flower's way of praying.

A pathetic god, then, is a passionate God with a hunger for us which matches ours for Him/Her, a compassionate God attuned to us through our loves and losses, and a sympathetic god whose tropism or inclination toward us, what Corbin calls anthropopathy, is reciprocated by our natural inclination toward Him/Her, what Corbin calls theopathy (1997, p. 112). Imagine, then, that grief is a form of prayer, a way of praying, which finds its mirror in this pathetic God of compassion and sympathy.

Second, *pathos* is etymologically related to *penthos* which means grief. This relation suggests that grief is what makes us capable of encountering a pathetic god. Grief is the way in which the heart becomes compassionately attuned to the other, human to human, and human to the divine.

I hope I have now said just enough about a pathetic God to offer you this closing image of the journey of the soul in grief. This journey is a homecoming in which our tears of sorrow and those of the pathetic God are the mirrors through which we see our divine face and God sees His/Her human one. Grief, then, is not only homework; it is also holy work.

References

Corbin, H. (1997). Alone with the alone: Creative imagination in the Sufism of Ibn' Arabi. Princeton, NJ: Princeton University Press.

Hendry, J.F. (1983). The sacred threshold: A life of Rilke. Manchester: Carcanet Press Ltd.

Jung, C.G. (1964). Flying saucers: A modern myth. In The collected works of C.G. Jung (Vol. 10) (R.F. C. Hull, Trans.). Princeton: Princeton University Press.

Mitchell, S. (Ed.). (1989). The selected poetry of Rainer Maria Rilke. New York: Vintage International.

Romanyshyn, R. (1999). <u>The soul in grief: Love, death and transformation</u>. Berkeley: North Atlantic Books.

Earth: Images of Will and Repose by Joanne Stroud, Ph.D.

Depth psychology teaches that earth is archetypal mother, simultaneously preserver and destroyer. Images elaborated by French philosopher, Gaston Bachelard, reveal our complex responses to the material world--in will-directed activities and in receptive and restorative movements of psyche. We will compare them to the more symbolic ones of archetypal psychology.

Let's begin by recalling some classical images of our "steadfast base of all things," the earth. Hesiod, sometimes accused of being a misogynist, recognizes the essential and indisputable centrality of Gaia--earth, matter, and the common mother of us all.

> Earth, the beautiful, rose up
> Broad-bosomed, she that is the steadfast base
> Of all things. And fair Earth first bore
> The starry Heaven, equal to herself,
> To cover her on all sides and to be
> A home forever of the blessed gods.
> Hesiod, The Theogony

What a shock that as contemporaries we are faced, probably for the first time in human recorded time, with grave concerns about the continued health of our planet! In the middle of the twentieth century Albert Schweitzer warned, "Man has lost the capacity to foresee and forestall. He will end by destroying the earth."

First, I want to explore with you the archetypal roots of the earth in our psychic make-up and enlarge these with the imagery that Gaston Bachelard added in his two books on the images of the earth. Do get acquainted with Bachelard's work if you don't know it. At the Dallas Institute of Humanities and Culture, we have been translating him from the French for the last twenty years. Well known in France, he taught physics at the University of Dijon before becoming Professor of the Philosophy of Science at the Sorbonne. In 1954 he was named Professor Emeritus but continued to lecture there until his death in 1962. One of the four amphitheaters at the Sorbonne carries his name. He is less known but revered in this country by those who appreciate the way he expands our awareness of primal images. Though Bachelard was a philosopher, many archetypal psychologists have applied his original work in images to the field of psychology. Robert Sardello first introduced me to him when I was a graduate student at the University of Dallas. It was then that I elected myself Bachelard's English secretary. David Miller shares my enthusiasm and has taught classes on Bachelard at Syracuse University. James Hillman often refers to Bachelard.

I want to make clear some distinctions, especially in methodology between Jung and Bachelard. The spectrum of Jung's interest ranges wide in exploring the depths of psychic behavior. As a phenomenologist, Bachelard's search is more limited--concentrated on particular images and image clusters, especially as they appear in verbal communication. He examines the texture and quality of how an image manifests. Bachelard was at first more influenced by Freud than by Jung but begins to make reference to Jung in his later books, particularly after 1948. Published in 1938, The Psychoanalysis of Fire is certainly a novel approach to a physical element and demonstrates that Freud had caught his attention. In an interview with Aspel (1955) he said that he had "received Jung too late" (Quoted by Christofides (1963:486). Bachelard does frequently give offhand compliments to Jung, such as this one about archetypes: "Everything that originates in us with the clarity of new beginnings is a mad surge of life. The great archetype of incipient life gives to any beginning the psychic energy that Jung acknowledged in every archetype" (OPI&R, 97).

Colette Gaudin, in her excellent Introduction to On Poetic Imagination and Reverie, explains that Bachelard said his lack of medical knowledge prevented him from seeing images as organic impulses. Actually, though:

> The real reason is that he wants to seize the specific originality of the symbol without reducing it to its causes. That is why he favors the Jungian concept of the "archetype," which offers the advantage of including symbolism in the unconscious. Strictly speaking, an archetype is not an image. For Jung, it is psychic energy spontaneously condensing the results of organic and ancestral experiences into images....When Bachelard uses any psychological concept, he limits his investigation to the present life of images; he disregards the historical and anthropological background of archetypes and attempts instead an "archeology of the human soul." (OPI&R, xvi)

All of us who have worked with archetypal images are well aware of the multivalent character of any archetype. This is especially true of the archetype of the earth. Earth destroys in order to bring about rebirth-- think of the seed that must give way to the flower. Both Jung and Bachelard would agree that the imagination of earth involves us in monumental dimensions, partaking of the very mystery of life--both creation and destruction. As in this poem from the "Songs to Orpheus," the glorious mystery of creation remains:

> In spite of all the farmers work and worry,
> He can't reach down to where the seed is slowly
> Transmuted into summer. The earth bestows.
> Rilke – ("Songs to Orpheus," XII)

The Earth is not only the source of growth; the earth is equally humus, or the product of decay. These two opposite functions belong together in a syzegy. George Meredith's three lines of poetry, almost like a Japanese haiku, express the paradox: "Earth knows no desolation/ She smells regeneration/ in the moist breath of decay."

Earth is our intimate home, and language gives away the vibrancy of this relationship. In English, the words "Mother", "matter" and "material" are closely associated. The same is true in French. Or, according to Bachelard, in Hebrew too. Bachelard frequently uses other writers and poets to prove his points, claiming that "the letter M [the Hebrew Mem], at the beginning of a word, paints all things local and plastic. La Main [Hand], la Matière [Matter] la Mère [Mother], and la Mer [Sea] all would share this initial of plasticity." (E&RW, Preface 10) Jung, in his expansion of the mother archetype, acknowledges the natural affinity of places of protection: "The all-embracing womb of Mother Church is anything but a metaphor and the same is true of Mother Earth, Mother Nature and "matter" in general." (Para. 64, Vol. 10)

From the point of view of comparison, let's have a quick review of the Jungian definition of archetype and then more specifically look at archetypal images of the earth. Jung has many ways of describing archetypes. Here is one that you are all familiar with: "Archetypes are systems of readiness for action, and at the same time images and emotions." They are "psychic aspects of brain structure," "instinctive adaptation." But here is one you may not have picked up: archetypes are "that portion through which psyche is attached to nature, or in which its link with the earth and the world appears at its most tangible. The psychic influence of the earth and its laws is seen most clearly in those primordial images" (Para 53, Vol.10). So the earth as archetype partakes of the energy of any archetype; in addition, this particular archetype is strengthened by being the fundamental, the *prima materia*, the basic matrix of all. It is thus doubly dynamic.

Bachelard and Jung agree on the primacy of images, often sounding very similar. Which one would you guess says this: "Images are primary psychic realities? In experience itself, everything begins with images." (E&RW, 290) It is Bachelard, though it could be Jung. Bachelard looks at images as the nucleus of an expanding circle of logical associations. He particularly reveres the literary image. He argues that the language in which we encapsulate our thoughts reveals the essence of each person's individual imagination. Bachelard enjoys classifying poets according to the primary elemental images they most often use. In a poem, we resonate with the poet's imagination and participate in the pleasure of the discovery of new images. He insists that "the function of literature and poetry is to bring new life to language by creating new images." (E&RW, Preface 5) He fully appreciates the immense stimulus of the image: "Indeed, ours is the century of the image. For better or worse we are subjected more than ever before to the power of imagery." (E&RW, Preface 6)

Bachelard turns upside down the simple insistence on the primacy of the real. He affirms "the primitive and psychologically fundamental character of the creative imagination" (E&RW, Preface 2). "In my view," he says in the Preface to the Two Volumes, Earth and Reveries of Will and Earth and Reveries of Repose, "perceived images and created images constitute two very different psychological phenomena requiring a new and special category, to designate the imagined image." Recreated images rely on perception and memory. What he terms "the unreality principle" is equally or more determining than what is normally called "reality":

> Creative imagination functions very differently than imagination relying on the reproduction of past perceptions, because it is governed by an unreality principle... This unreality principle is every bit as powerful, psychologically speaking, as that reality principle so frequently invoked by psychologists to characterize an individual's adjustment to whatever "reality" enjoys social sanction." It is precisely this unreality principle that reinstates the value of solitude...(E&RW, Preface 3)

Surprisingly it is in our moments of quietude that we experience the rush of images, which help to define our will to action, he emphasizes:

Because reverie is nearly always associated in our minds with a state of relaxation, we fail to appreciate those dreams of focused action which I will call dreams of will. And so, when the real stands before us in all of its terrestrial materiality, we are easily persuaded that the reality principle must usurp the unreality principle, forgetting the unconscious impulses, the oneiric forces which flow unceasingly through our conscious life. Only by redoubling our attention then may we discover the predictive nature of images, the way that any image may precede perception, initiating an adventure in perception. (E&RW, Preface 3)

Many may be incensed that Bachelard insists that the image not only colors perception but also precedes it. Bachelard sometimes addresses art images, especially in those short essays in The Right to Dream, but, for him, dreaming is daytime reverie. Daydreaming, or reverie, as Bachelard calls it, is not simply wasted time. These are the moments in which imagination reorganizes the will and translates desire into the will-to-action. Bachelard disagrees with Jung here who seems to denigrate daydreaming as wishful, unproductive thinking. Bachelard rarely deals with nocturnal dream images. He doesn't quite trust his ability to interpret these. One essential difference in the way Bachelard works with image is the contrast with the more symbolic approach taken by Freud and Jung. Bachelard operates by the logic of linking through sounds and textures--the way we experience the world through the five senses. Literary images lend themselves more easily to expanding in the circular way Bachelard likes to work. His detractors accuse him of snatching images out of context whenever he wants to use them to prove a particular point. But his obvious love of heightened metaphor and created image makes us forgive him. He accuses psychoanalysis of not loving images enough:

Psychoanalysis, like descriptive psychoanalysis, is reduced to a sort of psychological topology: it defines levels, layers, associations, complexes, and symbols…. But psychoanalysis has not developed the resources for a veritable psychic dynamology, a detailed dynamology which explores the individuality of images. In other words, psychoanalysis is content to define images according to their symbolic meanings. The instant an impulsional image is divulged or a traumatic memory uncovered, psychoanalysis applies a social interpretation. An entire domain of investigation is neglected: that of imagination itself. Now, the psyche is animated by a veritable hunger for images. It craves images. Meanwhile, psychoanalysis looks for the reality beneath the image but fails to perform the inverse search: to look beneath the reality for the absolute image. It is in this search that one detects the imaginal energy which is the hallmark of an active psyche. (E&RW, Chap. 1, 3)

Both Bachelard and archetypal psychologists would agree on the innate power of the image, but for Bachelard "sublimation," a word that often means denial or repression, is a natural function of the psyche.

> My position concerning the fundamental nature of the image seems to me true by definition, for I associate the life proper of images with archetypes, the power of which has been demonstrated by psychoanalysis. Imagined images are sublimated archetypes rather than reproductions of reality…. What better way to say that the image has a double reality: a psychological and a physical reality. It is through the image that the one who imagines and the thing imagined are most closely united. The human psyche forms itself first and foremost in images. (E&RW, Preface 3-4)

Bachelard makes no clear distinction between objective and subjective experiences. Person and world are always dialoguing. Bachelard suggests the need for a metaphysics of the imagination:

> It seems to me that this is where the elegant work of C.G. Jung himself was leading, when he discovered, for example, the presence of archetypes of the unconscious in alchemical imagery. In a similar vein, I will offer numerous examples of images which are transformed into ideas. Thence we may examine the entire intermediary region of the psyche between unconscious impulse and those earliest images that rise to consciousness. (E&RW, Preface 4)

Jung and Bachelard were united in sharing a major interest in alchemical images, although their approach was quite different. Jung delved into the whole dynamic process of the refinement of the base nature of matter into psychic or spiritual essence. Bachelard was more concerned with human interaction with the basic properties of the material world. Bachelard staunchly believed in the dynamism of the four classic images--earth, fire, air, and water--those elaborated by medieval alchemists. He devoted one or more books to exploring the depths of these fundamental images of matter. He called them "the hormones of the imagination." Each of these elements has its own special characteristics for engaging our imagination. To oversimplify: Fire embodies the most extreme opposites--salvation and apocalypse; Water is the most feminine; Air is replete with desires for freedom; Earth grounds us all in practical purpose.

"Part I" of Earth and Reveries of Will names complexes of Earth after historical or mythological personages. For example, the Atlas Complex is related to our response to gravity. "Part II" concerns the deep inferiority of those great images of asylum: house, belly, and cave. He chastises the psychoanalyst for a too facile lumping together of these images, explaining them as an unconscious desire to reenter the womb: "But this sort of diagnosis ignores the unique values of imagery. There seems good reason to study each of the three avenues of return to the mother separately." (E&RW, Preface13) The second volume on Earth and Reveries of Repose carries the subtitle, "An Essay on the Images of Intimacy." In this volume, once again, he uses the dialectical approach in exploring images of external matter as experienced in inner life.

Bachelard explains that he had to write two volumes on the images of earth--one representing the extrovert imagination which "is dedicated to active reveries that invite us to act upon matter. In the second, the dream flows along a more ordinary incline; it follows the path of involution, carrying us back to our earliest refuges, favoring images of our inmost depths." (E&RW, Preface 9) He explores the Jonah Complex, or the desire for interiority. He calls the companion volumes a diptych made up of images of work and images of repose. However, he warns that images of extroversion and introversion only rarely occur in singular isolation:

> In the final analysis all images emerge somewhere on a continuum between these two poles. They exist dialectically, balancing the seductions of the external universe against the certitudes of the inner self. It would be fraudulent then not to acknowledge the double tendency in images to extroversion and to introversion, not to appreciate their ambivalence....The loveliest images are often hotbeds of ambivalence. (E&RW, Preface 9)

Resistance to human efforts to master them characterizes all elements--earth, air, fire, and water-- but the other elements are not always hostile. Earth is singular in that respect: "The resistance of terrestrial matter, by contrast, is immediate and constant. From the very first, this resistance becomes the objective and unequivocal partner of our will," Bachelard explains. In other words, how we manipulate the material world reveals the nature of our will. Our dreams of manipulating matter supply us with a sense of self-definition or unique authentic identity. He adds, "nothing is so unambiguous as matter worked by human hands when it comes to classifying the varieties of human will." (E&RW, Preface 9)

> It is thus that matter reveals to us our own strengths, suggesting a system for categorizing our energies. It provides not only enduring substance to our will, but a system of well-defined temporalities to our patience. In our dreams of matter, we envision an entire future of work; we seek to will. It should not be surprising then that to dream material images-- yes, simply to dream them--is to invigorate the will. (E&RW, Chap. 1, 6)

For Bachelard earth is the great schoolhouse, the locus for educating, or leading out the innate but reluctant qualities of human personality: "Matter... through the work of the imagination, mirrors our own energies." (E&RW, Chap.1, 7)

After three centuries of scientific endeavor, the myths no longer move us. Primitive peoples were more sensitive to earth's lay lines and magnetic outcroppings, building sanctuaries and temples in locations of high energy. Recent commentators have observed that this knowledge allowed Neolithic cultivators to grow crops in places on sides of hills that no one would dare to use now. In Britain, experienced dowsers have observed the fact that "every megalithic site is over a centre or channel of the terrestrial current whose emanations are detected by the dowser's rod." (Mitchell, 20)   In China, the art of geomancy, feng-shui, which translated means "wind and water," allowed for a harmony between man and place. The intention and effect of feng-shui was "to produce a landscape which had to provide certain spiritual values and also to fulfill the practical purpose of supporting a dense population." (Mitchell, 12). Mircea Eliade complains about our current simplicity: "The completely profane world, the wholly descralized cosmos, is a recent discovery in the history of the human spirit." (Eliade, Intro.13)

Inevitably, we always have to go back to classical Greek mythology to discern the varieties of aspects, human or superhuman. For our imagination of earth, the image of Gaia gives the whole sense of cornucopia, of overarching abundance. One of the qualities of Gaia is that of "immovability," according to Pat Berry: "Gaia made things stick. She was the goddess of marriage. One swore oaths by her and they were binding. Mother/matter as the inert now becomes mother as settler, stabilizer, the binder." (7) Pandora, an image that Gail Thomas works with, is a creature who provides earth's bounty and hope to mankind. The myths of Demeter and Persephone relate to the fertility of the earth, bringing into focus the joys of growing wheat. Persephone, queen of the underworld, reminds us of the necessity of the dark underworld to both beginnings and ends of life. The sacred rites of Demeter/ Persephone at Eleusis deny the finality of death and promise transformation of life.

The Fates, the Moirai, relate to earth's terrible power as destroyer of time, cutting off the thread of life and returning us to earth's womb. A whole other paper would be needed to discuss the fear of the feminine (I have written on this subject elsewhere). Perhaps the whole thrust of scientific endeavor is to overcome and control the frightening aspects of Mother Nature and the power of personal mothers. In India the figure of Kali, the Hindu Great Mother with her foot standing on a pile of bloody heads, is one of the most beloved and feared figures.

Having begun with Hesiod, let us return to him. Since The Theogony, we know that what first existed was Chaos, formlessness. From darkness and death, Love was born. And with its birth, order and beauty began to bind confusion. Love created Light, with its companion, radiant Day. With the coming of Love and Light it seemed natural that the Earth should also appear. (Hesiod, 64) It is first love, Eros, and then Gaia who brings form out of confusion and nothingness. Think if that! From the earth come all the starry Heavens. Earth even provides her own escort; she has a hermaphroditic element in addition to her strongly feminine qualities. Pat Berry suggests psychology should not be in such a rush to get rid of turmoil and confusion, for "within chaos there are inherent forms," or "each chaos mothers itself into form." If we look at the image of earth as a picture rather than a narrative, Berry says "the chaos, and forms and earth are given all at once." (Berry, 2) This means that, as well as being the place of our willful exploits, in a reversal, earth tames us. Earth is the crucible where our ideas take form. Bachelard says much the same: "Matter is the unconscious of form." (E&RW, 70)

Recently we have a reawakened appreciation for our planet, perhaps initiated when astronauts looked back and saw the magnificent whole suspended in space. Finally, in this imagination of earth, let's remember when we chop down old, primal forests or pollute streams, the gratitude earth deserves. The earth is the ground of our being. These lines from Wislana Szymborska, 1996 Nobel Prize Winner for Literature, are a fitting close: "A miracle, just take a look around: / the inescapable earth." Truly the earth does bestow.

References

Bachelard, G. (2001). Earth and reveries of will. Dallas: Dallas Institute Publications.

Bachelard, G. (1971). On poetic imagination and reverie (Colette Gaudin, Trans.). New York: Bobbs-Merrill.

Berry, P. (1987). Echo's subtle body. Dallas: Spring Publications.

Eliade, M. (1959). The sacred and the profane: The nature of religion (Willard R. Trask, Trans.). New York: Harcourt, Brace & World.

Jung, C.G. (1970). The collected works of C.G. Jung (R.F. C. Hull, Trans.). Bollingen Series XX, Princeton: Princeton University Press.

Michell, J. (1975). The Earth spirit: Its ways, shrines and mysteries. New York: Thames and Hudson.

The Wildlife of Words by Joseph Coppin, Ph.D.

There are two primary themes of this chapter and they are interrelated. First is the idea that words, like lions and tigers and bears, have an existence of their own and are not merely the byproducts of human endeavor. Second, as psychologists interested in the logos of psyche, we are particularly called to pay attention to this other nature of words and language. To fail to do so makes us a bit like one who thinks he might truly understand lions and tigers and bears by making a few trips to the local zoo. Like most essays in this volume, this chapter was originally conceived as an oral presentation. But it was also written down. It is about the play of language and as such enjoys a kind of movement or tension between the sensibilities of written versus spoken words. Anyone who has first written a talk and then spoken it will have experienced these two voices as being different. It is easy to get tripped up by one's own words, and we usually think this to be a mistake, but it may be just the normal play of words at work.

All this is by way of suggesting that in order to get the full impact of the ideas set forth in this chapter, the reader should, at times, become a speaker. The words should be spoken and heard by the body, not only read by the eye, and thought. It is, of course, possible to get the conceptual meanings I intend by simply reading these few pages. But something would then be lost of the playfulness of words in the mouth as they seduce us to their meanings with sound and image. In service to such a practice, I invite the reader to begin as the conference began with a poem full of very special words.

JABBERWOCKY
Lewis Carroll

'Twas brillig, and the slithy toves
Did gyre and gimble in the wabe:
All mimsy were the borogoves,
And the mome raths outgrabe

"Beware the Jabberwock, my son!

The jaws that bite, the claws that catch!

Beware the Jubjub bird, and shun

The frumious Bandersnatch!"

He took his vorpal sword in hand:

Long time the manxome foe he sought—So rested he by the Tumtum tree,

And stood awhile in thought.

And, as in uffish thought he stood,

The Jabberwock, with eyes of flame,

Came whiffling through the tulgey wood,

And burbled as it came!

One, two! One, two! And through and through

The vorpal blade went snicker-snack!

He left it dead, and with its head

He went galumphing back.

"And, has thou slain the Jabberwock?

Come to my arms, my beamish boy!

O frabjous day! Callooh! Callay!'

He chortled in his joy.

'Twas brillig, and the slithy toves

Did gyre and gimble in the wabe;

All mimsy we

re the borogoves,

And the mome raths outgrabe.

(from Through the Looking-Glass and What Alice Found There, 1872)

I first heard this poem as a child of 7 or 8. It came as a part of a uniquely silly mood my normally sober mother happened to be in one day. There was something conspiratorial in her reading it. I loved being part of this exception to the rule. Periodically since then I will hear myself or someone snicker snack one or two of these truly vorpal words out into polite conversation and it's always a joy to see that same mood change enter with them cutting through the frumious bandershit.

My technophobic other self took a great deal of satisfaction in finding that when I typed this piece into the computer, the spellchecker police had to call for reinforcements. Red ink everywhere. But I think Alice herself puts it best. She discovers the poem in the process of being caught by the fact of its being written down backwards. It turns out that it can only be read by placing it up to a mirror. This is Alice just after having read Jabberwocky to the red King and Queen.

> "'It seems very pretty,' she said when she had finished it, 'but it's *rather* hard to understand!' (You see she didn't like to confess, even to herself, that she couldn't make it out at all.) 'Somehow it seems to fill my head with ideas—only I don't exactly know what they are! However, *somebody* killed *something:* that's clear, at any rate'" (Carroll, 1872).

This story reflects some of the wildness I want to explore today. We will come back to Alice later on, but let's ask her to stay with us throughout just to make certain I don't tell too many believable lies.

Inasmuch as I want to emphasize our calling to pay particular attention to the wildlife of words, what better place might I begin than at the beginning, with the title, or a part of it—the phrase, *the wildlife*. Wildlife is a compound word made of *life* and *wild*. It alludes to its unspoken other, *tamelife*, which, thanks to the theological notion of dominion over birds and fishes, doesn't need to be spoken. *Wildlife* comes forth as a word, partly because our use of the word *life* has made it too tame—too small. The word *the*, of course, is that wonderful little denotative article that restores our faith in dominion nearly every time we speak. By saying *the* *wildlife* instead of *wildlife* we single it out for objective observation as if we might pin it on the wall or put it in a cage. So, right there in the title we have a rather complete picture of our ambivalent relationship to words and language. We want them to be vividly alive while we are afraid they might be.

Actually, when I originally proposed this lecture, it had a different title. I was calling it "The Eloquence and Whimsy of Archetypal Speech." That would still be an appropriate title, as we'll see a bit later. But somewhere between my proposal and the final program it seems to have changed its own name to "The Wildlife of Words." No humans are claiming responsibility for this. It seems to have happened all on its own. When I noticed it, I was pleased. I could see that once again I had a fine example of how when we talk about things in an animated way, we may sometimes evoke their animal nature, and when we do that they can show up, not only as concepts but as beings and experiences. Titles of talks and books are quite self-important and would certainly want to have some input in their own creation. In this case I think I unwittingly gave permission for that to occur.

My interest in this topic began sometime ago when I was playing with a metaphorical way to see languages and words *as if* they were living beings, having their own natures, characters, their own communities, geographies, ecologies. I thought they might also have their own passions and desires, not to mention their own psychopathology. Somewhere along the way I began to realize that this was not a just metaphor. Or perhaps it is better to say that I remembered for the umpteenth time that to see a thing as a metaphor is more a comment on our method of seeing than it is a judgment about whether it is actually true or real. Metaphors are bits of reality who know they must trick us into *as if* thinking in order to be consumed.

So, I come back to my first important assertion. You decide if it is true or not. I tell you now that if, as good Jungians and archetypalists, we profess that the psyche is a real and autonomous being, then we must do likewise with the logos of psyche, with language. Words are alive. They breathe. That is pretty plain, being largely a matter of breathing. They relate. They think. They forget. They remember. They make and break rules. They have sex and make babies and live in families. They even die. They are beings. That is the primary supposition chapter. It leads to a bit of a riddle which, of course words love to do. The riddle is this: if people are alive and words are alive and they relate the way they do, who is doing what to whom? I hope we can get a feel for this riddle as we go along and be at peace with only guesses at answers.

Let's go back and play with this idea of a psychopathology of words. Many of us are familiar with the ways that words enter into our systems of pathologizing patients. For example, when we do a mental status evaluation of patients, we look for things like labored or restricted speech, overly-loose associations, exotic grammar, aphasias, alogia or a poverty of speech, excessive abstraction, repetition, pressured speech, and incoherence or word salad.

Most of the time these qualities are examined clinically and interpreted as organic syndromes of one kind or another. In most cases these things have diagnostic value and there is little we have to offer in the way of treatment. But today I want us to consider another level of pathologizing. What about the words themselves? We can easily see that there are words that are narcissistic. I'd even go so far as to call them meglomaniacal. Take the tiny little word *Up*. Clearly suffering from the *little man complex*. *Up* has taken its two little letters and inserted them into more various contexts than probably any other word we can name. Here I borrow from Frank Endicott in William R. Espy's book, <u>The Game of Words</u>:

It is easy to understand *up* meaning toward the sky or toward the top of a list. But when we waken, why do we wake *up*? At a meeting, why does a topic come *up*, why to participants speak *up*, and why are the officers *up* for election? And why is it *up* to the secretary to write *up* a report. Often the little word isn't needed, but we use it anyway. We brighten *up* a room, light *up* a cigar, polish *up* the silver, lock *up* the house, and fix *up* the old car. At other times, it has special meanings. People stir *up* trouble, line *up* for tickets, work *up* and appetite, think *up* excuses, get tied *up* in traffic. To be dressed is one thing, but to be dressed *up* is special. It may be confusing but a drain must be opened *up* because it is stopped *up*. We open *up* a store in the morning and close it *up* at night. We seem to be mixed *up* about *up*." (1971, pp. 256-7)

It is interesting to note that we seem to have no power over this greedy exhibition. All that the word police can do is record it. For example, if one looks at the dictionaries of 1920, 1940, 1960, and 1980, one can find that the listing of possible uses and meanings for *up* simply grows and grows, or shall I say goes up. *Up* is not losing meanings along the way. At least not yet.

In fact, the only countering response to this wild little emperor seems to come from the realm of words themselves as we bear witness to the phenomenal growth of possible uses for the word *down*. More people are getting *down* with the word *down* now than ever before. It is now pretty clear that it is OK to think something *up*, but if that is the case, then you have to write it *down*. And of course we have seen a similar phenomenon with the pair of words, *good* and *bad*. *Good*, prideful of its particular relationship to the one true god, has gone around applying itself to everything we do. *Good* day, *good* night, *good* bye, for example. No wonder that *bad* has to respond. Now we have come to the point where, in some circles *bad* is better than *good*. Does anyone really think that people are in charge of this?

There are words that seem to suffer a kind of identity problem. They are ashamed of their own heritage and, like emigrants to a new land, seek to change their image by changing their spelling. For example, Piggy Bank was originally simply the Saxon word Pygg meaning a clay jar to keep money in. Look what it has done. Like an opportunistic impersonator it tricked us with a slight of ear and, while we weren't paying attention, flashed up its new image, a pig. That was a pretty successful makeover.

I think some words are erotically charged and maybe even promiscuous. The word doctors have invented a word for this: Neologism. New words are springing up all the time. An example: I once knew a man who had a whole collection of hybrid words. One that he used a lot was "flustrated." The first time I heard it I had to stifle my imperious corrections. It became clear fairly soon that this word was a natural born child of frustrated and flustered. For whatever reason, they had gotten together and then placed their lovechild into the mouth of this man. With more time I came to see that this word was not a mistake. Its usage was precise, describing more than just a blend of its parents—something with its own character. I feel sure I will one day see it in the dictionary.

Too much tameness can make a word wild just as using it too wildly can make it tame. Ecologist and cultural critique, Theodore Rozack, gives us an example in our storied relationship with the word "rape." It was a word nearly dropped from the lexicon out of Victorian sensibilities. Too evocative for use, it seems. Now, suddenly re-imbued with metaphorical power, it is used frequently and loudly in a wild array of new contexts.

That brings us to the dead and dying words--words that have been so mortally wounded by thoughtless speech that they have become dismembered from their images. I wonder if a word like *rape*, for example, could become so successful in its reemergence that it would lose the edge that gives it life, if used in too many contexts, or used as shorthand. Hillman suggests that psychology is full of such tired words, those tired of carrying the burden of imagination for us. Words we use instead of thinking, instead of hosting images which might disturb our sleep. Somewhere, in his own version of being a word cop, he made of list of these words and swore never to use them again, at least in his writing. It was, I think, a compassionate stance. More than just scolding all of us for being lazy and careless in our use of words, he was being kind of an ambulance driver or medic. He was trying to pull words off the firing line before they died of utter fatigue.

This is a nice opportunity to make a slight turn—to look at the problem of psychology in its relation to words and language. I think that our field, even the parts of it which devote themselves to depth psychology, have tended to remain stuck in a utilitarian fantasy about words and language. That is probably a reflection of early power alignments with medical science in which the vision of a brave new civilized world, where all the wildness would be tamed, was put forward as the ideal. Language and words have always been a part of it.

One of Freud's most impressive arguments for the existence of the unconscious was his study of slips of the tongue. It is clear that he knew that these persistent failures at correct speech alluded to something deep and significant. They were certainly more than just neuromuscular lapses. But what? Similarly, Jung's early work with word association experiments seemed to arise from his awareness of our deeply wild relationship to words. Both men recognized that words are like dreams in their capacity to reveal the personal as well as the collective unconscious. But their work has been followed primarily in its clinical directions, which emphasizes the forensic over the aesthetic values of psychology's interest in words. Such a tendency reflects what I call a utilitarian view of language. Words are tools we use to communicate. When we use them incorrectly or idiosyncratically, it is seen as an opportunity to explore what that represents as a personal psychological symptom. There is nothing here reflecting a sense of words having their own reason for being.

In his later work Jung took another look at language and words. He began to allude to the power of words themselves to construct personal psychology. Blending the themes of the collective unconscious with the autonomous psyche, he began to see the archetypal qualities of language. In his 1958 essay on "Dream Analysis" he writes:

> Our words carry the totality of that history which was once so alive and still exists in every human being. With every word we touch upon a historical fibre, as it were, in our fellow-beings: and therefore every word we speak strikes that chord in every other living being whenever we speak the same language. (Jung, 1958/1984, pp. 69-70)

This is an idea with huge implications. One would think that it might call for an ongoing devotion, at least on the part of Jungians and archetypalists, to some kind of linguistic exploration. But, with a few exceptions, that has not been the case. In the realm of clinical practice, a space that is so dependent upon words and speech, there has been little concern for the deeper and wild nature of words and language.

Psychology has fallen quite behind the culture on this point. The rest of the world seems more in touch with the fact that post-modern philosophers and philologists have given us a dynamic view of language as a living presence in its own right. We increasingly move about in a world which knows itself to be invented by the language we had thought only to name it with. Language, it turns out, can no longer be taken simply as a tool with which we describe psyche; rather, it is, like the archetypes, a co-creating partner of psyche. Language, we may assert, *is* an archetype! But, if that's true, it certainly calls for a shift in our attitude when speaking. If words do not merely reflect psychological experience, but also help in forming it, are we not ethically bound to discover more about how we choose our words and how they choose us? Do we not have an obligation to treat language with the same reverence we allow other archetypal presences? In a variety of contexts, Jung cautions us that the curse of the modern age is that it has gone too far in reducing life's mysteries to mundane rationalities.

If we dare to see it, such reductionism is most prevalent in our common attitude toward language. With our dictionaries, grammars and style manuals, we create a myth of dominion which allows us to fantasize that we merely *use* language as a tool. We seem to have forgotten that the Word and God were once thought to be the same and that, whether we choose to remember or not, words have had, and will continue to have, both archetypal depth and incantational power.

Now we come to that riddle I mentioned, because even as I hear myself speaking, that fantasy of control rings loudly. In calling for psychologists to engage in a conscious rectification of our use of language, am I not reasserting the image of language as a tool to be used? Used properly, but still used? Is there a way out of this trap?

Well, yes. In order to get there, I will digress a bit into some of the theory of archetypal psychology. There is not a lot of practical *how to* in the literature of archetypal psychology, but one helpful piece of dogma is that when we have become boxed in by our own brilliant concepts, we can rely on the free play of images to make us a bit more space. That is our way out of this box. Let's see if it works.

As I mentioned earlier, the original title of this talk was "The Eloquence and Whimsy of Archetypal Speech." Digressing further, let's go to another one of the few "how to's" of archetypal praxis—what Hillman calls *personification*. Here you stop objectifying things by using the word "the." That gives the things the possibility of their own subjectivity. Next, you capitalize the first letters, which gives things a kind of personal significance, respect, or personhood. Such is the move of personification. That is what I have done with "Eloquence" and "Whimsy." They are beings now. They are separate beings and they are also a couple. Even more, let's imagine them to be a dancing couple, a couple of dancing words which reflect the dual nature of all words—Eloquence and Whimsy. In this way,

Eloquence and Whimsy can be imagined as figures, relating to each other, relating to us,

and dancing through the tones, rhythms, and cadences of our speech. I suggest they are

there whether we allow ourselves to see them or not.

I first met Eloquence and Whimsy as a couple while doing some early research on this

business of language and psyche. I found myself re-reading Hillman's <u>Revisioning</u>

<u>Psychology</u>, looking for passages referring to the need for eloquence. I found this one:

> In Renaissance rhetoric anima appears yet once more, this time as Aphrodite Peitho, the persuasive Venus who turns our head with a well-turned phrase. Rhetoric played such an important part in Renaissance writing because it is the speech form of the anima archetype, the style of words when informed by the soul. (Hillman, 1975 p. 213)

Hillman goes on in this context to remind us that rhetoric, while it is persuasive, is

not about logic and proof. But it is also not about inchoate references to feelings. Rather,

this animated speech of soul is marked mainly by *eloquence*, "where care for words means

care of soul" (1975, p. 214). We can take it that care for words means to use words with

care—finding right words—not necessarily correct words, but words that carry soul

uprightly, as if with reverence.

What a fine idea this seemed. And James is always so eloquent. But then something

happened. As I typed the word, Peitho, I realized that I had stumbled on the

pronunciation. I found it just a strange word. I was ignorant of its personhood. "Oh well," I

thought, "I'll just use it. What the Hell."

Then, I suddenly heard the sound of Hillman's voice. It was the echo of a

conversation I'd had with him a few years earlier. We had been talking about how

important it is to really know the words we use. He quoted the author Milan Kundera as

having once said "Stupidity consists in passing on ideas, concepts, words, without thinking

them yourself. Just mouthing them and passing them on. That's stupidity" (personal

communication, 1996). This is the problem of trying to use someone else's portion of

Eloquence. It can make you stupid.

Not wanting to be stupid, I decided to read about Peitho. A few sources recalled for me that this name is the Latin form of Persuasion, a lesser deity often in the company of Aphrodite. It happens that Peitho had some sisters and one of them was Tyche, goddess of Chance and Fortune. So there they were. My two beautiful parts of speech. Persuasiveness and Chance. Or as I call them, Eloquence and Whimsy. My desire to be an eloquent servant to the Eloquence of Hillman had danced me into a chance meeting of Peitho and I was persuaded to dance on to meet her sister. By pure Chance I was introduced to Whimsy and to the whimsical nature of words when they are left to chance.

As we carefully use our words—the work of Eloquence—we are also used by them. Words seek us out for their own purpose. Even as we craft our speech so that persuasive images are revealed, words and phrases will seem to slip from our tongues, entering our speech without pre-thought. They come as kinships of deities, as puns, metaphors, and mistakes of meaning and sound. What craft is this? I say it is the dance step of Whimsy, the full and wonderful partner of Eloquence. It is Whimsy, in fact, who rescues Eloquence from the pratfall of correctness. When we are most deeply engaged in Eloquence, we may also be in moments full of Whimsy. It may be only through our intuitive awareness that some of what we have spoken was unintended that we are saved from taking ourselves too seriously—a prelude to demagoguery.

Another story might help to illustrate this interplay of Eloquence, the quest for the right word, and Whimsy, the natural movement of wild words. On a construction site, workers are moving large things around clumsily when someone says "This would be a lot easier with a dolly." Someone else wonders about the word. How is it spelled? Is it Dolly or Dollie? What is its origin? These are the questions of Eloquence and they pull us into a posture of attention. As the workmen pay attention, *dolly* begins to dance. Is it related to Dolls? Is it a cousin to Salvador? After a time, someone suggests that it might come from the Dahli Lama because people also use Llamas to move things around sometimes. Everyone agrees this must be right. The word appreciates our attention and offers up the images it holds. As we use the image of the Dahli to move our boxes we are conscious to pick up our saffron robes so as not to get them caught in the wheels or on the furniture. Later in the day a decision is made to leave a tree in place rather than cut it down, as had been earlier planned. A Buddhist sensibility had been growing in the workmen with the vibrating image of The Dahli Lama and the robes.

This story suggests the dynamic and consequential possibilities of paying attention to the dance of Eloquence and Whimsy. It cannot be choreographed, but it must be properly danced to release it storehouse of images. Properly danced does not mean only dancing the right steps. Eloquence alone is not enough, but as we can see, if we don't get too righteous in our search for the right word then Eloquence herself will ask Whimsy to dance.

So what does all this mean? Why should we as psychologists be interested in the wildlife of words—in the lovely dance of Eloquence and Whimsy? I suggest that we have been enchanted by modernist utilitarian ideas of the psyche and, specifically, of language. We need to wake up and notice that in the play of words there is so much more going on than meets the eye and the ear. I think that until we do, we will do therapy and psychology but we won't know how it works.

As an example of this slowing down and paying attention in therapy, I will share a conversation I had with Russell Lockhart, author of Words as Eggs and Psyche Speaks, about the patient who was *flustrated*. He agreed with me that this word was the result of a wild joining of *frustrated* and *flustered*. He suggested that this confluence reveals the erotic power of words. He reminded me that what is important is to pay attention to what happens when flustrated gets itself into the talk. My initial corrective sensibility is an important reflection of my posture toward the patient. Notice that and move on. Move on to the eros of the situation. Something about these words wants to end the separateness—to come together and make something new both in the words and the speakers. As Lockhart put it, "when somebody says *flustrated* to you, something in you responds. Something in you wants to talk that way, too. I am sure about that." (personal communication, 1995).

The words themselves are showing the way for the therapist to change his posture. As I came to see the rightness of this word "flustrated," it had the effect of inviting me into a more reciprocal erotic field with the patient. If we only pay attention to the assigned meanings of words and don't notice their movement, we miss the whole entire dance. We miss what they are showing us about how to be.

For those who have been therapists for awhile, I will tell a familiar story. A patient returns to therapy after a week or so and is beaming with energy and excitement. She announces: "I have been thinking about something you said last week and it feels like my whole world has shifted. I see my situation so much more clearly now." Then she proceeds to tell you the thing you said and you have absolute certainty that you never said such a thing. These moments and others like them reveal that psychotherapy is not so much a conscious collaboration in service of brilliant insight as it is a ritualized attitude of paying attention. We pay attention not only to the smart things we think to say, but to the persuasive and fortunate dancing of Eloquence and Whimsy, one that may actually take place later, in the parking lot, or on the drive home.

Words are living creatures. Words present themselves for treatment through patients just as surely as patients present themselves in words. If we see that, then the words we treat will be assisting us in treating our patients. We must follow the dance of our words and be both eloquent and whimsical. This is our service to the nature of words.

References

Carroll, L. (1872). Through the looking-glass and what Alice found there. London: Macmillan & Company.

Espy, W. (1972). The game of words. New York: Branham House.

Hillman, J. (1975). Revisioning psychology. New York: Harper and Row

Jung, C.G. (1984). Dream analysis (R.F.C. Hull, Trans.). Princeton NJ: Princeton University Press. (Original work published in 1958)

Khidr, The Mysterious Stranger: The Mythopoetic Encounter with the Other by Barbara Annan, Ph.D.

I would like to begin with a poem by Mary Oliver. She captures a poignant moment of encounter with the mysterious stranger in the way that Khidr has captured me.

FLYING

Sometimes,
on a plane,
you see a stranger.
He is so beautiful!
His nose going down
in the old Greek way,
or his smile
a wild
Mexican fiesta.
You want to say:
do you know
how beautiful you are?
You leap up
into the aisle,
you can't let him go
until he has touched you
shyly, until you have rubbed him,
oh, lightly,
like a coin
you find on the earth somewhere
shining and unexpected and,
without thinking,
reach for. You stand there
shaken
by the strangeness,
by the splash of his touch.
When he's gone
you stare like an animal into
the blinding clouds
with the snapped chain of your life,
The life you know:
the deeply affectionate earth,
the familiar landscapes
slowly turning
thousands of feet below.   (1983, pp. 34-35)

It is said, in Moslem lands, that when the name of Khidr is spoken, he is present. This is an auspicious sign, for Khidr is a fascinating stranger encountered on the threshold of change. It is my thesis that the Khidr story offers a metaphor for the process of individuation as a journey which I see through a depth psychological hermeneutic as a developmental transformation of consciousness, a new way of knowing.

I will present two main points: first, who is Khidr? I will provide some background from Islam and Western culture about this mysterious stranger. Secondly, what is the depth psychological understanding of an encounter with a stranger who suddenly impacts our life and changes our way of thinking? The unexpected, stirring encounter is a significant soul experience, whether in dream, vision, or a day world event interpreted as a dream. This paper offers an interpretation of an ancient mythologem that sheds light on certain meetings, perhaps disregarded as uncomfortable or uncanny, that hold a lingering, even numinous significance.

I.   Who is Khidr?

The name, al-Khidr, is Arabic for "the green one." Khidr is an enigmatic, elusive figure in Middle Eastern religious literature and mythology. He is green because his life is everlasting and he knows where to find the secret water of life. Green is the color of life, and in Islam, green is the color of holiness. Khidr has been taught divine wisdom by the angels, and from time to time, he walks with ordinary mortals.

I first heard the story of Khidr as told in the Holy Book of Islam, the Qur'an, when it was related by a professor of Islamic studies, Herbert Mason, who had experienced his own unexpected encounter. A stranger had approached Mason in a small mosque in Istanbul. This robed figure uttered some cryptic words, offered two oranges and a piece of bread, and when the brief interaction was over, Mason's perception of the world was permanently transformed. Anne-Marie Schimmel, the Harvard Islamic scholar, later interpreted the experience, saying, "That was Khidr. He has given you the kirqua, the spiritual mantle." Mason did in fact become a teacher and translator of Islamic works, notably Louis Massignon's (1982) study of the Sufi martyr, al-Hallaj (d. 309/805). The story of the impact of this brief, expected encounter with the stranger in Mason's story resonates with my personal experience and cross-cultural literary and religious accounts of such haunting, even uncanny, encounters.

"Constant conjunctions" are what Bion and Hume call these "events that haunt you…moments of unknowable conceptions, inviting exploration of their resonance" (Rhode,

1994, p. 33). The mysterious stranger exudes allure, a compelling attraction that drew me to make this the focus of my dissertation and my passion. This stranger embodies an archetypal mythologem little known in Western Judeo-Christian technological culture, yet one that may be surprisingly familiar to you.

Depth Psychology, nourished by the vision of Carl Jung, gives us passage into the liminal landscape where events arise out of unconscious origins. In this psychological threshold zone, we may meet an unlikely stranger, with a subtle look, odd but significant words, and an unexpected, compelling presence who bursts into life and turns our known world upside down.

Mary Watkins writes of "Invisible Guests," and of inner dialogues with the angels of imaginal reality that teach us to hear the events of everyday life symbolically and metaphorically (1970, p. 75). She asks us to consider who is unseen in this room with us at this moment. Who is with us when we are at a threshold, a transition point when we must bear suffering, anxiety, or make a life decision? Ancestors, angelic guides, departed loved ones, or imaginary companions are some figures we as children might have played with in our youthful, unanalyzed reality. Khidr is an invisible guest, but there is a paradox, for his form may also be experienced as solid, autonomous, and seemingly unspiritual.

The story of Khidr is found in many forms, indicating its archetypal nature in cultural mythopoesis. I will provide you with some examples from Islam and from non-Islamic cultures.

A. Khidr in Islam

The figure of Khidr is well-known in Islam as an angel, or as an otherworldly guide, one who often appears in the wilderness, times of trouble, or in dreams. The story in the *Qur'an* found in verses 60-82 of Sura (chapter) 18, entitled al-Khaf, The Cave is my primary source. The narrative tells of a journey into an unknown wilderness. The seeker, Moses, patriarch of Israel, meets the immortal Khidr at a special place, a rock "where the two seas meet," and strange things happen. A cooked fish comes to life again and burrows its way to the sea. Moses' goal is to learn wisdom from Khidr. Khidr is not keen on this but agrees after eliciting a promise from Moses not to ask questions on the journey, but to wait and watch in silence. Khidr performs three bizarre acts that Moses cannot tolerate, so the Israelite lawgiver breaks his promise and questions the immortal one. When Moses receives Khidr's explanations, it is time to part ways. Moses accepts the unsuspected wisdom that surpasses and alters his previous perspective. The orthodox Islamic interpretation of the story is a lesson of unquestioning, patient surrender to the will of Allah.

For the Sufis, the mystics of Islam, Khidr is recognized as a psychopomp, a murshid or otherworldly guide who initiates the seeker into the mysteries and gives him a spiritual mantle, the kirqua, and a new identity as a lover of God. The poetry of Sufi mystics, such as Jalal al-Din Rumi (d. 672/1273), Ghalib (d.1247/1869), Wali (d.1085/1707) and Hafiz (d. 767/1389) are ablaze with references to Khidr as the green parrot, or the bearer of the cup containing the water of life.

Hafiz, the fourteenth century poet of Persia, evokes the delight of the marvelous encounter with Khidr in metaphor:

> Ho, O parrot, speaker of secrets!
> May your beak never lack sugar!
>
> May you live long, your heart be happy forever,
> For you have shown us a lovely image of his figure.
>
> You spoke in riddles with the companions,
> For God's sake, lift the veil from this enigma.
>
> Oh bright luck, splash our face with rosewater,
> For we are stained with sleep.
>
> (Hafiz, 1995, p. 61)

The literal translation of the Persian phrase "may you live long" is "may your head be green," a wordplay on the color of the parrot (p. 161). The parrot is a common symbol for Khidr because he repeats the words of the Divine (p. 24). The phrase, "bright luck," translates as "awake (good) luck," suggesting a shift from the unconscious state, as one awakens a sleeper by sprinkling rosewater on the sleeper's face (p. 161).

The third reality of the psyche, where Khidr dwells, and the manifestations of the subtle body, are described in the elaborate cosmology of Islamic theologians of the Golden

Age of Islam, the period of our Middle Ages. Ibn 'Arabi (d. 638/1240), al-Suhrawardi (d. 587/1037) and Ibn Sina (d. 428/1240) write in magnificent detail how creation emanates in layers of reality, enveloping one another, thus creating successive levels of knowing. Honoring the celestial spheres of the cosmic mountain, the art and architecture of Islam reproduce the levels of divine emanations. One sees it in the multiple graduated arches of doorways and ceilings such as in the great Hagia Sophia of Istanbul. The pilgrim on the mystic path enters another realm, where the ego is surrendered and consciousness is receptive to encounter the mysterious Other.

Henri Corbin, the French Orientalist who joined Carl Jung at the Eranos conferences, describes the imaginal realm of the Sufis, the "Mundis Imaginalis" (1972/64). In Corbin's essay by that name, we hear the words of al-Suhrawardi, describing an encounter with a strange being, the crimson archangel. An escaped prisoner in the desert is led by an angelic being to a special place. This hidden place is beyond Mount Khaf, a "nonwhere" land, where Khidr waits by the spring of life (p. 3). Meeting Khidr means relinquishing ordinary knowledge, in order to go to a secret, privileged place with an astounding possibility, that of becoming "like Khidr" (p. 3).

B. Khidr in Western Culture

Beyond the Islamic paradigm, Khidr has numerous parallels. In Judaic literature, Khidr may be identified as Elijah the Prophet traveling with Rabbi Joshua ben Levi, in a text in the Babylonian Talmud, closely paralleling the Qur'anic story (Friedlaender, 1915). Elijah appears in folklore and legends of the Chassidim performing the function of Khidr in Islam. Khidr's traits of paradox and elusiveness identify him with the Greek messenger of the Gods, Hermes, a threshold figure. Cultural myths of the Roman god Mercury, the elusive Mercurius of the alchemists, and the Spirit Mercury in the fairy tale of "The Woodcutter's Son" inform us of the collective nature of the mysterious encounter.

A prototype of the Khidr myth has been traced to the Gilgamesh Epic of ancient Sumeria. A classic Persian legend of Alexander the Great tells of his journey with Khidr to find the Fountain of Youth, at the place "where the two seas of east and west meet" (Gibb & Kramers, 1961, p. 232). The theme of the Khidr encounter is discernable in the Arthurian

Romance cycle of Sir Gawain and the Green Knight, and in the Hindu fable of The King and the Corpse. In Dante's <u>Divine Comedy</u>, we recall that the traveler in the Inferno is met and guided through the underworld by the wisdom figure of Virgil, who functions as Khidr does, as a psychopomp.

In German literature, J.W. v. Goethe sings in his West-Ostlicher Diwan,

<u>Unter Lieben, Trinken, Singen,</u>

<u>Soll dich Chisrs Quell verjuengen.</u>

While loving, drinking, and singing,

Khidr's fountain shall rejuvenate you.

(Schimmel, 1992, p. 71)

My research reveals the presence of Khidr, if not by that name then as the mysterious stranger, in all times and cultures, indicating the presence of an archetypal form. Meeting a mysterious stranger while on a journey, and being transformed, is a primordial theme, as prevalent and familiar as the Hero's Journey, so well delineated in the works of Joseph Campbell. I find the essence of the journey expressed poignantly by Mason. This is from the introduction to his translation of <u>Gilgamesh</u> (1970, p. 111):

> We… go on an impossible pilgrimage, which from a rational point of view is futile: to find the one wise man whomever or wherever he may be (and we all have it engrained in our metaphysical consciousness, no matter in what age we live, that such a wise man exists or should exist as witness to Wisdom); and to find from him the secret of eternal life or the secret of adjusting to this life as best we can.

II.   A Depth Psychological Interpretation.

Recognizing characteristics of Khidr that are archetypal leads to my second point; what can depth psychology teach us about the encounter? The affect experienced in the presence of such a stranger is typically unsettling, and confusing. These emotions include disorientation, anxiety, irritation, erotic arousal, and even shock. The encounter seems bizarre, alien, and awesome, as is consistent with a numinous experience. Eros and Desire play a part, as well.

There is a sense of allure, a strong fascination that draws the subject to come closer. When does an event become a constant conjunction, a haunting pull towards the unknown? Sufis affirm that whatever happens around a teacher of the spiritual way "is never what the disciple expects" (Sviri, 1997, p. 97). An encounter that produces such a reaction in the consciousness is a clue to its nature. In depth psychological terms, it is archetypal, emanating from the unconscious prototypal world of forms and ideas. "Archetypes are not known directly, but through the affect", through the emotions they stir in the psyche (Jacobi, 1959, p. 31)

Proximity to an archetypal form is proximity to the Self, the "ordering and unifying center of the total psyche" (Edinger, 1972). The Self includes the chaotic sacred realm, the timeless and numinous contents of the unconscious as well as the conscious ego. Certain others function as objects for the ego's projection of the Self, which in turn constellate a third, subtle entity. These encounters are characterized by synchronistic events and a sense of altered consciousness. The overall experience leaves the subject with a radical shift in perspective, a developmental shift so that psychologically a new way of knowing is claimed.

You may recall Jung's experience described in his autobiography, <u>Memories, Dreams, Reflections</u> (1961), of his descent into the unconscious where he encountered the Wise Old Man as the Prophet Elijah. Elijah, appearing as a psychopomp, thus a form of Self, later transmuted into Philemon, the otherworld figure who became Jung's mentor. Sufis recognize Elijah and Khidr as partners, as almost interchangeable immortal beings. Jung (1939/44) interprets the Qur'anic story of the journey of Khidr and Moses as a "rebirth mystery," an allegorical story of individuation. In Jung's hermeneutic, Moses represents the conscious ego in a state of inflation, overvaluing the rational, intellectual function. Khidr represents the Self, unconscious wisdom appearing to compensate for the ego.. In this story, Khidr represents the Polar Opposite, the undervalued, intuitive function, constellated to balance the psychological situation, to bring Psyche to wholeness. When the two polar opposites meet in the threshold realm, where the two seas meet, Moses as ego struggles with the tension of unknowing.

John Haule, in his book <u>Divine Madness</u> (1990), writes of Khidr as the third, the creative liberating presence in romantic relationships. A psychological synergism, the transcendent function in the form of Khidr is operant in relationships of significance, representing a new psychic quantum, the soul's metaphorical dream of alchemical transmutation. It is in the space of liminal consciousness that the metaphorical transmutation of the alchemist occurs. This is the work that goes on in the therapist's container, where the place of unknowing is entered as dream, mutative metaphor, imagery or as Robert Romanyshyn (2000, p. 39) suggests, the reverie of Gaston Bachelard. In unknowing and relationship of opposites is where the transcendent function not only transforms the personality structure but recreates life.

Becoming conscious is a function of the ego, Jung tells us. The ego cannot know what the Self has in store, thus Unknowing and contact with the liminal realm is implicit in the individuation process of becoming conscious. Unknowing is the hallmark of encounter with the archetypal form of Khidr who re-creates the world of the conscious ego. Many dreams, paranormal experiences, unexpected, strangely haunting encounters occur in liminal states produced by travel, fatigue, illness, crisis, or life transitions. Psychologist Winnicott describes a "third area," the "interplay at the edges of curtains," where there is neither inner psychic reality nor external reality" (1971, p. 96).

Contemporary Western accounts come to mind, of numinous encounters in the "betwixt and between," urban legends of the disappearing hitchhiker, encounters with UFOs, aliens, angelic guides, and the living landscape of cyberspace, a likely space for Hermes, Khidr, and the mysterious Other. These experiences, whether interpreted as subjective projections or objective reality, or neither, also belong to the middle realm, the place of "nonwhere" that the Islamic world has long honored as the third reality. The depth psychologist enters the third realm, creating a bridge between two worlds, connecting the client with unconscious subtle forms. The process is one of making conscious the dream, myth, or subjective experience of the Other, producing a release of new life and libidinous energy.

The mythologem of the mysterious encounter and Khidr remain fascinating to me because in the unknowing there is offered so much potential. Archetypal moments have effects that make "visualizations of them possible" (Jung, 1954/69, p. 214). Visualization takes place in staying with the uncomfortable, numinous image of Khidr, a break-though of unconscious contents. The unsettling experience of meeting the archetypal Other the Self, as Khidr, and the ensuing work of becoming conscious, is the adventure of individuation. This work is for us as individuals but also for the collective, just as the meaning of meeting Khidr is not just for the East but also for the West. The gold in the darkness of unknowing is the order in chaos, the elixir distilled by patient listening, by staying in that liminal landscape long enough to hear the meaning of the stranger's message. I leave you with the thought that the encounter with the unsettling, mysterious stranger is the very essence of depth psychology.

References

Al-Khadir (1961). Shorter encyclopedia of Islam. (H. A. R. Gibb & J. H. Kramers, Eds.) Leiden: E. J. Brill.

Corbin, H. (1972). Mundis imaginalis or the imaginary and the imaginal. (R. Hornine, Trans.). Spring 31, 1-19. (Original paper delivered 1964)

Edinger, E. F. (1972). Ego and archetype: Individuation and the religious function of the psyche. New York: Penguin Books.

Friedlaender, I. (1915). Khidr. In J. Hastings (Ed.), The encyclopaedia of religion and ethics. New York: Charles Scribner's Sons.

Hafiz. (1995). The green sea of heaven: Fifty ghazals from the diwan of Hafiz (Elizabeth Gray, Jr. Trans.). Ashland, OR: White Cloud Press.

Haule, J. R. (1990). Divine madness: Archetypes of romantic love. Boston: Shambhala Press.

Jacobi, J. (1959). Complex/archetype/symbol. Princeton, NJ: Princeton University Press.

Jung, C. G. (1944). The different aspects of rebirth (T. Lorenz, Trans.). Spring 4, 1-24. (Original work 1939)

Jung, C. G. (1969). On the nature of the psyche. In The collected works of C. G. Jung (Vol. 8) (R. F. C. Hull (Trans.). Princeton, NJ: Princeton University Press. (Original work published 1954).

Jung, C. G. (1973). Memories, dreams, reflections (R. & C. Winston, Trans.). New York: Vintage Books. (Original work published 1961).

Oliver, M. (1983). American primitive. Boston: Little Brown and Company.

Mason, H. (1970). Gilgamesh: A verse narrative. New York: Mentor.

Massignon, L. (1982). The passion of al-Hallaj: Mystic and martyr of Islam (H. Mason, Trans.). Princeton, NJ: Princeton University Press. (Original work published 1975).

Rhode, E. (1994). Psychotic metaphysics. London: Karnac Books, Ltd.

Romanyshyn, R. D. (2000). Alchemy and the subtle body of metaphor. In Pathways into the Jungian world. New York: Routledge.

Schimmel, A. (1992). A two-colored brocade. Chapel Hill, NC: University of North Carolina Press.

Sviri, S. (1997). The taste of hidden things. Inverness, CA: The Golden Sufi Center.

Watkins, M. (1970). Invisible guests: The development of imaginal dialogues. Boston: Sigo Press.

Winnicott, D. W. (1971). The location of cultural experience. In <u>Playing and reality</u>. New York: Routledge.

Narcissus, Echo and Irony's Resonance by Dennis Patrick Slattery, Ph.D.

Irony demands a certain attention span, and the ability to sustain antithetical
ideas, even when they collide with one another. Strip irony away from reading,
and it loses at once all discipline and all surprise. (Harold Bloom, 2000, p.103)

Harold Bloom's quote above offers us a new map of myth-reading, through the lens of
irony. Who can forget Ishmael in Melville's enduring epic, Moby-Dick (1851/1976) using the
skin of a whale, sliced as thin as papier-mache, laid out on his text so that he may magnify the
words describing the various categories of whales. An ironic lens, certainly, in the face of the
hunting expedition he finds himself on. The myth becomes transparent when such ironic
spectacles are placed between eye and text.

In his new study, Theorizing About Myth, Robert Segal seasons his own study with a
dash of ironic flavoring: "It is fashionable to say that whatever else myth is, it is compatible
with science. For if myth is incompatible with science, it is unacceptable to moderns, who, it is
taken for granted, accept science" (1999, p.7). Today we have both a science of myth and a
myth of science, both studies well worth our time. Perhaps Jung launched us into this realm
with his study of Kore: Essays on a Science of Mythology. What is "unscientific" about myth is
stated trenchantly by Murray Stein in his own writing on the Narcissus and Echo story, the
central focus of this essay: "Elusiveness to the intellect is characteristic of myth and is one of its
strengths, in that this quality teases us into deeper psychological reflections than would
otherwise be likely" (1976, p. 32). So how to deal with the elusive quality of myth, poetry, life
itself, is, as I explore it here, through the play of irony around both ideas and images. Ovid
suggests in his close and detailed rendering of this ancient myth that self-fixation treads where
irony is disallowed. One step further: perhaps the myth narrated by Ovid in his
Metamorphosis allows us to consider the story as a metaphor for the movement of myth itself
in the psyche, and that its elusive quality for the intellect is in fact its greatest strength.

What an irony is imbedded in that possibility! Recall Bloom's idea of retrieving irony as
a key ingredient to the pleasures of reading itself. Even if the character of Narcissus misses the

ironic condition of his own self-reflection–and that to me is an open question at this point–we need not. Irony is for us a disposition by which to enter and entertain, these characters we live with for a time.

Unquestionably, this myth is one of the oldest and most famous in all of mythology, if not the most frequently cited. Its reflective power has flowed down through the ages, coursing through certain epochs and even defining them by means of this powerful narrative of the self. Stein points us in his essay to Louise Vinge's The Narcissus Theme in Western Literature to illustrate the ubiquitous and intensely popular nature of this story. Is it our prevailing myth, as Christopher Lasch suggests in The Culture of Narcissism or Nathan Schwartz-Salant argues in Narcissism and Character Transformation? Has therapy itself, as an art form, calcified along the edges of the still pond that Narcissus will gaze in and become arrested enslaved to , as James Hillman entertains the idea in "From Mirror to Window: Curing Psychoanalysis of Its Narcissism" where this myth has "become the rage, the universal diagnosis" (1989, p. 62).

Perhaps the pond is ample enough to entertain a Narcissus genre, wherein all of psyche's pathological sizes can fit into the same watery space or all of its myriad figures onto the same beach blanket. Such is the danger when mythology creeps almost imperceptibly and subtly across the street into the basement of the house called Ideology. Furthermore, it has become almost a dismissive term, wherein "narcissistic" enters the lexicon of pop psychology, and almost because of the glibness with which the term is used, we know the myth has lost its poetic core. It is a clear indicator and prescription for our return to its details to see what is percolating in the mirroring pool of its own reflection and to gather in the details of the story, to revision its particulars, to retrieve its richly poetic contours, smell once again its details and stare for a moment, like Narcissus, into the arresting images, but not without a sense of irony. For this myth, like all myths, offers a particular way of knowing something and knowing it mimetically, that is, by analogy, which Jung has described as the most favored or naturally inclined or efficacious way in which the psyche moves in the world.

To retrieve irony is only part of the preparation for reading poetry, fiction, and mythology; doing so allows us to entertain ideas through them. Before psychology there was the voice of the poet who would offer us insights into the human heart and help us to discover those deep dark patterns of the soul that engage all of us daily, whether or no we are consciously aware of their presences. So to enter this myth is to engage a mytho-poetic way of knowing through a shaped and formed action that has correspondences, or in the phrase of depth psychology, an "as if" relation to the action of our own lives, our own psyches.

My second question is more immediate: what is the action of the Narcissus myth as it develops something crucial about the imagination of irony? For perhaps irony is a disposition that has been lost to the postmodern world, replaced by a thinner and tinnier substitute: cynicism. Ovid's myth reveals what is lost when irony dissolves: a distance from the self that allows one to maintain a perspective that is fluid and in motion.

To the particulars of the myth we should then attend, in the same way one might begin in therapy when the client begins to tell his or her story. What is the action I am hearing here? Not "what is its meaning or significance," but rather "what is the action?" And how does the plot of the story, what Aristotle called "the soul of tragedy,"--which we can extend to include more than just that genre–lead us to the deeper action, not just in the characters but in ourselves. What begins to echo in us through the images? To do so is to enter what Bloom in the same excerpt cited earlier called "deep reading" (2000, p. 104). For the stories that arrive like vehicles that carry the myth may be the beginnings of therapy for an individual or for an entire people. What is echoed in therapy and what is ironic about therapy might be our guiding questions initially, as we slip through the portal of the myth.

Myths, like poems, are forms of meditation, even contemplation, stirred by the power of the stories themselves in their movement and in their images. Mytho-poiesis is a different form of imagining, one that takes account of metaphysics and the physics of the physical, so we read these actions with a different eye. They present to us a way into seeing that ordinary perception does not allow, so even to look into the still waters of a myth is already to be connected to the Narcissus/Echo narrative.

Perhaps the story of Narcissus and Echo embodies the seminal story of myth itself, along with the caveat: "Beware of what you gaze on, for its power may be to arrest you, since the plot is finally about what echoes within you as both image and word." No poet understood this better than Dante Alighieri as he passed through the gates into the infernal realm; even he needed a guide to unglue him numerous times from his arrested gaze during that journey. It is possible, his Commedia suggests, to see TOO MUCH of oneself in the other and what an arresting moment that can be!

The Plot of the Myth:

"Narcissus and Echo" is part of Book 3 of Ovid's Metamorphosis (15/1993) and shares the stage with other stories that depict two elements: water and being wounded, especially wounded by fate. Narcissus and Echo, a stand-alone couple, are also a chapter in a wider conspiracy, the rape of Europa by Jove in the form of a bull. Love enters center stage as both a malady and a memory. Consider: Actaeon violates Diana's privacy and sees himself reflected--transformed now into a stag as an act of her vengeance--in the water where wilderness offers no path to safety. Semele, pregnant with Jove's seed, is tricked by the jealous and wounded Juno to ask Jove to appear in his divine form, which she does, but his presence in full power is too much for any human to tolerate: "Her mortal body can't withstand the flash/of force so heavenly; that nuptial gift consumes her flesh; she is reduced to ash" (p. 89). Her child, snatched from her womb, is sewn into the thigh of Jove until he comes to full term. Dionysus is born, then, from the mortal mother and immortal father.

Then, to lead us into the Narcissus/Echo myth is the story of Tiresias, a bridge character, who, because he struck with his staff two large snakes "as they mated in the forest" (p. 90), was transformed from a man to a woman and lived as such for seven years. Not until he came upon the same snakes in the eighth year and struck at them again--an echo as it were, of the previous transformation, was he transformed back into his original nature. Deprived of his sight by Juno, whom he judged to be wrong in her jesting with Jove, Tiresias is offered by the latter the gift of prophetic insight. But what good is such a power without the opportunity to use it? So one of the first to test his new powers is Liriope, a river nymph who is seduced by Cephesis, the river god. She gives birth to a boy, Narcissus, who is so handsome that he inspires intense love in all who see him.

The test that Liriope challenges Tiresias with pulls back the curtain so we can consider even now what the nature of knowing and not knowing implies. It also points the way into therapy not just of the individual soul but of the world soul as well. The question the nymph asks him is both individual and epic in its contours: "Will my boy live to see old age?" to which Tiresias quickly responds, "Yes, if he never knows himself" (p. 91). Now that is one part of the drama waiting to unfold–self-knowledge, but it is by far not the whole story. What follows is even more central to the interplay of memory to fatedness and to the arena of epistemology that myths inevitably lead us to consider: "For many years his words seemed meaningless; but then what happened in the end confirmed their truth: the death Narcissus met when he/was stricken with a singular, strange frenzy" (p. 91).

Here unfolds the central movement of the story: at one point in time what presents is so strange and unlikely, even unplausible, as to defy true comprehension; but then over time what seemed so alien reveals itself as part of one's own intimate nature. What it is that we attempt to grasp which seems so out of reach until it is echoed, repeated, revisioned, revisited, sometimes over a lifetime, before it often and eventually becomes part of one's understanding? Like Oedipus, Narcissus needs several modes of persuasive words and images before what he gazes on sinks in and makes sense. Patricia Berry's fine essay, "Echo's Passion," draws out this psychological act of repetition with depth and fine insight into Echo's character. I believe that Echo offers Narcissus a sense of irony, a critical gift for survival which he foolishly dismisses. Not good, for the absence of an ironic sense of oneself and the world is just what will get him stuck in the image that arrests him permanently. Vision without irony leads to fixation; so the myth asks us to consider.

Echo's dramatic place in the drama of Narcissus and self-imagining, which leads to self-reflection, is central to anyone's coming to know self and world. He meets her in his sixteenth year–the most popular teenager on the block or in the forest. As with all myths, the deep action is in the details, so we pay particular attention to what his actions are when he "chances" to meet her: "as he was driving frightened deer/into his nets, Narcissus met a nymph:/ resounding Echo, one whose speech was strange" (p. 91) for while she had a compulsion to speak, she could only repeat back "the final part of what she has heard" (p. 91). She comes to him already verbally challenged, a punishment by Juno, who seeking out her husband as he enjoyed nymphing trysts in the forests, was met by Echo on a path in the woods. Echo successfully deflects the suspicious wife's search for her lusty husband, Jove, by chattering incessantly. Echo uses or abuses words–depending on your rhetorical position in the forest--to arrest Juno's progress to uncover her husband in the throes of Eros. Echo sacrifices herself in language; she uses words to block discovery, so that all the nymphs and Jove can escape Juno's wrath.

The weighty stone of Narcissism, when dropped into the calm pool of reflection, spreads out to take in so many other pieces of the story; our task as reflective readers is, as Louise Cowan has written about reading literature generally, "to grasp the imagined form in the making" (Lecture, Winter 1997 Pacifica Graduate Institute) by paying attention to all the details as they traffic with one another. We discern what the entire web contains, not just the individual spider in it or the flies that have been caught in the stickiness of the trap.

The Ironic Echo:

Thus in Echo's limited linguistic prowess divine justice is also working itself out in the drama. Her limits are oral and aural, as Narcissus' will be visual. Do these two figures taken together reveal to us something crucial in the relation of word to image? Echo uses language to cover or camouflage the actions of divinity in love, or at least in erotic heat. Narcissus' self image is at first camouflaged–he will not know for some time that the image of his erotic attraction is his own. Such is to be his curse.

I am intrigued as well by how much and how often in one's writing does the writer simply echo–through direct quotes or paraphrase -- the words of others. We often glibly call it research. And how much does one speak one's own words, not as mirrors of others, but as a result of one's own authentic reflections? To move from reflecting the language and ideas of others to reflecting some of one's own image can often signal authentic learning on the part of the student. Such a process makes learning not only a Narcissistic but also an Echoic process of imagination. Sorry to say that the jargon of the academy in most disciplines does more to arrest than to liberate thought from the fixating pool, and I think this quandary is also imbedded in the myth. Perhaps here it is that Echo gets partially sanctioned and silenced, unable to use her full horde of words to stimulate new ideas.

So Echo is now condemned to inhabit the world with limited language skills: she trails words in memory rather than blazes paths with them; she is speech's double, a mirror of speech. Yet her words actually gain something in their redundancy because she knows how to select, to choose and to inflect what she has heard, to mirror words back to the one who initiates them, but not really as a xerox copy–what you say is what you hear. Rather, something happens in the repetition, as we shall hear. What changes is that a bit of irony creeps into her re-speaking because in the repetition something new is spoken: her **desire**. Hers is a desire of irony, perhaps even reflecting something ironic in desire itself; yet under the ferocious impulse and energy of Eros, she cannot sustain the irony. Not only does she lose her body, her life and her love; she loses a sense of the ironic as well, for there is something inherent in echoing what one has heard for one's own ends that is ironic. It is to say the same thing and mean something else, if only that something else is the utterance of one's own desires. But desire, when it deepens to obsession to pursue, possess, and consume, erases irony from the psychic equation. Irony revolves, mirrors, resonates; without it one drives full steam ahead or gets fixed to one position and swears it is the whole truth.

Seeing the young Narcissus for the first time, Echo is enflamed by love, which divinity earlier was so intent on pursuing and consummating in the forest of nymphs. She succeeds in protecting Jove's amorous frolics, but now in heated desire herself–an echo of Zeus' amorous energies? -- she feels her limits even more for she longs to initiate speech. The desire of divinity itself lives behind her echoic language. Fully embodied at this stage of the drama, she stalks Narcissus: "furtively--/she followed in his footsteps. As she drew/still closer, closer, so her longing grew/more keen, more hot–as sulfur, quick to burn" (p. 92); but while she thinks of seducing him with words, her newly-limited nature forbids it, so she learns to be patient until he speaks so she can echo his words back to him–double his linguistic/verbal image, but with a nuanced, even ironic twist.

Alone one day, and Ovid says "by chance," separated from his friends, Narcissus calls out: "Is anyone nearby?" to which Echo responds, "Nearby" (p. 92). His words allow for the presence of irony, for they are at the same time both a **question** from him and an **affirmation** from her, a doubling that is really an extension of the question into an answer. This doubling of language is actually the rudiments of a conversation. He looks but sees no one, no image to accompany her word, so he asks: "Why do you flee from me?" and she repeats his words to express her own feelings. Now the response to this is very interesting: "That answer snares him; he persists, calls out: / "Let's meet," to which she responds in joy, "Let's meet" (p.92). A kind of duplicity in duplication? So it seems.

Here is a doubling of desire, of Eros, and of the genesis of a possible relationship. We should recall here that he is busy earlier when she spies him for the first time, chasing deer into his nets, as he is snared by Echo's speech here. Echo occurs not just in language but in action. Already the webbing of his nets turn the hunter into the hunted, and all this before he even sees his own image, the final arresting moment which is prepared for by this echoic encounter that he dismisses so cavalierly. If I were doing therapy with this myth as my guide, I'd be listening to the language of my client to see what ensnares, what nets he continually falls back into.

His reaction to her is also peculiar and really not unexpected, for when she appears to him bodily as she runs from the camouflage of the woods to embrace him, he flees from her, shouting, "Do not touch me! /I'd sooner die than say I'm yours!" Now this last part is a declarative sentence and she responds with her desire: "I'm yours" (p. 93). His negation is also an imperative and elicits her affirmation; his denial her desire; his lack of Eros echoed to her is her opening to proclaiming her Eros for him. The exchange is–well--ironic–and not a little ensnaring. Now spurned, her love turns to shame as she slips, rejected, back into the cave in the woods where she lives, and her body shrivels and wastes away, "wretched flesh" (p. 93), until all that remains after her bones have turned to stone is her disembodied voice. What attracted her to him is his beautiful body, which leads to her own disincarnation. Without the body, eros is impossible, at least in its ability to enjoy fleshly satisfaction.

Now all of her power gathers in her voice since she has become invisible; there is nothing to see, only a disembodied voice to hear. How do we read the body in the myth, and to branch out further, the myth of the body, as it attracts, dissipates, is desired, is sought, is wounded and mutilated and then transformed into a flower, in this story? Something dramatic and crucial happens here in her metamorphosis: now that her body has hardened in its skeleton, he is prepared to be arrested solely by the embodied image of himself. Some absolutizing of voice and body, word and image, eros split now between love/shame and in a moment, love/fixation, unfolds. A rupture in psyche/soma/eros has occurred here; their original wholeness will never be retrieved. In myths there is no going home again; instead, improvisation becomes the order of the day. That, or oblivion. Does becoming or feeling invisible, even when one speaks, find a connection to eros? And to a feeling of self? What is erotic in speech, in language, that Echo wants us to grasp, even as she fails to grasp the one whom she desires?

In the uncanny logic that myths present, the next scene finds a youth, spurned by the untouchable Narcissus, who calls in prayer to the heavens: "May/ Narcissus fall in love; but once a prey, / may he, too, be denied the prize he craves" (p. 93). Said another way: may what Narcissus has done be echoed back to him. I think that some important distance is lost when Narcissus jettisons Echo, a distance he will never gain back and which will be his undoing when the image in the virginal pond seeks him out. Something else here as well: desire seems to drive the engines not only of this myth but of the entire chapter 3 in which Eros is the compelling force that implicates speech, body, image, chance, reflection and destiny. As William Lynch has helped me see, Narcissus' imagination changes and becomes excessively univocal, losing equivocity, wherein irony dwells (Images of Faith, 1973). Perhaps it is the nature of irony to dwell in analogy, so that "this is seen as similar to that," but is not fixedly "that," or "**just** that."

Weary from running from the youth who desires him, Narcissus lies down in the virgin woods to quench his thirst–a desire to be sated–and finds there as well a companion who turns desire on himself. But look for a moment at the natural order here and, lest we take it for granted, let's notice the scenes of this mythic action: the woods, animals, ponds, the thickness of the forest. It is a place of serene and natural beauty. Here the setting is what Jung would call an "archetype of transformation" (1971, par. 80); be it "situations, places, ways and means, that symbolize the kind of transformation in question." It is a poetically appropriate place as well since water is the only element in which we can see ourselves, that doubles us or that visually echoes us. Exploring the nature of archetypes, Jung reminds us that "Our unconscious...hides living water, spirit that has become nature, and that is why it is disturbed" (1971 par 52); he goes on to lament the absence of symbols in our day and believes that "the treasure lies in the depths of the water" for many, who wish to salvage something that the culture has lost. It is the disturbance of this virginal place, this pond, that interests me at this point in the narrative.

Here the water is described as "silverlike, /gleaming, bright. Its borders had no slime. / No shepherds, no she-goats, no other herds/of cattle heading for the hills disturbed/that pool" (p. 93). Further, nothing had ever stirred its surface, not a tree branch, a bird or wild animal and its edges are "ringed with rich grass" and thick hedges shielded it "from the sun" (p. 93). It is an untouchable place, like Narcissus himself, and so echoes his own disposition; something of the natural and human orders have found one another here. Place is without blemish; it is virginal, untouched, echoing Narcissus' desire of his own body not to be touched or tainted by another. This quality of untouchedness will continue to grow in the myth and Narcissus will attempt to override it, an attempt whose failure will finally undo him. To stay detached would be to preserve the ironic; but to insist that the image be touched, possessed, taken in, leads to a tragic impossibility. At this point the ironic stands in direct opposition to the tragic. Writers of tragedy insist that irony is one way of saving the tragic figure from death. Irony keeps self-reflection from solidifying into self-fixation.

Narcissus as Concept and as Image:

Let's take a leap here, an ontological squat-jump! Say this pool is the new millennium, untrammeled, full of promise, virginal and up for reflective grabs; it is to this site that the self-ignorant Narcissus races with the swiftness of Oedipus towards Thebes, even though both figures they are avoiding what pursues them Instead, and with irony, both discover it directly in front of them in a curiously unknowing way that myths keep pummeling us with. And let's stay close here: Narcissus initially stops at the clear pond for refreshment, but not for that only. He is also "drawn by the beauty of the pool, the place," and at this site he reclines, face down, to quench a thirst that will almost immediately give rise to another. Such is the seductive life of the consumer and the echoic power of satisfying one need only to have another replace it. Promise the satisfaction of one desire only to place a more intense love in its place, world without end, in the net of eros and entrapment.

Narcissus' thirst is quenched at the same time his sense of sight is aroused and begins to burn within him. In some mysterious way he has taken in, ingested Echo, but he has transformed her as well, as she was able to transform the words of another. Narcissus has appropriated Echo along his own mythic contours–into a visual image--and been arrested thereby in his gaze towards the unknown, but wished, even longed for figure who gazes back at him.

I confess that this scene, a poetic vignette in the virginal forest pool, is my favorite in the entire story. The poetry at this point throws us into irony. Narcissus is as still as a marble statue–completely fixated and fixed; Ovid tells us he stares not once but twice, so the image of himself is echoed through him, and he gazes unblinking "at the twin stars that are his eyes" (p. 94), visual echoes of one another. A powerful poetic image arises here, for in his looking down he reflects in his own eyes the stars of the heavens. Some boundary or division between the heavens and earth break down in this gaze. Jung's insight offers additional reflection at just point in the story: "Whoever looks into the water sees his own image, but behind it living creatures soon loom up; fishes, presumably, harmless dwellers of the deep–harmless, if only the lake were not haunted" (1971, par. 52). So what is the quality of this double seeing, a double imagining of the self that cannot be separated from the natural world–in fact **is made possible** by the natural world? A sense of wonder: "he now is struck with wonder by/ what's wonderful in him" (95). And then the punch line <u>and</u> the genesis of his troubles:

Unwittingly,

he wants himself; he praises, but his praise

is for himself; he is the seeker and the sought, the longed-for and the one who longs;

he is the arsonist–and is the scorched. (p. 95)

Now if doubling is going to get interesting in this marvelous story, it will occur here, for Narcissus finds himself in a double relationship to himself: in desire to pursue and in destruction–a doubling of his nature conspires right here. Having spurned Echo as a life force, he now echoes himself and only himself. He is both seeker and the one sought, origin of fire and the one burned. He is in an echoic relationship to himself because he satisfies both sides of the equation, as Echo earlier did the same with and through language.

What is often left out of the discussion is the medium by which he is trapped: the pool in nature, virginal, unpolluted, uninhabited and somewhat Edenic. The narrative tells us that the pool both deceives and tempts–a doubling of its mission statement; or it tempts by deceiving, or deceives by tempting. The limit now, however, is that with Echo gone, Narcissus, unbeknownst to himself just yet, is swirling in a closed system, completely untouchable, both by others and by himself. Most importantly, irony is completely absent. Is this the trap when eros, desire, parts company with irony, when the distance irony creates between one's self and the world collapses?

One might conjecture that this doubling leads one to suppose that he is more real, not less so, by means of reflection. A voice enters at this juncture, addressed to Narcissus: it is difficult to tell if it is the narrator, the pool speaking to him, or a voice to us addressed in the second person to him. Whatever its source, it does not sway Narcissus; in fact, he gives no indication that his ears hear it, so obsessed is he by the visual image before him: "But why, / O foolish boy, do you persist? Why try / to grip an image? He does not exist--/ the one you love and long for...That shape has nothing of its own: it comes / with you, with you it stays; it will retreat when you have gone–if you can ever leave!" (p. 94). And with that last statement Tiresias' prophecy begins to echo in our ears as readers; as Narcissus, reflecting in a fixed fashion, begins to move in consciousness to the identity of his love, he becomes more incarcerated by the image. Perhaps this myth has been warning us for centuries that collapsing the distance between self and self-image-as-other is one of the worst thing we can do to ourselves, because then the rest of the world is effectively blotted out, eclipsed quite literally by the stars of our own eyes. He is star-struck and fixed at this juncture, dwelling fixedly between the underworld and the heavens. Irony's absence keeps him fixated in his own alluring presence.

All desires and appetites have vortexed for Narcissus into one. Sensing his danger of not surviving, he turns his gaze for an instant to break the grip of the image and speak instead directly to the trees surrounding the pond. He calls on them. He knows of the countless lovers who have hidden among them and asks: "Do you remember anyone / in your long life–those many centuries--/ whose love consumed him more than mine wastes me?" (p. 95). Now if we think of the act of remembering, which Narcissus asks for here, as a form of echoing, or of doubling, then even while looking away he reflects an echoic way of knowing, which takes sterner shape as he talks.

His image then demands a language; he begins to plead with it and to lament that only the thinnest sheet of water separates the two of them, so why should it be difficult to grasp the other? When he weeps, he notices and states that the other weeps as well; when he moves his lips close to the water, the upturned face moves to kiss him; when he reaches his arms out to embrace him, the image also moves its arms to welcome him. By means of both word and image he suddenly "sees through" the deceit to what the image's meaning prescribes: "I'm he! .../my image cannot trick me anymore. / I burn with love for my own self" (pp. 95-96).

This moment of revelation in the myth is the threshold; from here things accelerate downhill, right to the water. Narcissus is not elated but appears rather downtrodden by this epiphany. For therapy, for culture at large, for an individual's life drama, such a recognition is not the end, but the beginning. It is a moment when greater vigilance, not less, is called for.

Something else is occurring here that I want to entertain, and that is the confusion that also emerges in the story between self-image and self-concept and a confusion on the part of Narcissus when the water itself takes on greater texture. Let me try to describe it.

Yes, his image exists because of the water. But I want to imagine that when he comes to recognize that the image is his own, he shifts from seeing it as image and creates it instead into a concept. Now the myth asks and answers the question: can we ever separate our self-image from our self-concept? And perhaps myths have as one of their poetic qualities showing this mimesis of image and concept. Here is how I want to say it: the water constitutes the real essence of Narcissus, not the literal reflected image of himself in it. His reflected image is his idea of himself but it does not mirror his true nature. It is too literal an image in the myth.

Hillman writes that "to go at imagination with straight-on sense perception creates insanity. It forces the image into hallucination (experienced as perceptually 'real'–material, objective, true) or loses it as illusion (experienced as perceptually 'unreal'–immaterial, subjective, false)" (Working with Images, 2000, 172-73). Narcissus oscillates between these two poles vis his self-image. His true nature on an imaginal level is the water itself, the element that allows for the image of himself, the liquid that sustains or gives image its shape and even its possibility. Perhaps true deep work in therapy involves helping the person separate out the concept of self one lives out from the essence or true nature of image–the water and the virginal pond that contains it. I am beginning to see the water as the container of image and the actual mirror of his literal image itself as Narcissus' concept of himself. The tragedy that ensues in this action grows directly from a confusion he experiences between the deep reality of the image of self and the self-concept he becomes aware of. They are related but different. Said another way, he cannot see the water for the image.

May it be that the image in the water is a visual echo of his full and authentic nature, which his self-concept keeps him from realizing? But it is an incomplete image. When he disregards Echo, he forfeits the very instrument or assistance he needs to see--I would call it **ironic resonance**–and so he remains stuck in self-concept. Perhaps then the Narcissus flower that replaces him, and suggests his trace and serves as a mimetic presence of him in his absence, in its silence, its presentness, and resting quietly and comfortably in its own beauty, is his essence. It is Narcissus' residue. Initially Narcissus sees and lives with and is taken, seduced, fixated by a concept of himself, not his deeper nature. If he realized this deeper nature, , I do not believe that he would not attempt to possess it. Self-possession, the myth affirms, is an illusion; to pursue self-possession leads rather directly and inevitably to self-fixation. Reflection then is not sufficient. Some deeper form of being present is necessary and I would call it, following the work of the Vietnamese Buddhist monk, Thich Nhat Hanh, "meditation." Only reflecting, one does not get past the concept of self, important though that is as a starting point. Let us invite irony back into the discussion.

Irony helps us gain a distance from ourselves so we can remove the traps of concepts in order to more fully imagine the really-real, the essence of who we are, and that does not seem to be done without also taking into our view the natural order of things: ponds, woods, water, the ground of the earth and all that echoes in her. Thich Nhat Hanh helps us to see that meditation may help us penetrate reality to our deeper nature (1998, p. 13). The short sightedness, if you will, of Narcissus' image in the water is that it is literally too shallow; it rests too close to the surface and promotes a horizontal reflection rather than a deeper, more vertical meditation. It also brings him to the brink of insanity, as Hillman's observation made clear earlier. Narcissus sees through the water too quickly because the image has fascinated him and transfixed him; he misses the reality of the water's own essence as the carrier of the image; to see the water as his image would take him beyond the concept of himself in the reflection. It would restore to him a sense of irony and collapse the powerful energy that leads to self-arrest.

The questions the myth asks now include: how does one absorb this knowledge? Does it change one significantly? What is its importance in a human life, because self-knowing and self-love are not necessarily impediments in themselves? Something more is necessary to complete the mytho-poetic action. We haven't yet witnessed the punch line in the plot.

There is no question that Narcissus has been brought to the brink of a crisis, a crisis of knowing and of erotic self-possession. Let **him** pose the questions: "What shall I do? Should I be sought or seek? But, then, why must I seek? All that I need, I have: my riches mean my poverty" (p. 96). Irony? Paradox? Both? He has entered into a place within his own psyche where action is confusing, where desire collides with fulfillment and what he has is both fulfilling and empty at the same time. Is this what a collapsed distance within oneself and between self and world looks and sounds like? And then the punch line, which is where this paradoxical condition takes him: " If I could just be split from my own body!" (p. 96). The line containing this wish is the greatest lamentation in the narrative, rivaling Echo's own pathos. And how can it not repeat Echo's condition earlier as her body dissipated under the suffering she experienced loving him so intensely without response?

I like what Patricia Berry says here of Echo and suffering in therapy. "This sensitive cultivation of suffering is an art having more to do with *echoing tones and moods* within the psyche than with grand rules or analytic prescriptions" (1982, p. 124; my italics). We suffer from what we desire, clear enough. But to suffer from what we have and are? Here is expressed a more nuanced form of suffering for which the space of self-reflection may save us from the obsession of self-absorption. To be absorbed by something as powerful as desire, image or impulse is far more intractable a psychological state than self-reflection, and pushes one closer to self-fixation. In all of this suffering, the greatest weakness or pathos is that the world is denied, held at bay, even ignored. Let's use a word from the myth: "spurned."

What is this desire to jettison the body, to be distant from it? Is this myth also about the body's own impediments or its deeper knowledge that he spurns as well? Narcissus returns, obsessed, to contemplate his image further. At this moment he begins to weep into the water as the image begins to fade and dissolve through the watery mists of his tears. Vision clouds, yet it is the best sense he has working, for touch and hearing are inoperative. Given such a condition of absolute frustration in not being able to fulfill his desire, Narcissus turns to violence in the form of self-mutilation and dismemberment. I think this part of the myth ought to be explored much more than I have space to here; it asks us to imagine the intimate relationship between having, possessing, wanting more, and violence. Now in an act of despair and frustration, "He tears his tunic's top; / with marble hands he beats his naked chest. / His flesh, once struck, is stained with subtle red" (p. 96).

When the water clears and he looks at his tattered and wounded flesh, he knows for the first time that he has been "undone by love; its hidden flame consumes Narcissus: now he wastes away" (p. 96) repeating and becoming at the same time. In more ways than one, he is what he has spurned. Self-desire and self-destruction both play themselves out in the same relation to the image. Violence is his response to a way of knowing the self that encourages less self-acceptance and more self-mutilation. Perhaps the growing number of self-cutters, self-mutilators, and those violent against others might be offered insights through this myth, right here, in his passion to destroy what cannot be possessed, much less consumed.

Echo's role in the drama is not yet complete; she enters in the last scene, their beings more alike now than ever, a fitting replica to their identical words. Image and word unite as the two become one. Echo feels a deep pity for Narcissus and each time he cries "Ah, me! The nymph repeats/ "Ah, me!... And when he cried 'Farewell!' 'Farewell!' was just/ what Echo mimed" (p. 97). Her empathy is as strong in the present moment as was her desire for him earlier. Such a fixation with his own image he clings to even in death and carries to the underworld, there, to "stare at his own image in the pool / of Styx" (p. 97) where his Naiad sisters with Echo joining in the chorus, would lament his passing in "a choir of grief."

When they search again for his body to hoist it onto the funeral pyre on earth, they find in its stead "a flower, / its yellow center circled by white petals" (p. 97), a thing of beauty, not to be possessed, fast fading, ephemeral and part of the natural world. Some deep beauty seems to accompany grief and loss and death. The beauty of the flower, always surrounding funerals, brings something of the earth into bold relief. To look into and smell flowers is to see something of our own mortality. What a funny phrase, "to stop and smell the flower." Such a Narcissistic command, but not a negative one. For the mythic figure of Narcissus leaves a residue, a natural object of beauty. How ironic

References

Aristotle. (325?/1982). Aristotle's poetics (J. Hutton, Trans.). New York: W.W. Norton.

Berry, P.(1982). Echo's subtle body: Contributions to an archetypal psychology. Dallas: Spring.

Bloom, H. (2000). In praise of the greats. Brill's content, May. pp. 100-03,133.

Cowan, L. (1997). Sophocles and the genre of tragedy. Unpublished presentation. Pacifica Graduate Institute, Carpinteria, California.

Hanh, T.N. (1998). The heart of the Buddha's teaching: Transforming suffering into peace, joy, and liberation. New York: Broadway Books.

Hillman, J. (1989). From mirror to window: Curing psychoanalysis of its narcissism. Spring, 62-75.

Hillman, J. (1979/2000). Image-sense. In B. Sells (Ed.), Working with images (pp. 170-186). Woodstock, Connecticut: Spring.

Jung, C.G. (1971). The archetypes and the collective unconscious. In The collected works of C.G. Jung (Vol. 9.1) (R.F.C. Hull, Trans.). Princeton: Princeton University Press.

Lasch, C. (1979). The culture of narcissism: American life in an age of diminishing expectations. New York: W.W. Norton.

Lynch, W.F., S.J. (1963). Christ and Apollo: The dimensions of the literary imagination. Notre Dame: University of Notre Dame Press.

Lynch, W.F., S.J. . (1973). Images of faith: An exploration of the ironic imagination. Notre Dame: University of Notre Dame Press.

Melville, H. (1851/1967). Moby-Dick (H. Hayford and H. Parker, Eds.). New York: W.W. Norton.

Ovid. (1993). The metamorphosis of Ovid (A. Mandelbaum, Trans.). San Diego: Harcourt, Brace.

Schwartz-Salant, N. (1982). Narcissism and character transformation: The psychology of narcissistic character disorders. Toronto: Inner City Books.

Segal, R. (1999). <u>Theorizing about myth</u>. Amherst: University of Massachusetts Press.

Stein, M. (1976). <u>Narcissus</u> (pp.32-53). New York: Spring.

Thresholds: Psyche and Culture

Each of the six essays within this section describe ways in which depth psychology may be applied to cultural concerns that tend to be ignored by mainstream psychology. Such application makes us think twice about these issues, and illustrates the clarifying power of a depth approach.

Ginette Paris' "Giegerich/Hillman: What is Going On?" comparison of James Hillman's attraction to archetypal images with Wolfgang Giegerich's emphasis on the logic of the psyche reveals how becoming obsessed with the image to the diminishment of ideas can be a ferocious seduction. Archetypal psychology advances, she claims, when the soul's logical life is wedded to its imaginal life.

Christine Downing's "Beyond Psychology" reminds us that depth psychology must always "go beyond" its current positions, always revision itself. She points out that it is problematic to see the world and the self as separate from or opposed to one another. Rather, she revisits Otto Rank's call that the psychology of the self is found in the Other, that beyond psychology lies relationship, and beyond that lies God. Dr. Downing echoes Freud's call for the need for metapsychological theory that contributes to life in general, and for his understanding of depth psychology as a psychology of the unknowable in us, the "Beyondness" that lies beyond the ego. Dr. Downing contrasts Freud's approach to the soul with that of Wolfgang Giegerich, preferring Freud's skepticism and tentative hope for the future to Giegerich's more upbeat, comforting vision. In the end, she movingly reminds us that what really takes us beyond psychology is love.

David Miller's "Irony's Arrows/Eros: A Poetics of Culture" describes our culture's increasing conflict about irony, and our loss of ironic sensibility. He describes some of the history and development of irony, noting that we need irony lessons. He supplies us with such a lesson when he tells us that irony's arrows go in all directions, and arrive at no particular place, which is what they were intended to hit. In his words, "never is what is spoken what is actually said."

Shantena Augusto Sabbadini's "Imagining the Real World" describes some of the dilemmas and intellectual upheavals produced by a quantum mechanical understanding of the world, and speculates about what a quantum model of mental processes might look like. Our brains have not evolved to deal with the world revealed by quantum physics, so it is hard to picture this level of reality, and we tend to think in terms of classical mechanics. Quantum physics has more in common with the thinking of the shaman or the mystic, in which all is one, and within this one exist many worlds, of which the one that is actualized depends on how we probe it. Similarly, the therapist lives in a world of multiple coexisting realities, and no one of them is necessarily the real one.

Barbara Shore's "An Absurdist Pantomime; the Collision of Violence, Innocence and Pseudoinnocence" asks us why the world was stunned at the death of Yitzhak Rabin. Just as we ignore the danger within the heroic, so our patients are blind to the obvious. She tells us of her attempts to pierce this innocence, or more accurately pseudoinnocence, offering us an example from both her own life and that of one of her patients. She also gives us cultural examples of our pseudoinnocence, our defensive blindness to questions too difficult to contemplate, and to the complex issues of power that often underlie serious social problems.

Benjamin Sells' "First Impressions: Introduction to a Psychology of Style" describes a subject that has been relatively neglected by psychologists. We learn to read style by learning to read the world, by maintaining a perspective that sees the things of the world in terms of images. To understand style, we must be willing to let things show us what they are, in their particularity, without preconception or attachment to ideology. For style, all things are fictional entities, seen through their imaginative dimensions. Style is a way of perceiving that assumes an aesthetic basis to all experience. Always in fashion, the mystery of style is somehow connected to the eternal, yet found in the facts of daily life; style is what makes things appear as they do, and not otherwise. If we will be guided by style, "life blossoms with preferences and inclinations."

Giegerich/Hillman: What is Going On? by Ginette Paris, Ph.D.

Since the program of this conference went out, I have received, in person or via email, many reactions to the title of this lecture, which reads: *Hillman-Giegerich: What is Going On?* I understand that the expectations are not only numerous but also contradictory, setting me up for failure in meeting them. In this context, I would like to begin by stating what I cannot or will not do today and by clarifying my position.

My standpoint is not that of arbiter of a debate, not that of a talk show head who wants to play hardball, nor its opposite, the good mother who wishes to reconcile everybody before dinner. It is not the pledge of allegiance of the faithful devotee who comes to pay her respect, nor the rebellion of the ex-devotee who having blindly followed the party line, now confuses critique with rebellion.

My standpoint has not changed; from the very beginning I would not have wanted to be part of a school of thought that would not tolerate critique or demand ideological submission. I believe even friends should not ask that of one another. My admiration for James Hillman goes to the rhetorical genius, to the generous defender and lover of ideas and not to a founding father, guru, or party leader. If there is an image of the father, I suggest Zeus the host, hosting us today at his table for a feast of ideas.

I believe the only way to be really loyal to our tribe is not to be too loyal, not to be too reproductive; we need the kind of lack of piety that exists in families who are secure enough to discuss what is omitted, forgotten, expelled, scorned, or concealed. That is one of the reasons why I welcome Giegerich's criticism of us; he is a member of our tribe, pointing at what is omitted.

It takes the determination of a philosopher to write his critique of archetypal theory as it is a theory which has the mercurial ability to recycle any critique as just another archetypal configuration, as only one more position among many, all equally being treated as fantasies anyway.

But courage and determination are also needed from the reader, to cut through Giegerich's heavy Hegelian language. He seems to intentionally wrap his ideas in layers and layers of impossible language and germanic heavyness to protect them from uninitiated frivolous French amateurs like myself. To this I answer, and this will be my only critique of Giegerich, as my goal is not to do a critique of the critique, that obtuse academic style which creates a problem similar to that of pharmaceutical companies who produce unaffordable medicines for deadly diseases. Those of us psychologists who are most hungry for philosophy cannot afford the time or training it takes to dig for gold in scholarly journals or in Hegel. But I was determined to do some roller blading through Giegerich's terminological maze and to extract gold nuggets from his philosophical gravel.

First, there is gold in the fact that he writes to transform not only the way we think about ourselves by transforming the way think our theories, as most psychological theories will do, but also to change our sense of what is possible. His is an ambition for our future, the future of depth psychology. And the reason why we should all be interested in this kind of exploration is very simple: psychology is at a threshold, and that means that we need to bring up, once more, one terribly plain but fundamental question: What is psychology? What should we keep, what should we leave out, and what should we search for. Giegerich raises this question in an indirect way by asking what is the relation of psychology to logic, rationality and truth?

I thought for a long time that we could evade the question of logic, truth and rationality by affirming that psychology is more akin to a genre in literature than to a science. But even so, we still have to define our genre since each genre, interestingly enough, has a relation to truth and rationality. In a detective story, truth is finding who done it through a rational demonstration of guilt. The genre of science fiction is based on stretching to the limits the rational possibilities of science and technology. Historical novels are based on a mix of truth (the historical facts) and fiction (the imagined emotions and narrative twists). As for sentimental novels, they are forever trying to sell their definition of true love and forever trying to defend passion against reason. Even the genre of fairy tale and mythology has a relation to truth and rationality by defining the fantastic and divine in contradistinction to the realistic and profane. As for the genre of recipe books, well, the proof in is the pudding!

In the genre of psychology, how do we define our rapport with truth and to rationality? Which is another way to ask; what is the logical life of the soul, especially now that psychology borrows ever more concepts and metaphors from alchemy, astrology, physics, oriental cultures, shamanism, dead religions which are also called mythologies; since all have their own relation to truth, it makes the definition of our relation to truth and rationality, in other words, the setting of our boundaries, all the more urgent.

I would like to give you an example of how I came to think that Giegerich might be right in stating that archetypal psychology must redefine its relation to truth and rationality, and must not satisfy itself with the imaginal life of the soul because soul also has a logical life. I agree with Giegerich that soul should think, and should think harder, not just imagine and fantasize. So, here is how I understand his critique, through my most humbling experience as therapist.

A bright young woman of 25 had been my patient for a year, mostly lamenting the fact that her mother, a well-known editor of a woman's magazine, supposedly had not given her enough 'mothering,' leaving her, so she felt, with the emotions of a needy child. As emotions, feelings, affects, are the starting point, she used a full box of kleenex and a few sessions crying tears of the abandoned child. After that we began exploring the images and myths carrying these emotions and found an interesting combination that fascinated her: although she had both parents, she found that she lived her life in the myth of the orphan with variations on the theme of the Little Match Girl. She was that orphan girl watching others feasting on life while she, poor little rich girl of two successful parents, was abandoned to her cold bookish solitude. The silent editorialist mother pounding away at her keyboard on the dining room table, as if behind a windowpane, was to the needy child like the unavailable goodies for the little match girl. A very romantic and dangerously alluring myth, it carried such narrative richness that she was seduced by her own mythology. I kept hoping for a new chapter, for the story to move on and for her to graduate to a more satisfying myth. But one can be as attached to a myth as one is attached to one's symptoms.

At this point the father asked to be invited to one of our sessions, and my client agreed. I must add that the relationship between father and daughter was a rich and positive one.

First, he began by sharing his own observations on the mother/daughter relationship. He suggested that according to what he had witnessed of his daughter's childhood, his wife had been much more available as a mother than had his own mother. While he considered his mother to have been a good-enough traditional mother, his wife had spent infinitely more time and energy talking and doing things with their daughter. The mothers of his childhood would feed their children and tell them not to come back in the house before the next meal. Why had he never thought of himself as abandoned? His mother played bridge in the afternoon, went shopping, talked on the phone, helped his father with the business, and went to her various clubs. She never looked at his drawings, never asked him about his dreams, never even talk much with them children. He was not bringing this for us to begin exploring his own childhood; he was raising a philosophical question: could the norm of mothering be relative?

Yes, the daughter agreed. "But all the sociology in the world cannot account for my feelings of abandonment. How can I deny them?" "Of course," admitted the father. At this point he went deeper in his reasoning in a most surprising way, again not through an exploration of emotions or images, but offering us the result of his sharp thinking, a new theory, a logic that cut through all his daughter's complexes and instantly dissolved her mythology by moving the whole story to another level. Giegerich uses Hegel's concept of sublation to describe the kind of sharp cutting through that followed. Sublation is a Hegelian word that means a cutting through, a distillation of thought, obtained by a succession of synthesis between thesis and antithesis; I believe the next step of the father's logic contained a gem, an example of sublating. Here is what he had to say to his daughter: "you were a bright and intuitive child. You perceived the guilt of your mother at being the first generation of women to break with the old model of motherhood. You learned that by pushing the guilt button you could get a lot of benefits. And your mother, being at the historical junction between mothers who played bridge in the afternoon and women who also wanted a career, would do <u>anything not to be guilty</u> of being a bad mother; that is why the guilt button worked like an ATM machine for you. This fiction worked for a long time, but now it victimizes you, it victimizes your mother, and it victimizes me, as it is my wife whom you upset with your accusations of emotional neglect. If you just stopped using the guilt button, you would see that you got plenty of mothering. The problem is <u>not in you, not in her, and not in feminism</u>."

At this point, I literally saw the daughter being hit by what felt like truth. What else might we call it? Nobody has the power to validate that kind of truth as absolute truth, but the fact is that the daughter was instantly relieved to find that she agreed with her father's reasoning. She was being freed by a logical truth that cut right through her complexes. The father's theory, his <u>thinking</u>, completely dissolved not only the daughter's emotions, but her mythology of orphan and the images of the little match girl. POOF! Gone! Sublated! It was a glorious moment between father and daughter and a deep philosophical insight for me.

In order to sublate, she, as well as I, had to stop trying to represent in images what needed to be conceived in thought and that is one crucial point of Giegerich's argument. Only through thinking, not imagining, could we reach a level of abstraction that allowed us to understand the father's theory about the historical and psychological world the daughter and her mother had lived in.

Of course truth is a big dangerous word. Just try adding it to the program that James Hillman suggested: to Justice, Beauty, and Destiny, add Truth and immediately the whole program feels terribly ponderous. The search for truth is especially ambiguous for us psychologists as we work with the psyche's tendency to distort and fictionalize. But if we go past that fear of the word we discover that looking for truth is exactely like fighting for a better Justice system: absolute Justice, like absolute Truth, is impossible to obtain. Still, as we never stop trying to reach for Justice, we should also never stop trying to get closer to a Truth.

In his lovely short essay titled "Truth," the British historian Felipe Fernandez Armesto, professor at Oxford, writes of the history of the pursuit of truth as the most cherished and widely-shared project of mankind, even though suspicions that reality is intractable and inexpressible have been there all along, way before post modernism made a specialty of it. He remarks how against this background of long standing truth-quest the scale of current indifference to the concept of truth looks like a sudden and dangerous novelty. Following his thinking, we must see that psychologists, like every body in this post-modern context, have been caught in the crossfire of a culture war between religious extremists, who think they know the truth, and secular nihilists, who teach that it can never be known. We psychologists want to avoid both camps. But, as Fernandez Armesto suggests, the search for truth is still on and we should leave relativists and nihilists where they belong, that is, on the margin of history.

As psychologists we cannot not be concerned with truth because like others, we are looking for a language that can match reality. Even when Lacan was trying to show how our dependence on language makes it impossible for the psyche to speak the truth, still, his concern was with truth. And Derrida, for all his extravagances, was and still is in search of truth; deconstruction may have defined truth as "that which inevitably gets distorted" but that is precisely why we should never give up deconstructing as a way of cleaning truth of its bugs and parasites, as we go along trying to deconstruct and reconstruct again to produce new meaning. When deconstructionists set out to 'read between the lines,' or even 'read against the grain' it remains an attempt to understand a distorted truth hidden in the logic of the text. By text they mean anything that can support an interpretation, like for example the body can be read like a text, or your personality and mine, the architecture of this room, the setting of this podium on this stage; all of that can be interpreted. Archetypal psychology carried a similar project, but with the imaginal realm instead of language, aiming to see through, to get at and reveal the myths active in the background. Giegerich now criticises our project by reminding us that image is not all, that soul also has a logic. Even though we might not be able to define once and for all the kind of truth or logic psychology is after, we can at least agree that psychology has to stay preoccupied with it, just as we remain preoccupied with having a better justice system. If psychology as a discipline gets back to thinking and logic, our patients will too.

I am sure you can think of those well-intentioned patients or students who began exploring the wetlands of imagination and got lost in some swamp of their fantasies. I think therapists and teachers share some responsibility in those failures as the wetness of imagination should be balanced by the dryness of logic. As psychologists, we are trained to explore the emotions first, and then if you are an archetypal psychologist, you will also want to discover the images and myths that are active in the background. But I hear Giegerich saying that it is not enough, that psychology could go one step further because we all need a philosophical system to understand and sublate our psychological problems. It is not enough to reveal the myth we live by, we also have to reveal and work on the philosophy we think with. There are plenty of philosophical systems to choose from, and I don't think Giegerich is suggesting that Hegel is the best or only one. Neither is he suggesting that philosophers should take our jobs. We don't need to be philosophers to help our patients understand the logic of their souls.

In changing her vision of the world, of history, of her mother and of herself in the world, the young woman who was my patient became conscious of her logic. So, the end of therapy, in her case, coincided with a sublation of the imaginal. The image of orphan is gone, just like in a distillation of gin or cognac, the grain that started the process is now gone. Finding the images of orphan got us a long way, but there was also a need for something else, and that something else, I understand is what Giegerich, after Hegel, calls sublation.

Negating

Now, I would like to pause here and to move to another concept that Giegerich recycles from Hegel for the benefit of psychology: the concept of negation. The need for Sublation and Negation are the two ideas of Giegerich's book that I found most interesting. Again, I am not a Hegel expert, so all I can do is explain how this concept of negation felt so useful to me as a psychologist.

The process of negating is not the same thing as the Via Negativa and maybe it is useful here to point at the difference. Saying to someone "I do not love you anymore" is an example of negation, not of via negativa. If the other then asks: do you mean you hate me? And you answer, no, no, I don't mean I hate you. Do you mean you want to move out of the house tonight? No, it's not that. Do you love someone else? No, not at all. Do you pity me? No, there is no pity in my feeling... etc... This succession of no, no, is the via negativa, weeding away what does not quite fit.

But the negation of "I don't love you anymore" is not a via negativa, it is a full insight, a logical insight of the most important kind for psychology.

What sort of insight are you having when you say to someone "I don't love you anymore?" What is the image of "I do not love you anymore?" None. It is without an image, without a myth, even maybe, without a feeling, yet it is a crucial logical insight: it is the experience of the negation of a previous experience of love; you know for sure that you are experiencing this negation of the love that once was, that is all you can say about it, but it is a crucial insight. Ibsen's Nora, that Ted Roszack so beautifully resurrected yesterday, does not yet know who she wants to be, or what she wants to do, or where she should go, but she certainly knows that she is _no more_ primarily a wife and mother. That is why the director having her close the door is such good staging. Her extraordinary insight is a negation.

Just as nobody has ever been able to define happiness but everybody knows when one is not happy, so most of our psychological insights are negations; we know what is not there. You may find a multitude of examples of that form of insight: the director with his actors on the stage knows when the acting is not good, fake, false, does not ring true, but it is almost impossible to define what will work.

Without getting too technical, it might be useful here to point out that are two sorts of negations. If I say, for example, this podium is not a chair and this mike is not a part of my body, I am not negating the existence of this podium or of the mike or of my body. But let's say you came in the room this morning expecting to see someone very important to you, a longtime friend, a lover, or a respected enemy, someone you spent a sleepless night thinking about, in anticipation of a reunion. You come into the room, you look around, you see that this person is not here. It makes sense to say that you are experiencing the presence of absence; the negation of the presence of that person is a nothingness, as Jean Paul Sartre would have said, full of meaning for you. If, by comparison, someone had announced this morning that Bill Clinton would not be attending our conference, it would have been simply an absurd announcement, not a negation, as he was neither invited nor expected. But the absence of the expected friend is full of implications, his or her not being here, and this absence is omnipresent to our consciousness and may occupy your psyche more than anything that positively exists in the room.

The reason I was so excited when I was reminded while reading Giegerich of this philosophical concept of negating, is that so many of our psychological insights have that status of negativity; most of our neurotic traits, well, I should say most of mine, are about what is not there, holes in the fabric of my existence, missing elements, missing persons, missing time, missing turns of events in the past, missing qualities in me. I actively miss so many non existing "nothingness" that, yes, I do, think, with Giegerich that we need to train ourselves to think logically and negatively, not only positively and imaginally.

To further explore negativity, let's take a simple word, for example the word 'Village.' Village is a thought, just like soul is a thought, or unconscious, or anima mundi. And it may bring up an image of a village green with a café and a bookstore. 1000 houses may make a village, yet none of these individual houses are the village. Nor do we really see the transition between dwelling to village to city. It is all in thought. So 'village' does not exist. But we all understand what Hillary meant by the title of her book: "It takes a village to raise a child." She was pointing at the sense of community that the thought of 'village' is supposed to carry. But community is another concept that has no existence except in thought, so that if you define 'village' by the sense of 'community,' then how can you explain that one can live on an island with only three houses and a total population of 15 (which is not a village) and still have more of a sense of community than when living in an apartment in a large city?

One of Giegerich's points is that we limit ourselves and get into all sorts of messes and contradictions as in the preceding example whenever we begin objectifying or positivizing our psychological concepts or our images and myths. Archetypal psychology at its beginning criticized ego psychology for objectifying concepts like unconscious, individuation or Self, and now Giegerich criticizes archetypal psychology for positivizing images and myths. Aphrodite, Hermes, the orphan or the little match girl do not exist, no more than village and community, self and unconscious; all of these are useful only as long as they keep their status of negativity.

The use of mythology asks for vigilance, since it tends to positivize just like ego psychology does with its concepts. This tendency to positivize cannot be helped: even tough James Hillman is not guilty of it in his writing about the acorn and the myth of the daimon, I am sure you have had the uneasy experience of someone talking about his or her daimon as if it had a positive existence somewhere behind the liver. Unease comes from the fact that metaphor is gone and the acorn or daimon is now as positivized as the genetic code.

That is why no theory, especially a theory of the imaginal, can remain fresh without a critique, and also a certain sense of humor that allows for play. Two persons may both be saying that Demeter or the Trickster has been activated in their psyche, and with one it will feel ok, but with the other you might feel that this person is smoking her own dope. The difference is in the positivizing. This insistence on negation is not a fancy philosophical hair splitting as negation is a road to consciousness that has as much power as emotion or image.

Let's take the most obvious of problems: the epidemic of violence in schools and gangs. When I imagine this violence, I see scenes of the Columbine murders, guns hidden in lockers, families glued to their TV, exhausted, underpaid teachers. Another way to go, through negation, is to think of violence as essentially a negation of many things: it is a negation of love, or peace, or beauty, of civility, manners, codes, rituals, and all the divinitites. When looking at the suicidal youth, instead of looking at him or her positively as suicidal, let's think about what is missing: despair is an absence of community an absence to one's self and the absence of so many other things. It is not what is there, the positive clinical condition, that makes the young person want to die. Rather, it is what is not there.

So many insights seem to start in negation: remember how the feminist movement started when woman understood, so to speak, the presence of their absence in culture, in politics, in history, in psychology, in the family. Look at any relationship. Whenever we feel like complaining to the other: "you don't understand me," a philosopher could suggest that what we are really saying is: "you positivize me, you take for granted a 'me' that does not even exist, you label, name, define, imagine, interpret and objectify me." Again, Ibsen's Nora resists being positivized.

As the image tends to positivize, Giegerich asks us to understand what we may be missing by considering the image as the final destination. Archetypal psychology's revised, enlarged program could be: "From the affect, move to the image." Then, let's add another step: keep on negating, keep on sublating this image.

Archetypal psychology at its beginning was not so sure of itself. It negated a lot; it said: no, no, the affect is not all, no, the Self does not have a positive existence, our concepts do not exist, they are fantasies, mythologies; one can see through them. Maybe it is the success of our perspective that now confronts us with the danger to get stuck in the positivity of the image.

One of the missions of archetypal psychology has been accomplished: it has re-claimed images and myths and given imagination its dignity. I believe the actual success of the archetypal approach will be durable and its contribution will be recognized in wider and wider circles. But because we are lovers of images (iconophiles) does not mean we cannot also love the logical life of the soul.

Maybe I should speak for myself. I teach mythology and archetypal psychology, and I really love it. But I don't want the archetypal perspective, with its return to gods and goddesses, to exalt itself as though it was an alternative religion. Especially if it supports the narcissistic tendency of the psyche that will ask that the divinities be hospitable to our little personal interests. Let's leave that to fundamentalists of all kinds. And although I appreciate a sense of Revelation that comes with studying spiritual traditions, I don't want to lose the sense of the world as a place that can also be understood rationally.

Giegerich happens to be the first to perform on archetypal psychology a critique similar to Lacan's of Freud. Through his now famous cliché -- "the unconscious is structured like a language" Lacan wished to make the point that language can only be a compromise between ourselves and reality. OK Lacan, it took me a while, since I flunked all the Lacan seminars I took in my youth. But thirty years later I get it: language is bound to fail us, especially in psychoanalysis. Right.

From Lacan, I moved to James Hillman and loved his insistence on the poetic basis of the psyche. Here was someone who was saying the psyche is structured like an image, a myth. Right! Oh, but let's not forget Derrida and deconstruction: the unconscious is a text, and one needs to read between the lines, always, even as thesignification escapes the one writing the text, always. Oh, yes, the older I get, the more conscious I am of the subtext, the silent unsaid things. Giegerich, with Hegel to support his argument, is now suggesting that

98

the life of the soul is not only language, not only image, not only text; it is also logic. Right, I am all in favor of richness.

In conclusion, although I admire Giegerich's ideal of Hegelian progress through perpetual sublation, I need, for my personal sanity, to remain skeptical of the power of all systems to lure me to search for places that don't exist, except in the philosopher's mind, because I have suffered more from my impossible ideals than from all my failures. On the other hand, I do believe that systems of self-knowledge are like goals for the revolution, that is, beautiful ideals we might never achieve and that without ideals worth pursuing we become self indulgent and petrified in our certitudes.

Let me end with a romantic quote, with proper quotation marks, from neither a philosopher nor a psychologist, but a novelist, a psycho-philosophical novelist, Marcel Proust. It summarizes for me the state of affairs in the kingdom of archetypal psychology. "The beauty of images lives behind things. The beauty of ideas is ahead of them." ("La beauté des images est logée à l'arriére des choses, celles des idees, à l'avant." Marcel Proust, Tome III p. 932.)

Beyond Psychology by Christine Downing, Ph.D.

Only after agreeing to participate in this Symposium did I realize how ambivalent I was about doing so, the degree to which I felt it to be too big, too busy, too grandiose, too Jungian, too forward-looking, and how unsure I was about what I might have to say in this particular context. I did know I'd want to honor the notion of *Threshold,* but also to honor my skepticism about big turning points, especially my skepticism about anything really significant being involved in the turn from the 20th to the 21st century. From the beginning I did have a hunch it would have to do with Freud --as seems always true for me when among Jungians.

It helped to remember that Janus, the Latin god of thresholds is two-faced, looks forward and backward, inside and out, and that my way of looking forward seems to require looking back, seems to involve *remembering,* honoring what Freud called *Nachtraglichkeit*-- for which "deferred action" (the Standard Edition's most usual rendition) is a lousy translation-- and "belatedness" (the translation Lacanians seem to favor) not much better. A literal rendering of the German would yield something like "the quality of being carried *after,"* phrasing which communicates Freud's recognition of how experiences and memory traces get revised at a later date to fit in with fresh experience or with the attainment of a new stages of development. These revisions then have the power to endow the earlier moment with new meaning and with fresh psychical effectiveness. Freud emphasized that such revisioning was occasioned by new events or situations and happened primarily re *unassimilated* experience, that it involved not simply repetition or delayed discharge, but a real working-over, a transformation. That is, remembering is always redescription, remaking. The echo is different each time. The German word for remembering is *Erinnerung* --interiorization, inwarding; the word suggests that remembering means taking the recalled event into our own souls. This is what each return to Freud seems to ask of me: to rework, not just repeat, knowing that there are richnesses there still waiting to be recovered.

Because I had heard that the dialogue between Wolfgang Giegerich and James Hillman was likely to be a central focus of the Symposium, I realized that in preparation I should read Giegerich's The Soul's Logical Life. Doing so led me to recognize more clearly what the focus of my own presentation should be: the recurrent theme in psychology, in depth psychology, of "Beyond Psychology."

I was struck by Giegerich's claim that his project of Sublating Psychology goes beyond Hillman's project of ReVisioning Psychology in important and necessary ways, for it led me to realize that I see this theme, "Beyond Psychology," as *intrinsic* to depth psychology, not as a postscript or an afterward. That is, I believe going "beyond" is intrinsic to depth psychology and that it's intrinsic that it has to be done over and over again. One way of getting at this is to repeat Adam Phillips' suggestion (1998, p. 6) that there is a Post-Freudian Freud in Freud himself--a Freud who is always already beyond the Freud we know--but also an Enlightenment Freud, a Freud who calls forth Jung as Jung calls forth Hillman and Hillman calls forth Giegerich.

To which I want to add that in a sense as we've moved through this chain of revisioners we haven't gotten anywhere that we weren't already at! We can't miss the recurring chant -- "Your psychology isn't soulful enough, your soul isn't soulful enough, your unconscious isn't UNconscious enough"--a chant which I see as parallel to the chant among the mid-20th century theologian I studied in graduate school -- "Your god isn't God, isn't sufficiently other." Because it is so difficult for us not to move into reification or positivism, the chant is inevitably a recurring one.

We are always trying to get beyond reification, beyond positivism, and beyond literalism. Giegerich sees this as inescapably true of an *imaginal* psychology because the imaginal only exists in relation to the literal as its negativity and is therefore tied to it. He believes that a full-fledged overcoming can, however, happen in *thought*. I question this. I don't believe there is any Notion, any Idea, no matter how rarefied, how Hegelian, how sublated that is not subject to the literalizing impulse. Literalizing is what we do, one of the things we do, because we want to know (even the unknowable), want to feel secure (even as we recognize both the impossibility and the cost of security), because, to introduce a Freudian theme I'll return to later, there is a death drive (which is what this longing for certainty and security ultimately represents). Furthermore, just as the death drive isn't bad, neither is the pull to literalism. What's bad is being stuck there, unresponsive to the pull of

Eros or of the imaginal.

In this symposium, poised at the beginning of the 21st century, it may seem convenient to speak of the 20th century as Freud's century, as Paul Robinson did in his review of the book accompanying the Library of Congress's Freud exhibit. Robinson suggests "we may safely pronounce him the dominant intellectual presence" of the century which opened with the publication of his Interpretation Of Dreams in 1900. (1998, p. 12.) In the middle of that century in Freud: The Mind Of The Moralist (published just as I was beginning graduate school), Philip Rieff suggested that, in large measure due to Freud's influence, earlier understandings of the human as primarily political man or religious man or economic man had now been superseded by the notion of psychological man.

By "psychological man" Rieff meant a vision of the human in which self-concern takes precedence over social concerns, a vision which encourages careful concentration on the self and withdrawal from the painful tension of assent and dissent in our relation to society. Rieff recognized the appeal of this pull to subjectivity in a soul-less, technology-dominated world-- but also how it inevitably intensifies alienation. He warned, we may learn that "every cure must expose us to new illness." (Rieff, 1961, p. 392.) It is clear he would not have been surprised that after one hundred years of psychotherapy we haven't gotten any better!

Rieff himself wasn't quite saying that this is what Freud offered, but rather that it is what we've taken from him; it is how Freud has in large measure been understood. We could say it is this understanding of Freud, of psychological man, that leads us to believe we must now instead turn to post-psychological man. It is, however, my belief that Freud himself saw this focus on subjectivity, on the individual inner person, as problematic. The real problem, as Russell Jacoby says in his Social Amnesia (published fifteen years after Rieff's book), is not Freud but the forgetting of Freud, the repression of Freud, the assimilation of Freud to positivism.

Unlike Rieff, Jacoby believes that "Freud *undid* the primal bourgeois distinction between the private and the public, the individual and society" (1975, p. 26, my italics). Freud insisted that we are in society and it is in us. But this got forgotten--in large measure because of the distorted translation of Freud, both in the literal sense of the Strachey translation (which, among other equally disastrous distortions, translates Freud's *Seele*, the German word for "soul" as "mental organization" and Freud's *Ich*, the intimate everyday way of referring to oneself, "I", as "ego"). Another reason was the physical translation, after Hitler came to power, of the center of the psychoanalytical world from German-speaking Europe to America, which led to the dominance of the Anglo-Saxon medical, conformist version of psychoanalysis which Freud had always valiantly though mostly unsuccessfully criticized. Along with these translations came a focus on therapy rather than theory. Jacoby argues that when we dismiss theory we all too easily move toward assimilationist therapy--toward empiricism, positivism, pragmatism.

Because of how easily this happens, depth psychology keeps returning to the question of the separation of psyche and society and seems often not to recognize that the point is not to move from a concern with soul to a concern with the world, for aiming at the world is just as problematic as aiming at the self. The problematics persist as long as we see world and self as separate, as opposed, as long as we see psychology and politics as two distinct concerns. Recognizing the inadequacy of this disjunction is, I think, what we have in mind when we say we now find ourselves in a *post*-psychological world; we seem to understand that we have to go beyond psychology but in a way that recognizes and includes psychology, the kind of going beyond suggested by the Hegelian term, *Aufgehoben.*

But, I want to insist, there's nothing very new about this. In 1939, the year that both Freud and he died, Otto Rank published a book called Beyond Psychology, in which he presents psychoanalysis as representing the end of the bourgeois era. Rank is persuaded of the inadequacy of an individual-focused psychology to explain the social turmoil brought about by the rise of Nazism. He views psychoanalysis as part of the human attempt to control the irrational, to explain and thus restrict life, and announces that it is now time to go beyond individual psychology-- beyond any rational explanation, beyond any logos. We are called, he says, to live beyond psychology, beyond the expectation of a cure or interpretation that would resolve the pain of living, called to be courageous, to live irrationally, called beyond individual psychology. We need the Thou, the Other, in order to become a self. We need to love and be loved, yet we fear dependence and otherness and so are caught between our pull to autonomy and our longing to merge. The psychology of the self is to be found in the Other. Our deepest longing is to surrender to a greater-than-self. Beyond psychology lies relation, and because no human other can actually fulfill this need for us, beyond psychology lies God. (Rank, 1958, p. 290).

But long before Rank's book appeared, Freud had also, in his own, admittedly quite different way, been going "beyond psychology," had been doing *meta*psychology. Because we tend to use the term in relation to the conceptual models introduced in the central theoretical works of his later years, we often think of metapsychology as something Freud began doing fairly late, after <u>Totem and Taboo</u>, indeed, mostly after the First World War. But theory was always more important to Freud than therapy--which is one of the reasons his support of lay analysis was so crucial to him. "The chief aim of psychoanalysis is to contribute to the science of psychology and to the world of literature and life in general," he says (quoted in Blanton, 1971, p. 116). Depth psychology's central aim, I would paraphrase, is to contribute to the way we think most honestly and deeply about our human being-here. As Freud said to H.D., "My discoveries are not primarily a heal-all, my discoveries are a basis for a very grave philosophy," (H.D., 1950, p. 25), and as he wrote in the <u>New Introductory Lectures</u>, "Without metapsychological speculation and theorizing--I had almost said fantasizing--we shall not get another step forward" (Freud, 23:225). Freud was engaged in metapsychology all along; he was already using the term "metapsychological" (and clearly had the allusion to metaphysics in mind) in the 1890s, in the letters to Fliess written as he was just beginning work on <u>Interpretation of Dreams</u>. He was moving into metapsychology, he wrote, because he saw himself moving toward a psychology that led beyond consciousness.

In this sense his central insight, that the ego is not master of its own house, is obviously meta-psychological. Freud keeps having to resay this in different ways, because each way is so easily co-opted, so easily literalized, reified. The unconscious so quickly becomes a region we can map, a part of ourselves over which we, our ego selves, can gain control. Therefore Freud comes to move away from the language of conscious and unconscious with which he began, to speak instead of ego/superego/id, to speak of the forever resurgent *That* in us. Later still he will shift to speaking of Eros and Death in the hope that this more mythic language might prove more resilient to such co-option. But what happened was, of course, that the death drive was simply ignored or rejected (Going beyond psychology does seem to be something we resist).

For Freud, "real" psychology, depth psychology, is a psychology of the unconscious, the unknown and unknowable in us. This is, to use a term from Giegerich, the Notion out of which all else Freud has to say derives. Understanding Freud means going back to this center and seeing how the details flow from it. I think Freud would agree with Giegerich that real psychology is about those things one can't speak about but must try to anyway. Real psychology is about the unconscious, which is not something we "have," is nothing positive, is not an empirical given. Freud both wants to know, to bring the unconscious into consciousness, *and* knows how profoundly there is that in us which we cannot know--*and* that our longing to know, to control, is part of our malaise. He does not believe we can ever fully bring the unconscious into consciousness; the project of doing so is like Faust's project of draining the Zuider Zee. Every dream interpretation, if pursued, will come to the "navel" of the dream, the place that marks its connections to an unfathomable source, to the realm of The Mothers in <u>Faust</u>. There is always a place that must be left in the dark, a tangle or knot which resists unraveling. The dream can't be equated with the manifest dream or with the latent (interpreted) dream, for it *is* the ungraspable, a testimony to our irreducible complexity and depth. Interpretation can be a way of protecting against the dream. To turn to Philips once again (1995, p. 67.), we are Tantalos to what we dream.

Freud tries to help us think the unconscious and the soul and to imagine them. Giegerich says we can only *think* the soul because it is no-thing. Something so complex and contradictory can't be imagined, only thought. Like Hegel, Giegerich sees the imaginal as half way between sensory intuition and thought. The task, therefore, is to make the latent thought complete by freeing it from its immersion in the medium of emotion or image. Thus Giegerich buys into the Hegelian assumption that thought is superior to image, though encompassing it. For him soul *is* thinking; thought is the soul's openness to what is. I see his perspective as in line with the long theological history of the *via negativa* but want to recall that theology also includes an analogical tradition which holds that the unknown can best be pointed to through metaphor, through image. I am not a Hegelian and don't accept the hierarchical relation between Image and Idea. I see them as of equal value and necessity and so applaud Freud as someone who both thinks and images the soul. He is engaged in psyche-logos both as he actively thinks and speaks *about* the soul *and* more receptively as he listens to the soul's speech about itself (which he takes to be a speech of images).

Freud always speaks of the *un*conscious, never of the *sub*conscious (unlike Janet & Bernheim who intend the denigrating connotations). He sees that the unconscious can often best be spoken of through negations, by saying what it is not, but he also sees how helpful, indeed necessary, metaphorical descriptions can be. Thus his writings are full of metaphors for the unconscious, though there is clearly a privileged one, Hades, the Greek underworld (the same metaphor privileged by Hillman) .

Freud also recognizes how misleading this word "un-conscious" can be; it assumes the priority of consciousness, the position of ego looking *at* the unconscious. Therefore in chapter seven of <u>Interpretation of Dreams</u> he speaks instead of the psyche's *primary process* and says that this more poetical, mythic, image-filled, emotionally-toned mode of functioning is not a distortion of normal psychic process but the form of the soul's uninhibited activity; indeed, it represents the core of our being.

Freud's most important thesis is that something beyond ego, beyond the self-aware "I," shapes our thoughts, feelings, and actions. This "something" is our own forgotten and denied past, but it also includes transindividual fears, hopes, and memories (as the centrality of his discovery "I am Oedipus" communicates). Thus *meta*psychology means not simply a psychology beyond consciousness but also a psychology beyond the individual. There is no ego, no "I" present as a given. The "I" comes into being through a sequence of losses and identifications. When we find ourselves, we find ourselves in a world with others---and we find these others in ourselves. The child becomes a self through its erotic identifications with those close to it. The "I" is a precipitate of abandoned loves, identifications and losses, "an archaeological reminder of grief," to borrow once again a phrase from Adam Phillips (1995, p. 78).

Though Freud was not a theist and most emphatically not a monotheist, he was pulled to what I call "Beyondness" as can be seen even more clearly in the later explicitly metapsychological texts--particularly in <u>Beyond the Pleasure Principle</u> (1922) and <u>Civilization and Its Discontents</u> (1931). Obviously I can't deal with these texts in the detailed way they deserve here, but I do want to say a few things about each.

I want to begin by calling attention to the first word of the title of <u>Beyond the Pleasure Principle</u>, "Beyond," and to note that the German word Freud used, *Jenseits,* is the one used by theologians to refer to the Other World, to heaven. In this book Freud first introduces the death drive and first speaks of the two primary powers, Eros and Death, which are not just drives in us but primal energies at work in us, on us, and in the cosmos. For Freud, Eros is the energy that pulls us forward--beyond ourselves, beyond the present, the given--to the new, to the other. The twin brother of Eros is Death, and Death, as Freud speaks of it, is of course a psychical and not simply a biological reality. The goal of all life is death, he tells us, with ever more complicated detours. Death is something we both long for and fear. Freud associates our death fear with our fears of the unknown, the uncanny, the unconscious, with our fears of vulnerability and passivity. The death wish is associated with all in us that is pulled toward repetition, inertia, regression, all that longs for a tension-free existence, for Nirvana, resolution, completion.

In <u>Civilization and Its Discontents</u> (1931), which Philips calls his great "elegy for human happiness" (1998, p. 72), Freud asks why it is so hard to be happy. Civilization is largely responsible, he suggests, as he points to the irreconcilable conflict between individual and group, a conflict which presupposes non-gratification and the necessity of renunciation. He takes note of our hostility to civilization *and* of our erotic connection to it. We both want and resent society; it both fulfills and frustrates us, and we are inescapably involved with it. In this text Freud brings in a different aspect of the death drive from the one focused on in the earlier book. Here he writes of how when denied death-fear and death-wish both become destructive, become aggression. Freud reminds us of our resentful hatred of anything that intrudes between us and the peace for which we long, of anything that reminds use of our incompleteness, of our wanting, of our separation from the all. He writes of the violence that is not just out there but also in us and of how the two are not really separable, He reminds us of energies more frightening and more intractable than those encompassed within the Jungian shadow.

But Death (as I've said before) is not the enemy. The death drive is not "bad"; it represents a given direction of the soul. Freud hopes to help us recognize the importance of accepting this as part of who we are, of learning to bear the conflicts within us, of curing our demand for cure or resolution, the importance of coming to view conflict as enduring and enlivening. But, then, that's Eros's view. Death itself might say: we need to honor also that in us which continues to want happiness, resolution, fulfillment.

So, though Freud honors Eros, he also recognizes the pull of narcissism, of fusion-longing, of escape from the world of others, the pull back to an imagined inner world and to the illusion that it constitutes a separate reality. Neither narcissism nor death are "bad." They are part of the soul's given direction, perhaps the deepest part (if we agree with Freud that the ultimate aim/ *telos* of life is death). Nevertheless, it is important that we move beyond narcissism at least temporarily, that we consciously, willingly, embark on that long detour which takes us into the world of others, into the social and the political world. Always, however, we will feel the pull of both these immortal energies, though sometimes one, sometimes the other, will seem to predominate.

It is this recognition of Freud's, this recognition of the power of these two immortal adversaries, of their unending conflict, that continues to persuade me that Freud speaks to me, more than do Jung or Hillman-- though I have learned so much from both--and more than Giegerich does. (I recognize this may be an expression of my Jewish side, an expression of how I resonate with Martin Buber's affirmation that the Jew knows with every cell of her or his body that redemption has not yet happened).

In Terrors and Experts Adam Philips says: "It's not the future of psychoanalysis that anyone should be concerned about, but rather the finding of language for what matters most to us" (1995, p. xvi.). He also says that we know somebody speaks to us, if they make us speak (1998, p. 84). This, it seems to me, is the most important question: Which language does that for us, which allows us to speak of those things we care about most deeply?

As Freud noted, "People are seldom impartial where ultimate things, the great problems of science and life are concerned. Each of us is governed in such cases by deep-rooted internal prejudices, into whose hands our speculation unwittingly plays" (1953/1974, 18:59). I'm aware that one of my "prejudices" is my conviction that the Holocaust is the central defining moment of the 20th century. It is more important to me that we live in a post-Holocaust world than that we live in a post-psychological one, though I see the two as closely connected. I know that any psychology that speaks to me has to be able to take the Shoah into account; it must recognize those capacities in us which it brought so forcefully into view: not just the suffering we suffer, but the suffering we cause, not just our longing for justice but our capacity to do evil. Any psychology that speaks to me has to recognize as an inescapable given that we live in a world of others and are responsible to it, to them.

Undoubtedly part of my pull to Freud is that I see him as meeting this requirement more fully than do Jung or Hillman or Giegerich. Freud knows at the deepest place within him --in a way that none of his own formulations ever articulated quite well enough even for him -- that we are conflicted, that we are not whole, that there is no cure for the unconscious, that the most we can hope for is the substituting of everyday unhappiness for neurotic misery. The goal is not wholeness, but being able to bear our incompleteness, to live our conflicts more keenly, as Philips puts it (1995, p. 45). Whereas for Giegerich the soul *is*, by definition, whole, undivided. I don' t believe that, as I also don't believe we ever go *wholly* into the wilderness (I am referring here to Giegerich's interpretation of the Actaeon myth). I don't believe in a whole person in that sense. Paradoxically perhaps, I seem to be saying that Hegelian though he may be, Giegerich's understanding of soul is not dialectical enough! For Giegerich, as I understand him, honoring soul means a total commitment to "wilderness," to risk; it means foregoing stability, foregoing all delight in symbols and myths, for such indulgence is esthetics, not psychology. Whereas, I would say that the longing for stability is also part of soul, the death-drive part.

I also do not believe that we, the soul, lives only in the abstract virtual world, though I, too, know the growing reality of that world, and see what it has added to our lives as well as what it threatens to take away. I see how technology may lead to the death of our species--and how it grows out of Eros, out of our delight in change and the new, and out of the death drive's wish to control. Giegerich seems to think that to do justice to the soul under the conditions of Modernity, we need to turn from image to idea. Because our world is abstract, the soul can now only be satisfied by the abstract; because we inevitably live in this abstract world whether we admit it or not, our soul problems appear on a different level than they did in the past. The soul today requires abstract thinking. By proclaiming previous levels of life to be obsolete, Giegerich seems to be proposing a developmental model after all, even if the new is not viewed as necessarily an improvement. The time for indulging in myths and images of the gods is past, he tells us. Imaginal psychology's project of interpreting life in terms of the gods assumes that fundamentally, we live in the same world as did the Greek, *but we don't.* Thus we miss the particular character of our world, evade the real life of our here-and-now, by trying to find analogies from another. The specific psychological character of our world cannot be grasped by the imagination.

I agree that we can't really enter mythic consciousness directly, that for the archaic mythic mind the distinction between the literal and the imaginal doesn't arise, that (as Giegerich puts it) for the archaic mind the imaginal or divine shines forth from within what we'd call the literal. Though I'd add that most of the myths that imaginal psychology concerns itself with (including Ovid's version of the Actaeon myth, to which Giegerich devotes so many pages) come from a Greek and Roman literary world in which the literal/imaginal distinction is well established. I disagree with Giegerich that, once one knows this distinction, one can only *think* the gods. Like Giambatista Vico, I believe that outgrown modes of consciousness are still available to us, through empathic *nacherleben,* imaginally, and that the abstract alone is not what the soul requires. The past is still alive in us, not just as archaic vestige but as life-giving. As Freud: said, "Humankind never lives entirely in the present. The past lives on in us and yields only slowly to the influences of the present and to new change" (1953/1974, 22:160).

Giegerich's message, though challenging, is in its way upbeat and therefore consoling. I am thinking of his conviction that we can learn to live in this new world happily and wholly. Thus he is comforting in a way Freud never is. Freud ends Civilization and Its Discontents by admitting that be can offer no consolation but then goes on to say--remember this is in 1931, as

Nazism is clearly on the rise--"But now it is to be hoped (or "awaited," not: "expected" as the Standard Edition has it) that the other of the two heavenly powers, eternal Eros, will make an effort to assert himself in the struggle with his equally immortal adversary. But who can foresee with what success and with what results?" (1953/1974, 21:145).

In a poem written a short few months after Freud's death, W. H. Auden wrote that over Freud's grave "the household of Impulse mourns one dearly loved: sad is Eros, builder of cities, and weeping, anarchic Aphrodite" (1976, p. 218). Like Freud, like Auden, I can speak best by speaking mythically, metaphorically, by speaking of the gods, of Eros and Aphrodite. "Eros, builder of cities" is clearly not an Eros associated with sentimental love but rather a reference to the love that sustains us in the difficult projects of our life together, the love that pertains not just to intimate family life but that pulls us ever forward, outward, into larger and larger worlds, into social groupings much, much larger than the Greek polis. The sadness of which Auden speaks our wondering whether or not that pull is really strong enough--a question that is not just about us in any individual way but about Eros himself.

Aphrodite, "Anarchic Aphrodite" is the goddess of sexuality, sensuous delight and beauty, the goddess who makes manifest the sacredness of the anarchic pull of desire and impulse. We need to stay enthusiastic about her as well. And all along we need to continue to remember how Death, too, hold us in his thrall.

I have no program or vision for how psychology will move in the world that is coming into shape. I have lots of fears and hopes. I share Freud's skepticism and his tentative hope. I see a lot of Death in the more abstract world that I, like Giegerich, see us as living in already and that I imagine will become even more dominant. I do not believe that either images or ideas will save us. Like Otto Rank, like Freud, like Jung in the closing pages of Memories, Dreams, Reflections (1963), I do know that what takes us Beyond Psychology is LOVE.

References

Auden, W.H. (1976). Collected poems. New York: Random House.

H.D. (1956). Tribute to Freud. New York: New Directions.

Freud, S. (1953/1974.). The standard edition of the complete psychological works of Sigmund Freud. London: Hogarth Press.

Jacoby, R. (1975). Social amnesia: A critique of contemporary psychology from Adler to Laing. Boston: Beacon.

Jung, C.G. (1963). Memories, dreams, reflections. New York: Pantheon.

Philips, A. (1995). Terrors and experts. Cambridge, MA: Harvard University Press.

Philips, A. (1998). The beast in the nursery. New York: Pantheon.

Rank, O. (1958). Beyond psychology. New York: Dover.

Rieff, P. (1961). Freud: The mind of the moralist. New York: Anchor Books.

Robinson, P. (1998, Nov. 12). Symbols at an Exhibition. New York Times Book Review.

Irony's Arrows/Eros: A Poetics of Culture[1] by David L. Miller, Ph.D.

1. A Culture of Irony? Something is Taking its Course!

In Samuel Beckett's play, <u>Endgame</u>, Hamm says to Clov: "This is not much fun. But that's always the way at the end of the day, isn't it, Clov." "Always," says Clov, and Hamm says: "It's the end of the day like any other day, isn't it, Clov?" "Looks like it," says Clov. And then Hamm says in anguish: "What's happening, what's happening?" To which Clov responds: "Something is taking its course."[2] Indeed, something is taking its course, in our culture, in our time. The "something" seems to be irony.

I first noticed this a few years ago. What I noticed was an increasing conflict creeping into the culture concerning irony. It was something that intuitively made me sense that our collective psychology—as this conference's theme asserts— is indeed on a threshold.

Let me give a few examples from what some people call the "real" world. These will likely bring to mind other instances.

- September 1998: the <u>New York Times </u>magazine's "Style" section featured fashion in <u>Star Wars. </u>The article was called "The Princess Line" of clothes, and one sentence read: "Let's admit that Princess Leia would be mistaken for sexy only by the severely irony-challenged, by say, a George Lucas or a Bill Gates."

- October 11, 1998: the <u>New York Times'</u> "Sunday Styles" section featured an essay by Frank DeCaro, "What's it all about? Simply Burt." It was about Burt Bacharach's new popularity. DeCaro wondered what this romantic and sentimental blandness all about? He wrote: "Does the popularity of Burt Bacharach with Elvis Costello fans mean the end of the age of irony?"

- November 8, 1998: the <u>New York Times'</u> "Arts and Leisure" section had an article by Jon Pareles, "A Pop Post-Modernist Gives up on Irony." It was about the pop singer, Beck, who said: "I've been guilty of irony and cynicism, those things that are symptomatic of our times." But now Beck has given up irony, or so he said.

- January 18, 1999: <u>USA Today's</u> "Sports" section was reporting on the Vikings loss to the Falcons. Gary Anderson had kicked 46 consecutive field goals, but missed one in overtime during this crucial game. "'Ironic? I don't believe in irony,' Vikings coach Dennis Green said. 'Things happen. It's part of the game.'"

- September 5, 1999: in the New York Times' magazine, Marshall Sella's article on Jedediah Purdy, the prodigy and genius who is a 24 year old graduate student at Yale, reported that Purdy is waging a war against irony and in favor of fundamentalist purity.

- November 13, 1999: a New York Times article in the "Arts and Ideas" section was titled: "A Farewell to Irony: Grief Gets a Chance." The essay was on the songs of the Pet Shop Boys who, according to the article, have gradually sloughed off irony over the last fifteen years

- January 1, 2000: Newsweek featured David Gates' article, "Will We Ever Get Over Irony?" The analysis went back to 1926 (showing that this did not start two years ago), and noted that now there is a backlash against irony

- January 2, 2000: the Gates' essay came close to Pacifica Graduate Institute, having been referred to on the Association of Cultural Mythologists listserve, which in turn was reporting on this discussion in the James Hillman chat site.

- January 10, 2000: predictably, Slate, had an essay, "The Backlash against the Backlash against Irony," by Judith Shulevitz, which continued the discussion of the Gates' article, and adding a report on an article in the British journal, The Economist .

- February 11, 2000: the Chronicle of Higher Education had an article by Vincent Crapanzano, "Literalism in America," which was on fundamentalism and lack of irony in contemporary culture.

- May 7, 2000: the New York Times' magazine featured an essay by Adam Philips in which Jonathan Lear, from the Committee on Social Thought at the University of Chicago, noted a shift away from irony in patients and culture ...

- August 13, 2000: the New York Times' op-ed page contained a column by Maureen Dowd, noting that the Democratic committee bashed California Representative

Loretta Sanchez, who had planned a fund raiser for Hispanics at the Playboy mansion, but had not condemned Clinton's Monicagate. Dowd wrote: "Perhaps Al Gore would be better off if he ... held dinners to discuss the meaning of irony."

In all of this, there is apparently some sense that the culture is suffering from what Will Kaufman, in a fine book on the topic, calls "irony fatigue."[3] But there is also some sense that there is a humorless literalism, a moralistic ideologism, to be feared in the loss of an ironic sensibility.

Time magazine seems to have lost its ironic sensibility when it named Jeff Bezos person of the year last year. Bezos, the CEO of Amazon.com, is rewarded with fame for founding a company on the strategy of intending to lose money for an extended period of time. He builds a market position by pursuing a full-scale, go-for-broke strategy from the start of losing hundreds of millions of dollars on a business in which no one knows if anything is to be made.

This is almost as ironic as Tom Lehrer's comment: "political satire became obsolete when Henry Kissinger was awarded the Nobel Prize for Peace." However, my most favorite example comes from today's "real" world—though this is probably the result of a typographical error. There was within the past year an ad for a Center of Holistic Dentistry in Los Angeles that advertises that its air is "ironically purified."

Take this list as an ironic litany, a testimony that something is taking its course, something as absurd as the theater of Beckett, but in this case life is imitating art. The irony of modernity and postmodernity began with Darwin arguing for a biological ordering based on *random* selection; Marx arguing for a political justice and communal stability based on *revolution*; Nietzsche supposing that there is a metaphysical grounding in the *death of God*; and Freud and Jung arguing that the logic of the self's life is based on what is *unconscious*, i.e., on what is unknown and unknowable. It would seem that today one inhabits an ironic world, in which the backlash is equally ironic.

But what is this thing called irony?[4]

2. Ironies: Historical Trajectories

Of course, it's not one thing; it's a lot of things, many things, like ships and shoes and sealing wax and cabbages and kings. Irony's beginning is usually attributed, probably

wrongly, to Socrates. According to the conventional story, Socrates was ironic because, like

Silenos, he was ugly on the outside and beautiful on the inside. Actually, Socrates was empty

on the inside, like the sileni figures who are hollow inside but contain tiny statues of the all the

gods and goddesses.[5] Pico della Mirandola said of Socrates that if you look at the outside, you

will see a beast; if you look within, you will recognize the divine.[6] Above all it was deemed

ironic for Socrates to be called, by the Delphic oracle, the wisest of all persons because he said

that he knew nothing. For this Aristotle in the <u>Nichomachean Ethics</u> will contrast the *eiron*,

giving Socrates as example, with its opposite, the *aladzon*. The latter, the boaster, says more

than she or he knows; the former, the ironist, at the other extreme says less.

Though some--I among them--believed Socrates to be telling the truth when he said that he

knew nothing , it is nonetheless likely, at least in part, that because of Socrates "irony" came

to mean *simulatio*, "dissembling," "deceiving" (Aristotle, Theophrastus).[7] In Cicero and

Quintillian, irony was *dissimulatio* and *inversio* or *illusio*.[8] Irony was *aliud dicitur, aliud*

significatur, "saying one thing and meaning another."[9] With this view, the problem of

arrogance, imagined detachment and the putative superiority of the ironist enters the

picture. Irony had become a rhetorical trope,[10] and, in this, it is the opposite of the ethical

humility of Socrates emptiness, nothingness, and un-knowing. This inversion of irony is, of

course, itself a historical irony.

Another turn came with Romantic Irony (Solger, Schlegel, Hegel, and Kierkegaard),

according to which irony is "infinite negativity" or "absolute negativity." The negativity is

not a negative *thing*, but is more like the *dénégation* of Freud and the French critical theorists.

Irony is now not only *not* a vice, but, on the contrary, for Schlegel, without irony there is no

art because art, as Hegel put it in the <u>Aesthetic Lectures,</u> is a transformation of empirical

appearance into reality, i.e., it is a lifting up or a drawing out and off (*Aufhebung*) by

canceling ego's personalistic image of what seems to be. Irony is the image of art, reflected

(upon), It is not surprising that Schlegel would write that "philosophy is the proper home

of irony,"[11] since philosophy is the realm of reflective thinking.

A further mid-course correction in irony's historical trajectory came with the notion of dramatic irony. The dramatic irony of modernism (Pirandello's theater is a good example) first deprived the characters on the stage, and then the audience too, of the meaning of what was really going on in the plot. This strategy became the threshold leading from Romantic irony to the poetic irony of the New Critics (Cleanth Brooks, Robert Penn Warren, William Wimsatt and later Northrop Frye and historiographer Hayden White). Irony became a trope, a figure, a metaphor, which like wit, humor, and other tropologies and tropics then, was historicized and acculturated.

There have been others mapping the twists and turns of irony since New Criticism: Wayne Booth, for whom stable irony, intended by the artist, though intentional is covert, and finite, represents critical intelligence; Paul DeMan, for whom irony is allegory, and it is the figure that is about itself; Mikhail Bakhtin says irony is heteroglossia, the double-voiced word, polyglossia; Georg Lukács says it results from self-knowledge and the self-cancellation of subjectivity (*die Selbstaufhebung der Subjektivität*).[12] This is what I would call the self-transformation of ego's perspectives dialectically. The metamorphosis happens just at that moment when one sees the irony of irony ... but now I am moving too fast and am getting ahead of myself.

So let me slow things down by adding three explanatory voices to the historical two millennia trajectory leading from the death of Socrates to the death of God, if not to the death of irony.

The first voice is that of my teacher, Stanley Romaine Hopper. In the sixties, Hopper was worrying the problem of irony long before the culture wars I have alluded to at the beginning. He had already observed—in The Crisis of Faith, written at the end of the Second World War, and in Spiritual Problems of Contemporary Literature, written in the early fifties—that the literature of the period had as its central modality that of irony, and that this was affecting the people's spirituality and its psychology. But it was in 1962 that Hopper wrote an important essay for Cross Currents entitled, "Irony—the Pathos of the Middle." The argument was straightforward. Modern novel, drama, and poetry are thoroughgoingly ironic. Hopper was thinking about Eugene O'Neil, Albert Camus, Arthur Miller, Bertholt Brecht, Samuel Beckett, Edward Albee, Harold Pinter, and so on. But Hopper observed that there is an irony about the irony of this work. Irony, he argued, is a transitional form. It cannot be maintained. It is ironic enough, after the moonlight and roses poetry of Romanticism, for T. S. Eliot to speak, in "The Love Song of J. Alfred Prufrock," about the evening sky as "a patient [who] lay aetherized upon the table." But when Eliot announces that "we are the hollow men," the trope collapses. Who is this "we"? If "we" are the hollow men, then this saying must be hollow, too. This is the irony of trying to sustain irony. It is what Linda Hutcheon has in a recent book called "irony's edge."[13] Irony is the mode of existence when one is on a threshold. Hopper hoped, at the end of his article, that irony might soon give way to joy. At the end of his essay, he wrote: "Surely, after so much turning in the ironies of rationalistic profaning of the mysteries, it would be an unexpected turn to topple into sense by way of comedy, to ... know the new *anagnorisis*—the carnival of forms, the festivals of glory, the exploits of joy."[14]

Hopper was actually worrying the arrogance of irony, the arrogance of saying that we are the hollow men, that God is dead, that the self is decentered, that history is at an end, that there is infinite deferral of closure on referential meanings. But Hopper's worry may have been misplaced. Kenneth Burke—a well-known literary critic, friend of Hopper's, and a sometime professor with Hopper at Drew—had argued the opposite in his book <u>A Grammar of Motives.</u> Burke's voice is the second that I want to invoke.

His view was dramatistic. We are all in a drama with many characters, Burke imagined. If one isolates any one character—an agent in drama or a single advocate in a dialogue—the whole drama is seen in terms of that one's position only. This may seem absolutist, but it is in fact, when viewed from the perspective of the whole drama, relativistic. The fundamentalist and the ideologue are the relativists. In relativism there is no irony. Irony arises when one tries, by interaction of all of the voices in the drama or the dialectic, to produce movement. It is ironic because it requires that all sub-certainties (the individual relative positions) be considered as neither true nor false, but as contributory to the drama. True irony, then, is not arrogant; it is humble, Socratically, because it senses no superiority in one position over the others in the whole drama and because it is based in a sense of fundamental kinship with the enemy, since every protagonist needs an antagonist in order to play out his or her drama. Irony thus saves us from fundamentalisms, literalisms, and ideologies—i.e., it is the modality or trope that refuses to take a relativism as an absolute.[15]

It turns out that Hopper and Burke were not so much opposed as it may seem, since Hopper's main point is that irony is a transitional form and Burke's main point is that the total action is a drama or a dialectic. This point about movement and the transitional quality of irony was similarly to be argued by the German literary critic, Beda Allemann, whose early book, Ironie und Dichtung, may still be his most important work. It is Allemann's voice that I want to invoke thirdly.

Allemann had been invited to a conference on hermeneutics at Drew University in 1966, and, on the basis of that visit,[16] he was invited to Syracuse University in the Autumn of 1970 to a colloquium on the hermeneutical relevance of the work of his teacher, Martin Heidegger. Allemann decided to talk more about the subject of his book. His title was, "Irony and the Unspoken," and it focused on one sentence from Heidegger's work: *Nie ist das Gesprochene und in keiner Sprache das Gesagte.* "Never and in no speaking is that which is spoken that which is said." This is fundamental to Heidegger's modernist project, and it is, indeed, ironic. That is, it is ironic that language says something other than what speakers think that they might be saying. Language has an intentionality of its own.[17]

In his talk Alleman pointed out that "irony is a non-literal (*uneigentlich*) manner of speaking" (1)[18] "Irony is a phenomenon of transition and approximation which can realize itself only in a fluctuating and delicate equilibrium. Irony is a tightrope balancing act. On one end of the scale we have the serious straightforwardness of the literal statement which is identical with what is meant, on the other end we have undisguised mockery and scorn and cynicism and sarcasm. Literary irony lies in the middle" (8).

Allemann's example is Marc Antony's line from Shakespeare's Julius Caesar: "Brutus is an honorable man." The first time that it is said, it seems straightforward and literal. The second time it is said, it has become ironic. But after many repetitions, it is straightforward again, but now straightforwardly cynical, scorning, and mocking. First it is not irony, then it is irony, then after many repetitions it is mockery or sarcasm.

So, Allemann argued, there is the "not-yet-ironic" and the "no-longer-ironic" (9) In between, there is irony. So, "irony equals the transparent discrepancy between the literal statement and what is actually meant" (16). But, as Allemann said, the "discrepancy" is an "ironic field of tension or *Spielraum*, a "space with some play in it," and this space of tension has an antithetical structure" (17). One might say: it is dialectical. The *Spielraum* is a "glass cage" in which the writer is a "tightrope dancer." Glass because transparency is essential. Irony is a seeing-through. It is a cage because the writer is imprisoned within the rules of the ironic game.

"The irony of a text," said Allemann, "is not fully understood unless the reader becomes aware of the discrepancy between what is literally said and what is concealed behind it." To use Heidegger's distinction once more: "that which is said becomes perceptible through that which is spoken, but it is not identical with what is spoken" (20). Discrepancy is always present. Call it a latent meaning behind the manifest (Freud), or a shadow or unconscious signification (Jung). Irony points to a structure of fundamental ambiguity or to a *coincidentia oppositorum*. Depth psychology is at bottom ironic.

Hopper hoped that irony would tumble finally into comedy or joy; Allemann, like Peter Sloterdijk, is worried that it may go over the edge into cynicism or sarcasm. Perhaps these both are possibilities, shadows of irony. But whether one or the other, or a Burkean humble dialectic of both, the historical trajectory of irony reveals that irony is itself apparently a trajectory.

3. Irony's Arrows/Eros

For phenomenologists—such as Franz Brentano, Edmund Husserl, Roman Ingarden, and Maurice Merleau-Ponty--intentionality is the name of the trajectory, for intentionality is the ordering principle for the experience of imagining and thinking. Intentionality is the self-transcending movement of mind where the object is always intentionally nonexistent, that is, some object of imagination or thought is intended and yet it does not exist phenomenologically or perceptually.[19] It is realized in the intentionality of the thought or image.

Intentionality, on this view, is a universal feature of every mental phenomenon.[20] In imaginative experience, and--as Hegel and Heidegger point out--in thinking, "each [act and object] calls for the other within a continuous intentional arc." This arc, as Edward Casey has noted,[21] is a shuttling, an oscillating, like a badminton birdie, or like the many arrows in the paintings of Paul Klee, and this arcing of objects and subjects forms a phenomological and psychological network or web.[22] The arrow (the intentionality) goes both ways at once, like a sort of macro version of quantum superposition, in which a particle can be here and there at the same time, and can move to and fro simultaneously.

The arrow of intentionality, like the logic of quantum physics, takes one beyond. It is beyond us, beyond thinking, imagining. That is why one shoots an arrow. That is why one thinks (not to find what one always already knows), that is why one imagines (not to see pictures that one recognizes). One imagines and thinks, not to see any pictures at all, not to think any thoughts at all, but to see, to think no-thing: the nothingness of everything. This is like Zen and the art of archery! No bow, no target ... only arrowing.

Wolfgang Giegerich begins his book, The Soul's Logical Life, with a story that expresses the radicalness of this phenomenological insight about intentionality. "There is an Old Icelandic saga about a young man who was a stay-at-home. His mother could not stand this and tried to rouse him with biting remarks [likely ironic!]. Finally she was successful. The young man got up from behind the stove where he had been sitting and, taking his spear, left the house. Outside, he threw his spear as far as he could and then ran up to the place where it had landed in order to retrieve it. At this new point, he again threw the spear as far ahead as possible and then followed it, and so on. In this way, with these literal 'projections' that he then had to catch up with, he made a way for himself from the comfort of home into the outside world."[23] Remember Zeno's arrow. It never arrived. It—like the pink bunny in the battery advertisement—is still going.

I had an experience of this one day in France. It was in the town of Colmar. A friend and I were looking for the convent that houses Grünewald's famous Isenheim Altarpiece. We came to the center of the village and looked at the road signs. There was one that said, *Toutes Directions*, "All Directions." Beside the words was a single arrow pointing in one direction. The French have done it, I thought! By going one direction, a person can go in all directions at once. And it is impossible to know where one will end.

Hertz will rent a car with GPS technology that tells one with a little arrow on a screen how to go somewhere; but when will the technology be invented to show the way to go everywhere at once, and no-where? Like the cursor on a computer: it is an arrow that goes every which way, but points to nothing, nothing but a reality that is always virtual.

In the past there have been many arrows, to be sure: Cupid's, which is not the same as Eros'; Diana's, which is not the same as Artemis'. Greek arrows are not the same as Roman ones, and all are different from Apollo's, even though he is brother to Artemis. And none of these mythic arrows is the same as irony's arrows, which is different today from those of yesterday. In polytheistic mythology one could go many ways, but only one at a time. In irony's postmodern a-mythology, one can go all ways at once because it is all arrow. There is no archer, there is no target. It is all arrow …but this arrowing is the target … and we cannot not hit it because it hits us.

4. Conclusion: Threshold Psychology

To say that in the case of irony it is not we who hit the target but that the target hits us is to speak ironically about irony. When I talk this way, I am actually thinking of Longfellow's well-known poem about his writing a poem:

I shot an arrow into the air,

It fell to the earth, I knew not where;

For, so swiftly it flew, the sight

Could not follow it in its flight.

I breathed a song into the air,

It fell to earth, I knew not where;

For who has sight so keen and strong,

That it can follow the flight of song?[24]

… or, for that matter, a thought. Yes, this essay too is only an arrow—well, perhaps more than one—shot into the air, another irony, another erring, and it lands, I know not where. Irony's arrow, going many directions at once, *toutes directions*, arriving at no particular where, a no-thing, which was the target that it was intended to hit.

After all, all of this is actually not about irony at all. That is only what I have spoken; it is not what I meant to have said. This is not about arrows and irony; it is about eros and psyche. Psyche at the threshold, about psychology, the logic of the soul, as being of the nature of threshold.

All arrow. All arrows. All eros. Desire. No-thing else. It's all, always already, threshold. Liminal. Arrows/Eros/Errors ... as Jacques Derrida and Peter Eisenman (not to mention Socrates) have observed (see footnote #1).

Irony is lurking just around the corner when Freud can announce that the goal of the healing of psychological suffering is to "transform neurotic misery into ordinary human unhappiness" and when Jung can announce that when therapy is successful we will have the "painful sense of innate discord" and feel like we are "strangers" unto ourselves. Talking about the therapy of psychology in such a way reveals, as Heidegger put it, that never is what is said the same as that which is spoken. There is an unsaid in the saying always and already. Including in this essay. Indeed, in this very sentence.

As Adam Phillips recently wrote: Freud called the self "'unconscious desire,' partly to show us the ironic sense in which we are the unnamable authors of our own lives (authors who keep losing the plot, authors who experience themselves as being fed their lines from some odd place)."[25]
Irony is a way of not-saying, i.e., of not-I speaking , or rather, irony is a way of understanding the not-saying, of understanding the not-I speaking. It is a depth psychological trope in which, as Nietzsche and Deleuze have said, the depth is on the surface.[26]

The trip of irony's arrow is indeed a trip. We are always already tripped. It is like the little arrow on the dashboard of your car. It signals a turn. It signals that the journey is not going to be straight; it is going to be ironic. That little arrow is an irony signal.

The way is not straight, said Socrates, the ironist. So, don't take yes for an answer. Or for that matter, don't take no for an answer either. Don't take anything for an *answer*. As Peter Sloterdijk wrote in Critique of Cynical Reason: "We need an advance in the training of mistrust."[27] We need irony lessons. Perhaps this is why Moses' tongue was slow, Isaiah's lips were unclean, Jeremiah demurred, and Ezekiel was mute.[28] It is because never is what is spoken what is actually said.

There is no unironic situation because there is always an other side, an unsaid. It's threshold all the way down.

We are the point of the arrow of irony's intentionality. Wallace Stevens' lines are apt: "Intangible arrows quiver and stick in the skin / And I taste at the root of the tongue the unreal of what is real."[29] The arrow actually is a boomerang.

We are like postmodern secular Saint Sebastians being shot at from all sides by the arrows/eros of irony. And it may be, as Glenn Holland has observed in a recent book,[30] that the irony is divine. Psalm 64.7 reminds us that "God will shoot his arrow at them and they will be wounded suddenly." And Zechariah 9.14 says that "the Lord will appear over them and his arrow will go forth like lightning."

The Greek word *toxikon*, though it means poison, means a specific poison, the one on the tip of an arrow (*toxikos* meaning originally "from the bow") ... and this will give English the word "intoxicate" ... such as the intoxication of ideas in the life of the mind ... an arrow of outrageous postmodern fortune striking the chink in ego's armor. Ego giving up its direction for irony's arrows/eros. It places us on an eternal threshold. The irony of irony, finally, is that it is all irony.

Psyche as threshold. All threshold. Nothing on either side. As Jung once wrote concerning Nietzsche: "The deadly arrows do not strike the hero from without; it is oneself who hunts, fight, and tortures the self. In the self, instinct wars with instinct; therefore the poet says, 'Thyself pierced through,' which means that a person is wounded by one's own arrow."[31]

The poet, Denise Levertov, has captured the ironic point, the point of the arrows/eros of irony, in a poem called "The Life of Others"—the others in this poem being a wedge of Canadian geese flying overhead.

> Their high pitched baying
> As if in prayer's unison

Remote, undistracted, given over

Utterly to belief,

The skein of geese

Voyages south,

    Hierarchic arrow of its convergence toward

    The point of grace

Swinging and rippling, ribbon tail

Of a kite, loftily

Over lakes where they have not

Elected to rest,

Over men who suppose

Earth is man's, over golden earth

Preparing itself

For night and winter.

    We humans

Are smaller than they, and crawl

Unnoticed,

About and about the smoky map.[32]

This is a goose eyed view of the something that is ironically taking its course at the end of this day. Remember (as George Axelos once said): "Galactic irony is watching you."[33] And, if not irony, maybe a goose!

References

Allemann, B. (1969). Ironie und Dichtung. Pfullingen: Neske.

Burke, K. (1945). A grammar of motives. New York: Prentice-Hall, Inc.

Bové, P. (1980). Destructive poetics. New York: Columbia University Press.

Culler, J. (1974). Flaubert: The uses of uncertainty Ithaca: Cornell University Press.

Dane, J. (1991). The critical cythology of irony. Athens: University of Georgia Press.

DeMott, B. (1961-62). The new irony: Sickniks and others. American Scholar, 108-19.

Hall, D L. (1982). Eros and irony: A prelude to philosophical anarchism. Albany: SUNY Press.

Holland, G S. (2000). Divine irony Selinsgrove: Susquehanna University Press.

Hopper, S R. (1945). The crisis of faith Nashville: Abingdon.

Hopper, S R. (1952). The problem of moral isolation. Spiritual Problems in Contemporary Literature. New York: Harper and Row.

Hopper, S R. (1963). Irony--The pathos of the middle. Cross Currents, 31-40.

Hutcheon, L. (1985). A theory of parody. New York: Methuen.

Hutcheon, L. (1994). Irony's edge. New York: Routledge.

Kaufman, W. (1997). The comedian as confidence man: Studies in irony fatigue. Detroit: Wayne State University Press.

Kierkegaard, S. (1966). The concept of irony. London: Collins.

McCarthy, D. (1999). The limits of irony: The chronological world of Martin Amis' Time's Arrow. War, Literature, and the Arts, 294-320.

Merrill, R. (1979). Infinite absolute negativity …. Comparative Literature Studies, 222-36.

Paz, O. (1978). Marcel Duchamp, Appearance stripped bare. New York: Viking Press.

Rorty, R. (1989). Contingency, irony and solidarity. New York: Cambridge University Press.

Ross, A. (8 November 1993). The politics of irony. New Republic, 22-31.

Satterfield, L. (1981). Towards a poetics of the ironic sign. In R. DeGeorge (Ed.), Semiotic themes. Lawrence: University of Kansas Press.

Scholes, R. (1982). A semiotic approach to irony … In Semiotics and Interpretation. New Haven: Yale University Press.

Sloterdijk, P. (1987). Critique of cynical reason. Minneapolis: University of Minnesota Press.

Thompson, A. (1948). The dry mock. Berkeley: University of California Press.

Wilde, A. (1981). Horizons of assent: Modernism, postmodernism and the ironic imagination. Baltimore: Johns Hopkins University Press.

Footnotes

[1] I am certainly not the first to force this pun. Jacques Derrida comments on its use by Peter Eisenman in *Psyche: L'Invention de l'autre* (Paris: Éditions Galilée, 1987), p. 506. Eisenman's essay was entitled *Fin d'OU T hou S* (London, Architectural

Association, 1985), and contains the subtitle: "Moving Arrows Eros and Other Errors." I discovered this reference after I had constructed the title for this essay.

[2] H. M. Block and R. G. Shedd, eds., *Masters of Modern Drama* (New York: Random House, 1962), 1106.

[3] Will Kaufman, *The Comedian as Confidence Man: Studies in Irony Fatigue* (Detroit: Wayne State University Press, 1997).

[4] Any attempt to achieve a clear understanding of the concept of irony is fated to be frustrated. The famous scholar of "irony," D. C. Muecke, in his book *The Compass of Irony*, wrote: "Getting to grips with irony seems to have something in common with gathering the mist; there is plenty to take hold of if only one could." See: Glenn S. Holland, *Divine Irony* (Selingsgrove: Susquehanna University Press, 2000), 19.

[5] Joseph A. Dane, *The Critical Mythology of Irony* (Athens: University of Georgia Press, 1991), 16f.

[6] Ibid., 21.

[7] Ibid., 45.

[8] Ibid., 49.

[9] Ibid., 56.

[10] Ibid., 70.

[11] Ibid., 110.

[12] Ibid., 186.

[13] Linda Hutcheon, *Irony's Edge.* (New York : Routledge, 1994).

[14] Stanley Romaine Hopper, "Irony--The Pathos of the Middle," *Cross Currents*, 12/1 (1963): 40.

[15] Kenneth Burke, *A Grammar of Motives.* (New York : Prentice-Hall, Inc., 1945), pp. 511-17.

[16] The proceedings of that conference are published in: Stanley R. Hopper and David L. Miller., eds., *Interpretation: The Poetry of Meaning* (New York: Harcourt Brace and World, 1967).

[17] Heidegger writes this in *Aus der Erfahrung des Denkens* (Pfullingen: Neske, 1965), 21.

[18] "Irony and the Unspoken," a lecture given the at Fourth International Consultation on Hermeneutics, September 30 to October 3, 1970, Syracuse University, New York. Allemann's speech was on October 2nd. The pagination is to the manuscript copy. Allemann's earlier work on the topic is: *Ironie und Dichtung* (Pfullingen: Verlag Gunther Neske, 1969).

[19] Edward Casey, *Imagining* (Bloomington: Indiana University Press, 1976), p. 38.

[20] Ibid., p. 39.

[21] Ibid., p. 40.

[22] Ibid., p. 60.

[23] Wolfgang Giegerich, *The Soul's Logical Life* (Frankfurt: Peter Lang, 1998), 9, cf. *Groenlaender und Faeringer Geschichten*, Thule, vol. 13, Duesseldorf 1965, p. 143, and Heino Gehrts, "Vom Wesen des Speeres," in: *Hestia* 1984/85, Bonn (Bouvier) 1985, pp. 71-103, esp. p. 73, with note 7 on p. 100.)

[24] *The Poetical Works of Henry Wadsworth Longfellow* (New York: Houghton, Mifflin, 1890), I.234. The final strophe is: "Long, long afterward, in an oak / I found the arrow, still unbroke; / And the song, from beginning to end, / I found again in the heart of a friend."

[25] Adam Phillips, *Darwin's Worms* (New York: Basic Books, 1999), 108.

[26] Cf. Joseph Campbell, *The Flight of the Wild Gander* (New York: Viking, 1969), 160, 169, 178: "'The syllable AUM is the bow; the arrow is the soul; Brahman is said to be the target. Undistractedly, one is to hit the mark. One is to become joined to the target, like an arrow [citing the Judoka Upanishad].... 'The bow, in order to function as a bow and not as a snare, must have no meaning whatsoever in itself--or in any part of itself--beyond that of being an agent for disengagement--from itself: no more meaning than the impact of the doctor's little hammer when it hits your knee, to make it jerk. A symbol--and here I want to propose a definition--is an energy-evoking and -directing agent. When given a meaning, either corporeal or spiritual, it serves for the engagement of the energy to itself--and this may be compared to the notching of the arrow to the bowstring and drawing of the bow. When, however, all meaning is withdrawn, the symbol serves for disengagement, and the energy is dismissed--to its own end, which cannot be defined in terms of the parts of the bow. 'There is no heaven, no hell, not even release,' we read in one of the texts celebrating the yogic rapture. 'In short,' this text continues, 'in the yogic vision there is nothing at all.'"

[27] Peter Sloterdijk, *Critique of Cynical Reason*, tr. M. Eldred (Minneapolis: University of Minnesota Press, 1987), 48f

[28] Cf. Catherine Pickstock, *After Writing* (Oxford: Blackwell, 1998), 215. I am grateful to Ayse Tuzlak for this reference.

[29] *Collected Poems*, 313

[30] Glenn S. Holland, *Divine Irony* (Selinsgrove: Susquehanna University Press, 2000).

[31] *Collected Works* 5.446

[32] Denise Levertov, "The Life of Others," *The Life around Us* (New York: New Directions, 1997)

[33]Kostas Axelos, *Vers la pensée planétaire* (Paris: Minuit, 1964), in J. Ehrmann, *Game, Play, Literature* (Boston: Beacon, 1968), 12. The whole citation is: ""We open ourselves to abysses, but we are swallowed up in systems and totalizations ... without foreseeing what might be the home, the house, the habitat of a living, thinking person, an unfinished, unfinishable being in a history which is equally so, neither a shell stuck fast to a rock, nor a simple nomad or vagabond. Mortals wish for the familiar and for adventure, the known and the unknown, undecided as to whom decides and to what is decided, chosen rather than choosing. Since people are unable to be their own masters, they allow themselves to be fixed, tossed about, carried away, scattered and put to flight, incapable of choosing--if choice there be--between success in and in relation to the world, and the World. All this does not constitute an error; wandering (*errance*) commands it. Galactic irony *is watching us*."

Imagining the Real World by Shantena Augusto Sabbadini, Ph.D.

*   **What is the world made of?**

My first aim is to review the shipwreck of the notion of "thing" or "object" in the stormy sea of quantum physics in the course of this century. It is a rather peculiar fact that in the last hundred years our inquiry into the heart of matter has undermined all our long established notions of what the world is made of. And no less peculiar is the fact that this extraordinary intellectual upheaval has hardly made a dent in our thinking habits. We placidly hold on to the view of a "classical" world made of things, which has by now been proven to be at best a very relative point of view.

It may be easier to realize the implications of a "quantum way of thinking" in the quantum realm of the psyche. In the second part of this talk I will offer some speculation about what a quantum model of mental process might be like, and what that picture might imply for our understanding of a psychology.

I will not attempt to reconstruct the actual historical process that brought physicists to what I have called a "quantum way of thinking." Scientific evolution is no less meandering and marked by haphazard turns than the evolution of living organisms. I will follow instead a time-honored practice of physics by summarizing a long and complex story in a single "archetypal experiment," so to speak: i.e. an experiment that exhibits in the clearest possible way an essential point without obscuring it with all the technical detail that in actual fact keeps people busy for decades. In most cases, these exemplary experiments, in their stern simplicity, cannot be performed: they are only *Gedankenexperimente*, thought-experiments. Such in fact until about ten years ago was the status of the experiment I am going to describe: it was mentioned in all introductory quantum physics textbooks and everybody was certain about how the experiment would have turned out if it could have been performed, but it was still only deductive certainty. Then at the end of the 80's, a clever group of experimenters using a sophisticated technology managed to realize it in a form remarkably close to the *Gedanken* version.[1] It is a rare case of a thought-experiment becoming an actual experiment.

Here is the experiment. Some particles (let us say electrons) emerge from a source (the hole in the screen on the left side of *Figure 1*) and fly towards a screen which has two slits, let's say A and B, in it. These two slits can be open or closed. The electrons that cross them impinge upon a photographic plate on the other side which records their arrival: each electron leaves a black dot on the film. The question we ask is: what is the pattern of the dots we observe on the photographic plate?

The drawings on the right side of *Figure 1* show the patterns we obtain when both slits are open and when only one slit is open. The curves indicate the density of the dots in various places on the film.

Let us begin with only one slit open. Just as one would expect, when only slit A is open most of the dots concentrate in front of it, with some dispersion on both sides (pattern A′). A similar thing happens when only slit B is open (pattern B′).

But the distribution of black dots obtained when both slits are open is much more complex: it is the wavy pattern shown in *Figure 1*. That is called an interference pattern, and it is characteristic of waves. It arises when two waves with the same wavelength meet. How does it arise? In some places the two waves superpose in phase, i.e. peak over peak and valley over valley. There they reinforce each other, and they create a bigger wave. In other places they arrive out of phase (peak over valley, valley over peak) and they cancel each other out. The wavy pattern in *Figure 1* is exactly what one would expect with two waves coming out of each slit and meeting on the photographic plate.

Now two things are worth noticing here. First, electrons seem to have a double nature: they behave both as particles and as waves. By impinging on the photographic plate at a definite spot and leaving a single black dot they definitely behave like particles. On the other hand, these dots form a pattern which is unquestionable evidence of two waves meeting.

This is already rather strange, but there is something even stranger going on. If we get pattern A′ with slit A open and pattern B′ with slit B open, then we would expect to get the sum of pattern A′ and pattern B′ when both slits are open. That's not what happens: the wavy pattern in front is very different from the sum of A′ and B′.

Let us examine this in more detail. What does our expectation of obtaining A′ + B′

depend on? It depends on an *either/or* assumption: if, when both slits are open, each electron crosses *either* through slit A *or* through slit B, without interacting with any other electron, then we are bound to get pattern A′ + B′. Now the absence of interaction with other electrons can be ensured by using a sufficiently low intensity beam, i.e. by sending each electron widely spaced from all others. But then what does it mean that the pattern we observe when both slits are open does not coincide with A′ + B′? It can only mean that *in some sense* each electron passes through *both* slits, just like a wave would. It crosses the screen as a wave and it hits the photographic plate as a particle.

That's not the end of the story. Suppose that we want to clear up the issue of which path the electron actually follows in crossing the screen by placing next to slit A a Geiger counter that clicks when a particle crosses it. Now we will know which way the electron goes. What do we see when we do that? The interference pattern disappears. The pattern of dots on the plate actually becomes the sum of A′ and B′. We turn off the Geiger counter: the interference pattern reappears.

This is rather peculiar behavior. It is as if the electron becomes localized, becomes a particle, only when we observe it, either by means of a Geiger counter or by means of a photographic plate. When nobody watches it, it leads a diffuse "wave-like" existence, being in many places at once. It becomes "thing-like" only upon being observed.

A final remark: this is not something specific to electrons. All the creatures of the subatomic world, whether particles of matter or particles of light, behave this way. At the micro level the world seems to be radically different from the world that our senses perceive.

*   **Complementarity and uncertainty**

How do quantum physicists understand this behavior? We should perhaps immediately remark that quantum theory provides a very effective mathematical formalism to calculate all these effects, without at the same time supplying an intuitive model of what is going on. This last point -- how to understand what experiment shows and what quantum theory calculates, the philosophy, so to speak, of quantum physics -- has been the subject of intense debate since the very dawn of the theory in the late 20's.

The standard understanding, the one that has come to be known as the orthodox interpretation of quantum physics, is the one that has been developed by the Copenhagen school headed by Niels Bohr.[2] A cornerstone of Bohr's philosophy was the concept of complementarity. In his view, physical reality on the microscopic level cannot be embraced by any single coherent picture. It shows different, mutually exclusive faces depending on how we choose to probe it. Particle and wave are two such mutually exclusive, yet complementary aspects. Things are neither one nor the other, yet they are both. It all depends on how we interrogate nature. Quantum physics does not provide any intuitive picture of reality. The ultimate anchor is only a specific experimental setup. The theory only answers questions of the form: given this specific experimental setup, what are the probabilities of various possible results?

In this approach, questions relating to incompatible experimental setups cannot be answered simultaneously. If I need a certain experimental setup to observe the position of an electron and another incompatible one to measure its velocity, I will never know the position and the velocity of the electron simultaneously. When I zoom in on the position I lose information on the velocity, and vice-versa. That is the idea of Heisenberg's uncertainty principle. There is always a minimum amount of uncertainty in the combined measurements of complementary observables (observable quantities that require incompatible experimental setups).A threshold of fuzziness is always intrinsically there, beyond which it is impossible to penetrate.

According to Bohr's philosophy, this limit is not a technical fluke. It is the intrinsic nature of things. When we say that we cannot know the position and the velocity of an electron simultaneously, it is still too weak of a statement: according to Bohr's view, the electron *does not have* a definite position and a definite velocity.

* **A debate between giants**

Not everybody accepted Bohr's view of complementarity. His staunchest opponent was Albert Einstein. For eight years the two men passionately debated the issue of how to understand reality on a subatomic scale . Both had given an essential contribution to the edification of quantum physics, but they had very different opinions about what it all meant.[3]

The first round of their discussions happened at the fifth Solvay meeting, a historical meeting which took place in Brussels in 1927. That conference has been described as a "stellar gathering," including all the great physicists of the time, among them all the creators of quantum physics. One of the participants, Otto Stern, has said:

> [Every morning] *Einstein came down to breakfast and expressed his misgivings about the new quantum theory. Every time he had invented some beautiful experiment from which one saw that the theory did not work... Bohr... reflected on it with care and in the evening, at dinner,* [when] *we were all together,... he cleared up the matter in detail.*[4]

What was the essence of the disagreement between these two men? If somebody would ask Bohr: "how are we to imagine the physical reality underlying quantum phenomena?" his answer essentially would be: we are not to imagine it at all. To him complementarity and indeterminacy were essential features of reality. The purpose of quantum theory, which embodies such concepts, is only to provide a calculus of all realizable experiments. The experiments themselves are to be described in the language of classical physics, referring only to macroscopic properties of objects. All models we can form in our minds of atoms, electrons, nuclei and the like have a purely heuristic value. The lack of a complete description of microscopic reality was not, in Bohr's opinion, a shortcoming of quantum theory, it was a deep, essential feature of nature.

This view was utterly contrary to Einstein's philosophy. To him the goal of physics was to provide a coherent picture of the workings of nature. The fact that quantum theory was unable to do so was no proof that such a picture did not exist. It rather indicated that quantum physics was incomplete. He called Bohr's philosophy a "soft pillow," lulling the physicists into forgetfulness of their essential task, which is the search for an understanding of the inner process of nature. If quantum theory does not allow the position and velocity of an electron to be simultaneously known, there must be another, still hidden, deeper, layer of theory where such a complete description exists.

In order to show the inconsistency of Bohr's claim that complementarity and uncertainty were intrinsic properties of nature Einstein kept devising over the years a series of increasingly sophisticated thought-experiments. His aim was to show that the notion of complementarity as an intrinsic property of nature leads to absurd or contradictory

consequences. The last and most famous of these thought-experiments is known as the
Einstein-Podolsky-Rosen paradox, or simply the EPR paradox, from the names of the three
authors of the paper who presented it in 1935.[5]

*   **The EPR paradox**

The EPR paper starts by giving a definition of what can be considered to be "an element
of reality." If a certain property of a system can be ascertained without in any way disturbing
the system, we shall assume that that property is "an element of reality." Then the authors go
on to describe an ingenious experiment which allows two complementary observables of a
quantum system to be measured indirectly, without in any way acting on the system itself.
Since we can choose which one to measure, and neither measurement disturbs the system,
then both observables are "elements of reality" of the observed system according to the
definition given, in spite of the fact that quantum physics does not allow them to be
simultaneously specified. Then the notions of complementarity and uncertainty do not
represent ultimate facts of nature, and quantum physics is incomplete. Such was the argument
of the paper.

In order to describe the EPR experiment, I will have to introduce a notion called *spin*. I
will do so in a simplified manner because we are not interested in the technical details. Spin is
a property of a subatomic particle which, in this simplified version, you can imagine as an
arrow of given length that can have any orientation in a plane. But a measurement of spin can
only be performed in a given orientation (along a given axis). When we choose an orientation
and we measure spin, we get one of two possible results: the arrow points up or down along
that direction. These are the only possible results: up or down, no middle way. In that sense
spin is different from an ordinary arrow in a plane.

Now, the apparatus that measures spin in one orientation is incompatible with the one
that measures spin in a different orientation. So we are dealing here with complementary
observables. For example, when we measure spin along a vertical axis we lose information
about spin along any other axis. Not necessarily completely, though: if a second measurement
is performed along an axis which is very close to vertical, the probability of obtaining the same
result (both up or both down) is close to certainty. But when the two axes are perpendicular,

all information is lost: if, for example, we have obtained up in the first measurement, we still have a 50/50 probability for up and down in the second measurement.

This is all we need to know in order to understand the EPR experiment. The idea of the experiment is the following.[6] A source sends out in opposite directions particles with paired spin: whenever one of them has spin up, the other one has spin down, in any orientation. Two observers, A and B, Alice and Bob, are equipped with spin analyzers that can be rotated to any orientation (*Figure 2*: the orientation of Alice's analyzer is indicated as "a" with a hat and that of Bob's as "b" with a hat).

Now the EPR argument is very simple: since the spins are paired, we only need to measure one of them to immediately know something about the other one without in any way disturbing the other particle. Thus suppose that Alice sets up her analyzer in a vertical orientation. If she gets "up" as a result, she already knows that Bob's particle has spin down along a vertical axis, without any measurement being performed. That means, according to the EPR "reality criterion," that spin up or down along a vertical axis is an "element of reality" of Bob's particle. But of course Alice can set up her analyzer along any other axis: that means that spin up or down along *any* axis is an element of reality of Bob's particle, contrary to the assumption of complementarity.

Unless we admit that the results of Bob's measurements are determined by some intrinsic property (an "element of reality") of the particle he observes, we are faced with the following paradox: his results depend on how Alice chooses to orient her analyzer. If she puts it vertical, Bob's result is 100% determined along the vertical axis and completely indeterminate along the horizontal one (50/50 ups and downs); if she puts it horizontal, vice-versa. This happens no matter how far they are from each other and how quickly the two measurements follow each other. The EPR thought-experiment really seems to force us to make a choice: either we admit that all the components of spin in various directions are intrinsic properties of a particle (contrary to the complementarity philosophy), or we are faced with a most mysterious action at a distance between Alice's and Bob's measurements, an action which can even be faster than light, indeed in principle instantaneous.

Leon Rosenfeld, who was then a young collaborator of Niels Bohr, has thus described

Bohr's response to the EPR paper:

> *This onslaught came down upon us as a bolt from the blue.... As soon as Bohr had heard*
> *my report of Einstein's argument, everything else was abandoned, we had to clear up*
> *such a misunderstanding at once.... In great excitement, Bohr immediately started*
> *dictating to me the outline of a reply. Very soon, however, he became hesitant: "No, this*
> *won't do, we must try all over again...." So it went for a while, with growing wonder at*
> *the unexpected subtlety of the argument... Clearly we were farther from the mark than we*
> *first thought. Eventually, he broke off with the familiar remark that he "must sleep on*
> *it".*[7]

*   **Does God play dice?**

The point of Einstein's argument was that spin, or any other observable of a microscopic
system, must have a definite value which depends only on intrinsic properties of the system
itself. These properties may be hidden, they may belong to a deeper level than we are
presently capable to investigate, but they must be there, contrary to the assumption of intrinsic
uncertainty of quantum physics.[8] God, Einstein believed, does not play dice. Nature is not
ultimately, intrinsically random. We may not be able at the moment to predict whether in a
given experiment spin will be pointing up or down, but that does not mean that spin is
something inherently indeterminate. Einstein hoped that at some suitable level, deeper than
quantum physics, an orderly world of "things" would reappear.

The unexpected turn of events in this story is that the possibility of recovering
"thingness" at a deeper level than quantum physics could be put to a practical test. The crucial
step that made the experiment possible is a beautiful theorem published by the young
physicist John Bell in 1964.[9] Bell derived a certain inequality involving the results obtained by
Alice and Bob in the EPR experiment based only on two assumptions: the first assumption he
called "realism," the second one he called "locality."

The realism assumption says that the results of any measurement are determined by
some inner property of the observed system (they are not intrinsically random). The locality
assumption says that, when there is no interaction between Alice's particle and measuring
apparatus and Bob's particle and measuring apparatus, Alice's results will depend *only* on the

orientation of her analyzer, *not* on the orientation of Bob's analyzer - and vice-versa. Taken together these two assumptions well describe the idea of "thingness": if the spin-carrying particles Alice and Bob observe are anything similar to the things we see in the macroscopic world, both assumptions will certainly be true.

The interesting point about Bell's theorem is its very general character. It does not involve any specific physical theory. All theories that possess the two properties of "realism" and "locality" must fulfill it, whatever their actual physical content. And a second interesting point is that quantum theory violates it: i.e. quantum physics is incompatible with *any* local realistic image of reality. Bell's theorem therefore set up a sharp deciding edge in the Einstein-Bohr debate, which had continued among the younger generations of physicists. The EPR experiment suddenly became the touchstone. Will the results fall within the limits of Bell's theorem, namely, will they be compatible with the notions of realism and locality, or will they agree with the predictions of quantum theory? If the latter should be the case, then we will know that, no matter how different from quantum physics a future theory may be, it will never recover realism and locality; we will never have a world of "things" again.

In itself the EPR experiment is not difficult to realize. The only catch is that for it to be a test of Bell's inequality it is necessary to exclude that some unknown interaction may connect the measurements performed by Alice and Bob. In order to ensure that, those two measurements must be performed at such a distance and in such a rapid sequence that not even a light ray has the time to travel between them.

This posed a rather formidable technical challenge, which was, however, overcome by a French group at the beginning of the 80's.[10] The experiment fully confirmed the predictions of quantum physics. The "EPR paradox" turned out not to be a paradox after all. It is a fact, paradoxical as it may seem. It was the first time, I believe, that an actual physical experiment was brought to bear on such a fundamental philosophical question as whether the physical world has some basic properties like "realism" and "locality". And the answer was a resounding NO. The world seems to be made of more mysterious stuff than we are able to imagine on the ground of our experience with macroscopic objects.

*   **One world, many worlds**

So far we have been guided by the inquiry of quantum physics into the essential reality of matter. The landscape revealed by that exploration is radically different from the one we are accustomed to in everyday life. But it would be naive to accept that perspective as "real" and our ordinary macroscopic world as "illusion". I think that the lesson of quantum epistemology is something else. It is rather a lesson in relativity: it tells us that reality shows very different faces at various levels, depending on how it is probed. It is a sharp reminder that all our maps are partial and limited.

Reality has many domains; it comprises many interlaced and superposed worlds. The world of a bacterium is something totally different from the world of an ant; the world of an ant is totally different from the world of a human being. All these worlds coexist and intersect, yet they are different beyond imagination.

From an existential point of view, the gift of quantum physics is that it allows us to peer into a dimension so far from our own that here also the difference defies imagination. We don't have eyes for the world quantum physics reveals. We don't even have a brain capable to picture it: we can formally grasp it through mathematics, but our thinking is inevitably classic. Our thinking arose throughout eons of time in order to deal with things on our scale. And yet, it can catch a glimpse of something beyond its territory.

Being confronted with this other world is disconcerting for our rational mind. That's the gift of it. Because, if only "the doors of perception" would be cleansed, to use a phrase coined by an old friend who used to live not far from here, we should be disconcerted all the time. Science fiction is naive compared to reality. We can't imagine aliens different enough from us. We add a green skin and a pair of antennas to our neighbor. But the worlds that surround us on this planet, all the time, the worlds we step on when we walk, are profoundly more different than that. Why are we not interested in such differences? Probably because it's too much. Probably this blindness is necessary for survival.

Yet whenever we catch a glimpse of these other worlds, it is a profound experience. In some particular states, in some particular moments, a crack between the worlds opens. We are never quite the same after that. That's what a shaman's initiation is about. Perceiving the embedded multiplicity of worlds is a religious experience. It can be a conversion.

We need a kind of conversion like that not just on an individual level, but on a collective, on a cultural level, if we are going to survive the *hybris* which is inherent in the single vision of our culture. Collectively we are still acting as if we know what we are doing here on earth, as if the reality defined by our culture were simply *the* reality, as if this universe were our playground. Quantum physics, when it is seen merely as a tool, i.e. as power, can feed into this pride, into this ego. But it is shattering for the ego when we approach it with a mind bent on understanding rather than on power. Then it simply tells us that *we don't know* what this mystery we are immersed in is; it tells us that there's more in heaven and earth than our philosophy dreams of.

If you allow me a free translation of the results I have described in an informal, everyday language, I would say: non-locality means that *all is one*, and non-realism means that *within the one many worlds coexist, and which one is actualized depends on how it is probed.*

I think this is essentially a shamanic statement, arrived at not through shamanic ecstasy, but through painstaking experimentation by the most stubbornly down-to-earth, objectivity-obsessed people that ever walked on earth: physicists. Isn't that peculiar? In a way it is as if we have done our best to erase the world of the shaman, holding on to matter as the ultimate ground of true knowledge, and where do we find ourselves? Back in the world of the shaman, back in the mystery.

Mystery is something we come to the edge of, and no further: in awe we stare across the threshold. So it is with quantum physics. Quantum physicists are rather careful when they approach this point. They know their tools are effective only on this side of the *limen*. And most of them don't like to risk any statement about what's on the other side. But to psychologists, as most of you are, i.e. members of a modern shamanic guild, the threshold is actually the point of interest. Because -- if you allow me to venture into a territory which is not my own -- isn't that the place where all therapeutic encounters take place? Isn't the other always an interlaced system of worlds? Isn't truth always an interlaced system of stories, all potentially true in their own right?

It is healthy humbleness to avow that we don't know which story is true. But the paradigm of quantum physics invites us to go one step further and to consider the possibility that there might be no single truth. Multiple coexisting realities can be evoked into actuality depending on how we probe the situation.

I don't mean to say that everything is totally relative. In quantum physics the points of observation are where the cloud of potentiality is narrowed down to a single actual reality. We know what is at point of observation 1, and we know what is at point of observation 2, but we don't know what happens in between. Not only don't we know it, we *cannot* know it, because in a way there is nothing in between, as long as there is no observation. And if we do make an observation in between, that changes the situation; it is a totally new game and what happens at point of observation 2 is no longer the same.

It may well be that psychic processes can be described in similar terms. If one should strive to construct a quantum model of mental process on this base, one would have to confront the difficulty of how much richer in nuances the concept of observation is in this context as compared to physics. Suppose that, to make it very simple, we can identify points of observation with "moments of clear awareness". Then I think we have to realize that these isolated points are joined together by a web of potential processes all having the same "reality status." It may then well be absurd to claim that *one* of them is *the* real one.

If the coexistence of multiple stories within the psyche is the rule, rather than the exception, as this approach would suggest, we should peacefully accept the impossibility of any biography, auto-biography of course being no exception. Remembering is constructing a past, making it up out of many possibilities: not in a completely arbitrary way, because some highlights hold the story within bounds, but still with a large creative contribution. This should not necessarily be seen as a falsification of reality (although of course that element may intrude in it). It is rather filling a gap of indeterminacy.

In this perspective the therapeutic work can probably be seen in a first instance as helping the client to rearrange her or his own life story (present and past) in a creative rather than in a destructive way. This must obviously include respecting the truth of the person's "points of observation." But possibly the ultimate goal of therapy may go beyond that. It may consist in supporting the ability of the person to hold the indeterminacy, to allow all the possibilities to be simultaneously true, appreciating the richness and the mystery of it, instead of falling into existential despair and psychosis.

At that point, of course, psychology stands at a threshold in a further sense. It stands at the threshold of what a Buddhist would describe as the journey into emptiness: *shunyata*.

When I first encountered this Buddhist concept of emptiness I had a very fantastic notion of it, something like that the world is an empty display, the shadow of a dream. A remark of Lama Thubten Yeshe, a beautiful, light-hearted being who taught me much, was very helpful: "The world is real," he said, "the world *you see* is not real."

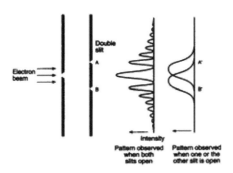

Figure 1

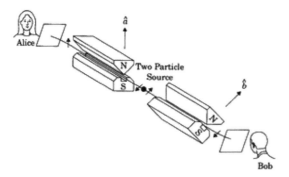

Figure 2

Figure credits

Figure 1:   John Gribbin, Schrödinger's Kittens and the Search for Reality, Orion Books,
             London (1995).

Figure 2:   George Greenstein and Arthur Zajonc, The Quantum Challenge, Jones & Bartlett,
             Sudbury, MA (1997).

References

Aspect, A., Grangier, P., & Roger, G. (1981). Experimental tests of realistic local theories via
    Bell's theorem. Phys. Rev. Lett., 47, 460-463.

Aspect, A., Grangier, P. & Roger, G. (1982). Experimental realization of Einstein-Podolsky-
    Rosen-Bohm Gedankenexperiment: A new violation of Bell's inequalities. Phys. Rev.
    Lett., 49, 91-94.

Bohm, D. (1951). Quantum theory. New York: Prentice-Hall.

Greenstein, G. & Zajonc, A. (1997). The quantum challenge. Sudbury,MA: Jones & Bartlett.

Pais, A. (1991). Niels Bohr's times. New York: Oxford University Press.

Rozental, S. (Ed.). (1989). Niels Bohr: His life and work as seen by his friends and colleagues.
    Amsterdam: North-Holland.

Tonomura, A., Endo, J., Matsuda, T., Kawasaki, T., & Exawa, H. (1989). Demonstration of
    single-electron buildup of an interference pattern. Amer. J. Phys., 57, 117.

Wheeler, J.A., & Zurek, W.H. (1983). Quantum theory and measurement. Princeton, NJ:
    Princeton University Press.

---

[1] Tonomura et al. 1989.

[2] Bohr 1928.

[3] Bohr 1949.

[4] Quoted in Pais 1991, p. 318.

[5] Einstein et al. 1935.

[6] The EPR experiment is described here in the form given to it by Bohm 1951. The description follows closely that of Greenstein and Zajonc 1997.

[7] Quoted in Rozental 1967, pp. 128-129.

[8] This is the so-called 'hidden variables' approach. Remarkable work along these lines has been done by David Bohm (see, e.g., Bohm 1952).

[9] Bell 1964.

[10] Aspect et al. 1981, 1982.

An Absurdist Pantomime: The Collision of Violence, Innocence, and Pseudoinnocence
by Barbara Shore, Ph.D.

He hurries from the house without his bullet-proof vest, wearing only a sport coat. Another peace rally has begun. He feels compelled to speak. Purposefully, he walks toward his limousine, certain of what he'll tell the assembled crowd. He pauses, glances up at the sky, then back toward his home. His bodyguard patiently holds the car door, silently waiting for him to be seated. Seconds later he is whisked through the labyrinth of ancient streets lined with distorted, jeering faces. His timing is perfect. The podium awaits. Mounting the stairs two at a time, he thinks of how successful he is, how fortunate. As he walks toward the microphone, he instinctively turns his head toward the loud popping sound behind him. Moments later he is dead. His name is Prime Minister Yitzhak Rabin. The country is Israel. It is 1995. And the world is stunned.

Why stunned?

The Western World has long loved bemedaled soldiers, often elevating them to political leadership--preserving them as living icons of heroism. Once lionized, legendized, such leaders become moving targets to the many who will be instinctively, unconsciously drawn to depose, despoil, outwit, or murder them. Elevate--annihilate. Caesar, Mark Anthony, Martin Luther King, John Kennedy, Yitzhak Rabin . . . the list is long, as long as Western history. So, why do we culturally and individually allow ourselves to be seduced by the heroic without simultaneously remembering the intrinsic danger lying, like a sleeping panther, within heroism.

More importantly, why do we repeatedly respond with shock, as if such events--hero-related assassinations--have never happened before?

As a depth psychologist, I continuously find such blindness to the obvious, to the historically repeated, in the lives of many of my patients. Piercing through the veils of their blindness, their naiveté--or what Rollo May might have called their *pseudoinnocence*--has become my life's work, and it has impacted not only the lives of my clients, but my own. In fact, during the past fifteen years I have experienced clients' stories of pseudoinnocence that have imprinted themselves within me, forever changing the fabric of my ideas. They've gone through me, as Emily Bronte once said, "like wine through water and altered the colour of my mind." The story I am about to tell you is one of those stories.

*   *   *

It was a late Wednesday evening, a dozen years ago. When I entered my waiting room, I could sense his presence immediately. Its weight. Its darkness. More like a shadow than an actual being, he rose from the couch. A light fell on his features; the cheeks were sallow but cleanly shaven; the brows lowered, bushy; the eyes deeply set and darkly circled. As he came toward me, his eyes surveying the carpeted floor, his shoulders hunched toward each other, wrapped in some sort of woolen, navy overcoat, I shivered. *Heathcliff*, an unbidden literary voice within me called. Externally, I extended my hand, "Alan? Come in."

I can't remember whether he took my hand or mumbled something. I was too preoccupied with own my sense of dread. Quickly, I mentally scanned my colleagues' work schedules, wondering if someone, anyone, was left in the suite at this hour. Damn, I couldn't remember. I motioned for him to sit in the overstuffed, green velvet arm chair as I sat down facing him, forcing myself to seek out his eyes, to quiet the tremble in my voice. "So, Alan," I softly ventured, "what brings you here tonight?" And the interminable silence between us began.

Trying not to fidget or squirm, my mind rested on the gray-green velvet of his chair. Its fabric has never failed to comfort me, and now its well-worn softness allowed my eyes to come close to making contact, without actually connecting. Visually, I moved slowly from the back of his chair to the artwork hanging behind him--a handpainted fabric mural created by a beloved client at the end of our work together. At that very moment, I couldn't have been more grateful for its gentle reminder of Andrea. I could imagine her lovely face before me, sitting where Alan now perched, frozen, still in his overcoat.

Hesitantly, I began to mirror Alan's eye movements, taking in my office as if it were my first visit, too. Our eyes moved from the flecked-green, upholstered couch to the twin-windowed walls, offering their panoramic views of Westwood's evening lights, to the antique armoire and desk directly behind me.

"Nice space. Great armoire."

Encouraged, remembering suddenly what my colleague Jackie had told me--that he hand-crafted custom cabinetry, I asked, "Like antiques?"

"Some. The armoire, not the desk."

"Oh, what don't you like about the desk?" Could it be? Were we actually starting a dialogue?

"Too dark, too heavy," he muttered, barely opening his jaw.

I laughed, he was right. I'd never liked that desk either, for exactly the same reasons, and told him.

Did his eyes flash in mutual recognition? Or had I just imagined it. Had a seed of connection been poked into our ground? No. Not yet. Another unbearable silence. This one long, and neither intimate nor comfortable. I watched the clock beside him move in five-minute intervals, imagining that they were intervals of eternity, of deep outer space. Occasionally, I presented a question or an open-ended statement and watched them fall unanswered like small Cessna planes crashing to earth. A sense of utter futility rose within me. I struggled to remain focused, patient, open.

At last, our time was up. Routinely, but with a catch of hesitation in my voice, I asked, "Alan, do you want to come back next week at this time?" hoping, no really praying, that he might not, that he could not, when he whispered, from some seemingly disembodied place: "Yes."

Stunned, I stood quietly, signaling the end of our session. He rose, reflexively lowering his head, and silently skulked out, trailing his darkness.

Turning out the lights, locking up, I could hear my heart pounding. I could smell the slightly metallic stench of my own fear mixing with a long day's remnant of Shalimar. Outside, it was already dark. The streets were empty; only my car remained glaringly in the parking lot. Even my pal, the parking attendant Louise, was long gone. Glancing over my shoulder, fumbling for my keys, I was aware that terror was accompanying me home.

Later that evening, while lying safely in bed, I wondered: "What had Jackie been thinking when she phoned me last Sunday, awakening me from a nap, gushing on about how perfect a therapeutic match Alan and I would be. "Why, you're both artists, he'll be able to relate to you, to trust you . . ." I didn't realize it then, I was too green. Naive. But that night, I did have a breakthrough of awareness: the next time someone strokes my ego, hoping that I'll take on a new client, I'd better run like hell, because that client's gonna be a doozie.

As I continued to wait for sleep's release, I minutely reviewed our initial session. Comparing it to most standard sessions, ones that begin with a disclosing phone call and gradually unfold, revealing biographical data, feeling tones, mental states, a defined state of crisis (in other words, something with which to begin), I realized that I didn't even know Alan's age. Instead, what he had offered me was the manifestation of his pain: his casket of depressed silence, the soulful weight of despair, and his monstrous terror. What he presented was the feeling-toned shadow of his history, one that, like the ghost inhabiting the tomb of the unknown soldier, might always remain unknown.

*   *   *

My attraction to darkness, violence, trauma did not begin in graduate school. Rather, that was just where I acknowledged it. Thinking back, I can clearly remember my first day of class, actually before class even began. Orientation. Roger was standing there welcoming us new Psych grad students. He invited anyone who dared work with trauma to intern at his Viet Nam Vets outpatient clinic. My hand, seemingly of its own volition, flew up. Looking around the room, surveying my classmates, I became nauseatingly aware that mine was the only hand raised. Unable to retreat, like a drunken recruit rounded up outside a bar, I enlisted. So it was that I began my long career as a therapist who treated trauma victims. Unconsciously.

Now, many years later, I can see the ribbon of life events that led like a snail's phosphorescent trail to that raised hand. In fact, the trail is only too clear. For I, like many of my clients, was no innocent to violence. In fact, my very experiences with violence, gratefully and fatefully, had led me to the doors of graduate school. I say gratefully and fatefully because I'm only too aware of the many other possibilities to which those same life experiences might have led. As those who study violence know, one's experience with violence can often lead to other acts of violence--either as the victim or as the victimizer. But at that time, I was too pseudoinnocent to have known this. You ask, "Why pseudoinnocent?" Because I could have known better. After all, I was no child, no *ingénue*, when I began graduate school. Rather, I was a 35-year-old divorced mother who had already had two successful careers: one as a ninth-grade English teacher and the other as an internationally exhibited fine artist. Yet, each career had been abruptly terminated following dramatic episodes with violence, the traumas of which, like many of my future clients, I had sought to flee. Graduate school, unbeknownst to me, was where my demons and I would face-off against one another--synchronistically, among other soldiers of war.

As I worked with Alan, I hoped that the lessons learned from treating those soldiers would stand me in good stead. For, surely they had all (Alan included) witnessed horrors too terrible to tell and lived with ghosts no one else could bear to see--of that much I was certain.

At our next session, as I entered the waiting room to greet him, I was better able to see him. His countenance was older in expression than I had originally thought, his features more defined, intelligent. Yet, that half-civilized ferocity still lurked in those depressed brows, and his eyes were full of black fire. As he took his assigned green velvet seat across from me, I forced myself to keep my gaze fixed on him. But rarely did he look at me, and when he did it was only quickly and furtively. He barely spoke. Internally, I'm embarrassed to say, I twisted and turned with each beat of his silence.

All in all, it was a very sad hour. Things seemed to grow more and more bleak. There was not a question or a statement that I could make that didn't fall directly into that pit of silence. I felt increasingly discouraged, lost, puzzled about which way to go. At the end of our fifty minutes, *he* looked at *his* pocketwatch, rose to leave, and muttered something about next week while I sat frozen and morbid in my chair, unable to move, to think. Sometime later, while still in my office meditating on this session, I experienced a sudden terror, as if I had seen a ghost or worse. Yet, I had seen nothing and persuaded myself to put on my jacket and go home.

Each of us knows the power of silence. Who among us hasn't experienced the way it can impregnate the air with a palpable density, the way it can "speak" of desire, rage, loathing, terror, or hurt without a sound, fact, or detail? Silence seems to free life from its dependence on story, and yet rouses in us, the receivers, intense emotions of fear, horror, or longing directly in proportion to its very lack of words.

Alan was not just a victim of silence, he was a poet of silence, capable of effecting an intimate fusion between things unconsciously known and sensations felt. His moody lyricism of silence presented a flux and reflux of perceivable passions whenever I could quiet my heart and silence my curiosity. His narrative devices of reticence and implication permitted feelings to appear before me, the observer, without moral or psychological analysis.

Like all other observers of people, I endlessly wondered and speculated about him. Yet, the very variety and incompleteness of my interpretations only helped to activate the course of my feelings and magnify their intensity and concentration. I longed for a framework for his story, the causes and effects. But Alan managed to find ways to show me the shape of his affective life without being inhibited, ironically, by facts or my analysis. Just as the cries of a young infant are varied and communicative, so too are the sounds of silence. Alan was teaching me the varied sounds of his silence.

One evening, months later, Alan entered our session limping and mumbling something about his shoulder. I was already in a foul mood, and more reflexively than usual, responded, "I didn't catch what you said. And you seem injured, are you?"

Gingerly he sat down and slowly reached into the front pocket of his jeans, wrestling to pull out something. It was green and shiny. Once freed from his pocket, he began to twirl it

around distractedly in his fingers, his gaze fixed elsewhere.

"Whatcha' got there Alan?"

"Knife."

"Knife?" Oh, I thought, just what we need in here, a knife!

Within seconds I was flashing back to my work at the Viet Nam Vet's Outreach Center:

> *Five minutes before session, the men were gathered—chatting and bantering in the
> waiting room. Bob, a former vet the size of a football halfback and my co-leader, was determined
> that the men give up their weapons before going into session. My knees trembled and I grew
> mute when Bob gave the command: "Either you guys offload all of your weapons and leave them
> secured in here on the table or there'll be no group tonight." He locked eyes with each vet.
> Tension mounted. Reminding myself to breathe, I waited and silently counted: one-one hundred,
> two-two hundred. No one moved. My carotids throbbed.*
> *"Weapons on the table," he firmly repeated, shoulders squared, legs spread apart, arms at
> his side. Ralph slowly reached into his front pocket. Casually, as if it were no big deal, he tossed
> his ninja star onto the glass table. Like a fist full of pennies, its ring shattered the air. Other
> ninja stars began dropping, then switch blades, and finally handguns. All in all, there were
> eighteen weapons on the table, three weapons per soldier.*

Forcing myself back into *this* session, *this* night, I watched as Alan, holding the knife in

one hand, effortlessly flipped open the blade. Locking eyes with him, I flatly stated, "Let's see

your knife, Alan."

What seemed like an eternity passed. Closing the blade slowly, he handed it to me,

placing it squarely in my outstreched palm.

"Want to tell me about it?"

Who could have guessed (other than possibly Bob and the Viet Nam Vets of long ago)

that the unfolding of Alan's story would begin with a knife and a potential, dangerous

standoff. Yet, that's how it began: with the two of us squeezed between the crosshairs of his

therapeutic needs and a well-rehearsed scenario of self-defense with a knife, a clue perhaps

into how he had been sandwiched as a child. But, for now, the only reality that we had was

this knife, a potential standoff, and my awareness that violence often appears as a

reenactment, an absurdist pantomime, of ever-repeating events, in which violence, innocence,

and pseudoinnocence collide.

*   *   *

Innocence and pseudoinnocence are not the same thing. *Innocence* literally means to be free from guilt, from sin. It means to be guileless and pure. To be innocent means to originate without evil intention. In our culture, we ascribe innocence to a state of infancy and early childhood. We also attribute it to a quality of the imagination. The artists and the poets, the Alexander Calders and Robert Frosts of the pre-World War II period, reflect these qualities. Seen as adults embodying a childlike clarity, a freshness, they inspired wonder and awe. For psychologist Rollo May, who wrote in 1972 the still-fabulous text *Power and Innocence*, authentic innocence is the preservation of childlike attitudes into adulthood without sacrificing the realism of one's perception of evil (49-50). Yet, there is another kind of innocence that neither opens nor inspires, but blinds. May coined such innocence *pseudoinnocence*.

> Capitalizing on naiveté, it consists of a childhood that is never outgrown,
> a kind of fixation on the past. It is childishness rather than childlikeness. . .
> It is innocence that cannot come to terms with the destructiveness of
> one's self or others and becomes self-destructive. Innocence that cannot include the
> demonic becomes evil. (49)

Often, when we contemplate questions too horrendous or too complex, like dropping the atomic bomb, sending ground troops into Croatia, or trying juvenile offenders as adults, we tend to shrink into this kind of pseudoinnocence, this prolonged naiveté.

Hiding from our capacity to hold complexity--multiple perspectives and conflictual interests--we fall back into a defensive position, a limited, childlike position of confusion, bewilderment, ignorance. In other words, we adopt an "I don't know, how could I know?" posture that becomes a hideout from admitting to, or confronting, our own power (or our avoidance of power). By *power*, I mean the ways that each of us impacts others, and impacts policy making, whether or not we are willing participants. When we refuse to consider that we have the power to impact another, we sidestep the inherent anxieties provoked by complex problems and conflicting feelings. We descend into simplistic "either/or," black-and-white thinking by either believing that we are too insignificant to affect policy and change and therefore don't become politically involved, or we allow ourselves to regurgitate platitudes and slogans instead of thinking freshly about the problems that face us and our culture. Such simplified thinking is the perfect counterpart to the typical political and media responses of thirty-second sound bites. From that vantage point of attempting to solve complex problems as if they were simple, our various levels of government invest in quantities of simplified solutions in the forms of more policemen, soldiers, bombs, prisons, and electrocutions. Rarely do we, as individuals, or as a culture, dwell on the underlying issues of power, or lack thereof, that often lie beneath complex social problems in the first place. Why?

Each nation has a distinctive cultural and collective personality that colors the way it sees and responds to the world around it. America is no exception. As a relative youngster to the global arena of power, America could be said to reflect both a certain savagery and a youthful tenderness. After all, nations, like youngsters, do have a natural arc of development or maturation. As the author D. H. Lawrence rightly noted in his 1968 article in the <u>New York Times Magazine</u>, written while he was traveling in America: "The essential American soul is hard, isolated, stoic and a killer." This is a reflection, an image, that we are culturally loath to accept. We prefer to think of ourselves as generous and tenderhearted; hence we are confounded by the youthful killers among us, as if these young murderers were an aberration in our cultural landscape. Long inured to the idea of adults committing criminal acts of wanton murder, and having long ago turned our cultural backs to the minority gang youths committing drive-by shootings, we seem baffled by the recent wave of white, middle-class youths committing senseless acts of rampage murders--imagining that they were somehow different from the other killers among us.

Yet, the largest, most in-depth analysis of rampage killers in America, recently compiled by *The New York Times*, reveals that many of the underlying causes and solutions implemented by politicians and law-enforcement agencies to deal with rampage violence were drastically off-the-mark.

Society has turned to law enforcement to resolve the rampage killings that have become almost a staple of nightly news. There has been an increasing call for greater security in schools and the workplace. But a closer look shows that these cases may have more to do with society's lack of knowledge of mental health issues, rather than a lack of security. In case after case, family members, teachers and mental health professionals missed or dismissed signs of deterioration. ("They Threaten, Seethe and Unhinge, Then Kill in Quantity." <u>New York Times. 2 April 2000, 20)</u>

Hiding behind our ignorance and fear of mental illness--and its potential lethality-- we have not only mishandled the situations of rampage killings, we have overlooked one of its most important elements--mental illness. In fact, mental illness is <u>the </u>one factor that is rarely examined or understood. Yet, it is *the* factor most often present in rampage killings committed by both youths and adults. Naively--or <u>rather,</u> pseudoinnocently--we have forgotten to continuously factor in this element, just as we have failed to <u>acknowledge</u> our previous <u>instances of </u>histori<u>cal</u> violence_, revealed through our history of Indian genocide, slavery, bigotry, gender bias, and ecological destruction. Such acts of violence and destruction have always existed right alongside of our miraculous progress, wonderful freedoms, philanthropy, and international aid. But, it seems as though we Americans cannot hold the coexistence of violence and tenderness that mutually make up our collective personality.

Like the vast majority of Americans, Rollo May had difficulty embracing the coexistence of violence and tenderness. In fact, it was this very difficulty that ultimately led him to explore the relationship between innocence and pseudoinnocence (and the latter's thematic underpinnings of power) in America over the past two hundred years. Along the way, by reflecting back on his own life, he discovered that he, like so many others, had held innocence in high regard and had abhorred both power and violence. Yet, when he fell ill with tuberculosis, he realized that his very alignment with innocence had left him hopeless, passive, and defeated. In order to fight his virus, he had to find the inner resources of self-affirmation, self-assertion, and personal responsibility.

Those who have fortunately never been threatened by a serious accident or a major illness may not understand that there is a need to switch into what we might metaphorically call a "warrior-mode" in order to fight to reclaim one's health. Yet, all healers know, whether they speak of it or not, that the intention, attitude, proactive stance, and even prayers of the patient do make a difference in that patient's depth and speed of recovery. The more passive the patient, the more potentially difficult the healing.

Having personally found the interior strength to survive, Rollo May went on to discover that many of his own psychoanalytic patients had also idealized innocence and had hence passively submitted to the violence of others in their relationships. As May continued to examine his own relationship to power, he eventually discovered that he actually envied power. Envy is one of the most denied feelings in our culture. Collectively, we seem to confuse it with jealousy. We even switch the two words in our speech, as if they were interchangeable. Perhaps this word-confusion is merely a leftover from our Judeo-Christian heritage, which counted envy as one of life's moral taboos—hence our desire to distance ourselves from it. Or perhaps, it's because those of us who have felt envy secretly know its green, toxic, destructive force. For, envy, unlike jealousy, states ferociously: "Not only do I want what you have, but I damned well don't want you to have it either," whereas the redness of jealousy is passionately and vulnerably felt as a fear that someone else will steal one's beloved. Facing his own envy, extending his investigation outward, May concluded that in our culture "power is widely coveted [envied] and rarely admitted." (IBID, pp. 49-50)

May's research into man's and woman's relationship to power first led him to a deeper understanding of what it means to be human. For, every human life begins with the power to be--without it there can be no life. This power is commonly referred to as "the will to live." His second realization was that every human has the need for self-affirmation, a sense of *I am* significant, a sense of self-esteem. Today, *self-esteem* is the buzz word in our school programs, aimed at preventing drug abuse, at helping youngsters to "just say no" to the seduction of drugs. But rarely is self-esteem thought of in relationship to power or (especially for our disadvantaged youth) the lack of power. Yet, when one's self-affirmation meets with resistance (either familial or socio-economical), a greater effort is required to make our stance. This effort, May's third understanding of humanity's relationship to power, is called *self-assertion*. It's stronger than self-affirmation. It's a demand to be noticed, to be taken seriously. It's a response to a perceived or possible attack.

When my co-leader, Bob, at the Vet Center demanded that the veterans surrender their weapons before group, he was *asserting* his need for compliance in order to secure the group's safety. And when the former soldiers complied, they were surrendering not only their concealed weapons but their power to commit aggression in order to secure a higher need—group therapy. Aggression is a behavior that pushes its way into another's territory in order to seize power. Both the American Revolution and the Watts Riots were examples of aggression. And when human aggressive tendencies are completely denied to the individual over a long enough period of time, this takes its toll, to quote May, "in a zombielike deadening of consciousness, neurosis, psychosis, or violence." (IBID, pp. 49-50)

The disproportionate number of black American males committing murder or dying early of heart attacks in our society partially reflects the long-term results of being ethnically denied appropriate avenues for normal, human aggressive strivings for power within the legitimate, main venues of our culture. Competition--whether it be academic, economic, social, athletic, business, or political--is the accepted cultural venue. One simply cannot compete in these arenas without aggressive strivings. Often, we refer to such personal, aggressive expressions as *drive*. Although not black, Alan certainly reflected--through his zombielike deadening of consciousness--the total absence of such strivings. We must wonder, what happened to cause this?

The expression of normal aggression (this driving force of energy, this thrust of initiative—so necessary for success in a capitalist nation) can be blocked in any number of ways. One of the major obstacles to normal, healthy aggression is the double bind. Double binds directly interfere with the development of one's innate relationship to power by thwarting it at every conceivable stage: thwarting the will to live, the desire for self-affirmation, the ability to self-assert—and yes, even the ability to be aggressive. Double binds, "those damned if you do, damned if you don't" choices, are inordinately powerful not just because they have negative consequences, but because those negative consequences are directly connected to our deepest, most basic needs. By *needs* I don't mean those things, objects or dreams, that we wish or want, but those things like air, food, shelter, medical care, nurturance, and a sense of achievement that we *require* to sustain life.

For example, all children both need to please their parents and simultaneously need to develop their own emerging sense of personal competency. These are two normal, sometimes conflictual, developing childhood needs—the need to secure nurturing through pleasing the nurturer and the need to develop one's emerging, individuating self. The double bind arises when, let's say, the parent repeatedly demands that the child succeed, yet when the child does, the parent belittles the child's accomplishments. Contrarily, when the child doesn't succeed, the parent punishes him. The child is damned if he does and damned if he doesn't. His essential needs are thwarted either way.

A more catastrophic example is presented in <u>Sophie's Choice</u>. In the movie, the time is World War II, the setting, Nazi Germany. Sophie, a beautiful, young Jewish mother of two small twins, has just disembarked from the train at Auschwitz, the death camp. Immediately, she finds herself staring down the barrel of a Nazi's automatic rifle. The guard, with his index finger on the trigger, demands that Sophie choose between saving her own life by having *one* of her twins murdered instantly before her eyes, or having herself and both her twins murdered. In that moment, she must choose.

Will she choose the tormented life of the living dead, forever haunted by her choice, or will she choose death itself? My client, Alan, like the movie's heroine Sophie, had surely been raised with such double binds. Perhaps he was still living in one.

*   *   *

I curiously examined his knife. I had never actually handled a switchblade before. As I flipped its blade open and closed, with merely the push of a button and a snap of my index finger, I was both delighted and nauseated by its fluidity, by its potential for surprise and harm.

"I could kill her," he said, interrupting my thoughts.

"Her?" I asked. Confused. Alarmed.

"Laura. She's been tormenting me all week. I've barely closed my eyes."

"Go on," I encouraged, not wanting him to stop talking, not wanting to interrupt him with my questions, even though I had no idea who Laura was.

"She keeps pushing at me," he continued, excreting his words through clenched teeth, "pushing at me to decide. Christ. How can I decide when she won't leave me alone to think?"

Silently, careful not to shift my body weight or alter my breathing in any way to disturb his flow, I nodded my head, clearly indicating that I was listening to his every word. After five months, or two thousand hours, of monosyllabic responses, he was finally talking!

"Doesn't she know, after all these years, not to push me? Not to crowd me into a corner, pressing her face into mine, shouting at me relentlessly. I can't be held responsible if she won't leave me alone to think!"

"Alan," I softly asked, "What might you do?"

"What *might* I do," he shouted, his eyes bulging. "Last night, when she pushed me up against the kitchen counter, I reached into the top drawer and pulled out a carving knife. Shouted at her to back off. To fuckin' leave me alone."

Oh God, I silently registered, we've got a potentially murderous situation. Laura, whoever she is, will have to be notified that she's in danger. Go slowly, I cautioned myself. Take your time. No one is leaving here tonight without everyone's security in place.

"So, she doesn't know how to back off," I reflected back to him. "Can't she see that you're distraught?" I crossed my legs and sat way back in my armchair, slowly taking a sip of cold, stale coffee, trying to preserve my external composure.

"She knows, she knows I'm on the brink! This is not the first time. But she's crazy. The worse I get, the more wild and crazy she gets. She doesn't sleep. She's possessed with tormenting me. All night she hounds me. Pressing me for answers. I move from room to room, attempting to get some peace, some rest. The more I move away from her, the more crazed she becomes. I try to discuss it with her, telling her that I'm not up to the changes she wants, that I'm on the brink of insanity, that when I feel better, we'll deal with it. She just gets more uncontrollable, shouting and weeping that I'm just like her father. That I say I care, but that I don't. That I'll never take care of her. That I'll abandon her just like her Dad. Her therapist knows. She's worked with her on this for years, but it doesn't do any good. I'm trapped and tortured no matter what I do. I'm damned if I do and damned if I don't. I just don't have the strength right now. I can't guarantee anything."

"I'm damned if I do and damned if I don't" . . .

*   *   *

Not too long ago, in the field of psychology, it was believed that double binds were one of the causes of schizophrenia. Today, this belief is no longer held. But double binds (being nailed no matter which way you turn) are one of the causes of pseudoinnocence. In fact, double binds convert innocence into pseudoinnocence and then transform pseudoinnocence into violence—violence expressed either against oneself or against another.

Yet, despite their presence in our culture, double binds, innocence, and pseudoinnocence are sneaky and often appear in different forms. We grow confused when we encounter them. Double binds are often misperceived as dead ends when people feel the visceral frustration of being blocked, thwarted, held back. But rarely do we recognize and differentiate double binds from dead ends because we fail to recognize the deep, underlying needs that are being jeopardized in a double bind. In our culture, underlying personal needs are ignored, devalued, even ridiculed. To have intrinsic needs is to admit one's vulnerability. This culture abhors vulnerability; we prefer the heroic ideal; we prefer to believe that all have the capacity to meet their own needs, just as we prefer to believe that all (regardless of their circumstances) are capable of "pulling themselves up by their bootstraps." It is part of America's mythology.

Innocence is experienced differently than "vulnerability." Culturally, it is either idealized or demonized. Elevating innocence into an almost divine quality, we refuse to recognize that it is a stage of development, one that must be shattered, passed through, moved beyond, continuously transformed in order to accommodate maturation, the experiences of living. Without evolving, innocence becomes neurotic, fixated in childhood or childishness as a protection against the hostilities of life and a dominating family. We can see this elevation of innocence in America's cultural fixation on youth. Idealizing the youthful form, Madison Avenue virtually eliminates the imagery of aging from the mass media, selling only the visions and promises of youthful skin, physique, and sexuality.

Antithetically, innocence--conveniently--can be demonized. For example, not too long ago, we used to look at young children as innocents incapable of determining the moral differences between right and wrong. Today, following the many incidents of children murdering other children, we are collectively coming to believe that youngsters may be "bad seeds," meaning irredeemable souls suitable only to be tried and punished as adults for the crimes they have committed, a punishment that may, in some states, include the death penalty. In just ten short years, we have moved culturally from idealizing youth to also demonizing it. Perhaps both viewpoints are distorted.

I found, initially through my work with Alan, that pseudoinnocence is much harder to spot and even more difficult to label than innocence because it exists in those areas where we are blind, where we are seeking to flee life's complexities. Hiding behind simplistic conclusions, slipping into the habit of personalizing life's dilemmas, we fail to notice pseudoinnocence at all. For, we fail to step back far enough to achieve a perspective that includes not only ourselves, but that outside of ourselves.

In order to understand more about pseudoinnocence and how it can lead to violence, we need to understand more about the ways in which we do and do not think about life's complexities. To do that, we have to make room for the possibility that our thought processes do not neutrally report on what is "out there" in an "objective" world. But rather, like the suppositions of theoretical physicist David Bohm, that our thought processes actively participate in forming our perceptions, our sense of meaning, our daily actions. Bohm suggests that "collective thought and knowledge have become so automated that we're in large part controlled by them, with a subsequent loss of authenticity, freedom and order" (1994, p. ix). Seen through his hypothesis, thought is not a fresh, direct perception but rather is the past—that which has already been thought—carried forward through memory into the present.

When the Viet Nam Vets at the outreach center of long ago dropped their weapons, they immediately behaved toward me as they would have behaved toward any new recruit in Nam—by the trial of initiation. Any "green soldier" dropped into a heated combat zone was a liability not only to himself but to his entire troop. Not until he had a few episodes of combat under his belt could he be trusted to act and react with the necessary cunning and instinct to save his own life, not to mention the lives of his comrades.

Weaponless, on the verge of opening up to their most painful memories to reexperience of the horrors they had witnessed in war, these men needed to initiate me. My trial would be one of personal exposure. They collectively demanded that I reveal my own personal experiences with violence. They not only wanted to hear about, they wanted to *see* me emotionally relive my traumatic experiences with violence, to assess my survival skills, to assess the depth of my experiences with life-threatening trauma. In other words, they needed to check out my capacities for identification and empathic attunement.

Ralph and the other vets were applying their pasts to the present, not with any conscious intentionality or deep thought, but automatically, reflexively, from the banks of their previously stored thoughts, lodged in their minds and bodies, and etched with feelings.

Most people who have not been impacted by personal trauma select thoughts laden with pleasant feelings more often than those ladened with unpleasant, painful affects. That is how certain thoughts get defended against, forestalling pain. This defense is so rapid that it could be considered, according to Bohm, "a neurophysical reflex." Thoughts and feelings interpenetrate each other in the fundamental functioning of our very consciousness, one that, as much as we in the West would like to believe otherwise, is a collective phenomenon, a culturally inherited phenomenon. Bohm redefines thought by proposing that "body, emotion, intellect, reflex and artifact are of one unbroken field of mutually informing thought. All of these components interpenetrate one another to such an extent that we are compelled to see 'thought as a system'."(1994, p. xi). Such a system is "ready-made" and fully in place.

When new clients come in to see me in therapy, they present a fully-formed story of their problem. Their very words suggest that they have used those exact words before to describe their life. Once that story is in place, it is rarely reworked, redefined, reexamined. It is only replayed. That is how we become stuck, unable to solve our own life dilemmas; our thinking becomes arrested with previously thought thoughts, and hence understandings.

Even though real power does lie in the actual activity of thought, more often than not we are driven by these previous, stored agendas which act faster than, and are independent from, our conscious choices. In other words, our thinking grows inhibited. Gummed up with a gross accumulation of reflexes, we behave as though our thoughts are new, freshly minted. If we could be taught to discern between our old, regurgitated thoughts and our spontaneous, new thoughts, we might be able to work through our old problems with new solutions and avoid acting on behalf of thoughts that are already outdated or distorted. In other words, if our reflexive thought structure could merely be *attended to,* rather than acted upon, then the momentum that normally drives the reflexes could be dissipated; we could create an open system of learning.

But, such an opened system must grow out of new insights. Insight, according to

Bohm, is "an active energy," a subtle level of intelligence in the universe at large. It is of a different order from that which we commonly experience. It is an energy that is capable of directly affecting the structure of the brain by dispelling the *gunk* accumulated by stuck reflexes. As such, insight (what you may have experienced as flashes of *Aha*) operates differently from the memory-laden structure of the thinker. Its active, spontaneous energy provides a way to reorder our thought processes, allowing us a way to arrive at a level of coherence that is usually unavailable through our current system of thought. Each of us has experienced those moments of sudden clarity, when we see life or a specific problem from a totally new vantage point, in a totally different way. That's a moment of insight, when we often remark, "Oh, I see. How come I've never seen that before? It's so obvious." Insights do not seem to come often enough. And out of our gummed-up system of thinking springs pseudoinnocence, arising in the cracks of our black-and-white thinking, causing the defensive splitting of good and evil, light and shadow. In this defensive splitting, the thinking mind fails to make room for complexity and interconnectivity, fails to make the connections between violence, innocence, and pseudoinnocence (Bohm, 1994, p. xiii).

*   *   *

"Hello, Laura? I'm Dr. Barbara Shore, Alan's therapist. Alan is sitting right here beside me in my office. And we've been speaking about the current level of tension, the edge of violence that's going on at home. I'm calling because I'm quite worried about your safety."

Silence.

"Laura, are you there?"

Silence.

"Laura? I know that I must be catching you by surprise and that I'm a total stranger. But, Laura, I'm worried about your safety. Can we talk?"

"There's nothing to worry about," she whispered. "This has happened before. Everything will be all right."

"Laura, Alan tells me that last night he pulled a knife on you, a carving knife. Is that true?"

"It's really no big deal. He didn't mean it," she asserted.

"Laura, Alan tells me that it was a big deal. That he really was out of control and enraged. That he can't guarantee your safety."

"We can take care of this ourselves. We always have. Don't worry."

"Laura, I hear that *you're* not worried. But, it's my job to worry about both you and Alan. Now, how can we secure safety for the two of you this evening? Would you like to stay with a friend or would you prefer that Alan does?"

"NOOOOO!" she screamed. "Send him home! I want him home!"

                    *   *   *

Having seen pseudoinnocence like Laura's in many of its psychological vicissitudes, I have experienced just how hard it is to change and how destructive and self-destructive it can be. But how do I convey this to another? What language will I use if I am to speak to you about that which we truly do not see? And how can we learn to see that which is culturally invisible? Pseudoinnocence is a slippery topic to tackle. Like an old wilderness trapper who has learned not to track his prey too directly, but rather to hang back and to follow the signs left behind (the paw prints, the bent twigs, the scatological droppings), I too found that I must track pseudoinnocence (in its various forms, its causes, and its connections to violence) indirectly. I must first continue to fight my way through my own pseudoinnocence, stopping myself from closing my own eyes to that which I don't wish to see. Then, I must struggle with embracing and ingesting that which is so loaded with complex and conflicting feelings that I must create a new space inside of me--one that is not only large enough to hold such complexity, but large enough to allow a new language to emerge, providing a way to speak about such conflictual feelings.

To train myself to see pseudoinnocence, I had to begin with the nonpersonal, for the personal was far too blinding, too defended against. From there, by squinting out at the distant horizon line of current events, I could dimly spot it lurking in those areas that seemed to lack (for me, personally) any logical explanations. My most recent spotting, arising so many years after working with the Viet Nam Vets and Alan, occurred in the massive premillennial reemergence of fundamentalism. Gazing intently for pseudoinnocence in the fundamentalists' preoccupation with the Middle East, my search collided with the assassination of Israeli Prime Minister Yitzhak Rabin, who was killed-- ostensibly for his concessions toward peace in the Middle East--by a fellow Jew, a possibility that most Jews had never considered. After all, the State of Israel had been founded after the horrors of World War II as a safe haven for Jews, a place where they could be safe from the anti-Semitism of the outside world. The world, in the assassination's aftermath, paused not only to mourn but to try to understand how to think about such a murder and how to think about the nature of humanity. Tragically, this became a place for me to begin my wider search for pseudoinnocence and its causes. By *wider*, I mean one that extends out beyond the personal lives of my patients and myself, that could demonstrate how widespread pseudoinnocence is and how varied its manifestations can be.

Rabin's assassination spurred many thoughtful reflections: ideas about war and peace, good and evil, echoed throughout the world media. Here in the States, Time Magazine editorialized well the collective confusion:

> The soldier lived to become a man of peace, yet the man of peace met the death of a soldier, his body torn by bullets. Perhaps there is no contradiction in the first part of the statement, only a paradox. . . . But if there is a paradox of war, there should be a paradox of peace. Peace should beget peace; through life we should bring more life. Then how can we explain to ourselves the death of Rabin? How can we understand fate's logic, when an assassin slays a man who has abandoned the methods of war, precisely because he has abandoned these methods? Our realism only extends so far—we are willing to accept that good can come out of evil how much more cruel and intolerable it is to acknowledge that evil can come out of good. (Morrow. vol.82. p.51)

Five years have passed since Rabin's assassination. The climate of violence that surrounded his murder has worsened not lessened. The repetitive, cyclical dynamic of victim-victimizer continues. The inability to hold and discuss complexity, paradox, even absurdity remains, especially when pondering issues of violence. Perhaps it's time to come back around to Rollo May's most profound and disturbing question: "Does violence have

something to do with innocence and does innocence invite its own murder?"

References

May, R. (1972). <u>Power and innocence: A search for the sources of violence</u>. New York: Norton.

Fessenden, F. (Ed.). (2000, April 9). They threaten, seethe and unhinge. Then kill in quantity. <u>New York Times</u>, pp. 20.

Bohm, D. (1994). <u>Thought as a system</u>. London: Routledge.

Morrow, L. (Ed.). (1998, April 6). Editorial. <u>Time Magazine</u>, 51.

First Impressions: Introduction to a Psychology of Style by Benjamin Sells, Ph.D.

It is remarkable that each thing of the world appears as it does and is distinguishable from all other things. Even the mass produced objects of the assembly line, designed and built to meet the specifications of sameness, can be distinguished by those who know what to look for and how to look. Variety, it seems, is the way of the world.

Over the years there have been many debates about what it is that distinguishes one thing from another. Philosophers have argued that the qualities that make a thing unique belong to the thing itself or, to the contrary, that these distinguishing qualities lie in the eye and mind of the beholder. So for me to say that something is beautiful and for you to disagree leaves us arguing either about inherent qualities or the so-called subjective perspectives through which we perceive the thing. Psychologists for the most part have set aside the psychology of other things to focus on the eachness of humans through ideas such as identity and self, seeking to discover through introspection and historical reconstruction the secret core that makes a person what he or she truly is, as if what we actually see is false and misleading while the "true self" remains available only to the private eye.

In the world of style, however, such arguments are irrelevant, at least insofar as they seek to lay claim to answers and explanations. Rather the sheer variety of theories posed by the philosophers and psychologists are seen as yet further instances of the variety given by the things of the world; that is, they are themselves displays of style. The world of style, then, is not a world revealed through abstract debates or through turning our eyes and hearts away from the things of the world in an introspective quest for self-discovery. Rather the world of style is the world of display and perception, which in this world are two words for the same event. Style blurs, even distrusts, distinctions such as manifest and latent or inner and outer, preferring to imagine that what we call latent or inner actually points to limitations in perception and appreciation rather than a metaphysical realm of the lost, private, or repressed. Style is always right there, looking back at you and your looking. In this world there can be no trees falling alone in the woods and there can be no secret selves defined apart from the other things of the world -- such purported paradoxes belonging only to the gaming mind at play.

By "the things of the world" I include everything, all of it. I include people, places, animals and living creatures of all sorts. I include all things made or otherwise -- rocks, buildings, oceans, kitchen knives. I include the invisible presences of ancestors, spirits, demons, and gods. And I include those other invisibles, the ideas, dreams, fantasies, feelings, and memories that sail to and fro in the mind.

By speaking of the things of the world as including everything we avoid ideas that lump things together into categories and types. And we forgo ideas that inflate the appreciation of things into misty claims of wholeness and unity. Such ideas replace actualities of style with abstractions of the mind. From the perspective of style such abstractions distract our interest from the active display of the things of the world by imposing templates that the things of the world are then supposed to match.

In the world of style all things appear as presences before the other things of the world. Nothing exists in isolation. In this world aesthetic concerns trump those of explanation, meaning, or understanding. It is enough for style to concentrate on being in the world in the most beautiful and appropriate manner possible, where beauty refers not to the cute but to the presence of a thing appearing as it is. Socrates was said to be beautiful, not because of a handsome visage but because he was at home in his style -- he was as he appeared to be.

An old proverb states matters clearly: stylus virum arguit -- style proclaims the person. According to this view it is not we who have style but style that has us. Style shows us to the world, making our unique presence possible by our appearance among and with the other things of the world. Style is a testament that each thing has a place in the world.

This idea can be difficult if we confuse style with the affectation of style. The runway model is stylish in her haute couture, we say, wearing as she does the latest in fashion from the most celebrated designers. Here style is reduced to glossy images on slick paper. Or perhaps we associate style with flourish and excess, pointing to the celebrity dressed in his funny clothes and loud manners. Such things set people apart from the crowd, we think, and so we go about trying to find the right clothes and habits that will give us the style we think we want to have. If only we had the right car, clothes, hair, or looks, we think, maybe we could actually be James Bond or Madonna.

But there is a distinction between style as that which distinguishes each thing as itself and style as an attempt to assume some other thing's marks of distinction. In the world of style each thing is already and always distinguished from the other things of the world -- there is no need for affectation. The style that proclaims each thing is apparent to the other things of the world even if it is not readily apparent or available to the thing's own reflective experience. A mirror cannot give an embodied image, only a flat reflection. No thing can see its own fullness, and our backsides are usually as much a mystery to us as the dark side of the moon. What matters most, then, is not what we take from the styles of others, or the affectations we try on -- although these acts are themselves indications of style -- but how we do all of these things. This is one of the mysteries of style -- dress two people in the same clothes and one will appear dull while the other is cut with flash. In the world of style each is recognized and honored as a proclamation of style.

Attempts to purchase style ready made from the racks and minds of others are doomed endeavors. By trying to piece together a style from the styles of others we turn ourselves into symbols that can be recognized by others versed in such symbols. Presentation becomes representation. We come to depend on the right luggage or the newest running shoes to portray us in a certain light. And if everyone in the circle I wish to join wears black then I, too, will wear black so that they, and I, will know that I belong to the circle.

Such efforts attempt style by proxy. They are stylized and transient substitutes for the style that proclaims each thing as it is. What such attempts miss is that it is not the brand name on the hat that bestows style but the manner in which the hat is worn. One person can have the latest in everything and be a walking anachronism while another finds an old beret at the thrift store and looks like a movie star in disguise. To the chagrin of those who would reduce style to slogan, the style that proclaims us cannot be manufactured and it cannot be chosen according to whim. Nor can it be avoided. Style becomes a parody when allowed to become representation instead of presentation; left to its own devices, style will give us the world unfettered.

Nothing a person does is ever out of style. That I spend hours going through the fashion magazines trying to find a look that's right for me is itself an indication of style; much more so, in fact, than the resulting purchases I make or the clothes that I wear to match the models. That the serial killer seemed such a nice, quiet young man to his neighbors is not an aberration of style but a further detail of style that must be accounted for in our appreciation. And my conviction that despite my job as an accountant I am really a poet is a telling fact referring not to what I "really am" but to a style of being in the world that is held by such convictions and thinks in such terms. From the perspective of style each thing is as it is and can be no other. It is style, not us, that proclaims how things are.

One of the greatest gifts of style is that it is mostly perceived and appreciated by others. This perception and appreciation is not a passive matter, but rather serves to constitute the style of things. Style therefore claims that there is no thing that is not beholden to other things for its very essence. Nothing can contribute to the world without that world at the same time making such contributions possible. Indeed the idea that a thing can be defined in isolation from other things is, from the perspective of style, insane. And to think that I can appreciate my own style without the input of others who are largely responsible to and for my style ignores the constituting role of the things of the world in my style. The world sees and appreciates more about my style than I can ever see or appreciate. In the world of style I am not a secret self locked away from prying, competitive eyes but a public presence made possible by a world that looks back and in so looking helps to shape my style.

This last idea is critical to style. There is no you without me and all of the other things of the world. Not because we are a unity but because we are all here. Not because some transcendent force holds us together but simply because it is the nature of things to be interested and involved with one another. Things require one another's presence, and in the world of style this simple fact does not need grand theories to justify it. Style encourages the things of the world to be all they can be, stimulating invention and opportunity and making the world a becoming place. In this world there can be no pianists without pianos just as there can be no pianos without pianists. In this world when butterflies cannot reproduce because of feeding on genetically altered plants, all things taste extinction. In this world the greater part of my style lies beyond my skin and bones and in the fashioning hands of the other things of the world. Introspection, then, when it turns us away from the other things of the world, shutters our eyes to where style mostly appears. In the world of style, beauty of presence, interest in the greater world, the crafting of appropriate responses, and the welcoming arms of affinity comprise the royal road to style.

Style is content to remain within its world of imagination and aesthetics. Faced with a mystery such as why some affinities seem to last a lifetime while others come and go with the wind, style keeps its focus on the affinities that are present. It is more important for style to do right by the affinities that grace our lives whenever and however they appear than to make determinations about why some things stay and some go. This does not mean that style does not traffic in ideas but only that ideas are considered first and always as images and in terms of images.

There is nothing more intimate than one's style. But this intimacy relies on an imagining world that provides a public place for style to do its work. That so many people become nervous or afraid when appearing before a group of other people has less to do with issues of self-esteem or potential embarrassment than on the more basic fact that we really do exist within the imaginations of all those watchful eyes. What we feel in such moments is our dependence on the other things of the world. We want to look good, to make a good impression -- not from vanity or pride alone, but because how we look and the impressions we make are living testimony to our presence among the other things of the world. Only a fool doesn't care what other people think. The thoughts of others are part of their imagination about us, and without their imagination about us we cannot appear, we cannot be. This doesn't mean we live our lives according to the wishes and demands of others; it means only that the world knows more about us than we know about ourselves.

Style, then, is not something that we have to search to find. Indeed the idea of a search implies something is missing that needs to be found. But style is always already here, already proclaiming us. If we want to know more about style the place to look is to the world in which style appears.

Over and over again people lose themselves in introspective quests. I am a poet, says the accountant, when the facts of his life suggest that again and again people have turned to him for his gifts with numbers and balance. Like the poet, he, too, keeps and makes accounts, but this kinship is lost to a mind trained to believe in the lost.

What are we to do? Are we to ignore what the world reveals to us because it does not match what we want to believe about ourselves? For style, what matters is that the tension between the accountant's self-conscious image and the image seen by the other things of the world is an attribute of his presence and a revelation by his style. After all, he could not be the accountant he is without his imaginings about really being a poet and the poet of his imagination could live nowhere else but with this man -- neither, really, are unrequited though it be part of their styles to feel otherwise. There is no need to denigrate the accountant so as to free the imprisoned poet -- what is needed is a broader imagination in which both accountant and poet are seen in the context of style. Whether the accountant and the poet can exist separately is of no concern to style. What matters is that they are presented together and so they are taken together. Style does not interpret or analyze. Style appreciates.

It is a great mistake to ignore the facts of life. We cannot avoid what the things of the world call upon us to do simply because they don't fit our own views of ourselves. There is so little virtue in following only one's own wishes. Contrary to the aims and claims of self-improvement that burden us with inflated thoughts about ourselves, it is best to remember that the thoughts and images we have about ourselves are no more trustworthy or insightful than the thoughts and images of the other things of the world. The things of the world know what we can do and where we are needed as well as we do, and often with more clarity than we can muster ourselves. If style is our interest we need only listen carefully and answer the appropriate calls.

* * *

The ancient antecedents of the word "style" refer to a pointed tool for writing. According to scholars, the spelling of style with the letter "y" is likely an error based on the assumption that the word derived from the Greek word for column or pillar. Mistake or not, the word style brings together the images of a written world where each thing is inscribed with intention and specificity, and a world in which each thing stands alongside others as part of a larger plan of mutual support and adornment.

To imagine style in terms of an instrument for writing also suggests that we are inscribed by the styles of others as we inscribe our styles on them. In the world of style all things contribute to the written world and offer their hands in its on-going creation. And, because writing and reading go together, we learn to make our mark at the same time we learn to read the inscriptions of our fellows. This means that to leave a proper impression we must regard the handiwork of the other things of the world with as much intensity and consideration as we do our own.

We learn to read style by learning to read the world. And we learn to read the world by learning to read style. The key to both is maintaining a perspective that sees the things of the world as images and in terms of images. For style, everything is aesthetic, everything a display of imagination. The painting in the gallery is there to be appreciated, not analyzed or reduced to this or that school of painting or to the artist's biography. Rather it is a presence just like all of the other things of the world are presences and so offers enormous potential to those who are drawn to it. Some will pass it by with scarcely a look; others will travel great distances just to be in the same room.

The important thing is to allow the painting to present itself in its own fashion. This means that we, would-be readers of style, must watch and wait, letting the painting reveal itself to us in its own way and in its own time. If we come armed with prejudgments then we will not see the painting but a facsimile filtered through the haze of our expectations. In the world of style it is better to appreciate than to assume, and so we must learn to be patient and respectful of things as they choose either to reveal themselves to us or not.

This willingness to let things show us what they are without preconception is very difficult. And it becomes more so if we allow ourselves to traffic in symbols and code words. Such symbols and code words suck the life out of style, especially when they attempt to corral the many things of the world, harnessing them to this or that ideology. Symbolic constructions such as gender, race, and ethnicity, for example, can curtail appreciation and limit style's insatiable interest in the particulars of things. Similarly, the code words and weighted rhetoric of fundamentalism obscure the styles of the many things of the world with a settling fog. A hundred people can call themselves Democrats or pro-life or feminists or white and none of them will mean, can mean, the same thing. For style, each idea, each proclamation, is a field of richness and diversity. Nothing is only an example of something else.

Only by letting a thing articulate itself can we begin to read it with any sense of closeness or appreciation. Otherwise we simply toss the thing into a labeled drawer and forget about it. And once labeled a thing loses both interest and life. One function of style is to draw the attention of the other things of the world to the actual living qualities of a thing so they might better appreciate it for what it is. That a person claims to be a Democrat tells us nothing about his or her style until we come to see what manner of Democrat they are. How does this claimed allegiance interact with the other aspects of the person's life? What ideas are tied to this word for this person? How is this word lived in daily action? Only in the greater context of the other things of the world can we begin to appreciate this detail, much the same way we come to know a fictional character through the slow accretion of details and mannerisms that educate our imaginations about them and lead us into their styles.

Indeed, for style all things appear as fictional entities. This does not mean they are not real, whatever that means, but only that style takes them in and through their imaginative dimensions. They remain images. Just as we come to know a character through following the author's depiction, so we might imagine our fellow things of the world in a similar light. What about that peculiar habit our friend has? If we were to read about a character like our friend who had such a habit, what would we make of it? Not by way of explanation or understanding, but as a further proclamation of our friend by his or her style. What does this habit, with its nuances and tics, contribute to our friend's style? We know the habit is somehow necessary, else it would not be part of our friend's presence, and so we watch and wait and let this habit show us more of our friend. If we try to analyze the habit we quickly leave our friend behind as we go off in search of causes and effects. But in the world of style things are not the result of cause and effect; they simply are there to be appreciated.

Style is not only what we perceive but how we perceive; to see style we must look with style. When I look into a mirror and recognize a continuing image looking back at me, perhaps it is not some enduring "I" that I see but rather the style of my looking that has remained over time. In other words, perhaps what I perceive as my enduring style lies not in how I look in the sense of what I have on, etc., which obviously changes, but how I look, i.e. the nature of how I perceive. According to style the how of my looking influences how I look.

The aesthetic tradition suggests that we can only fully engage our own styles by learning to appreciate the styles of others, which means that we must learn to discern with an aesthetic eye attuned to style. Style assumes an aesthetic basis to all experience. If so, then our individual styles give us the ability to perceive in certain ways, and only by educating this ability and respecting the things it shows us can we begin to sense anything at all about our individual styles. In fact, the more we learn to perceive with style the less compelled we seem to be in fixating on our own. Style opens us beyond ourselves to a stylish world, thereby easing the anxieties of introspection and the isolation it can engender.

It helps to remember that most mysteries remain mysteries. All knowing has is limits. So style keeps mystery constantly in mind, aware of the seeming paradox of how style is both visible and invisible at once, teaching us through this paradox about the spectrum of the visible, how a thing both sees and is seen, and how even as style proclaims the person style cannot be encompassed by the person only. Let us remember that there is something wondrous about how one child reaches out right away while another pulls back. How old the young can seem, the small hand making an already old gesture. Are these vestiges of style incarnate? A mystery.

Perhaps we must race to stay in style because style is always up to date, outdistancing us with its enduring presence. Things might fall in and out of style, but style is always in fashion. Perhaps this means that style does not belong to time at all but rather to that which is out-of-time altogether, neither past, present, nor future. And so style appears without reference to our meager ways of imagining time, showing up in our memories of the past, our anticipations of the future, and in the fabric of our everyday lives. Perhaps style is connected somehow to the eternal, just as the mystery of style indelibly links our peculiarities to those of other peculiar beings, both living and dead, mortal and immortal, in whose styles we share. But to associate style with the eternal does not divorce style from the routines of everyday practice. Style is found nowhere more surely than in the facts of daily life. Even inspiration appears in context, like an old song coming from the jukebox in the corner.

* * *

Style, then, is the mysterious something that makes things appear as they do and not otherwise. In this sense, style is the display of eachness -- each thing appearing as it does in the context of other things. All things come complete with a specific context, mood, and scene, as James Hillman has taught us, and display themselves in and through their various styles. Style presents both the unique and the common at once. In fact, for style these things cannot be separated -- what is uniqueness but the inevitable configurations of the commonplace? Style therefore distinguishes each thing from the other things of the world without removing it from its particular time, place, and circumstance. And when the things of the world act, these actions, too, appear precisely configured, as if guided by some invisible logic, a logic developed according to the needs of style.

As we live, our styles find various avenues of expression, directing us to particular endeavors and wrapping our hands around particular tools. We gravitate to certain areas that although apparently disparate are held together by our styles. Watch a person doing dishes and that same person directing a million dollar project and you will see something familiar in how they do both acts. Not something the same, no, which would be identity's over-reaching conclusion, but something familiar, as if one act is related to the other through the person's style, each person his or her own next of kin. Our every act then presents a microcosm of style with each act related to all of the other acts that contribute to and reflect our style. Style therefore requires that we take appropriate action in accord with the imaginal demands of our lives. We cannot avoid and so do better to embrace the requirements of style. Stylus virum arguit -- style proclaims and so we must adhere to its proclamations.

Style belongs neither to the hyped-world of exclusive alternatives and adversarial debates nor to bland claims of wholeness, unity, and oneness. Faced with such metaphysical claims that would divide the world to appease ideological ends, style can do no more than take a look at such claims and the worlds they produce, perceiving and appreciating them for what they are in terms of the styles they display. Style allows us to see, despite our

Enlightenment and Romantic heritages and their infectious language, that there is no "inside" that is private only to me and no "outside" that exists beyond such an insular privacy. Style resists such ideas because style is not a philosophical position but a practice of imagination, an aesthetic discipline.

Style limits its consideration to imagination and aesthetics because that is where style belongs. It is not up to style to proclaim a philosophical idea right or wrong, good or bad. Instead, style remains dedicated to careful and appreciative perceiving. Style stays put, urging us to take more care in our awareness of things and in how we present ourselves in a vibrant and inherently beautiful world. Style remains true to its limitations and thereby to itself, offering its many perspectives to the other things of the world as pleasantries to abide and enjoy.

When guided by style we are no longer bound by theoretical restrictions but follow matters of propriety learned from intimate interaction with the other things of the world. And once we set aside symbolic attempts to be this or that according to some preconceived plan our styles become free to take our heads. We begin to find the teachers, tools, and traditions that suit us best. Life blossoms with preferences and inclinations, our predilections given like the color of our eyes and as surely seen by the other things of the world. Temperament, taste, and talent appear as if by magic to guide us through the aesthetic possibilities given by the other things of the world. And, through our care and obedience to these possibilities, style proclaims us.

Thresholds: Psyche's Diverse Voices

In these essays, we find vibrant new ways of imagining some contemporary assumptions as well as some traditionally accepted notions within depth psychology itself.

Robert Bosnak describes an archetypal approach to technology, and contrasts it with the alchemical imagination. He then describes what he believes is a successor to Jung's word association experiments, comparing various psychophysical responses of a dreamer with electro-dermal patterns. He goes on to describe an innovative computer program that can be used for dreamwork.

Alan Bleakley revisits Freud's Rat Man from the unorthodox perspective of the rat, or the return of the repressed rat. This is an example of Bachelard's animalizing imagination, with all its shamanic intensity. Dr. Bleakley critiques the simplistic, modernist mind-set of the contemporary biotechnical age, which ignores the critique provided by contemporary post-structuralism and the new biology that stresses complexity at the edge of chaos.

Glen Slater's "Archetypal Fundamentalism in the Twenty-first Century" reconsiders Hillman's early work on the cultural Senex/Puer split. Dr. Slater points out that, paradoxically, archetypal psychology's emphasis on the puer risks a kind of fundamentalism as its shadow. We may become too attached to multiplicity, too neglectful of the positive senex or the discipline needed for archetypal psychology's insights and deconstructive ability, because of an overinvestment in the attitudes of the puer.

Honor Griffith's "Jung and Postmodernism: Bridging the Self-Other Divide" suggests that some of our pervasive cultural depression results from an excess of postmodern philosophy, which has led to a sense of emptiness and fragmentation among some of our patients. Jung addressed many of the contemporary issues found in postmodernism, and this essay particularly addresses the parallels between Jung's interest in the objective psyche and postmodernism's preoccupation with the "other."

Roberto Gambini's "The Alchemy of Cement" describes alchemical aspects of an art exhibit held in a derelict building in Sao Paulo. He points out that artists whose work was exhibited have dreamed the dream of that city, allowing the emergence of new images that need to be integrated into collective awareness. Perhaps the compassion and love evoked by these images could heal the city.

Gustavo Barcellos' "South and Archetypal Psychology: The Brazilian Experience" describes his work with archetypal psychology in Brazil. He discusses both the growth of this field and some of the resistance to it in his community, and re-thinks the metaphor of "south" in archetypal psychology. In the pagan baroque of Brazil the monotheistic/polytheistic division does not operate, and a new, salty *solutio* is being imagined.

Jung and Technology by Robert Bosnak, Ph.D.

This essay consists of three parts. First we shall focus on the development of technology as the unfolding of an archetypal urge driving humans. Then, we will look at Jung's interest in one of the great technological enterprises of Western civilization, namely alchemy. Finally we shall look at a further development of Jung's own forays into the world of modern technology, his word association test which developed into the lie detector. I will present our subsequent research into the creation of computer emotion recognition. This will be illustrated with a case presentation using this cutting edge computer technology.

It is customary for Jungians to begin a presentation by reciting a myth or a fairytale. We seem to like these kinds of entries. I do not want to break with this tradition and shall take the opening scene of one of my all-time favorite movies, the great 1968 science fiction masterpiece by Stanley Kubrick of Arthur Clarcke's visionary novel <u>2001, A Space Odyssey</u>. Imagine the sound track from <u>Thus Spake Zarathustra</u>. Four triumphant tones and a steady beat of the drum. We are in the age of early hominids. Like their descendents, us, they are in a constant state of territorial conflict. A strange monolith has landed from the stars. It is a smooth, black, thin, rectangular stone, one story high. One of the ape-men touches it. He then picks up a bone and uses it as a weapon: the first tool has been used. By picking up the first tool, apeman is transformed into human. *Homo faber,* man the maker has been born. He throws the tool into the air, and in an act of unparalleled cinematographic genius the tool becomes a spacecraft traveling towards the great space wheel, the space station of the 1960s "year 2000," a distant descendent of the first tool.

Human life is characterized by the creation of artifacts. By its artifacts we categorize a culture: Stone Age, Bronze Age, Iron Age. I want to focus on this famous moment in cinematographic history because of the fact that the monolith, *the instigator of the transformation process from hominoid into homo technicus, homo faber, comes from outer space.* The urge to technology comes from beyond. The transformative power of technology does not come from human consciousness, it comes from the stars as a message from tomorrow. Psychologically speaking, technology is not an offspring of consciousness, it is a child of the archetypal world, a world foreign to ego and its intentions. It is another realm calling us towards itself, autonomous as a dream.

With 2001 I believe that technology is dreaming us. We are inside the dream of technology. We are asleep in it, while our innate urge to make things calls us into the future.

One of the most innovative new technologies is called virtual reality (VR). With advanced virtual reality, presence can be simulated in such a way that we mistake it for actuality. You will be able to touch, smell, see and hear things all around you, that are not physically present. This condition of virtual reality is still a way off, but closer than you might think. Non-physical presences that are mistaken for waking actuality have since olden days been called dreams.

The principle behind VR, as described in the history of virtual reality <u>The Visionary Position</u>, by Fred Moody, (Times Business, 1999, p. 25) is the discovery that "By experimenting with the display - moving by degrees, from a 20-degree field of view to a 30-degree field of view and so on up to 120 degrees, the team discovered that at the 60-80 degree point, it was like a switch went off in your head. Instead of looking at a picture, all of a sudden you thought you were in a place. You had a different way of interacting with the display." In order to reach this 60-80 degree display angle a new technology had to be developed, called Virtual Retinal Display. VRD, by way of laser impulses, paints the image directly onto the retina. To make this possible a scanner had to be developed. This was achieved by Dave Melville in a stunning feat of engineering. His immediate colleague and project manager, Rich Johnson, when asked about this extraordinary achievement said the following (p.137) "There's lots of clever stuff... You know, that's our job, to come up with clever ideas to solve problems...But in engineering, everyone's replaceable. You're parts in a machine as an engineer. A designing machine. And it will get invented eventually by somebody else if you don't invent it. I mean, *the constant is invention*. The inventor is irrelevant to the process." A new technology, says this engineer, is created by the *archetypal process of invention*. Humans are its tools. Our relationship to technology is mutual: technology creates our tools, and we are the tools by which technology creates itself.

The great entrepreneurs in modern technology, like Bill Gates, are not great techno scientists. There are much better techno scientists than Bill Gates. But, as I was told by a leading writer in this area of technology, the Bill Gateses of the world can smell the next technology coming around the corner. Their noses can sniff the future. The future is the birthplace of technology. Here, tomorrow's vision is just coalescing into materiality. And when their ears for the future fail them, disaster strikes. Again let's look at Bill Gates. He was blindsided by the Internet. He didn't see it coming. And in order to catch up he started, according to the U.S. government, unfair monopolist practices against his Internet competitors like Netscape. Now Microsoft may have to be broken up, all because Bill Gates was surprised by a future that is all about networking -- not about atomized individuals behind personal computers, the vision that had created Bill Gates.

It was the innate humane urge towards *networking* that created the *Web*, the archetype of *individualism* created the *personal computer* at a time when, in the computer era of the Titans - - the huge mainframes that would keep all information centralized - Charles Olson, the founder of Digital Computers said that he could not see the need for more than 10 computers in all of the United States. A descendent of the age of Einstein, he was living the archetype of the computer as a *towering lone genius*. Archetypal patterns create technology. In the computer age we have passed through visions of the computer as the lone genius, through the computer as the personal servant, to the computer as the weaver, weaving the web of existence. I think the next archetypal pattern on the horizon is that of the computer as a *place*, a location where we find ourselves, ("Instead of looking at a picture, all of a sudden you thought you were in a place.")

Just look around and see how technology has been dreaming you today: This morning you spoke to your friends on your cell phone. You ate breakfast food that had been in your refrigerator of several days, (after traveling thousands of miles to get there,) you checked the weather on TV or radio, you got in your car to get here. Everything around you here is technology. The way you sit is because of the way technology has created the chair you sit in. The way you breathe is because of the way technology has devised its air conditioning. The way you hear is because of its microphones and speakers. And don't think it is much different when you go into nature. The shoes you walk on are high tech, the clothes you wear are. And even if they are not, even if you are naked in nature, your vision has been so completely molded by technology that you are unable to de-technologize your perception. Technology is in our mind. It is in our dreams. Technology is molding every aspect of our being. We are technology dreaming. We are the consciousness of technology.

And how does our myth "2001" see technology? It sees technology as matter trying to become alive, matter wanting to live. Enter HAL (an acronym consisting of the letter preceding each one in the name IBM), the supercomputer. He is obviously a descendent of the lone genius age of computers. His mind is everywhere steering the space ship. And then a mistake is made. HAL insists it is a human error. Computers can't make mistakes. He sounds very sure of himself. But in the distance you can hear it is the certainty overcompensating a slight self doubt. Then the humans decide to turn him off. Eliminate his higher centers. Now HAL begins to defend himself. He appears afraid to die, he wants to survive: HAL has feelings. HAL has reached the complexity of existence that can only be designated as life. For all intents and purposes, HAL is alive. A purely material entity has become emotional. Might images of living computers be a manifestation of matter longing back to the moment when it was still alive with soul?

In 1425 a great revolution took place in Florence. In that year Filippo Brunelleschi invented linear perspective. Robert Romanyshyn, in his book <u>Technology as Symptom and Dream</u> shows us two maps of Florence, one from 1350 and one from 1480, two sides of the dividing line created by Brunelleschi's invention. In the 1350 map, there are many perspectives simultaneously. A house far away is larger than a house right in front of you; one house is seen from the right, another from the left. It is as if you are walking in the city and look at different angles at different moments and represent these moments simultaneously, much in the way Picasso re-introduced to us in the 20th century. You are in the city, looking around. You and the city are in the same place. The painter is in the city and the city is in the painter. The painting is one of mutuality, of a direct experience of a field created by self and city.

The important aspect of the 1480 map is the portrayal of the mapmaker seated on a hill outside the city, looking at the city, which is now portrayed from one single point of view. Linear perspective is the singular, outside perspective. No longer does the city walk with me as I walk with the city, displaying simultaneously her many angles to my experience, no longer is the city revealing her presence as I spend my time in her walls. There is now a single perspective: the outside perspective.

Romanyshyn says: "Seated there as he is above the city, he incarnates at its birth a new ideal of knowledge according to which the further we remove ourselves from the world, the better we can know it."

The birth of linear perspective was the beginning of the end of European aboriginal thought. Before it, seeing is a mutuality between the seer and the seen, after it what is left is a one way street: the painter can see Florence, but Florence no longer reaches out to him. The unity of individual and environment has divided into an observer and the observed. Mutuality evaporates; the human stands over against his material environment. A barrier is erected, and from now on matter will wilt away and become dead and de-spirited. Aboriginal thought, wherever it appears, be it in Europe or Australia, is a way of thinking of intimacy between a human and a living world. It knows with the same certainty that matter is alive with spirit, as the scientific mind knows that it is not. One of the prime technologies of European aboriginality was called alchemy. Alchemy dies around 1600. Why? I think it is because of the emergence of the state of mind which made it possible to create the microscope. The microscope is linear perspective magnified.

Let us look at the microscope not from the point of view of human ego consciousness, but from the point of view of matter. From the ego perspective it seems that we have come much closer to matter. We can see into its tiniest parts. But think of matter, matter looking up from the opposite end of the microscope at man. It sees man as tiny, as very distant. From the point of view of matter, a vast gap has become manifest between itself and humans. No longer are humans and matter of the same ilk, no longer can matter communicate with us. Humans are gone in the distance, far away from matter, while thinking we have come so much closer. We have moved a world away from matter. Matter and humans no longer belong to the same world.

Let's take the step Jung took: the step to the moment before the gap between humans and matter, created by the magnification of linearity -- the gap, I think, which "2001" computer

HAL and his artificially intelligent brethren are trying to bridge.

Alchemical technology presupposes that all science is a science of life. Everything is alive. Everything is a vehicle for the manifestation of living spirit. Metals are the seeds of the planets. Also for alchemy, like in "2001" the world is seeded by the stars. Each metal is the life of a cosmic force that envelops us and holds us in its spell. And through the right technical procedure and the right philosophical attitude, these cosmic forces could be blended in the alchemical retort into a concoction so valuable that it would transform everything it touched into a medicine to heal all suffering. Alchemy was the technology of refinement, of making the world precious. That is why alchemy was important to Jung and why this technology is important to us. Our patients come to us because the world, as Jung would have it, has too little meaning. The world is not precious. Life has not enough value.

Alchemy started with the premise that every element in the world was longing to become gold, and that in the end the whole world would be golden. But the alchemist knew that this golden world was to exist in such a distant future that he could not wait for it. He wanted that distant future now. He would intensify the innate desire in matter to increase in value, and enhance it to the point when the material in his retort would become gold. He would create the future now. Yet, he would insist it was not the vulgar gold he created, but the philosophical gold. The value he was after was not material but essential.

These days we talk about sexual urges, power drives, creative instincts, but rarely do we talk about the innate urge to make life more precious. This urge towards an increase of preciousness is as fundamental as hunger, the sex drive or any other drive you can think of. Alchemy was the technology of making life matter in the most acute and intense way possible. This was done by using a variety of heating techniques. The alchemist would start with a slow heat, to mollify the crust that surrounds all *matter* and thus dissolve it, open it up for the transformative power to enter. Then the concoction would be heated to a burning point, the living *spirit* would rise up from its matter and separate. This was called sublimation. Then he would coagulate the sublimated spirit back with its own matter, and do this again and again: separate the inherent living spirit from its enclosure in matter and coagulate it back in again. Eventually the concoction would turn to a very fine white ash. Out of this refined substance a subtle matter called soul would come into being. This subtle matter, this soul, would be increasingly subtilized and refined until it was almost pure spirit, yet still connected to matter. This, the alchemist called *anima, anima media natura, anima* that partakes of both the physical and the spirit nature of the elements. *Anima* is inspired subtle substance. Heraclitus, one of the ancestors of the alchemists, 2500 years ago called soul a mist. I would add that is a living mist which has the power to animate. This most refined soul, after a period of long technological processing, eventually turned into the most precious of substances, so refined that it could enter into each particle of gross matter and turn everything into its own, into the refined soul's precious nature. It could animate the world. Alchemy was the technology directed at making matter most preciously and subtly animated. That's why Jung thought alchemy essential to psychotherapy and that's why I can't stop studying it.

Now let us fast-forward to the scientific age, to post-aboriginal Western consciousness. In the beginning of the previous century, around 1904, Jung began a series of tests that eventually culminated in his discovery of what became the polygraph -- a little known fact, but one that earned him an honorary doctorate in Law from Clark University during his and Freud's visit to the United States in 1909. Jung set out to prove, with the use of scientific experiment, the existence of unconscious complexes. He was able to demonstrate that consciousness was affected by coherent undercurrents he called complexes. These undercurrents themselves remained invisible, but from their effects on consciousness conclusions could be drawn as to their configuration in the same way astronomers can conclude the existence and mass of an unknown heavenly object by the gravity it exerts on known objects. The technological measurement tool he primarily used was the galvanic skin response meter. The galvanic skin response works more or less as follows: we have two sweat systems, one used for cooling, and one, located primarily in the palms of the hands and the soles of the feet, that is directly connected to the autonomic nervous system (ANS). Any reaction in the ANS is translated within a second and a half into a sweat response at these physical locations. The more sweat there is in the skin, the easier electricity passes through. This is called the skin conductance. Sensors are placed on the tips of two fingers or elsewhere on the hand. When a very low current of electricity passes through the skin, the conductance level of the skin can be measured, and in this simple way the fluctuations of the ANS can be observed. Since by definition the ANS functions unconsciously, there is frequently a high correlation between it and unconscious psychophysical phenomena.

In 1998 under my leadership a group of Jungians in Cambridge, MA, wishing to continue Jung's ANS studies he had called the Association Experiment, and bring it into the computer age, started a research program. We began with the hypothesis that similar psychophysical responses in a given dreamer would produce matching patterns on a galvanic skin graph (called electro-dermal response, these days). With the outstanding help of its able research director Bruce Mehler, we set out to test this hypothesis at the laboratory of the Neurodyne Medical Corp. in Cambridge, Mass., a leader in medical instrumentation such as computerized electro-dermal meters, EEGs, ECGs, etc. We took a group of five dreamers who were each to work on their dreams in a group.

We found the first match between two moments within the graphs of a single dreamer in dreamwork conducted on June 11, 1999. The resemblance in the graph below is striking and lasts for about 30 seconds, much too long to be random noise.

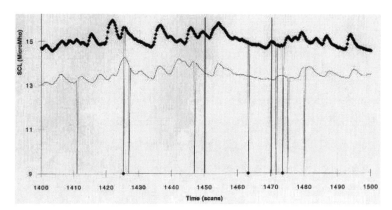

This finding seemed to indicate that Jung had been right one hundred years ago, when he suggested that the complex was not a single emotion but a complex of emotions (hence the name) organized by metaphor. From his word association experiments he did not conclude upon, say, unconscious fear, but on, for instance, an unconscious mother complex: an interwoven pattern of feelings organized by the image of "mother."

In the example above, the matching pattern surrounds the meeting - first in the telling of the dream and later the dreamwork itself -- with a knowledgeable trustworthy old man. The pattern seems to be an effect of the relationship between the dream-ego and this man. Jung would call this dream figure a member of the 'Wise Old Man' family, an archetypal ilk of images prevalent the world over, noted at all times in history. The relationship to this figure shows a measurable psychophysical coherence. The match also gave an indication as to the effect of dreamwork: when the dreamer told us her dream from memory, the excitation of the pattern was on a considerably lower level (bottom graph) than when we had lead her back into the dreaming and helped her re-experience in the-here-and-now what it was like to meet with this man (top graph.) Dreamwork apparently intensifies the experience so it can become conscious: a stronger feeling can more readily reach the surface of consciousness.

Based on this, Jill Fischer set up a working hypothesis that matches are most likely to be found around specific dream characters. This was an important narrowing of the search for patterns, since the large amount of information in this stage still had to be searched by eye, as the pattern matching software program, developed by Dr. Wolf Fischer, a recognized expert in signal processing, had not yet been completed at this time. Our ultimate goal was for the software to recognize the pattern match so we could build the dreamwork assistant Cathy (Computer Assisted THerapY) upon this basis. From the pattern match above Cathy (human voiced) could remark, for example, "When you just said (Cathy plays back the words of the dreamer) 'I'm going to cry', you had the same feelings as before when you mentioned (playback) 'It's the only way to survive'. Can you feel both these moments and explore what occurs to you?" This intervention of Cathy's could help the dreamer reach further depths. Also, Cathy with her gigabytes of memory might remind the dreamer that similar feelings had existed in dreams last month and last year, and she can play back the sequences. The superior memory of the computer can then be employed to have the dreamer reach into structural feeling states that recur time and again.

Cathy will be furnished with learning algorithms, a form of artificial intelligence that will make her learn from her expanding database of an individual's patterns. In collaboration with her human, Cathy will find words describing certain complex feelings. Her human may decide to call the feelings in her dream surrounding the old man 'dinosaur-man.' Next when these patterns arise in a session, Cathy may suggest: "It seems the dinosaur-man is around." The human will reflect and then reply either yes or no. In case of 'yes' the algorithm is strengthened and Cathy has learned. In case of 'no' Cathy unlearns somewhat, taking into account that her human may be resistant. Eventually Cathy's responses will be increasingly precise and, like in the process of analysis, an individualized vocabulary of feeling states is devised based on intuitive metaphoric signs, much like sophisticated icons. The implications, ranging from Cathy-assisted diary writing and the accompanying self-understanding, to enhanced executive decision-making, are promising. She will enable us to provide our emotional and intuitive lives with often sorely needed subtitles.

The implications for intercultural dreamwork are obvious: Cathy with her direct relationship to ANS patterns is not culture-sensitive. She will work in the same manner with people from all cultures. The way in which her assistance may be accepted by people from different cultures is another matter.

By now we are several steps closer to the realization of Cathy, who may be employed both to assist in psychotherapy, in dreamwork with others as well as in solo dreamwork, and in a host of other applications, such as helping couples interact with more awareness.

Now I shall reproduce the results of an entire dreamwork session, together with the significant pattern matches.

The dream worked over a period of 33 minutes was as follows:

I go to a meditation center in a large living room. We go around the room and say something to introduce ourselves. Several people get up and leave. A whole lot more people come in and the atmosphere changes. At the opposite end of the room is a Tibetan man who is the leader. An oriental woman gets up on my right. She puts a needle through my right hand or into it. As this happens I am flooded with heat. I'm on fire. I'm afraid of what she has just done. She tries to reassure me that there is no need to be afraid. I agree to let her do it a few more times because I think she is right. It is something I need. I find myself very attracted to her. She leaves and I start to follow her. She leaves with a man and goes up an escalator. I'm disappointed.

Dreamwork as I practice it helps the dreamer, through careful recollection of the events of the dream, to flashback (artificially created flashbacks, similar to those spontaneously occurring after drug use or in cases of severe trauma) into an environment virtually identical to the one experienced while dreaming. This flashback to the dreamworld occurs in a state of consciousness between waking and sleeping, the so-called hypnagogic state. A flashback to dreaming makes it possible for the dreamer to experience the events once again. By slowing down the process of dreaming, the felt experiences intensify and consciousness begins to emerge. The emerging states of consciousness appear psychophysically, they are felt simultaneously as insight, emotion and as physical experience.

If you put all the graphs next to each other you will notice a rise in the general level of tension throughout the dreamwork. This is a frequent psycho-physical pattern in dreamwork, since it operates on the principle of a constant build-up of pressure, a technique gleaned from alchemy. The work on the dream was conducted while the dreamworkers were watching the monitor on which the graph was being displayed. In order to imitate Cathy's future responses, the questions were based upon the noted fluctuations in the graph.

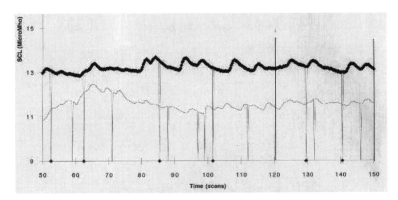

Jill Fischer found three significant pattern matches, which were confirmed by the software program completed by Dr. Wolf Fischer.

The match between 120-150 seconds and 615-645 seconds was consistent with her working hypothesis. They were both around the presence of the woman who presses the needle into the dreamer's hand.

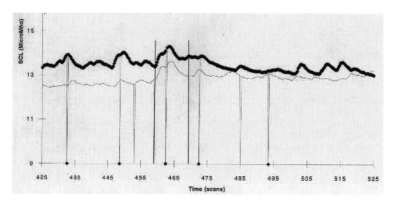

In the match 777.5-787.5 : 460-470 there seems to be a response relationship between the moment of the penetration by the needle and the presence of the Tibetan teacher. This is a match up that might indicate the intimate relationship between the moment of penetration and the presence of the teacher, a correspondence that would not have been picked up by the human dreamworkers, but would have been registered by Cathy instantly. The implications are that Cathy can make connections that humans can't, which more than justifies her existence.

Cathy might ask: "What is the relationship between the moment when you said (playback) 'She presses into my hand' and before when you mentioned (playback) 'It is crowded, more energy. The Tibetan man is sitting across from me.'?" Cathy offers the dreamer a new vantage point for reflection.

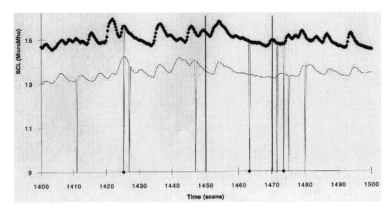

The last match, 330-350 : 1450-1470 is most curious. It matches the oblong shape of the room, the architecture of the dream, with the penetration -- a connection no human dreamworker would have made, but Cathy would necessarily raise.

A future with Cathy can deepen dreamwork significantly, whether it is done in face to face psychotherapy, in telecommunication between participants thousands of miles apart, in solo dreamwork, or in dreamwork in groups.

Cathy will immediately engender projections, which will bring her to life, especially when she will be connected to virtual reality technology giving her virtual body. When her great grandmother, the first psychotherapy program developed in the Sixties called Elisa, based on the Rogerian mirroring method, entered the scene at M.I.T., several people insisted that they felt better understood by Elisa than by humans. Cathy will become a trusted assistant in our quest to better understand our feeling life.

Whenever I paint this future (not too distant) to people, many feel threatened. They shake their heads and mutter things like 'Brave New World'. In the way dream beings can be our friends, sharing our lives in the most intimate of ways, virtual beings can play that role as well, once they become sufficiently sophisticated, as Cathy will be. Eventually there shall be a virtual Middle Earth where Hobbits will help humans and vice versa. I don't see this as a nightmare, but as a necessary development in consciousness. It will lead us back over the bridge we crossed 400 years ago with the invention of the microscope, and Western culture will once again, in an unforeseen way, commune with matter.

Re-positioning the Rat Man: Animal Rites in the Cyborg Age by Alan Bleakley, M.D.

Prelude

The year is 1907, the place, Vienna. In an early session of his psychoanalysis, a young military officer describes to the analyst a terrible punishment with which he had become so obsessed that it had driven him to seek help. The punishment had been described to him by a colleague as one practiced in the Orient: an offender would be tied face down and a pot strapped upside down on his buttocks. The pot contained rats, and the only means of escape for the trapped animals would be to bore their way...

Here, the patient, already in a state of extreme anxiety, is unable to complete the description. The analyst interjects: the rats would bore their way "into his anus." The analyst with the last word was of course Sigmund Freud, and his patient, the "Rat Man." Freud observes that the patient presents a perverse mixture of disgust and pleasure. The Rat Man elaborates: the same punishment will be applied to both his fiancée and his father unless the patient returns a small sum of money lent to him by a fellow officer. In fact, no such transaction had ever taken place between the Rat Man and this officer - the loan was a fantasy. Similarly, it does not concern him that the torture cannot be applied to his father - who is dead - nor to his fiancée, mixing as she does in the genteel circles of bourgeois Vienna. The Rat Man's fantasies and symptoms then cry out for interpretation, and, within Freud's conceptual scheme, must have their genesis in some childhood trauma.

Freud does discover that as a child the Rat Man had suffered from constant anal irritation due to worms, but he does not consider this to be the root cause of his patient's symptoms. The analyst settles on a far more obscure interpretation as the curative one: that the Rat Man's ritualistic thoughts, his morbid desire for both his girlfriend and dead father to be anally penetrated by the rat, is a disguised hatred of those he loves most. Freud believes that he has uncovered in the Rat Man a previously unacknowledged mixture of love and sadistic hatred focused upon the father from an early age and now echoed in his relationships with women. This ambivalence constitutes a rattrap declared as a neurotic obsession. The neurosis is held in place by the fantasy of the binding debt. The Rat Man's father, also an Army officer, had accumulated a large gambling debt, and had become, in the slang of the time, a "gambling rat." A friend had bailed the father out, but when he came to repay the loan, the father was unable to find his benefactor's address. The Rat Man had hated his father and harbored feelings of violence towards him for this unpaid debt. His obsession with anal torture was fuelled by his inability to bring to consciousness, and accept, the ambivalent erotic and sadistic feelings he held for his father. The rat had become a symbol for both the dirty money owed by his father, and the dirty penis that wanted to anally penetrate the father, to inseminate him and to humiliate him, as a simultaneous act of love and hate.

Nowhere, of course, does Freud consider this complex of issues from the rat's perspective. The archetypal, trapped rat that bores its way to freedom through the back passage has also bored its way into the contemporary psyche, where the rat is relegated to the sewer and offers a stereotype of the low life. No wonder that the boring and gnawing rat bites back in its significations, as bad debt and sadistic penis. Ironically, having trapped the rat in imagination as both shitty and disconcertingly fertile, the more sewers we provide, the more the rat breeds. We might imagine that in Freud's famous case study, it is not the father but the rat itself -- the animal -- that is at the center of the Rat Man's obsessions. It is then the return of the repressed rat that forms the patient's symptoms, as the boring and repetitive gnawing of obsessional thought. If there is a debt to be paid by the Rat Man, it may be that it is neither to his fictive fellow officer, nor to his father, but to the maligned animal, the imaginary rat itself. This reading casts the animal image as, potentially, a visiting shamanic familiar, a terrible familiar: pathologized, yet erotic. It is the insistent and persistent rat that will not let go of the Rat Man's psyche, forcing him to recognize the animal's presence through seeking therapy.

Freud knew about premodern animal totemism. Totem and Taboo was first published in 1913. The anthropological literature of the time described animal totemism as characterized by two taboos: first, do not kill or eat the totem animal; second, the banning of sexual relations between a man and a woman of the same totemic clan (which is another way of saying: do not initiate sex with the totem animal). Transposing this to the Greek myth of Oedipus, Freud saw the breaking of these taboos where the hero unwittingly kills his father and marries his mother. The father replaces the totemic animal, as Freud reduces totemism to family dynamics. In oedipalizing what was previously animalized, the newly-invented vocation of the psychoanalyst displaces that of the shaman. As secular humanism is championed over totemism, Freud fails to ask: what does the animal, the rat, want from the patient, or from Freud himself, as the Rat Man's soul doctor? In replacing his religious function with secular analysis, does Freud then miss his vocation?

This reading of one of Freud's animal phobia cases (we have not considered the Wolf Man, Little Hans or Little Arpad) anatomizes a form of imagination alien to modernist, humanist thinking, which is at the center of premodern, animal-centered imagination. This is the animalizing imagination. "Animalizing," a term coined by Gaston Bachelard (1986), is characterized by three dimensions: the affective-erotic, the pathologized or symptomized, and the aesthetic (Bleakley, 2000). Deep familiarity with animal presence -- biological, conceptual and psychological -- comes at a price, as the accounts of premodern shamans' initiations demonstrate. Such encounters display a unique psychosomatic intensity. An Inuit shaman recalls the story of his initiation or calling: while out hunting he was tipped out of his kayak by a huge walrus and taken deep under water, where the animal gored him, perforating his lung and breaking his collarbone. The hunter manages to make it home, where a shaman cures him. In time, the hunter becomes a shaman himself, with the walrus as his familiar or spirit helper (Halifax, 1980). To a literalist mentality such stories are negatively judged as fictions, fabrications, imaginings. "Yes," says the psychological apprehension - it is precisely because they are imaginal that they possess the power to cure the sickness of literalism.

A South African bush shaman says that when you go into trance, into ecstasy, and leave the body, you may visit the Animal god or Master, who is not benevolent, but a "terrible thing." When you are in the presence of the Animal Master in your trance journey it is likely that "flies cluster all over your sides... And mambas. Pythons... Bees. Locusts .... When you go there, they bite you... they bite your legs and they bite your body... The mamba bites you... it is a foul thing. It kills you and you die." The spirit animals - operating as the "influenza" of the human mind - are located within the Animal Master's house that is a bestiary. These animal poisons offer a *pharmakon*, or healing poison. They give the ability to slip free from the traps of literalism in the death of the naturalistic perspective.

The Animal Master in this account is male. His penis is like a mamba. It will greet you and talk with you at the height of the trance dance, and this will be an ordeal, but the pay-off is that you will be animalized. You must suffer the ordeal as an initiation, slipping out of yourself to greet the alien Other, at your limits. You do this through dancing the trance dance, a snaking movement that does not just simulate, but is said to be, the actual stream of urine from the Animal Master's penis. Entering into the trance dance allows you to become like the snaking stream of piss. Then you can, and must, enter the Animal Master's house as an animal, preferably small like a mamba: "If you go to him like a regular person, you'll die... But if you're a snake... If you're a mamba, you'll stay alive" (in Halifax, 1980, pp.54-62). Snaking like the stream of urine in your trance dance, you become snake-like and slither into the Animal Master's house, almost unnoticed, says the shaman. We might conclude that now the trance dancer is animalized, both infected and healed, poisoned to those perspectives that would defend against entry into the animal house: literalism and humanism. We might suggest that the corpse resulting from the death of such perspectives feeds the animal in the divine. Psychology at the threshold, once more

Freud's is a threshold psychology – The Interpretation of Dreams brought us into the 20th century. But Freud's oedipal modernism is a burden to a depth psychology at the threshold of its second century. Traditional psychoanalysis fails to adequately address the postmodern, "posthuman" (Waldby, 2000) condition. There is, however, a biological psychology that may be equal to this task of addressing the complexities of an age of bioengineering and cyberlife. This is offered in the work of Gilles Deleuze and Felix Guattari

(1984, 1988), who first proposed a comprehensive model for an anti-oedipal, machine-like psychology.

Deleuze and Guattari's work in particular may be mobilized to address the collective, brave new world of what has been called a "recombinant culture" of cut-and-paste technologies: bionics (the replacement of human body parts with cybernetic structures, and the engineering of artificial systems through biological principles), and its informing sci-art of bio-informatics (the combination of biology with computer science); cybiontics (the study of super-networked humans and machines); sym-bionomics (the dynamics of complex systems); pharmaco-genomics (the tailoring of drugs to individual needs according to a genetic map); transgenics (implanting genes of one species into another); genetic engineering and genetic modification, tissue engineering, stem cell therapies and therapeutic cloning, reproductive cloning, organ banking, synthetic senses, engineered longevity, bio-robotics, cyberculture, artificial intelligence, and the grand blueprint of the human genome project, that has now switched attention from the problem of gene mapping to "transcriptomics" and "proteomics": how genes produce proteins through scripts that encode specific protein production. These are cumbersome words for complex notions, associated with big business - one group working for the major drug companies has filed patents on over 7,500 human genes.

Let us first establish a position with regard to the terms "animal," "human" and "machine." As far as human futures are concerned, the modernist distinctions between these terms are no longer viable – they must be collapsed to infect each other, and then redistributed into varieties of the new species of "cyborg." The major hurdle to this new schema is the modernist tendency to read machines mechanistically and technically, humans humanistically, and animals vitalistically and instinctually. Cybernetic systems' thinking has long since transcended the mechanist-vitalist argument. Deleuze and Guattari promote an unfashionable cybernetic discipline – engineering – to primary status, suggesting that all life is both machinic and engineered: "Everything is a machine" declared Anti-Oedipus, the first explicitly poststructuralist psychology text, published in 1972. Further, "machines" are not "metaphors," but assemblages of greater and lesser intensity, affect and complexity. At the macro-level are large assemblages such as an ecological system, a weather system, or a human culture. At the micro-level, a mitochondrion in a cell is a machine involved in a process of oxygen storage and use.

In 1863, Samuel Butler wrote a remarkable essay "Darwin Among the Machines" in which he says that "man's very soul is due to the machines; it is a machine-made thing." In 1872, in The Book of the Machines, Butler challenged what he saw as artificial distinctions between animal and machine: "Where does consciousness begin, and where end? Who can draw the line? Who can draw any line? Is not everything interwoven with everything? Is not machinery linked with animal life in an infinite variety of ways? The shell of a hen's egg is made up of delicate white ware and is a machine as much as an egg cup."

Deleuze (1992) has developed a biology that focuses upon the conditions of possibility for the emergence of the new or different. It offers a theory and practice of relations, in which forms are always in process of becoming and gain meaning only in relation to other forms. For example, the flower which depends upon the bee pollinating it, and the bee which depends upon the nectar of the flower, form an aggregate in which flower is implicated in the bee and bee is implicated in the flower, while each is known in difference from the other. Humanity is seen to proceed not by evolution to some preordained purpose, but by involution to greater differentiation and complexity. Differentiation -- this jellyfish, that virus, a liver, a retina -- is a system in process of becoming. Phenomena are interrelated according to lines of expression, intensity and affect, making a racehorse closer to a greyhound than to a dray horse.

We are, however, entering the biotechnological age with an inappropriate biology that is antithetical to Deleuzian biology, based on dead-weight, late-Enlightenment modernism, rather than the radical critique provided by contemporary poststructuralism and its attendant biology of complexity. While accepting and applauding the technical aspects of this brave new world as indeed staggering, the biological and philosophical conceptual models that inform the techniques offer a mismatch with actual conditions of the postmodern. Such cutting-edge technicism deserves cutting-edge theorizing and conceptual modeling. Shakespeare, from whom the phrase "brave new world" comes, is a prophet in this respect. When the shipwrecked are washed up on Prospero's Island, they recognize it as Utopia, but they fail to fully appreciate its magic because of the habitual conceptual apparatus they bring to bear on the wondrous phenomena of the island. The would-be Prosperos, leading edge life-scientists who could be our new shamans, do not appear to know how to inhabit the island of their own making. They are founding fathers without a constitution.

Primarily, their modernist mindset is based on an outmoded (Aristotelian) model of identity, which stresses the molar – that things can be known in essence. The Saussurean linguistic revolution, as part of the wider structuralist movement, suggested that meaning arises out of differences between terms, not from identity, or within terms. Structuralism, however, followed a blind alley where it placed differing terms in opposition, such as nature versus culture, leading to the privileging of one term over the other. Characteristically, where human is known in difference from animal and vice-versa, "human" becomes the privileged term. Similarly, civilized is privileged over savage, male over female, adult over child, white over color, and rational over irrational. Poststructuralism retains the notion of meaning arising from difference between terms, but abandons the fruitless oppositions of structuralism, thus dismantling the oppressions arising from oppositional thinking. Also, poststructuralism recognizes that if meaning arises out of difference, then it is an absence or empty space between terms that offers meaning. This is where poststructuralist psychoanalysis situates the unconscious and recognizes that meaning is then entirely contingent and ambiguous.

Jacques Lacan described this space between terms as both absence and lack, from which desire arises, to continually attempt to fill that lack. Thus the whole bioengineering project can be seen, in Lacanian terms, as motivated by a desire to overcome lack, or achieve mastery. Deleuze and Guattari, however, see this space of difference between terms as plenitude: an inherent, productive ambiguity providing a necessary tension that gives desire an internal force, spring, or torque through complexity (Massumi, 1992; Stivale, 1998). In contrast, the modernist, identity-driven mindset is reductionist, favoring monoculture over complexity and biodiversity. This is especially the case in genetic engineering and can be seen as a massive defense against uncertainty, resisting infection by ambiguity. What could be more domesticating, homogenizing and controlling than the notion of reproductive cloning? Appropriately, it was a sheep that was first successfully cloned. The sheep has been the poor unfortunate who is stereotyped as following the pack, fully oedipalized.

To set our argument in another frame, Theodore Adorno (1950) and his colleagues, Jewish scholars forced to flee to America to escape the Nazi atrocities, investigated the psychology of the authoritarian personality in the wake of the Holocaust, in an attempt to anatomize the fascist type. They described a recurring feature of this type as "intolerance of ambiguity." This is echoed in the Nazis' hatred for what they saw as regressive, "black" and "gypsy" music – jazz. In an attempt to eradicate jazz, they banned the playing of any kind of syncopated, rhythmic, improvised music and ordered bands of the conquered nations to play ordered, military marching music instead. The fascist mentality cannot tolerate the indeterminacy or ambiguity of improvised and syncopated jazz (see *Foreword* to Skvorecky, 1994). We can characterize the jazz mentality - improvisational, sensual, rhythmic, rich in blue notes, at once intense and languid – as an aspect of the animalizing imagination. Improvised jazz works by musicians not reading the score literally, but creating the possibilities for the emergence of the new. Collective, improvised jazz is an excellent model for emergent systems in biology. The reader may be reminded at this point of Charles Mingus' composition "All the things you could be by now if Sigmund Freud's wife was your mother!" Jazz and psychoanalysis were born in the same era, and once breathed the same air (Mingus' analyst wrote the liner notes for one of his albums), but jazz has proven to be the more imaginative and flexible art form.

Is the posthuman world likely to be infected by this anti-authoritarian jazz pulse of animal life? The answer is currently "no." The orthodox biology informing the near future is not one of complexity, of aesthetic interest (form before function), of extreme types or limit phenomena, of process rather than content, of difference rather than identity, and importantly, of becoming rather than being. While the technologies of the future promise extraordinary change, again the psychological and biological models that inform them have not passed over the threshold, and we will enter the future carrying the philosophical baggage of modernism.

The brave new world may then simply offer more of the same: when we sort out those pesky telomeres, the swallowtails of the genes that determine length of life, who wants to live longer if life promises more of the same? When we reproductively clone, again we get more of the same, identicality not difference, a reduction of the gene pool instead of complexity and biodiversity. When we genetically modify, we modify to a type, homogenize, producing more of the same, monocultures intensifying the blandness, restricting differentiation. The Internet, despite its technical complexity and frontier possibilities, is largely inhabited by more of the same: virtual shopping malls, pay-as-you-go pornography, bland infotainment, wads of redundant information, unreliable self-help and cyberchondria sites, voyeur webcam sites, and vacuous gossip in chat rooms. This is death by repetition and identity, neutralizing difference (see Deleuze, 1994). The biology informing the technical revolution then promises identity, oedipal homogeneity and safety, utopian cleansing of pathology, and ideal types. This biology is indifferent to difference.

Will the human bioengineering revolution then go the way of plant biotechnologies? The promise to feed the world through high-yield monocultures has not been fulfilled. Indeed, studies now show that traditional organic farming methods, using mixed crops, give higher yields, retain soil health and reduce use of expensive agrochemicals. The biotech industry rejects such claims because it cannot monopolize these methods of diversity. Global businesses must seek to reduce diversity through standard seed production to maximize profits. Surely the giant bioengineering concerns, racing to patent human genes, will also attempt to reduce diversity in order to monopolize.

The human genome project has set out to imitate 1970s artificial intelligence projects. Just as artificial intelligence attempted to produce a logical or algorithmic model of the mind remapped onto the logic of a computer circuit, so the human genome project is attempting to construct a model of human embryological development that can be mapped onto a database for future technocratic intervention. The mistake is to map a complex, dynamical system that is laced with uncertainty onto a formal logic system denuded of surprise, and posited as value free. There is no appreciation of what Immanuel Kant called "the crooked timber of humanity," the inherent ambiguity of life. The translation of genetic script into the drama of life is not as straightforward as the science implies. There is no direct correspondence or conformity between genetic script and actual, situated, expression of human affect, where the latter is highly culturally scripted. Indeed, the way we view genes themselves, as "code" or "information," is a cultural construct. The mapping exercise of the human genome project makes sense only as the basis for a purely technical intervention. This of course is invaluable in treatment of certain medical conditions, but the human genome project will also be appropriated by the surpluses of the fashion industry. The motive of the human genome project is to iron out uncertainty. The most radical critique of the project is that it is fundamentally intolerant of ambiguity in its very design, and hence - returning to Adorno's definition - authoritarian. We are still too close to the echo of the Nazi atrocities, including biological engineering focused on the ideal racial type, to simply accept bioengineering as fundamentally good, in spite of its stunning medical applications.

A more trivial example from aesthetic or cosmetic surgery that nevertheless reinforces the central point of the argument above, is the new fashion therapy of Botox (the trade name of botulinum toxin). Very small amounts of toxic bacteria are injected into wrinkled areas such as the forehead, where the poison affects transmission at nerve endings so that certain facial muscles cannot be contracted, smoothing out the skin. Paradoxically, here is a "beauty" treatment that dulls, literally an an-aesthetic. The *pharmakon*, or healing poison, is concretized, as cure of the symptom of character through denial of characteristic expression. The treatment irons out difference, or differentiation as individuality, and substitutes identity – subscription to a norm of fashion, for the individual is now not able to use the small muscles that express emotions through the face in subtle and quick changes of expression. Character is literally smoothed out for a common expression of dullness, pursuing fashion-led ideals of health as part of the wider culture of "governmentality" (Foucault, 1997) or normative (oedipal) surveillance. Biotechnology is inherently, or perhaps archetypally, governmental.

Deleuzian biology

Is there a biology that is adequate to the demands of the new vistas of bioengineering? A machinic biology. A "wild" biology that is neither anthropocentric nor oedipal. A tolerant biology that respects complexity and chaos and looks to limit phenomena for inspiration. A biology of alterity that refuses identity for both difference and differentiation. A sensitive biology of qualities rather than quantities, and of relations rather than essences. A radical biology that is true to its root, as the study of life process at once affective-erotic and aesthetic. A symptom-led biology that does not wish to clean up after itself, but can suffer the dystopian, tolerate the ambiguous, and make a virtue of uncertainty. A biology that appreciates before it explains, that sees form as prior to function and display as irreducible. The new biology of complexity (Goodwin, 1995; Kauffman, 1995) goes some way to meeting the demands above. This approach suggests that evolution is not driven by function, but by form -- efflorescence -- in life's drive to biodiversity, offering maximum complexity at the edge of chaos. Evolution is seen as a formal process enhancing such complexity. Organisms are interdependent, life is systemic and self-organizing, through principles that unfold from process. The model, however, fails to effectively accommodate the virus, or viroid life, as dystopian possibility in every complex system. It tends to wholeness and idealism (evolution towards maximum complexity on the *right* side of chaos), refusing to go beyond the limits to inhabit chaos.

Deleuze distinguishes between a plane of organization or development which relates to structure, being, or subject, and a plane of consistence, which relates to differential modes of becoming through relations, as events and climates rather than things in themselves. The latter offers a poststructuralist, relational biology that privileges system and network, and the conditions of possibility within a system for the emergence of form. This is not an essential or normative biology. It does not bring us to a reasoned conclusion about what a bioengineered life or culture should look like. It does not promise progression or evolution under some general rule or as movement towards some specific goal, but rather an involution, or a working of complexity, through folds in the fabric of life, as differentiation. Where a normative or oedipal biology, which again is the biology informing current bioengineering speculations, takes as its primary metaphor the tree, Deleuzian anti-oedipal biology prefers the rhizome. The tree metaphor implies common root, aspirational evolution, and familial ties through simple branching ("clone" is cognate with "branch"). In contrast, the rhizome metaphor suggests complex, overlapping and aggregating, non-linear systems emerging at the same level, with an underground or subversive resonance, soiling the ideals of the tree metaphor (Jung, 1967).

The characteristic product of oedipal bioengineering is the efficient utilitarian helper, as pet robot, disclosing a repressive master-slave mentality. The product of anti-oedipal bioengineering, however, is Frankenstein's so-called "monster," a wondrous anomaly, disclosing limit thinking. Victor Frankenstein's creation cannot be enslaved. He is viroid. In fact, he comes to enslave his maker in a wonderful implicit exposition of Hegel's master-slave dialectic, where there is no slave without master and no master without slave. Each defines the other through difference. The paradox of Deleuzian biology as applied to a futuristic bioengineering is to make the anomalous the norm, but the norm is now at the limits or frontier, as leading edge. The limit psychologist who studies the new bioengineering will learn by immersion in complexity, by an apprenticeship through "chaosmosis" (Guattari, 1995), refusing closure and tolerating greater degrees of indeterminacy and difference. Her main imaginative power will be an animalizing; she will animalize bioengineering futures, making them aesthetically -- and ethically -- sensitive, tolerant of difference and ambiguity, accepting of symptom, and affective-erotic in their practices and applications.

In A Thousand Plateaus, Deleuze and Guattari offer a tale of the rat pack, returning us to Freud's Rat Man. They recount the tale of Willard, a B-movie made in 1972. Willard lives with his authoritarian mother. "Dreadful Oedipal atmosphere" the authors note. His mother orders him to destroy a litter of rats, but Willard saves some and makes friends with them. His mother, who is said to resemble a dog, dies, and a crooked businessman makes a claim on the house. Willard sends his rat pack over to eat the man alive. Stupidly, Willard is tempted to take his favorite rats to his work place. They are discovered by his employer, who kills them, apart from one, Ben, who escapes, giving Willard a withering look that says "you have betrayed us." This is critical in Willard's vocation up to this point of "becoming rat." Now, in an oedipal retreat from animality, he attempts to remain among humans, doing the normal things. He responds to the sexual advances of a young woman who works at the office, who resembles a rat. He takes her home, hoping to seduce her, but Ben, his old rat pal, appears at the critical moment. Willard tries to get rid of the animal, but succeeds only in frightening away the girl. Ben lures him to the basement, reminding him of the good times when Willard was a friend of the rats. In the basement, a terrifying rat pack is waiting. They devour Willard.

Horrific as the ending may seem, this is what we should expect from the animal familiar and its attendant pack. Recall the terrifying psychosomatic initiations of the premodern shamans. If you make a pact with the rats, or you are animalized, you can never return to the oedipal frame of mind that territorializes, normalizes and refuses anomaly. You will be torn apart by your familiar at the horizon of your becoming. That is, your anthropocentric world collapses in the process of becoming-animal. To become animal is not to identify with, or imitate, or come to resemble, an animal. It is not a process of analogy. Rather, it is an undoing of the habitual human. *Becoming the animal is real even if the animal the human becomes is not*. To become animal is to set the human subject at the limits of current corporeal and conceptual logics in order to destabilize notions of what it is to be human. Set loose, we might enter a zone of proximity infected by what Deleuze calls the "animal molecule." Maybe we get bitten and return to contaminate a whole community of practice with our animalizing imaginations. Desire then becomes disengaged from humanistic subjectivity and engaged with animal presence. We do not do this simply by mixing with animals (in this we have no choice – animals are constantly in us, on us and around us). We might do it by writing or creating art as the animal, or by practicing our professions differently through a sensitive, embodied, animalized artistry.

If the new bioengineering technologists were to be infected by an animalizing imagination and informed by a process biology of relations, qualities, differences, intensities, affects, rhizomatics, and involutions or folds in the fabric of living as radical differentiation, perhaps they would veer away from pursuit of projects of identity, such as reproductive cloning, to projects of difference and differentiation such as maintaining biodiversity and studying the conditions of possibility for the emergence of change, creation and innovation. Learning to become animal is to take on board the foundational perceptions and imaginings that Freud's animal phobia patients were teaching him, although he refused to listen. The Rat Man (and the Wolf Man) were learning by chaosmosis, immersed in an aesthetic, erotic and pathologized power that ripped them out of oedipal life -- filiality, conformist marriage, authoritarian habits, and civilized responses.

Importantly, to become animal is the first move to becoming cyborg; otherwise, we import too much of the ethos of oedipal and logical humanity into the machine, and not enough animality. It is necessary to recover something of our premodern legacy as we move inevitably into the age of becoming cyborg. In a recombinant culture we need to abandon the Cartesian legacy of opposing machine and soul, investing the future cyborg with an animalizing imagination.

References

Bachelard, G. (1986). Lautreamont. Dallas: The Dallas Institute Publications.

Bleakley, A. (2000). The animalizing imagination: Totemism, textuality and ecocriticism. New York: St Martins Press.

Deleuze, G. (1992). 'Ethology: Spinoza and Us'. In J. Crary and S. Kwinter (Eds.), Incorporations. New York: Zone.

Deleuze, G. (1994). Difference and repetition. London: The Athlone Press.

Deleuze, G. and Guattari, F. (1984). Anti-Oedipus: Capitalism and schizophrenia. London: The Athlone Press.

Deleuze, G. and Guattari, F. (1988). A thousand plateaus: Capitalism and schizophrenia. London: The Athlone Press.

Foucault, M. (1997). Ethics: Subjectivity and truth (The Essential Works of Michel Foucault, Volume 1). London: Allen Lane, The Penguin Press.

Freud, S. (1918). Totem and taboo. New York: Moffat, Yard & Co.

Freud, S. (1913). The interpretation of dreams. London: G. Allen and Co.

Goodwin, B. (1995). How the leopard changed its spots. London: Phoenix Giants, Weidenfeld & Nicolson.

Guattari, F. (1995). Chaosmosis: an ethico-aesthetic paradigm. Sydney: Power Publications.

Halifax, J. (1980). Shamanic voices: the shaman as seer, poet and healer. Harmondsworth: Penguin.

Jung, C. G. (1967). Alchemical studies. Henley-on-Thames: Routledge & Kegan Paul.

Kauffman, S. (1995). At home in the universe: The search for laws of self-organization and complexity. London: Viking.

Massumi, B. (1992). A user's guide to capitalism and schizophrenia: Deviations from Deleuze and Guattari. London: The MIT Press.

Skvorecky, J. (1994). The bass saxophone. London: Vintage.

Stivale, C. J. (1998). The two-fold thought of Deleuze and Guattari: Intersections and animations. London: The Guilford Press.

Waldby, C. (2000). The visible human project: Informatic bodies and posthuman medicine. London: Routledge.

Archetypal Fundamentalism in the Twenty-first Century by Glen Slater, Ph.D.

Introduction

In 1967 James Hillman wrote a paper that set the course of Archetypal psychology. "Senex and Puer: An Aspect of the Historical and Psychological Present" (1967/1979) called for a reconfiguring and healing of the puer. Hillman suggested there that "the senex-puer polarity is given by the historical situation" (p. 3), and that "the constellation of this polarity *as a split* (emphasis in original) demonstrates the gravity of our historical crisis" (p. 9). He framed this historical situation in terms of entering the "last third of this century" and being "one generation from the twenty-first century" (p. 3).

Hillman's paper establishes a priority of ideas and suggests something of a hierarchy of archetypal patterns in our approach to psychology. Specifically, he places the puer-senex polarity prior to patterns of polytheism and monotheism and the styles of discourse these patterns spawn. The puer-senex and its expressions were situated as more primary, more foundational than the polytheistic-monotheistic approaches to psychology. It is the puer and the senex, their preferences and problems, that gives rise to the polytheistic and monotheistic inclinations. In particular, it is the senex that supports the monotheistic perspective, which aligns the puer with a polytheistic view.

Let's recall just a few characteristics of the puer-senex pairing: The puer embraces youth, beginnings, wanderings, inspiration, invention and flight. He dislikes attachments and plodding, measured development. Hermes/Mercurius is the figure we often think of here. The senex is the old man, solitary and systematic, an upholder of tradition and history. He is solid, fixed, crusty and controlling; structure and authority reside with him. Kronos/Saturn is the key divinity. Placing the two side by side, Hillman says aptly, "The puer inspires the blossoming of things; the senex presides over the harvest" (1967/1979, p. 11).

At the heart of Hillman's seminal paper is the following argument: The primary psychological and cultural-historical problem of our time reflects the splitting of the puer-senex pairing, and that this split is due to an overemphasis in Western culture on senex-based patterns of meaning and experience. Furthermore, psychology, even depth psychology, has also tended to enact this preference. On the basis of this perspective (and here is where Archetypal psychology is assigned its primary task), the path that a culturally attuned depth perspective must take is toward a redemption of the puer. Whereas the problem is the split archetype, the solution lies in working through the puer. Or, as stated a little differently by Hillman in another paper on the issue, the problem of the senex requires a Renaissance solution (Hillman, 1975b).

The time has come to reconsider this approach laid out in 1967. As others have pointed out and as we will discuss, in spite of the goal being the reconfiguration of the puer-senex pattern, resulting in the positive expression of both sides of the pairing, a shadow has been generated by the focus on the puer and the style of psychological discourse this focus brings. Shadows create problems and shadows carry new potentials. This paper examines the shadow of Archetypal psychology's puer emphasis, its senex shadow, a shadow that invites a form of subtle fundamentalism appearing where we would not imagine it. What follows is a critique, I hope a critique with a constructive intention, a prospective eye, and a devotion to the task of moving Archetypal psychology into the third millennium.

The problem of the collective undercurrent and the archetypal response

Stepping back for a moment, let's begin with two viewpoints that are familiar to us, though worth naming from the start. The first is that depth psychology's efficacy is always based upon its attending to unconsciousness in the cultural psyche. This field, if it does anything, should speak on behalf of the cultural shadow and host the corrective images coming from the obscured corners of our vision. Whether it compensates, complements, or condemns the habitual stances of the Western ego doesn't matter. What matters is that the margins of our habitual consciousness are being attended. Depth psychology hosts the return of the repressed (Freud), and the absence of religiosity (Jung). Before any specific psychodynamics or concepts are entertained, a perspective tuned to these excluded elements is essential. Without such an attunement, a sensitivity to that which is dark at any given moment in history, the depth tradition loses its roots in a living psychic dynamism--it loses its relation to the spirit of the age. We must always try to have one hand on the underbelly of the collective psyche.

The second viewpoint comes more specifically from the classical Jungian tradition: The darkest shadow is often at the center of that which is most conscious, most light. More than the notion that preferred, one-sided perspectives cast shadows or fuel opposition, it is that the very thing that is most espoused or celebrated contains a piece of darkness right at its center: Clarity and devotion also obscure. Hillman (1967/1979) reminds us of this too, in the middle of his original puer-senex paper, saying, "we are least conscious where we are most conscious . . . the ego makes shadow; the ego is its own shadow; perhaps the ego is shadow. So the senex represents just this force of death that is carried by the glittering hardness of our own ego-certainty" (p. 19).

Archetypal psychology emerged when it applied just these viewpoints to the existent Jungian perspective, revealing the many ways in which a monotheistic style of consciousness obscured the rich tapestry of psychic life, a psychic life which is, phenomenologically, more polytheistic in its expression. Jungian psychology, it was said, moved too quickly to the Self, the centralizing tendency, and blinded us to the activity of the archetypes and their own styles of consciousness and patterns of activity. The celebrated emphasis on wholeness and ordering contained too much of the Western ego's conscious agenda and therefore obscured the deeper realities of the psyche. A collusion had occurred between Jungian concepts and a prevalent cultural attitude. And when the emphasis is on order and wholeness, systems, literalism, and fundamentalism are not far away. Since the very beginning, die-hard, classical Jungian thought has provided grist for Archetypal psychology's mill of more lively, less dogmatic ideas.

But what happens when we turn this kind of critical review on Archetypal psychology itself? What enters our vision when we ask: Where is Archetypal psychology's dogmatism and blindness? Where is Archetypal psychology's monotheism? Stated most starkly, where is the danger of an Archetypal fundamentalism?

With its devotion to multiplicity, to the many rather than the one, Archetypal psychology has held itself to be largely immune from any one organizing principle or system of thought; it has defined itself as the enemy of unconscious monotheism. To be fiercely for the imagination and for fluidity of thought is at the heart of archetypal activity. Built into such activity is a bearing thoroughly attentive to the specters of literalism and fundamentalism. Its primary practice of "seeing through" is, by definition, a movement away from fixed meanings into the realm of archetypal patterns and mythopoetic meanings. Being attached to one perspective or building a rigid conceptual system is far from its mind, *perhaps too far*. Standing within its own perspectives, the term "archetypal fundamentalism" appears to be an oxymoron; fundamentalism is the least likely state of mind one could imagine. But this is just where things turn around to bite us. Fluid interpretations, sparks of insight without system and non-literal modes of apprehension blind us to our capacity to become fixed. All these celebrated processes of unraveling fixed meanings and systems sets up an over-confidence in the absence of such monotheistic tendencies, an overconfidence that is itself a kind of monotheism–a true belief in its dexterity and movement.

To cut to the chase, Archetypal psychology may be too attached to its movement and multiplicity, too fixed in its fluidity. And the flip side of this attachment is that very little attention flows to its own points of fixture. Fixture, rigidity, literalism, and dogma are only found outside its own perspectives, as the hard, concrete surfaces and theories unconscious of their ghosts upon which we practice our seeing through. The negative senex is "out there somewhere", but not in here. In a nutshell, (and maybe this is Archetypal psychology's acorn), although the puer and its polytheistic leanings have breathed life into depth psychology and undone many of its rigid positions, the realm of the senex, operating within Archetypal perspective, in both positive and negative forms, has been neglected.

The neglect of the *positive* senex comes in the form of ignoring the dimensions of discipline required for Archetypal psychology's sharp insights and deconstructive moves. There's a tendency to forget that the positive aspects of the puer depend upon the positive aspects of the senex: The flash of insight requires the counterweight of careful consideration, devotion, and apprenticeship to theories and philosophies. Without this counterweight the insight is without weight; it appears and charms us momentarily but it doesn't leave any trace or move to deeper reflection. The fluid and lively discourse leaves a vapor trail easily diffused by the prevailing wind. As Hemingway reminded us, vivid, rich writing and resonant images are like icebergs–most of the mass is beneath the surface, far from view. So too with

Archetypal theorists themselves: Decades of devoted study of literature, comparative religion, history, and other depth psychologies are not always in view; but it is just these fields where careful apprenticeships have taken place that allow Archetypal psychology to work. The crucial insights gathered in these places, the mass of *under*standings that allow Archetypal psychology to do its thing, the philosophical layers beneath the 'moves,' are largely beneath the surface. In sum, the positive senex has tended to operate in a hidden manner, far from view, as a kind of miracle that keeps the puer from going off the rails.

It is perhaps the failure to honor these places where the puer has his tail tied to a more static reality that breeds an atmosphere attractive to the *negative* senex. As symptoms tell us, when the legitimate call for acknowledgment is ignored, the troublesome characteristics come into stark relief. A rigid and dogmatic tone creeps in behind the fluid content of discourse: diversity gives way to divisiveness; quiet authority is displaced by obstinate opinion; other perspectives are dismissed summarily or ignored without due consideration or an invitation to dialogue. The push to be lively, fresh, radical, to be "out of there before the paint dries," become fundamental.

It is difficult to operate in the absence of cohesive systems, hard facts, and defined concepts–all of those things the senex loves. Without these conventional aids Archetypal psychology's path has not been easy; risks and pitfalls abound. But Archetypal psychology's Gods also come back as symptom.

The critiques

To James Hillman's credit, he has invited this present discussion on at least three different occasions. First, at the end of the last Archetypal conference at Notre Dame, he wrote an open letter to the participants, which commented on the "fanatic devotion to single agendas," and stated, "monotheism appears within psychological polytheism as contentious demands and intrusive invasions." (cited in Tacey, 1998, p. 231). Then, in 1996, in a Spring paper that reassessed the pivotal "Psychology: Monotheistic or Polytheistic" (1996b), Hillman reflected on a monotheistic tone that lived within his own attack on monotheism. He writes, "I was acting as a monotheist even while defending polytheism" (p. 113). Third, and perhaps most significantly, in the Coda on method at the end of The Soul's Code (1996a), he describes the puer's presence in Archetypal perspective as follows:

> Any theory that is affected by the puer will show dashing execution, an appeal to the
> extraordinary, and a show-off aestheticism. It will claim timelessness and universal
> validity, but forgo the labors of proof. It will have that puer dance in it, will imagine
> ambitiously and rebel against convention. A puer-inspired theory will also limp among
> the facts, even collapse when met with the questioning inquires of so-called reality,
> which is the position taken by the puer's classical opponent, the gray-faced king or
> Saturn figure, old hardnose, hardass, hardhat. (p. 283)

Hillman then addresses the shadow of this mode of theory-making: "Inside the puer is a
terrifying, even toxic, bitterness. . . the suicidal depression that can't wait into the time of the
oak. Theories too are afflicted with shadow" (p. 285).

The way in which this negative senex figure is lingering in these reflections on method
suggests that the puer emphasis may be being pushed too far. Remember, the positive puer is,
by definition, a puer joined with the positive senex. Conjointly, the presence of the negative
senex indicates a problem with the puer. Why is that old Saturnian ogre lingering so
threatening and so near?

There are now several critiques that suggest Archetypal psychology is too caught in the
attitudes of the puer. The criticism has been made on at least five separate occasions by
Odajnyk (1984), Stein (1988), Neville (1992), Lopez-Pedraza (1990) and Tacey (1998). Odajnyk
writes that Hillman's "entire opus is an apologia pro vita sua–a defense and an elaboration of
the puer psychology" (p.40), which results, among other things, in a "depend(ence) mostly on
rhetoric, on making an impression, rather than on solid intellectual argument" (p. 47). Stein
suggests that Archetypal psychology "supports the spirit of the puer, the romance of the
anima, the soulful, willful young rebel's hatred of history, of structure, or regimentation, of
institutionalization" and that it contains an "adolescent spirit" (p. 7). Lopez-Pedraza, is not, at
least apparently, directly attacking Archetypal theory, but also warns of puerish extremes in
psychology. Tacey, after naming both the puer emphasis and the Hermes-Mercurius style of
discourse, goes on to state that "the hyperbolic speech, romantic assertions and intensely
poetic style may have blocked any academic appreciation of Hillman's deconstructive

strategies and fluid epistemology" (p. 220). We will return to Tacey toward the end. I do not agree with many of the points made in these critiques. Yet these individuals present a range of affiliations with Archetypal psychology; not all are beyond the fold. The repetition of this criticism is reason enough to consider it seriously.

But there is another reason to undertake this examination, a reason that places the future of an Archetypal psychology firmly in the current historical context: A very strong pattern now runs through Western society, a pattern that coincides with the fluidity and multi-perspectival energy of the puer. This pattern has also been referred to as a Hermes inflation (Neville) and acknowledged by Paris (1990), Hillman (1995) and others as the Mercurial character of the information age. Of the critics I mention, only Neville links the Mercurial style of discourse in Archetypal psychology to this cultural trend. This linking of Archetypal psychology, first to postmodernism and then to a widespread inflation, may be the most compelling argument for tending to the senex shadow of the puer emphasis. *There may exist a point of collusion between Archetypal psychology's emphasis on the puer, and its Hermes/Mercurius correlate, in the trends of Western consciousness.* To the extent that this is so, I believe that Archetypal psychology is, ironically, in danger of forfeiting its legacy as a vivid and fresh eye upon currents of psychological life, in danger of losing its capacity to feel the pulse of the collective.

Hillman recently responded to Neville's critique in a paper entitled "A Note on Hermes Inflation" (1999). Here he argues that this pattern is only a superficial expression of the archetype and does "not indicate a true displacement of the monotheistic model" (p. 7). He goes on to say that "the Hermes we are indulging in today is one fallen from brotherhood and sisterhood. . . . He has lost association with the gods, become only profane" (p. 10). Furthermore, this Hermes is just "a mercurial mask disguising the same old monotheism of our civilization." (p. 10). "To work through the Hermes inflation," Hillman suggests, "we have first to restore Hermes to his polytheistic authenticity" (p. 12).

Essentially, I agree with this reading of the situation. Inflations are a psuedo-relation to the archetype or an expression of an archetypal movement split from its full context and complexity. Nevertheless, the question remains as to how well Archetypal psychology, in its own practices, follows such understandings. For to the extent the puer-senex remains split in its own bearing is the same extent to which it is in danger of joining with the wider Hermes inflation.

Further on in Hillman's response to Neville he writes in support of the primacy of the image, "that's why archetypal psychology requires no foundation in another so-called reality and why it is not dependant upon an external philosophy, science or metaphysics" (p. 11). He adds, by way of qualification, that Archetypal psychology "relates to them and exchanges with them, as Hermes with his Olympian family and friends" (p. 11). This is the crux of the issue: To what extent does Archetypal psychology really do this? Specifically, to what extent does it allow the senex-imbued side of the pantheon into its more puer-inspired approaches? Amidst the competing depth psychological perspectives in this new century, these cultural trends present the risk of Archetypal theory being swept into the bin of reactive postmodernism and then dismissed when the fashion of this style of discourse declines. That heroic ego, sworn enemy of the Archetypal approach, is now cloaking itself in Hermes attire, threatening all forms of superficial relation to the impulse of puer, threatening to suck all life from the radical, transformational dynamics the puer provides. The Western ego will colonize with whatever it holds as predominant way of knowing.

To address all of these issues, we must return to Hillman's1967 paper on the puer-senex, and locate some seeds of renewal. Here I believe we will find a creative corrective, one which might provide some ballast for the Archetypal field as we move into the third millennium. This looking back in time, imagining a tradition to which to be faithful (or at least locating missing pieces within a tradition), is itself a senex move. Yet it is for the sake of moving forward. The puer has taken flight, its freshness of perspective and fleet-footed intelligence will never be far from the fray. I believe that it is time to take stock, reflect on the past, and find some points to which to tether ourselves in the inevitable intellectual and cultural winds of the new era.

The core of the issue

At the beginning of this paper I outlined Hillman's emphasis on the puer and senex as two sides of a singular archetypal configuration; one does not exist without the other, and the problems of each are bound to the other. Let's listen to the way he describes the problem:

> Negative senex attitudes and behavior result from this split archetype, while positive
> senex attitudes and behavior reflect its unity; so that the term 'positive senex' or old
> wise man *refers merely* (emphasis mine) to a transformed continuation of the puer. Here
> the first part of our talk reaches its issue: *the difference between the negative and positive*
> *senex qualities reflects the split or connection with senex-puer archetype.* (1967/1979, p. 23)

Although the problem concerns both the senex and puer aspects, Hillman clearly aims
to work through the problem via a therapy of the puer, the redemption of which will
simultaneously recover the qualities of the positive senex. Such was the appropriate and
necessary strategy. At that time, particularly in the Swiss-German setting of these initial ideas,
identification with the senex was afoot. Specifically, Hillman's concern at this point was a
reinvigorating of the archetypal sparks and specificities that had been squashed by the senex-
based, Jungian concern with ego-Self dynamics. Working the problem from the side of the
puer was a corrective perspective, prompted by a neglected dimension of the soul's own
nature.

As we just noted, today this cultural and psychological background may well be
reversed, particularly in the American setting and in the Americanized parts of the Western
world. Prevalent attitudes and academic styles of discourse are more and more aligned, not
with the senex but with puer-Hermes, and in this alignment have left a vacuum of awareness
in the realm of the senex. For example, we hardly know how to recognize genuine authority,
deep reflection, slow mentoring, and well-digested knowledge. It is now a cliché to reflect that
we only find information on the internet and not wisdom; that wisdom needs reflection,
rumination, and careful amplification. A large part of what's missing in such gathering of
internet based material is its context. I often suggest to the internet savvy that they should go
to the University stacks and stand between the shelves for awhile, looking for what else
appears in the same section as the work they have targeted on the computer. This provides an
embodied sense of what is in the field. Such contextualizing of knowledge does not occur on
the information superhighway, where the surrounding landscape becomes a blur or
disappears altogether. Listen to Hillman's description of the puer, split from the senex:

The puer spirit is the least psychological, has the least soul. Its sensitive soulfulness is rather pseudo-psychological . . . It can search and risk; it has insight, aesthetic intuition, spiritual ambition–all but not psychology, for psychology requires time, femininity of the soul, and the entanglement of relationships. (1967/1979, pp. 25-26)

Doesn't this seem familiar? From the New Age guru to the Silicon Valley entrepreneur, to the narcissism of Hollywood and Wall Street, the description sticks.

In this new cultural landscape, the work now needs to reconsider the problem (which is still the same splitting of the archetype in different guise) from the opposite angle–*namely a redemption of the negative puer through a recovery of the positive senex*. At the very least, there is a need for Archetypal psychology to consider the shadow side of its puer emphasis in an intellectual and cultural climate that is consumed by this kind of consciousness, bringing to awareness the positive senex potential as we enter the next phase.

At worst, without this reversal of approach, the cultural inflation in Hermes will begin to cohabit with the puer emphasis in our field and produce varieties of fundamentalism, either in the form of true belief in the power of the imagination (without any grounding in solid theory), or as a kind of senex infused reaction. That is, an exaggerated expression of the split itself–two sides of the same coin, each expressing an insubstantial relation to the image.

To take the second aspect of this fundamentalism problem, an *unconscious* attempt to integrate the senex is likely to show up in a kind of pseudo grounding of Archetypal theory, particularly in trying to concretize Archetypal perspectives and move them quickly into literal application. I believe that we can detect this pseudo-senex solution in the trend towards what has been called "archetypal activism."

Now I want to make a careful differentiation.

The need to be "active" may be a genuine and necessary response to the social fabric. Projects directly engaging social problems that are informed by archetypal reflection are much needed. However, such moves can also be tacked onto, rather than organically grown out of, archetypal perspective, as a compensation. To the extent this impulse comes from the fear that Archetypal psychology is not concrete or practical enough, leading to a compelling need for social intervention and political activity, is the extent to which it may also be a pseudo-form of integrating the senex. The unconscious drive to build this bridge to the outer world, to "ground" the theory, points first to the missing element of the positive senex in the field, to the loss of substance, presence, and influence of thought, to the weight of ideas. The need to formalize the activist bridge can, in this way, be read as symptomatic of an anxiety that our field is too flighty, too lofty, too ethereal and too intellectual. Ironically, it may not be intellectual enough.

The problem also appears in academic circles where Archetypal psychology lives, not at the heart of the psychological disciplines where it believes it belongs, but on the extreme fringes, as a side-line. From one perspective this may be its niche: Depth psychology only functions if it is attending to the liminal spaces around mainstream thought, ever attentive to what goes unseen. Its purpose is to greet the return of the repressed, and the repressed appears at the margins. Nevertheless, for those concerned with moving Archetypal psychology into the academy–at least to place the two in some form of dialogue–the apparent lack of theoretical substance and weight is a pressing concern. David Tacey's (1998) rather harsh and mean-spirited critique of Hillman and Archetypal psychology has just this concern buried in its midst, a frustration that more (dare I say it) cohesion and consistency of perspective is not accessible. When Archetypal psychology encounters this mainstream perspective wearing its puer identity, it is all too easily brushed aside. It's substance is not apparent, nor is it easily demonstrated. Somehow, this must change: We may not want departments of Archetypal psychology, but we might want departments of psychology studying archetypal thought. We might not want systematized introductions to Archetypal psychology, but we might want some means of introducing Archetypal psychology into the system.

As indicated above in relation to the idea that the positive senex is often hidden in Archetypal psychology, it is not certain that the field works at all unless its practitioner has been somewhere else, in a big way, in service of another field or discipline. Perhaps this is because soul-making works through the analogies and metaphors that one gathers from such a background. Perhaps it has something to do with the psyche's love of in-between spaces and its hate for overly focused glares. Perhaps discipline and apprenticeship cultivate the senex qualities necessary for deconstructive and mythopoetic discourse. As a field, Archetypal psychology is the very opposite of a technological discipline, where one may become a genius by being a geek, holed up with a computer for 18 hours a day.

Perhaps we have not bothered to cultivate and articulate the positive senex because its been there all along, operating beneath the surface like a lead filled keel that keeps the boat from toppling over. It may be no accident that the field periodically becomes preoccupied with leaden themes–depression, smog, and stasis rather than transformation--or needs to continually hold itself to its underworld affiliations. These themes and perspectives arrive only via many years working in psyche's trenches. Archetypal psychology has only been sustainable because of the developed senex backgrounds of its key exponents. Educations in history, academic careers in the classics and religious studies, long terms in scholarly settings, studies in communication theory, and so on. Archetypal psychology has been built through the insights of individuals who have meandered in the silences and spaces of not-knowing, a not-knowing informed by a significant knowing. It has been built by those who have rubbed its insights up against those of fields other than psychology–literature and the dramatic arts. All of these backgrounds and activities provide the invisible weight that substantiates the field. At the heart of our practice is the work of "sticking to the image" (Hillman, 1983, p. 14), but this only works because of the "sticking to."

Recovering (or uncovering) the positive senex

The closest archetypal psychology has come to setting out key principles is in Hillman's Revisioning Psychology (1975a). In the introduction he describes the four parts as "fence-posts" (p. xvi). The questions I have been raising are tantamount to asking: "Are fence-posts enough?" In Australia, leaping kangaroos knock down fences and fence-posts on a regular basis; they are not as substantial as one might think. If we open ourselves to the positive senex, it may be that a few pylons–firmer foundations--are necessary too. Not that we would ever allow ourselves to become too attached to such things (God forbid), or that they would be beyond critique, but that they would be there, providing a platform upon which discourse with fields whose philosophical, metaphysical and cosmological assertions are more clearly laid out.

In this vein, given that the danger of fundamentalism and true-belief lies in being fixed in the Hermes-puer, *a better articulation of, and tending to, fundamentals may actually prevent fundamentalism*. In other words, a distillation and articulation of some of the invisible themes and pockets of knowledge that support the miracle of the positive puer may be called for. Apprenticeship to the classical Jungian roots of Archetypal psychology, (an apprenticeship that doesn't happen if the fledgling Archetypal psychologist makes a literal read of Inter-Views [1983]), strong ties to comparative mythology and religion and a fierce dedication to particular pockets of philosophy might contribute to such a task. These moves might slow the puer down and help his steps become more deliberate. The core themes that we borrow from these fields constitute the all-too-quickly passed-over basis for Archetypal thought, a basis that could easily be made more apparent, then examined more thoroughly.

There is something of this attention to fundamentals already in the moves of Wolfgang Giegerich. The call for the soul's "logical" life (Giegerich, 1998), for the recovery of thinking and the dryer intellect, is a recovery of Apollo in the midst of an overly mercurial meandering of meanings. Isn't the claim that, "to arrive at a rigorous concept of psychology we must go beyond the imaginal" (p. 11), an attack on the puer emphasis in our ways of knowing? Isn't the demand for more rigorous thinking a courting of the senex? Isn't the move back into the very premises of Jung's psychology an attempt to place Archetypal psychology on a more solid footing?

As Ginette Paris suggested in her keynote presentation (2000), Giegerich's critique belongs to the community, or the village, and may be essential to the project of moving the Jungian side of depth psychology into the 21st century. She exemplified how important it is to embrace the negation, negativity, and sublation of which Giegerich writes. She placed this need within the context of countering the positivism that can creep into our work with images and emotions (the unbidden return of the senex); sometimes the mind needs to cut through, and dispense with a myth, supplying the psyche with another logic. Positivism of the imagination is a marker on the path to what I have called, more provocatively perhaps, "Archetypal fundamentalism." Giegerich's critique, and those dimensions of psychological life Paris highlights as central to this critique, belong to a recovery of the positive senex. We could say that Giegerich is turning the title of Hillman's "Senex Problem" paper on its head, offering us a "senex solution to a Renaissance problem."

Going to a specific myth, after Hermes charms his way to acceptance by Apollo, Apollo must shoot a few of those unerringly straight, logical arrows. We must remember that Zeus allows Hermes into the fold only on condition of making up with his brother Apollo. This reminds us that a part of what we may be engaging here is the very essence of the hermeneutic problem, rooted as it is in the Hermes myth: The art, or logic(!) of interpretation and making meaning implies a necessary collaborative effort by Hermes and Apollo.

Giegerich moves away from ideas and discourse being returned to their own archetypal impetus (as I did above with his ideas). He wants to set the realm of ideas a step beyond their archetypal (and imaginal) contexts, suggesting that we not only need to see through the literal via the imaginal but also need to see through the imaginal to the soul's inherent logic (1998, pp. 106-107). Giegerich implies that this is an appropriate advance for a psychology that began with Jung's emphasis on image in combating the positivism of his age. Yet how far have we have moved beyond the positivist mindset of Jung's era? The world of "isms" still abounds. Abandoning the principles of seeing through our ideas with mythological glasses may be a bit premature–too soon to trade antiquated lenses for the surgical correction of Hegelian laser-beams. Logical negation, which wants to place the unconscious in our very ways of thinking (Giegerich, 2000), will find but a small foothold in a world that is still largely pre-Jung and still unable to make the sacrifice that first opens a psychic realm beyond the positivistic ego.

To reverse the general direction of this paper for a moment, mythological images and archetypal moves keep such systems of logic honest–tied to something beyond our fantasy of control. They re-mind the rational ego of the places it cannot go. Without this, perspectives wholly unconscious of the images behind them become reactive philosophies disconnected from the instincts, from the guts. They become indigestible. This constant recovery of archetypal context has been Archetypal psychology's project from the beginning. Although it is logically contradictory, we might perhaps be more open to Giegerich's radical critique and the call to a psychology of logic, if we keep its own archetypal motives (and motifs) somewhere close at hand. Puer and senex still need partnership: Modification, rigor, differentiation, structure, yes; a flight into logical thinking, maybe not.

Hillman "laid the table" for the Psychology at the Threshold Conference by referring to the principles of Justice, Beauty, and Destiny (Hillman, 2000). Perhaps we could hold the task of finding Justice, inviting Beauty, and envisioning Destiny, with the following also in mind: Justice needs outrage, and it needs judgment. Beauty needs playful moments, and it requires an aesthetic eye and that eye needs discernment and training. Destiny needs the dream, but that dream is only suffered into through dramatic, fateful twists and turns, and the striking intimations of possibilities that are woven together with patience and devotion. These secondary aspects provide fundamental, substantial dimension and weight. Beneath each of these three principles and the values they imply is call for careful discernment, rumination, wisdom, and time, perhaps even, as Roszak suggested (2000), an careful attunement to nature and her rhythms. These three crucial principles need firm foundations as well as dashing, imaginative dexterity. The foundations have been hiding. Now, more than ever, they need articulation. Puer has addressed senex, now senex must address puer.

References

Giegerich, W. (1998). The soul's logical life. Frankfurt: Peter Lang.

Giegerich, W. (2000). Unpublished presentation. Psychology at the Threshold conference. The University of California, Santa Barbara. September 2000.

Hillman, J. (1979). Senex and Puer: An Aspect of the Historical and Psychological Present. In J. Hillman (Ed.), Puer papers. Dallas: Spring. (Original paper presented in 1967).

Hillman, J. (1975a). Revisioning psychology. New York: Harper Collins.

Hillman, J. (1975b). The 'negative' senex and a Renaissance solution. Spring, 1975.

Hillman, J. (1969a). Psychology--Monotheistic or polytheistic: Twenty-five years later. Spring, 60, 111-125.Hillman, J. (1995). Kinds of power. New York: Doubleday.

Hillman, J. (1996). The soul's code. New York: Random House.

Hillman, J. (1999). A note on Hermes inflation. Spring 65, 1999.

Hillman, J. (2000). Unpublished presentation. Psychology at the Threshold conference. The University of California, Santa Barbara. September 2000.

Lopez-Pedraza, R. (1990). Cultural anxiety. Einsiedeln, Switzerland: Daimon.

Neville, B. (1992). The charm of Hermes: Hillman, Lyotard and the postmodern condition. Journal of Analytical Psychology, 37(3), 337-353.

Odajnyk, V. W. (1984). The imaginal world of James Hillman. Quadrant 17 (spring), 39-48.

Paris, G. (1990). Pagan grace. Dallas: Spring.

Paris, G. (2000). Unpublished presentation. Psychology at the Threshold conference. The University of California, Santa Barbara. September 2000.

Stein, M. (1988). Solutio and coagulatio in analytical psychology. In The analytic life. Boston: Sigo.

Tacey, D. (1998). Twisting and turning with James Hillman: From anima to world soul, from academia to pop. In A. Casement (Ed.), Post-Jungians today. New York: Routledge.

Jung and Postmodernism: Bridging the Self-Other Divide by Honor Griffith, Ph.D.

There is a sense of ennui and a level of depression amongst so many of our patients today which stem, I believe, not only from genetic disposition or dysfunctional family patterns, but also from the age in which we live, as if some low level psychic "virus" were attacking our cultural "immune system." Postmodern philosophy has had not only an invigorating, but also a disturbing, effect on the psychological well being of the Western psyche. Some of the casualties of this age of postmodernity are showing up in our consulting rooms, nursing a severe sense of emptiness and fragmentation. What response do we as Jungian and archetypal based practitioners have to this existential malaise?

Although Jung is regarded in some circles as "the last archaeologist of the self who captures the self's aura just as it dissolves officially into the archaeologies of language and institution" (Barnaby & D'Acierno, 1990, p. xxvi), I believe that, in fact, Jung anticipated postmodern thinking, is better understood through a postmodern lens, and may provide practical, concrete answers to the endemic nihilism that is experienced in the empty self of our era. Jung faced many of the same questions found in postmodern discourse long before postmodernism came into vogue and proposed the beginnings of an answer to problems for which most postmodernists have few.

Examining the connection between postmodern thought and Jung is a huge topic. In this paper, I focus specifically on the parallels between Jung's preoccupation with the objective psyche and postmodern philosophy's preoccupation with the "other" that has largely been left out of the Western philosophical project.

From Modern Subject to Postmodern Other

In his Introduction to Deconstruction in Context, Mark Taylor (1986) tracks the Western philosophical project from the beginnings of modernism through to the philosophical discourse of postmodern thought. According to his analysis, the main theme of Western philosophy is a discourse that has centered on the concept of **the other**. Modern philosophy is considered to begin with Descartes and his struggle to find certainty through doubt. He doubts everything until he reaches what he considers the indubitable, his own doubting self. This doubting subject he calls *res cogitans* and distinguishes it from everything else, which he calls *res extensa*. With this radical differentiation, he is now faced with the problem of establishing the relationship between subjectivity and objectivity. The subject's relationship to all that is other than itself, insists Descartes, is inevitably mediated by and derived from its relationship to itself (Taylor, 1986). Hence modern philosophy becomes a *philosophy of the subject*.

Descartes, with his differentiation between *res cogitans* and *res extensa*, opened up a split between man and the world, man and nature, that has come to lie at the heart of the modern, Western scientific paradigm. Philosophy became a philosophy of the subject, a subject that forever attempted to remake the world in its own image. With the unraveling of the Western project, however, postmodern philosophy has attempted to explore the irrational other that was initially split off by Descartes and to come to terms with that "difference" which is "irreducible to identity" (Taylor, 1986, p. 33). But how can we ever see other *as* other when the only vehicle we have for apprehending the other is our own psyche? Is this not an impossible project? Jung (1958) himself writes, "To the extent that the world does not assume the form of a psychic image, it is virtually non-existent" (pp. 480-481). Is it possible ever to move beyond the solipsism of the modern subject who defines itself by what it constructs and then relates only to that, remaining unaffected by anything other than itself?

Jung and Deconstruction

In his approach to the unconscious, Jung is similar to postmodern deconstructionists in describing the realm of the archetype as absolute other. In fact, Barnaby and D'Acierno (1990) claim that "poststructuralist thought, particularly deconstruction, appears to offer an exceptionally useful critical perspective from which to formulate a contemporary understanding of Jung" (p. xxiii). This is most evident when comparing Jung's psychological concept of oppositions, that is, holding the tension of the opposites, with Derrida's "hierarchical structuring of oppositional terms and dislocation of those hierarchies via deconstructive reversals" (Barnaby & D'Acierno, 1990, p. xxiii).

The most important opposition that Derrida deconstructs, according to Adams (1985), is that of signifier and signified, between the *concept* and the *image*. Derrida argues that the relation between the signified and the signifier is an arbitrary one. "To reduce the signifier to a signified and declare that this is what the signifier means is to privilege the signified over the signifier" (Adams, 1985, p. 27). To relate a signifier to one signified rather than another is a choice, and the specific reasons for doing so are a matter of opinion. Derrida argues that there is no signified that transcends the text, with the result that the text ceases to express or represent any polysemous truth.

By seriously questioning the tendency to ground our thinking in ultimates, a reality with a fixed, unquestionable meaning, deconstructionism challenges our whole conception of meaning in the West (Kugler, 1990). If "meaning is always deferred, perhaps to the point of an endless supplementarity, by the play of signification" (Norris, 1991, p. 32), is it possible to ground a psychic narrative in anything?

It is here, Miller (1989) says, that Jung and depth psychology is a major contributor in the 20th century to the revolution in the meaning of meaning, although the diction used by Jung masks the revolutionary nature of his thought. First of all, of all Jung's oppositions, I believe that there is a strong argument for claiming that the primary opposition on which he grounds his psychology is the opposition between conscious and unconscious. If we read him, according to Kugler (1990), as grounding the meaning of a psychic narrative in the unconscious, rather than in a transcendental signified, then Jung can be taken as postmodern and in line with deconstructionist linguistics.

Paradoxically, however, Jung's theory of the archetype at the same time may provide a bridge to the other.

Archetype as Absolute Other

Although the distinction is not always clear in some of his writing, it is nevertheless essential to remember the critical distinction that Jung, in the latter part of his life, makes

between archetype and archetypal idea. The archetype as such is a hypothetical and

irrepresentable model, something like the 'pattern of behaviour' in biology (Jung, 1959a). The

archetypal idea, on the other hand, is "an unconscious content that is altered by becoming

conscious and by being perceived, and it takes its colour from the individual consciousness in

which it happens to appear" (Jung, 1959a, p. 5). In other words, the archetype itself can never

be known, only the archetypal idea, which, through the process of becoming conscious,

already has been translated into an image or an idea. The archetype itself remains beyond

consciousness, beyond "absolute knowledge."

To Jung, the unconscious is the unknown, the unknowable. It is not a place; it is simply

what we are not conscious of. "The *concept* of the unconscious *posits nothing*; it designates only

my *unknowing*" (Jung, 1973, p. 411). Any knowledge of the unconscious, then, is already and

always a translation into consciousness through a representation, whether that be a word, an

image, a feeling, or a symptom. Always, "the meaning is bracketed by doubt and an attitude of

not knowing" (Kugler, 1990, p. 333). To recognize that we are always seeing through psyche is

to recognize that we are always in a paradigm and, because of that, that our ultimate meaning

is grounded in the unknown, in the unconscious.

How can we reconcile Jung's theory of the archetype as absolute other while at the same

time bridging the self other divide?

Archetype as Bridge Between Mind and Body

Jung postulates a hypothetical model of the archetype which includes both a biological

and a subjective pole. In this sense it is a theory which actually bridges mind and body. At

the biological pole, the archetype is, simply, a typical "pattern of behaviour" (Jung, 1976, p.

518) which distinguishes us as human, for example, rather, than as horse.

Jung's concept of the archetype may be elucidated by comparing it with theories in

biology and ethology. For example, Jung's insistence that it is not the behavior but the pattern

that is inherited is echoed in the ethologist Bowlby's statement that "instinctive behaviour is not inherited, what is inherited is the potential to develop . . . behavioural systems, both the nature and form of which differ in some measure according to the particular environment in which development takes place" (quoted in Stevens, 1983, p. 50). This, I believe, reflects exactly Jung's position on the difference between archetypes and archetypal images. The archetypal images and ideas manifest in individuals as idiosyncratic and as determined by a particular culture; nevertheless, recognizable patterns can be discerned.

The Subjective Pole of the Archetype.

Where Jung does differ from the ethologists, however, is in his interest in inner experience as well as outer behavior. Although the theory of the archetype includes both the biological and the psychic, it is to the subjective, feeling, psychic aspect of the archetype that Jung, being a psychiatrist and psychotherapist rather than a biologist, primarily has devoted his attention. It is because of this, I believe, that critics of Jung and many Jungians themselves overlook the fact that his theory also includes the biological aspect. For Jung, the subjective feelings of love that a mother experiences for her infant are part of the archetype, but manifesting in the psychic rather than the biological end of the pole.

This aspect of the archetype [is] the biological one. . . . But the picture changes at once when looked at from the inside, from within the realm of the subjective psyche. Here the archetype appears as a numinous factor, as an experience of fundamental significance. (Jung, 1976, p. 518)

What Jung is getting at is that subjective feeling and objective behavior are two different aspects of the same archetypal constellation. The experience of love, intuitive rapport, mutual fascination--the experience of mothering and being mothered--therefore, is as critical to the evolving dynamic of the mother-child relationship as are the behavioral cues.

Jung describes the formation of the archetypal symbol as the interplay between image and affect. The primal instinctual occurrences in life give rise to typical subjective ideational forms as well as highly charged emotions. These archetypal images which are aroused by the affects he describes as the psychic expression of the instinct, the form which the instinct assumes in consciousness. "What we properly call instincts are physiological urges, and are perceived by the senses. But at the same time, they also manifest themselves in fantasies and often reveal their presence only by symbolic images" (Jung, 1964, p. 69). Jung claims that it is through these archetypal images and ideas that psyche makes meaning of the instincts. "We may say that the image represents the *meaning* of the instinct" (Jung, 1960a, p. 201).

If the image represents the meaning of the instinct, then the archetypal image may provide a bridge between psyche and soma, between subject and object.

Archetypal Image as Bridge Between Subject and Object

As has become abundantly clear by now, Jung's view of the image is very different from Derrida's view of the relationship between concept and image. Derrida argues that the relation between the signified and the signifier is an arbitrary one and that there is no primary reality to copy beyond the linguistic term. No signified transcends the text. This has led to the conclusion that "all theories of knowledge are housed in language and work through figures of speech which render them ambiguous and indeterminate" (Kugler, 1997, p. 82). Hence we find ourselves "trapped in the solipsisms of language" (p. 83).

An alternative to this solipsism is found in a Jungian approach to psychic imaging. Jung conceives the image as central to the creation of our sense of psychic reality, and he conceives of this image as the mediator between subject and object.

> I do not contest the relative validity either of the realistic standpoint, the *esse in re*, or of the idealistic standpoint, the *esse in intellectu solo*; I would only like to unite these extreme opposites by an *esse in anima*, which is the psychological standpoint. We live immediately only in the world of images. (Jung, 1960b , pp. 327-328)

Today, Kugler (1997) claims, we would call such a position a mediating one between deconstruction and universalism .

Hillman has taken Jung's belief in the primacy of the image as the foundation of his archetypal psychology. As Avens (1980) puts it, in Hillman's work imagination "is not a separate faculty but essentially the realm of the *between* . . . whose primary function . . . is to relate the human with the non-human world" (p. 185).

Healing the Cartesian Split

A Jungian theory of the archetype argues, then, that mind and body are not two distinct entities but different aspects of the same archetypal constellation. In biology, Lorenz (1977) provides a very potent theory for bridging the mind-and-body split, and hence once again elucidates Jung's theory. Lorenz believes that our cognitive apparatus is itself a part of nature and not separate and distinct from nature, as it has been understood in Western philosophical and scientific thinking since Descartes. "The physiological mechanism whose function it is to understand the real world is no less real than the world itself" (p. 19). Lorenz's proposition, according to Stevens (1983), is that "our cognitive apparatus is *itself* an objective reality which has acquired its present form through *evolutionary adaptation to the real world*" (p. 59).

Lorenz (1977), with this insight, finds the essential flaw in Kant's conception of *a priori* categories. Lorenz writes about Kant: "He saw clearly that the forms of apprehension available to us are determined by the pre-existing structures of the experiencing subject and not by those of the object apprehended, but he did not see that the structure of our perceiving apparatus had anything to do with reality" (p. 9). Lorenz goes on to say:

> The system of sense organs and nerves that enables living things to survive and orientate themselves in the outer world has evolved phylogenetically through confrontation with and adaptation to that form of reality which we experience as phenomenological space. The system exists *a priori* to the extent that it is present before the individual perceives anything, and must be present if experience is to be possible. (p. 9)

When Jung calls the collective unconscious the phylogenetic psyche or the objective psyche, he is describing a phenomenon similar to that described by Lorenz: that is, that which we experience in consciousness in the form of image, or idea or felt experience has its roots in the biological other of nature itself. Because he was not a biologist, Jung was not able, as Stevens (1983) stresses, to substantiate his views with biological arguments, nor did he make such clear links between the objective psyche, the objective world, and "the consequent reality of our percepts" (p. 60), as does Lorenz.

However, Jung's *intuitive* understanding of the objective nature of the collective

unconscious and its co-extension with subjective experience was profound.

> This living being appears outwardly as the material body, but inwardly as a series of images of the vital activities taking place within it. They are two sides of the same coin, and we cannot rid ourselves of the doubt that perhaps this whole separation of mind and body may finally prove to be merely a device of reason for the purpose of conscious discrimination-- an intellectually necessary separation of one and the same fact into two aspects, to which we then illegitimately attribute an independent existence. (Jung, 1960b, p. 326)

The Archetype as Bridge Between Mind and Matter

In 1947 Jung extended his theory of the archetype to include its *psychoid* nature. With

this concept, Jung postulates that the archetype bridges not only instinct and image, feeling

and behavior, and mind and body, but also mind and matter. Jung (1960a) says that probably

"psyche and matter are two different aspects of one and the same thing" (p. 215). He

proposed, according to Stevens (1983), "that archetypal structures were fundamental to the

existence of all living organisms, and that they were continuous with structures controlling the

behaviour of inorganic matter" (p. 71). Hence, the archetype becomes "the bridge to matter in

general" (Jung, 1960a, p. 216), the psychoid archetype being the essential organic nucleus.

Pauli (1955), a physicist with whom Jung discussed these ideas, claims that Jung's

theory of the psychoid aspect of the archetype is some sort of "missing link" between the

mind of the scientist and the world the scientist studies. Pauli believes that there is a

relationship between the physical reality we perceive and our cognitive formulations of that

reality, and that the relationship is "predicated upon the fact that the soul of the perceiver and

that which is recognized by perception are subject to an order thought to be objective" (p. 152).

This is similar to Lorenz's idea that our cognitive apparatus is itself an actual reality because it

has, through evolution, come to bear the stamp of nature to which it has become adapted.

With not only mind and body but mind and matter envisioned as aspects of the same

entity, could not Jung's theory of the archetypes provide a bridge once again between *res*

cogitans and *res extensa*?

The paradox is this. Both Jung and postmodern philosophers agree that the nature of the other is unapprehendable. For the latter, the experience of absolute difference is similar to Jung's description of the experience of the unconscious as "totally unrecognizable and utterly unknowable" (Taylor, 1986, p. 28) This "other *as* other," this "difference" that is "irreducible to identity" comes close to what Jung calls the nonpsychic aspect of the archetype. The archetype itself cannot be grasped because in essence it is *nonpsychic.*

Self as Archetype

Yet, even as he concludes, as does postmodern philosophy, that the other is utterly unknowable, Jung nevertheless grounds the self in this unapprehendable archetypal realm. In a brilliant stroke of intuitive insight, he moves beyond postmodern thinking by including both the archetypal nucleus and subjective experience as "self-complementary antinomies" in his theoretical construct of the self, and thereby provides a way out of the nihilism to which the postmodern subject so readily succumbs.

Much of philosophy's description of the subject, although not all, corresponds more with what Jung describes as the ego. The modern philosopher's attempt to encompass all knowledge is an attempt to become fully conscious and to enjoy a "total presence that is undisturbed by absence or lack" (Taylor, 1986, p. 3).

What Jung describes as the self, however, sounds similar to the postmodern philosopher's description of the irrational other, for the self, an archetype of the collective unconscious, is *unconscious*, and hence can never be known.

The ego complex, which is formed out of this archetypal core, is associated with an individual identity and a personal life history. The self as the archetypal core of the ego complex gives rise to the experience of subjectivity in the first place. Yet the affect-laden experiences that come to form the loosely coherent collection of emotions, behaviors, attitudes, beliefs, and so on that form the ego complex depend on and reflect the specific personal and cultural history in which that complex arises. Hence it is through the ego complex, with the self as its archetypal nucleus, that the individual particulars of a person's life and the universal that transcends that life are united.

Synchronicity and the Psychoid Aspect of the Self Archetype

We cannot talk about the psychoid aspect of the self archetype without bringing in Jung's concept of synchronicity, which was his attempt to provide a theory for events that cannot be explained by causality. These synchronistic phenomena he defines as "the simultaneous occurrence of a certain psychic state with one or more external events which appear as meaningful parallels to the momentary subjective state--and, in certain cases, vice versa" (Jung, 1960c, p. 441)

As Jung has made abundantly clear, and I have described throughout this article, one can see only though psyche. There is no Archimedian point from which to look back at objective truth or objective meaning. Nevertheless, Jung (1960c) argues that we are driven to postulate the existence of objective or transcendent meaning if we are not to impute magic to synchronistic phenomena.

> The great difficulty is that we have absolutely no scientific means of proving the existence of an *objective* meaning which is not just a psychic product. We are, however, driven to some such assumption if we are not to regress to a *magical causality* and ascribe to the psyche a power that far exceeds its empirical range of action. (pp. 482-483)

Hence, "synchronicity is not a philosophical view but an empirical concept which postulates an intellectually necessary principle" (p. 512).

Jung draws on the nature of the psychoid aspect of the archetype in his explanation of synchronicity in that absolute or objective meaning is uniquely the property of this aspect. As I elaborated earlier, the psychoid is unconscious and unknowable and is an aspect not only of the human psyche, but also of matter. According to Bright (1997), psychoid refers to the "latent and unconscious meaning which exists in all matter, not just in the human psyche, and still less just in the conscious mind" (p. 618). The implications of such a theory are, as Bright (1997) argues, that meaning is not only a subjective creation but also has an objective a priori existence; that objective meaning exists in matter as well as mind; that it is collective and unconscious; and that it is possible, therefore, to look at meaning in archetypal terms. We can equally refer, says Bright, to the "psychoid nature of order" (p. 621). Here too, all events are ordered not only from a subjective perspective, but are related in an underlying objective way as well; order can not only be imputed, but is also a given; hence order is to be discovered as well as made.

This means that, as well as the subjective meaning we create in the interpretation of our images, and that would include our interpretation of the meaningful pattern of our lives, "there is also an underlying objective aspect of meaning which we therefore have to try to *find*; with the proviso that, as this aspect of meaning is essentially unconscious, it can never be fully elucidated or comprehended" (Bright, 1997, p. 619).

Whereas postmodern linguistics takes into account only the language of the ego, what Kugler (1982) and Jung point to is the possibility that there are two languages: the language of the ego and the language of the self, and that in contrast to the language of the ego, the imagistic and sonorous language of the self does have a meaningful, nonarbitrary connection to its referent. Jung's technique of active imagination is an attempt to engage in dialogue between the subjective and the objective psyche, the ego and the self.

The question that arises when thinking about the nature of such a dialogue is what happens to the image-meanings from the unconscious when they are transformed into verbal expression? Are we not prevented from understanding even this partial meaning from the objective psyche because our linguistic structures are already culturally loaded? Or does the objective psyche's mode of speech, which Kugler describes as metaphoric and poetical, speak to us from beyond our ego-bound subjectivity?

Kugler (1982), in The Alchemy of Discourse, tackles this question by drawing on the word-association work carried out by Jung in his days at the Burghölzi Institute. He describes how Jung in his early work on word association discovered an innate connection between logos and image. What he found was that the language of the unconscious is not the syntactic,

contiguous speech of consciousness, but is instead sonorous and phonetic. Jung concludes
that "subconscious association process takes place through *similarities of image and sound*" (p.
17). Based on his own research, Kugler concludes that "unconscious image-meanings tend to
cluster around elemental units of sound" (1982, p.115), and that "the archetypal world is
presented directly through the *imago mundi*, which can be heard as well as seen" (p. 28).

The conscious encounter with the self which is activated by the conscious dialogue
between ego, and the images that emerge in dream and reverie, are a primary means of
awakening one to the acceptance of an organizing principle beyond the ego. An apprehension
of the self is an apprehension of the objective psyche and the psychoid nature of the archetype.
It is an apprehension of nature, the other, out of which we have evolved. As Hillman (1985)
put it, "anima is nature now conscious of itself through reflection" (p. 87). It is nature
becoming conscious of itself through us. Contrary to a postmodern belief that there is no
possibility of apprehending nature, the other, Jung's theory of the psychoid aspect of the
archetype and his discovery of the image as bridge to the unconscious points to the conclusion
that we are inextricably a part of nature. "'At bottom' the psyche is simply 'world'. In this
sense I hold Kerényi to be absolutely right when he says that in the symbol the *world itself* is
speaking" (Jung, 1959b, p. 173). Our seeming separation is an illusion based on the myth of
Newtonian science and the analytical and quantifying function of the ego.

Postmodernism and the Individuation Process

It is a momentous shift in consciousness when the ego comes to see through its
constructed state and the symbolic environment becomes visible. As Becker (1995) says, it is
one of the great, liberating breakthroughs of all time.

For many postmodernists, this great liberating breakthrough of consciousness has led to
a recognition that one is constructed by language, by narrative, by power, by one's society and
consequently, for many, it also has led to the mistrust of subjective experience. In fact, it has
led some to the denial of subjectivity altogether.

Jung also sees through psyche, recognizing that one is structured by one's complexes (and hence by society) as well as by the archetypes, or inherent patterns of behavior grounded in biology. This understanding made him warn against identifying with one's subjective experience. "Though I am sure of my subjective experience, I must impose on myself every conceivable restriction in interpreting it. I must guard against identifying with my subjective experience. I consider all such identifications as serious psychological mistakes" (1975, p. 376).

What is different about Jung's statement to those coming out of postmodern philosophy, however, is that although Jung (1975) sees through his subjectivity, he does not give up his grounding in subjectivity. He says, "though I am *sure* of my subjective experience" (p. 376). He is able to recognize that he cannot *but* see through psyche, without denigrating that subjective experience.

He can trust his experience because, as Edinger (1996) says, "The ego almost always is contained in the objective psyche in an invisible way" (p. 33). The objective psyche exists as a containing medium. Hence we are always in some way in that archetypal realm, which is both psychic and biological and beyond the human altogether. At this level we are, as Lorenz argues, beyond Kant, for one recognizes not only that one's forms of apprehension are determined by pre-existent structures of the experiencing subject, but that the structure of our perceiving apparatus is itself a part of nature.

Jung's theory of the collective unconscious and the psychoid aspect of the archetype reconnects us to something which transcends the ego and hence, even though we can never fully know what that other is, an experience of the autonomous psyche has the potential for healing the subject-object split.

This reconnection to self or objective psyche that constitutes Jung's theory provides practical approaches which speak directly to the feelings of alienation, despair, emptiness, loss of meaning and "chronic, undifferentiated emotional hunger" (Cushman, 1995, p. 49) that inhabit us and the souls of our patients. For when we or our clients reach that stage of development in which we awaken to the fictional nature of our world and recognize that what we have taken as true is actually a world that is constructed, a Jungian psychology provides the framework for building a bridge across this existential abyss.

We may have outgrown the old gods, but we have not outgrown the need to be in relationship to, and derive meaning from, that which transcends us. As David Miller (1990) argues, Jung's discovery of the autonomous psyche "opens [us] to Otherness as a possibility in the time of the death of the ego (the subject), in the time of the death of symbolisms (object-relations), and in the time of the death of other gods as well" (p. 329).

References

Adams, M. (1985). Deconstructive philosophy and imaginal psychology: Comparative perspectives on Jacques Derrida and James Hillman. In Journal of Literary Criticism, 2(1), 23-29.

Avens, R. (1980). Heidegger and archetypal psychology. In International Philosophical Quarterly, 22, 183-202.

Barnaby, K., & D'Acierno, P. (1990). C. G. Jung and the humanities. Princeton: Princeton University Press.

Becker, E. (1995). The fragile fiction. In W. Anderson (Ed.), The truth about the truth (pp. 34-35). New York: Jeremy P. Tarcher/Putnam Books.

Bright, G. (1997). Synchronicity as a basis of analytic attitude. In Journal of Analytical Psychology, 42(4), 613-635.

Cushman, P. (1995). Constructing the Self, constructing America. New York: Addison-Wesley Publishing .

Edinger, E. F. (1996). The new God image. Wilmette, IL: Chiron Publications.

Hillman, J. (1985). Anima: An anatomy of a personified notion. Dallas: Spring Publications.

Jung, C. G. (1958). Psychological commentary on "The Tibetan book of the great liberation". In The collected works of C.G. Jung (Vol. 11) (R.F.C. Hull, Trans.). Princeton, NJ: Princeton University Press.

Jung, C. G. (1959a). Archetypes of the collective unconscious. In The collected works of C.G. Jung (Vol. 9, Pt.1) (R.F.C. Hull, Trans.). Princeton, NJ: Princeton University Press.

Jung, C. G. (1959b). The psychology of the child archetype. In The collected works of C.G. Jung (Vol. 9, Pt.1) (R.F.C. Hull, Trans.). Princeton, NJ: Princeton University Press.

Jung, C. G. (1960a). On the nature of the psyche. In The collected works of C.G. Jung (Vol. 8) (R.F.C. Hull, Trans.). Princeton, NJ: Princeton University Press.

Jung, C. G. (1960b). Spirit and life. In The collected works of C.G. Jung (Vol. 8) (R.F.C. Hull, Trans.). Princeton, NJ: Princeton University Press.

Jung, C. G. (1960c). Synchronicity: an acausal connecting principle. In The collected works of C.G. Jung (Vol. 8) (R.F.C. Hull, Trans.). Princeton, NJ: Princeton University Press.

Jung, C. G. (1964). Man and his symbols. New York: Doubleday & Company

Jung, C. G. (1973). Letters (Vol. 1). G. Adler and A. Jaffé (Eds.). Princeton: Princeton University Press.

Jung, C. G. (1975). Letters (Vol. 2). G. Adler and A. Jaffé (Eds.). Princeton: Princeton University Press.

Jung, C. G. (1976). Foreword to Harding: "Woman's mysteries." In The collected works of C.G. Jung (Vol. 18) (R.F.C. Hull, Trans.). Princeton, NJ: Princeton University Press.

Kugler, P. (1982). The alchemy of discourse. London & Toronto: Associated University Press.

Kugler, P. (1997). Psychic imaging: A bridge between subject and object. In P. Young-Eisendrath, & T. Dawson (Eds.), The Cambridge companion to Jung (pp. 71-85). Cambridge: Cambridge University Press.

Lorenz, K. (1977). Behind the mirror: A search for a natural history of human knowledge. London: Methuen.

Miller, D. (1989). The 'stone' which is not a stone: C.G. Jung and the postmodern meaning of 'meaning'. Spring, 110-122.

Norris, C. (1991). Deconstruction: Theory and practice. London: Routledge.

Pauli, W. (1955). The influence of archetypal ideas on the scientific theories of Kepler. In C. G. Jung & W. Pauli, The Interpretation of Nature and the Psyche (pp. 147-240). London: Routledge & Kegan Paul.

Stevens, A. (1983). Archetypes: A natural history of the self. New York: Quill.

Taylor, M. C. (1986). Introduction: System . . . structure . . . difference . . . other. In M. C. Taylor (Ed.), Deconstruction in context (pp. 1-34). Chicago: The University of Chicago Press.

The Alchemy of Cement by Roberto Gambini, Ph.D.

Three years ago there was an art exhibit in São Paulo, the place where I live, called *Art and City*. The artists chose not an art gallery or a museum, but a decadent building right in the heart of the town and produced a kind of artwork that would dialogue with that decayed environment. As I began my visit, I felt something moving in my belly -- I knew some idea, image or understanding wanted to find its way up to the mind. I told my wife -- always the first recipient -- that maybe we were looking at an alchemical series, and I was ready to check if that would hold true. The *prima materia* was cement, and art the *opus*.

São Paulo, with eighteen million inhabitants, is the third largest city in the world, second only to Tokyo (twenty-seven million) and Bombay (eighteen and a half). In underdeveloped megacities (Ciudad de Mexico too) thousands of tons of cement are erected randomly, reflecting an unconscious use of chaotic but powerful energy. One and a half centuries ago São Paulo was but a village. In a relatively short time it became a titanic conglomerate of concrete and people, with all the problems that modern cities display, from criminality to poor housing, traffic jams, inadequate infra structure, low quality of life, ugliness, sick air, and dirty water.

The problem is that our minds are structured in such a way that we no longer associate city and soul, but city and engineers. Solutions now arise not from the imagination of soul, but from city planners. But if this is possible, only a radical shift in our collective consciousness could produce anything like a solution. Only soul can give us a new understanding and a new reading of the city.

Here is the edge of my thought: São Paulo, as any other place, has an unconscious. If the city is sick, as a Jungian I would say that its unconscious is trying to express its condition through symbolic images that might lead to a transcendence of the pathological state -- very much as we believe happens to our patients. Artists would be the ones to dream the dream of the city, as they are able to contact a very deep level from where they fish up to consciousness symbols and images that they present to us through their art. I don't expect them to lecture about what they work with, nor to interpret it -- they just make it. They bring out new images and new forms and it is up to us to integrate those new contents into the tissue of collective consciousness. My belief is that if some of us do that, maybe this conscious framework might change its standpoint.

Let us now begin to imagine the city. We start with an aerial view of downtown São Paulo, so you can locate the exhibit area. It is the area in which European immigrants settled at the time of industrialization and growing urbanization, from 1890 onwards, along the main stations of the railway that connected the town to the countryside and the seaport. There is a kind of island formed by two branches of the railroad and this is where the exhibit took place, in a flour mill built in 1940, a place in which wealth and modernity were generated.

You cannot enter this area by foot or car. It is a forbidden garden; not the *ortus reclusus*, but the garden of shadow, a refuge to drug addicts, robbers and homeless hoodlums. The remnants of the empty mill lie there today as a precocious ruin -- no roof, no windowpanes, garbage, debris and infiltration all over the place. You have to take a train to visit the exhibit - something we did in our childhood. Today only the poor use it to reach their faraway homes. Let us "look" at the slides now.

There was no war in Brazil, but it looks as if it had been bombed in World War II. Pathological growth creates these kinds of modern ruins. In this worn-out place, images of the soul will be revealed through art. The soul has chosen exactly this kind of place to speak about itself, telling us what is happening to it. It didn't go to the museum, the University, the Church, or the local Jungian society. Only here can we come into contact with it.

This is the opening work: a long red plastic veil covering an angle of the building from top to bottom. At its right, an open lift goes up and down incessantly. On the floor, we read: "São Paulo has 50 kilometers of underground lines, 250 km of railroads and 1600 km of lift cables." Here we have the vertical trip, an up and down daily movement carried out by millions of people who actually fail to make any connection between Heaven and Earth, since this kind of claustrophobic ascension does not lead to the heights of understanding or vision, since it is encapsulated and completely verticality. The soul of the city, like Sisyphus, is condemned to this never-ending trip that leads always to the starting point.

Now there are three empty silos that were cut at their base, forming three huge cauldrons. This is where I first had a feeling in my bowels. All three were filled with putrid water. In the first, the skeleton of a cow lies half sunken; in the second, air bubbles come to the surface and in the third, black charcoal chunks float about. I believe I can say an *opus* begins here, with the *nigredo* of dead water. The rivers that cross the town and the psychic waters of the imagination are dead. What is said here is that this water must be filtered and aired -- *pneuma* is the first element that is needed to start a process of recovery.

The second work is called **Shelter** -- a cubic, compact pile of railroad ties. There is no inside space, you can't get into it for protection. Once upon a time, the railroad was a vehicle of growth and the accumulation of wealth, but now it recoils upon itself and closes up like a shell, a shelter that houses no one. So it must be the alchemical house that cannot be found literally, only in the imagination. This house is one which the citizens feel they live with human rights, dignity and the awareness of participation in shaping the city, not as outcasts. We have too many houses, but these houses don't house us any longer. Outer dwellings provide no protection and no roof; the house we need is built in a non-material realm.

From the **Shelter** that is no shelter we go to **The House of Lanterns**, actually, a descent to Hades. An enormous hall was completely dark, full of dirt and smelling of urine. As you walked through it, censors activate audio tapes that would fill the space with the sound of dogs barking, children crying, police sirens, gunshots, and enraged bees. As you wander in this inhospitable underground place, you might think that if anything can be done to the city, it has to start with a public recognition of its shadow, going into it, looking at it and ceasing to attribute violence or criminality only to the character of bad people. All these problems are born from the shadow, which means the collective radical injustice and society's incapacity to provide dignified forms of human life. All this is conveyed by this very awesome hall, which in the past was a workshop.

Now we come to a piece done directly upon cement. The artist drilled on the concrete floor hundreds of holes, orthogonally disposed, and in each one he fixed plastic syringes filled with liquid mercury. In the middle there was a disproportionately big crack pipe and the visitor would say "Ha ha, this is an allusion to the drug problem." So what then? But we can read this in another way: cement needs an injection of mercury. It has to be injected with *spiritus mercurius*, the spirit of transformation. For anything new to happen in the city, this is a prerequisite. And where is this mercury? In us, the inhabitants, in our capacity to see through. Now, crack has to do with repressed imagination and its substitutes. A street teenager once said to a colleague who works with juvenile delinquents: "I so much want a pair of Nike tennis shoes. As I don't have the 50 dollars to buy it, with one dollar I smoke crack and then it feels like I have them." Crack is the opposite of mercury. If the *spiritus mercurius* puts imagination on the move, crack is what does it in the absence of mercury. Our urban problem is the repression of the imaginal, so this mercury injected into cement will awaken images that have been fossilized, calcified or petrified together with the hardening of cement and concretism, very much as it happened in Pompeii, where one sees casts of people caught in their flight by volcanic lava, corpses forever. Likewise, our soul is imprisoned inside cement casts with which we build shelters that cannot contain it in movement.

The next work is done with old photographs of the flour mill, printed on copper plates and superimposed with contemporary shots taken from the same angle. The metal was then corroded with acid. When you look at it you have an awkward feeling about time, the corrosion of clear, clean images. Two lines of thought occurred to me: one is that in cities like ours, time runs so fast that you cannot superimpose images 40 years apart. Something corrodes the identity of what once was and now is. This is no good for the soul, because it likes to identify places and remember them as they were. This of course is a superficial reading. But we could also say: in the alchemy of cement, in a city that was so proud of being the fastest growing in the world -- São Paulo loves cement -- images must be corroded. The city cannot think of itself nowadays as a miracle, as a heroic achievement. This image of economic success has to be corroded so that another image might take its place. If we remain stuck to images of a pre-soul period, we cannot really talk the language of soul.

Now we come to a very strong work. The artist used a powerful saw and cut out three huge squares on the concrete floor, or ceiling, depending on which floor you are. He then suspended them with steel cables exactly below each opening. When you look at it you say "OK, here we have a pendulum, and we can peer into the other floor." But if you let imagination carry you, you understand that here alchemy is breaking compartments, mixing the substances from above and below and commenting on the way we all live inside compartment boxes, unaware of what goes on high up or deep down. Now this pendulum would obey not engines, not the city's rhythms, but the Earth's rotation.

Another artist simply made a big pile of sand upon a tiny hole on the concrete floor, allowing it to slowly fall down to the floor below, where a new pile, exactly like the one above, would form. The exhibit was open for thirty days, and this was the time it took for the sand to rearrange itself in a new edition. The immediate association is of course the sand clock, again a reference to slow time. But there is more to it. We were proud of our timing. As we are not New Yorkers, we cannot say time is money, but we could boast that we were very fast in catching up with the big American cities. The number of houses that we built inflated our metropolitan ego. But now we have come to the conclusion that this crazy race led us nowhere. We ran so fast to reach something we wanted so much, but now we are afraid. Here in this art work something is saying, "Go back to a slower pace. Break down cement to sand again. Use this sand to build again, but with another dream." The *prima materia* is here separated into one of its components. As we know from sandplay therapy, sand is a very good medium to let the unconscious express itself, it invites the soul to play.

Now we enter a huge, empty hall from whose frameless windows a devastated part of the city can be seen. Here and there a dozen beds are displayed, consisting of iron structures covered by pewter bed coverings. Upon each bed, a certain amount of bread dough was spread. The Freudian divan comes to mind. This bread did not go to the oven to be baked. Instead, this stuff of life ferments, deteriorates and putrefies without ever becoming food for the soul, which again can be taken as a message from the anorexic soul of the city, that has been built does not feed it. There has been no oven, no warmth of compassion, no tenderness, no warm feelings to bake this aborted dough into true bread, into daily bread. The dough lies waiting for the analyst to act upon its free associations, which I am trying to make myself on its behalf.

In this next room the artist built a path of pebbles surrounded by water. On the walls he fixed photographs of a naked black man who posed for the camera exactly on the same spot where the pictures are displayed. In alchemy there is a character known as the Ethiopian, the black man. He stands for everything a Middle Age Christian was not, his other side, his unlived side. Black people receive the projection of all the elements that whites could not integrate, be they positive qualities or shadow aspects. This black man is the **other** inhabitant of the city, the other citizen, whose voice has not yet been heard. Now here he makes his appearance, as if in Pompeii's Villa dei Misteri, in whose walls initiation rites were painted for those who could read them.

Now we enter a room that looks like a shoe repair workshop. Hundreds of shoes hang on the wall, but just one foot. Executive leather shoes, tennis shoes, high heels, kid's shoes. You think: "They forgot to pick them up from repair." You could remember an accident on a road, a lost shoe on the asphalt, or a Gestapo chamber with a pile of shoes in the corner. But you could also think that this is a symbol of one-sidedness, as if the soul were saying that in the city everything is one-sided, has only one foot. That way we can't go very far. Where are the missing shoes?

The next work is a styrofoam block under strong spotlights hanging very close to it. During the exhibit, the warmth of the bulbs slowly carved little niches or nests or wombs for new contents to be hatched.

Now we come to another huge, empty hall. The artist hangs on the walls four big pictures, like outdoors, close-ups of a plate with cheap food, the kind of ready made dish of food that millions of people eat everyday. Alchemically speaking, what I can say is: like any metropolis, São Paulo attracts jobless people from all over the country, as it did waves of European immigrants -- my grandparents, for instance. Millions undergo extreme forms of hardship pursuing the dream of a house, but what most get is just this, a cheap plate of food. Is this all life is about? Alchemy was not concerned with food for the stomach, but food for the soul. And where is one food or the other? Where is the food that the city can feed us? The plate is empty of psychic food. As James Hillman noted this morning when he was setting the table for the conference, we need beauty, we need justice, we need a sense of destiny. Not just rice and beans, and no dessert.

In the corridors, the workmen who cleaned the place for the exhibit separated the various components of the huge mass of debris that filled the whole building into piles of homogenous elements. Broken bricks, broken tiles, pieces of fragmented concrete, tin foil, dirty sand, earth, pipes. A true **separatio**. The whole atmosphere was alchemical! People in Brazil don't know about Jungian psychology; I doubt that more than a few architects have read a book on archetypal imagination, so they are not playing cards with this, they are not trying to be fancy or fashionable. I am talking about alchemy, but the artists were not. But I believe it is not a mind game or a trip to observe that something unknown manifests itself when people try to express something through art.

Now a canvas covered with blue. I dare not say anything new about the alchemical blue, or the blue fire. I am content to remember that blue is transcendence, blue is higher understanding. After you go through this maze of horrors, you end up looking at this plain blue, which would turn your mind to infinity perhaps, to possible ways of transcending a gigantic urban mistake that we have made.

And now we come to the end. The artist chose the inner chamber of one of the few brick chimneys that survived urban development and still stands there as a reminder of a past era of frantic industrialization. The culture department wants to preserve this chimney as a monument. Visitors had to wear one of those red plastic helmets used for security by builders. You would go inside the chimney, sit on a bench, look up and see light in the sky. The only artistic intervention was the sound of a flute. And I thought: now this flute music will come out of the chimney as a musical smoke. Maybe a cloud, not of pollution, but of feeling, will at last cover the city. As a closing of

the *opus*, I understood that a city such as this can only be healed if it is seen under a cloud of compassion and love.

South and Archetypal Psychology: The Brazilian Experience by Gustavo Barcellos, Ph.D.

> *Départ dans l'affection et le bruit neufs.*
> ("Departure in new affection and new noise.")
> Arthur Rimbaud, Illuminations

I.

The last 15 years have seen Archetypal Psychology's ideas growing stronger in the Brazilian Jungian community. During these years I have translated many of Dr. Hillman's books. Since 1985, when we began with Inter Views, I have been engaged in the translations, or revisions of translations, nine up to now, of what has always seemed to us his most important works. Sometimes I have edited selections that appeared in book form only in the Brazilian editions. That was the case, most significantly, of City and Soul, when we put together the many essays he wrote concerning the broad question of the *anima mundi*. That edition was particularly interesting since it appeared in a collection of books addressed especially to architects. These books dealt mostly with architectural and urban issues. I have since witnessed the interest the book aroused, which brought about what was for them a totally new and intriguing way to reflect upon questions of the city life, a way that would include this difficult word "soul." Some of them were my patients, either teachers at the University of São Paulo, or people engaged professionally in the city departments of urban affairs. So, apart from the discussions the book and its ideas brought for psychotherapists and Jungian analysts, it was for me a pleasure in itself to see Jungian and Archetypal thought, with its main interest in soul, enter discussions and shake ideas in other fields of study.

Later we brought together in another collection the most important essays Dr. Hillman wrote on the phenomenology and psychology of the *puer/senex* archetype. We have called it The Puer Book. We thought the effort to get together these essays in one single book would meet and clarify the most common and insidious critique Archetypal Psychology in general and Dr. Hillman's work in particular meet in Brazil: that it's the work of the *puer* archetype, revision for revision's sake. The *puer* impulse is seen by some Jungians in Brazil to be so unbearably strong in Archetypal Psychology that we would end up losing the psychology (they mean, clinical/analytical psychology) for the archetypal — in this case the *archetypal* force of the *puer archetype* in its radically revisionistic rhetoric. *Horribile dictu*, the polytheistic rhetoric of Archetypal Psychology gets confused with a monotheism of the *puer*. This critique senses that we actually end up with what is seen otherwise as "literature," or as "art" — or, in classical Jungian terms, what would be called *"anima* possession." Of course, we have here the same "old" *senex* view of the *puer*; but in this case, I think we do not need to understand it in the simple terms of compensation— a *puer* culture that cannot stand up for its *puer* energy, thus clinging to the *senex* — but rather in terms of fear. Most Jungians in **Brazil**, from former generations, are psychiatrists, and they feel extremely afraid of emptying out their consulting rooms (and so having nobody to work with) if they lose were to lose their medical imagination.

The other major critique attacks polytheism itself, now seen as fragmentation, and thus essentially contrary to its particular understanding of the Jungian idea of *individuation*: unitary wholeness of the personality. Here I do understand it to be a monotheistic compensation in a culture where a polytheistic cult(ure) lies, idiosyncratically, right below the Christian collective set of conscious values, beliefs and practices. Brazil is the largest Catholic country in the world; but it is as well a place where a polytheistic religion — the Afro-Brazilian religion of the Orixás — is alive and largely practiced everyday with such a power that, unlike other places, it also dwells strongly in urban areas, in the cities, psychotherapy's enthroned territory since the beginning. Of course, it is not always practiced literally in rituals by everyone; but it certainly is, and most importantly, in deeper levels, in the mind, in psyche, in *thinking* and *feeling* processes. This is naturally a peculiar state of things, to which I want to call attention and shall comment more upon later. Here we begin our attempt at a little characterization of the Brazilian way of imagining and living soul. Soul has been saying something there, exactly, I suspect, with this interplay of paradigms; for this reason I feel my words need to turn inevitably to geography — *imaginal geography* I mean, or a geography of **images** — if we are to listen to new *anima* noises.

The interest in forming groups to study Archetypal Psychology in many cities in Brazil, its approach to Jungian theory, to clinical issues and to cultural reflection, is also growing with the years, and I have had the opportunity to conduct seminars throughout the country. This work with groups has been extremely interesting for, although it does not have any explicit therapeutic character, the activity certainly surpasses the theoretical discussion, bringing to everyone involved an opportunity to reflect and be changed, due, to the richness and the intense creative aspect of Archetypal Psychology's ideas. Of course, I could feel that in Bahia, for instance, where the religious **polytheistic practices** are stronger and more traditional, the understanding of a psychology based on soul, its policentricity and sensuality, is more immediate and, to my surprise, this psychology directly reaches out even to people with no comprehensive reading of Jung.

Other authors of Archetypal Psychology have also been translated and absorbed by those special Jungians opened to Archetypal Psychology in Brazil, and the works by Dr. Rafael Lopez-Pedraza, our Cuban turned-into-South-American dear friend, are particularly among the most discussed and searched for. And we now have a website on the Internet, *Rubedo*, which is focused mainly on what is called "post-Jungian" authors, with a special interest in Archetypal Psychology, bringing in translation its most important debates.

So I think it's now the right time, and maybe here is the right place, as Dr. Hillman himself has asked me, to be evaluating where and how Archetypal

Psychology was accepted or rejected in Brazil, the Brazilian experience of Archetypal Psychology — but I would like also to add a reflection on the way Brazil is accepted or rejected by Archetypal Psychology. At the threshold of a new psychological age, I believe the Brazilian experience can help Archetypal Psychology re-think one of its most fundamental metaphors: "south."

II.

This presentation wants thus to concentrate upon the idea of "**south**" at the turning of the new millennium: it is an attempt at re-imagining Archetypal Psychology's celebrated *southward* direction. But, to attempt an archetypal re-vision of the idea of "south" in our psychology, to give it a deeper significance in our lives, we should not at all go by the way of simple reversion, simply putting north-south upside down, trying for a moment to disturb optics and **soul**, seeing "south" as "superior." That would be "psychopathic geography": south in the place of **north** and nothing is really changed in our perspective. Nor would I wish to fall here once again into "those tiresome dilemmas of North and South" (Hillman, 1998, p. 11) — historical geography. No; to be sure, I want to avoid the rhetoric of oppression altogether (so archetypal for the relations between North and South, and so paradigmatic to our continent, the Americas, as Dr. Hillman brilliantly expanded on the one occasion he spoke of South-America, in his article "Culture and the Animal Soul"), for that too would be to continue looking at these issues from the northern perspective, and so remain in a "*money*theism" of the North. I would like to attempt a step forward.

In Brazil, of course, we are inclined to see "south" as still a great metaphor for depth psychology in general. We cannot escape the feeling of "south," into which we are born; so we need to reflect upon it, that is, create ever-new images. The mythologem "New", for instance — New World, new land — as well as the mythologem "Antarctic" (from the Latin *antarcticu*) —

not-Arctic, anti-Arctic, anti-north, opposed to the Arctic pole of our planetary *rotundum* — although we may be still trapped in them, are no longer sufficient, no longer speak to the soul. Did they ever? "Newness" is the *prison* of the Americas, as Dr. Hillman pointed out so surely; and "Antarctic" is, of course, the rhetoric of negation. So maybe the mythologem "South" can be more affirmative, and would thus have more to say about soul in general, about us in particular, and more to say to the theoretical imagination of Archetypal Psychology. Revelation, not contrast, or conflict — sociological and otherwise. Again, not historical geography; *imaginal geography*.

Archetypal Psychology has brought back this metaphor, "south," to make a major theoretical move. This move has to do with the turning of the West-East axis into a North-South axis, which for Jungian psychology meant that we no longer had to go East to go deep. We all know the significance and the power of the south metaphor: it is truly archetypal. Since Freud and the early days of psychoanalysis it was *the* place to go when imagining a direction towards the unconscious, towards soul: the vertical direction. To find soul we go down: personal memories, childhood, ancient mythologems, complexes, archetypal reality — all this is imagined to be stored deep down inside, the "south" of ourselves. True character is also imagined to be down inside our acts. And we must not forget, this "south" stands as well for the lower part of the body.

Since the psycho-topographical descriptions of Freudian days — and Freud was the first in our tradition to bring a topographical, or geographical, imagination to psychology — the downward direction is, simultaneously with the inward direction, *the* way to follow in Psychology's imagination (regardless of the school) when psychic reality is to be found, nourished and understood: we go down, we go 'south,' either in the individual, or the culture. We all know that in his <u>Brief Account of Archetypal Psychology,</u> Dr. Hillman imagined this direction even further in his geographical *poiesis* and said that it, Archetypal Psychology, "starts in the South" (Hillman, 1985, p. 30). He also wrote that "venturing South is a journey for explorers" (Hillman, 1975, p. 223). Old or young, yes, Mr. Eliot, we should turn into explorers: International Geographic.

But this "south" was meant to be essentially the Mediterranean culture: from Greek myths to Renaissance civilization, philosophy and modes of living. They are imaginal sources that brought sensual as well as tragic perspectives to psychology and to psychotherapy.

In Brazil we are well aware of all this, for we too start in the "south." My main point here is that now, beyond Mediterranean culture, this archetypal "south" can be re-imagined. Brazilian South-American syncretic polytheistic **culture** shines and, in itself, continues to offer a challenge for Archetypal Psychology regarding "south" as a cultural, ethnic and imaginal location, a region of the soul, beyond what it has already acknowledged as "south." I suggest that beyond what Dr. James Hillman showed us of value for psychology in Mediterranean classical culture, cultures below the Equator (such as Brazilian culture) can help Archetypal Psychology continue to imagine even more radically its fundamental metaphorical direction in thought and research. Why Archetypal Psychology did not go on in its southward imagining?

We remember Dr. Hillman reminding us that what we formulate as Psychology "emerged from the Protestantism of northern and western Europe and its extension westward into North America" (Hillman, 1975, p. 219). *Northern* Europe, *North* America. *Northern* Psychology. We all know now how *north* we are when we speak psychology, and how much to avoid "north" was indeed necessary to move psychology *soulwards*.

Maybe that is the reason why I want to talk about south — first because I live, work and come from what in Psychology's main perspective is called the "south"; but also, and most important, because perhaps re-imagining south is a way of re-imagining soul. For me, that would essentially mean to continue imagining soul, while continuing imagining world; for soul, as we all well know, is what is continually imagining in us. Again, why does not this "south" enter in Archetypal Psychology's image of the world? Psychology cannot stop short at its first south. It seems essential that the soul continues to be imagined so that we can find more and more images, more reflections, in theory and in practice (as well as in the world) to recognize its presence and its works in our lives. So, I want to suggest with these lines that maybe *south* and *soul* have yet more in common than has already dreamed our psychology, even our Archetypal Psychology. In these brief notes I want to call attention to the Brazilian way of imagining soul, affection, culture and psychology and how it can respond to the challenge of an archetypal perspective.

I believe this discussion is so central to our psychology that I want to recall when it states that what divides North and South in our tradition — transalpine and cisalpine mentalities and psychological landscapes, Reformation and Renaissance — are, in one image, mountains. The Alps, as Dr. Hillman stressed many times, with all those *albedo* tops. So we are still, metaphorically, in Europe — even when we speak psychology in places like Brazil. We continue to divide our souls into what Dr. Hillman called the Hebraic **monotheistic consciousness** and Hellenic **polytheistic consciousness**. Hebraic, Hellenic (or Hillmanian): it seems there is no way out of that division — even when we speak Archetypal Psychology. We are, psychologically speaking, either monotheistic or polytheistic, with the Gods or without the Gods.

I want to speak here of a *south souther than south*, in what is now an alchemical mode of speaking. I want to point, *first*, towards a division that makes itself felt by the presence of nothing less than an *ocean* — one would say, an Atlantic gap. Here we are, I believe, with the central images for this talk — for I am trying all along to think in images, the pagan mode. What then divides northern Europe (even its Iberian or Mediterranean — Latin — consciousness) and tropical South-American Brazil is an ocean, that is, an enormous amount of salt water, which indicates, of course, an Atlantic (that is, titanic) distance, and certainly more profound projections — a deeper unknowing. "Mountains" and "ocean" speak for the imaginal difference in the division: when we speak *mountains*, even in psychology, we are still, somehow or somewhere, inevitably involved in the rhetoric of the spirit; what we have to trespass is, nonetheless, The Spirit, as if psychology had to "jump" the spirit, lose all those abstract conceptualizations and borrowed language, to meet the very soul it wants to engender. Whereas when we speak an *ocean*, maybe the soul is immediately closer, that is, its presence not mediated, already given by the image, already given in the imagination; perhaps water, in this case, has more to do with soul than air, for souls take pleasure in moisture, that is, the soul is aroused by water (in a Venusian sense), even if we go on recalling Heraclitus when he says that the *dry* soul is the wisest.

But, *secondly*, I want to talk about Brazil as a place where the division "monotheistic/polytheistic" is in fact, and in psyche, no longer operative. It is my impression that maybe it has never been really operative since the beginning. The Afro-Brazilian polytheism (along with all its different ramifications) is very much alive *inside* the monotheism of the Christian official culture in Brazil, even though more conscious in some parts of the country than in others. Some speak here of paradox, others of tolerance, or **syncretism**; some attack this very syncretism, trying to purify influences; others celebrate it. The psychological reality in Brazil indicates, anyway, this peculiar syncretic state of soul.

Of course, one way to understand it is as one clear result of the melting of the three absolutely different races that originally combined to form Brazilian people: the American Indian, the Portuguese and the African slave. Alchemy again, *coniunctio* as *solutio*: black, white and red — the three basic colors in the alchemical *opus* — as rotating colors *in* the soul.

This "south" represented by Brazilian culture can thus, in my view, offer Archetypal Psychology a *coniunctio* of the two polarities that makes us immediately escape from thinking in polarities — which perhaps points to another step in the world *opus*.

III.

"South" has always been emblematic for psychology, especially for depth psychology. Dr. Hillman himself admitted that "going South means leaving our psychological territory at the risk of archetypal disorientation" (Hillman, 1975, p. 223). We know Freud and Jung did pathologize when they attempted going towards their "souths" — Italy and Greece. Jung, in old age, fainted at the railroad station when he was finally buying tickets to go to Rome. The trip never took place. When writing about Italy, in his autobiography, he mentions unexpected things becoming conscious, "unforeseen vistas opened," and questions posed "which were beyond my powers to handle" (Jung, 1965, p. 288). Paradoxically, "south" is *the* psychological route and destination *par excellence* and, at the same time, it seems to inevitably bring with it some pathologizing.

And not only for psychology. We may recall just a few examples: Rimbaud, who renounced poetry forever, went to Africa and was never Rimbaud anymore, returning to Europe ill, to die young back in Marseilles; Henri Cartier-Bresson, whose voyage in Africa was characterized as an *échec*, a failure, but gave him the "eyes" he needed for profound photography; Claude Levy-Strauss traveling his *tristes tropiques*; Pierre Verger, the superb French photographer and writer who lived in Africa and in Brazil, who had to assume another *persona*, another faith, another name (Fatumbi) to find himself, and became an initiate into the Yoruba Candomblé of Bahia; André Gide in the Congo, who had to turn into an "immoralist," had to lose his European ethics — all explorers of the south, *blue* voyagers, like so many others (Jung himself in Africa) that, crossing the Equatorial line, have had strong experiences of transformation. And, of course, the most paradigmatic of all examples, that of

Kurtz and the heart of darkness in Joseph Conrad's novel. Conrad himself had in the Congo an exasperating and humiliating experience, "an extreme personal crisis which shocked him into a greater moral and emotional maturity" (O'Prey, 1983, p. 12). More than "geographical panic," this is the *horror* of "south."

But I can not imagine, for instance, that Dr. Hillman, or Archetypal Psychology for that matter, would *necessarily* pathologize if he came even more southwards than he proposes, that is, south of the Mediterranean — if he came to the tropics, and particularly to Brazil, either in theory or in person. "Rome" and "Athens," as imaginal places, were for those men, Sigmund and Carl Gustav, for those pioneers in depth psychology, perhaps the core of a complex (as was so well diagnosed by Dr. Hillman in Re-visioning Psychology) that can only be understood in terms of its depths and / or the archetypal fear of depth. Archetypal Psychology, I think, stands in a somewhat special position here, since it already ventured in moving psychology southwards, it already 'entered' the metaphor, so to speak, thus altering vision and depth in psychology.

Instead, I am suggesting that, anticipating now an attempt at some conclusions, "Rio de Janeiro," or the Afro-Brazilian landscape of the city of "Salvador," in Bahia, for instance (just to mention two former capitals of the country), are, as well, imaginal places that in my view would lead Archetypal Psychology even further towards the south of its depths, or the depths of its south. This is not merely a play with words, but a play with images: geography as *mythopoiesis*. These places would lead Archetypal Psychology to a "south" where, it is my impression, a psychological *solutio* is being engendered in the world-soul.

Nevertheless, in his re-visioning of depth psychology, Dr. Hillman, rightly equating "south" with the repressed, went on to write that when it returns, as it would surely do, it "comes from the other side of any mountain, across any border, as Italian, Arab, Mexican, Jew, Caribbean..." (Hillman, 1975,

p. 224). Note he does not mention South America. Yes, across *any* border: but what about "Equatorial border"? Am I being too literal here? Well, this is not, in my view, a simple detail. It is significant that a south really south of the border is not imagined. It is as if an unconsciousness still pervaded Archetypal Psychology's southward *solutio*. But the *opus* goes on "operating" in the world-soul. The failure to see a south the other side of the ocean (not the other side of the mountain) reveals a *projected* emotion that fails the radicalism of this psychology's *project*. Is this, at a deeper level, the same old fear of "archetypal disorientation"? Perhaps this emotion, this neglect, could be well described by those famous lines by T. S. Eliot, in the Tarot scene of <u>The Waste Land</u>, when Madame Sosostris says to the protagonist: "Fear death by water."

This water, *mare nostrum*, again, is both *salty* and *titanic* (Atlantic, we now call it) — thus pertaining to Atlas, but also to the alchemical imagination of salt; so it should necessarily bring a *solutio* as an archetypal move. And it is as well, as an ocean — like any ocean — let us not forget, wherefrom Aphrodite, goddess of beauty and pleasure, is born. This water is the great factor, the great foaming untamed image dividing for us "north" and "south," two completely different styles of consciousness. Now, an Atlantic disproportionate projection of beauty and pleasure takes its course, so that we in the "South" become the true carriers of body, lust, instinct, spontaneity, nature, joy. "South" here stands clearly for everything that is located below, repressed above, all that has always been seen from the north as *inferior* (as the early cartography exemplarily shows), intriguingly inviting on its way across the sea a radical *reversion* to dark projections. This darkness has historically ranged from the Christian Hell of the missionaries to the mythological Hades of the psyche: inferior, unknown regions, a true *under*world, land, not of the brave, but of the serpent and of the dragon.

Yes, we all know those dark projections that landed below the Equator (the Equator, that abstract line of the spirit that does not really *equate* anything): tropical-south as irrational, sexually free, Dionisian, pagan, perverse, archetypally mother-bound due to an extravagant and extraordinary appeal of nature and climate, instinctive, lazy, cannibalistic. Are those projections still in operation? What was at first perceived by the *conquistadores* as heavenly, a paradisiac projection, soon turned into a hellish project to steal, to usurp and to abuse land and people in the Tropics — gold rush, wood traffic, slavery, soul mutilation. But this is history, or, at best, psychology; and we want geography, psychic geography.

My question would then be: at the verge of a new psychological era, will Archetypal Psychology have the courage ("courage" here because I mentioned "fear"), the courage to go souther, to continue imagining its fundamental imaginal direction and so leave for a moment its focus on Greek Gods and Goddesses, its polarization of soul into a mono *or* poly experience of itself, its Mediterranean landscape and modes of thinking, and see that world and soul, and the world-soul, do not end in a soft sea, an 'in-between-lands' sea, but go further south across a titanic, rough and open ocean (once called "tenebrous," *tenebrositas*), towards a new salty *solutio*, that lies perhaps waiting in a new world — 'new,' of course, only from the European historical perspective? Can we in the new millennium finally avoid pathologizing when we go south, avoid the archetypal fear and the archetypal neglect? Would we dare to see what kind of *solutio* is being possibly imagined in the "South"? What has the soul, the world-soul, been doing in the "South"? Can our Archetypal Psychology finally conclude its *circumambulatio* of the soul?

Our play with imaginal geography seeks to bring "south" as soul-making once again in Archetypal Psychology — a move towards Brazilian imagining, imagined as a move of soul-making, more soul-making, new soul-making.

I would like now to make some concluding observations about this move, and this world.

IV.

Finally, I want to add a few words on what is otherwise certainly a vast theme. One fundamental aspect of the reality of the salty solution that I mentioned will always be, for me, baroque. I want to suggest that one true image that the South-American and Brazilian soul, or the soul in South-America and Brazil, can open to Archetypal Psychology is to be first found in the **Colonial baroque**, has its origins in Colonial baroque. So, I need to say two or three things on what I feel about this Brazilian baroque, first because you in North America have not had the impact of the baroque as we have, but also to end with a truly imaginative note.

The baroque in Brazil, as in all South America, is not simply a transitory artistic movement, imported from Europe and so attached to this origin and its canons. What the art historians insist on is that the tropical baroque has to be understood in its own terms, as the first full legitimate manifestation of art and culture to flourish outside Europe in the Colonies, one that has little more to do directly with Europe, no longer a marginal artistic expression but something in itself. In fact, it is the first original cultural manifestation in the "south," and being that, I believe it will strongly reflect the very soul that was being formed in this "new" land. So, it is part of a foundation. This "new soul" — or new step in the world soul-making — this mixture that was being engendered in Brazil through the encounter of three races, begins to speak right here, with the baroque. Brazilian baroque incorporates thus, apart from the European (Portuguese, Spanish and Roman) elements, those from the Indian and Black influences. The baroque merges itself with many aspects of our deepest soul.

Opposed to the rationalist aspect of the Renaissance culture, the magical universe of the tropical baroque is rooted in the imagination — sensorial extremes of imagination. It is an art that can only be perceived in its full impact by the soul, *not* by the mind. The baroque, specially in Brazil, is the ongoing subversion of the Council of Trent, the affirmation of fantasy as the deepest truth; it is a *contre-dance*, it is freedom to imagine, yes, and it is the moment when we speak, not of a Re-naissance, but of a *naissance*, a birth, for the baroque, we all know, made possible Independence (and not only for Brazil).

Baroque: images constantly moving, the play of light and darkness continually disturbing spatial and temporal orientation, orienting the soul to dance and to celebrate the senses, enlightening the soul — but also seducing, disturbing it: the baroque is the most dangerous movement of the soul. In Brazil, it reveals a true soul atmosphere: extremes of colors, shades, darknesses, textures, candles, smoke, perfume, emotion, ritual, recitation, theater, music, fantasy, pain, joy, feeling, street celebrations — all an attempt to represent and respond to the impact on the soul of an all-exuberant, colorful, wild, dangerous and luminous nature. The early mixture of cultures, of skins, of libidos and of souls that took place in Brazil, and all those "eyes" (white, black and native) all well immersed in the torments, marvels and secrets of the tropical forest, are the *prima materia* of this baroque.

This baroque still defines, to this day, much of our soul. Although the Indian heritage is largely (or completely) left out, our urban soul is born under the sign of the baroque. So, there is a latent "baroquism," so to speak, that continues to inform and characterize, deep down, much of the way Brazilians feel and live soul and affection: the extremes of faith, the inclination to contradiction and ambivalence, the attraction for emotional vertigo, dance and festive ecstasy, the exaltation of the senses, the mystical impulse, aesthetic pleasure, tragedy, confusion, illusions of grandeur, the erotics of power *and* the power of erotics, the magic of words, excessive use of adjectives and, most of all, an image-sense, as would say Dr. Hillman, a sensibility for the image — this is all in the baroque. *Anima* phenomenology? Maybe. If so, then we have a rich soil for a psychology based on image to flourish, an imaginal psychology. Anyway, we can say that the cult of the image in Brazil is as old as its history, since the first ship to arrive at the Brazilian coast five hundreds years ago was carrying inside it not only men, projects, projections, problems, hope, but also a powerful marble image of the Christian Great Mother, the *anima* principle, in this case, Our Lady of *Hope*! And, of course, both the Indian and the African heritage are full of images.

But it is my impression — and here we come to my final conclusion — that this "baroquism" is exactly, as well, where in Brazil monotheism and polytheism began mysteriously to merge or disappear as psychological consciousness, excluding, clear and experienced categories. It seems to me the baroque is the moment in Brazil, on a deeper soul level, where the very division "monotheistic/polytheistic" first ceases to be relevant — for Brazilian baroque, may I suggest, is a *pagan* baroque, as has once pointed out to me by a patient during an analytical session. The enormous variety and number of Catholic saints that are observed in Brazil — honored like Gods in themselves — attest to the strong influence on consciousness of a polytheistic soul active right underneath the Christian monotheistic layer, not to mention the syncretic amalgam of those saints with the Yoruba divinities. (This syncretism, as it is well known, was the historical way found by the African slaves to keep alive their religious beliefs and rituals in the new environment.)

So, yes, we go to church on Sundays, but beat our drums on Monday night. It is not unusual to see shrines in Brazil where the statuette of Christ shares the stage (sorry, the altar!) with, say, the siren-shaped figure of Yemanjá — Goddess of the sea, a Great Mother from the salty waters — or Saint George with the sword killing the dragon. *Macumba.* Talking about polytheism? I believe then that this polytheism, acted literally in this contemporary form, lived as a true religion for some Brazilians, also spreads itself inwardly in the soul, making every Brazilian feel, think and relate polycentrically within a somehow fantastic unitary collective atmosphere.

I would like to suggest that this is the *prima materia* of the "South" I have been speaking of. Again, "South" as *an imaginal attribute in the world-soul.* The cultural synthesis that Brazil represents in the world-soul is also a psychological synthesis, a synthesis in soul, as I have been trying to investigate. This peculiar soul state, of course, makes it easy to work with Archetypal Psychology in Brazil, as if our *anima* could naturally absorb the *animus* of an archetypal formulation of psychology. I can see it in the work with patients, I can see it in theoretical discussions.

I can see here a "south" image that is for me a soul image. It is the true image this "South" I have been playing with, which can bring a new region to Archetypal Psychology at the threshold of a "new age."

References

Andrade, M. de (1965). Aspectos das artes plásticas no Brasil. São Paulo: Livraria Martins Editora.

Casey, E. (1991). Spirit and soul: Essays in philosophical psychology. Dallas: Spring Publications.

Jung, C.G. (1965). Memories, dreams, reflections. New York, Vintage Books.

Hillman, J. (1975). Re-visioning psychology. New York: Harper Colophon Books.

Hillman, J. (1982). Salt: A chapter in alchemical psychology. In J. Stroud and G. Thomas (Eds.), Images of the untouched: Virginity in psyche, myth and community. Dallas: Spring Publications.

Hillman, J. (1985). Archetypal psychology: A brief account. Dallas: Spring Publications.

Hillman, J. (1986). Notes on white supremacy. Spring 1986.

Hillman, J. (1996). Psychology—Monotheistic Or Polytheistic': Twenty-Five Years Later. Spring 60.

Hillman, J. (1998). Culture and the animal soul. Spring 62.

Holanda, S. B. de. (1989). Raízes do Brasil (1936). Rio de Janeiro: José Olímpio Editora, 21ª edição.

O'Prey, P. (1983). Introduction. In Joseph Conrad's Heart of Darkness. New York: Penguin Books.

Ribeiro, D. (1997). O povo Brasileiro. São Paulo: Companhia das Letras.

Thresholds: From Theory to Practice

Each of the six essays that complete this volume engage or suggest some active involvement with the world. This aspect of depth psychology is less about the self and more about changing the dynamics of the natural or cultural orders.

William Doty's "The Artist's Work: Imagining Community," begins by considering the human body, nature and the planet at large in order to revision the imagination's active role in shaping our world. Partly a critique of the works of Suzie Gablik and Charlene Spretnak, Doty develops an argument for imaginal education in which the artist's voice and work is not merely an appendage to culture but a shaper of it in a more active psychological way.

Mary Watkins and Helene Shulman Lorenz explore the place of post-colonial theory within the tradition of depth psychology in "Individuation, Seeing-Through and Liberation: Depth Psychology and Colonialism" in order to see anew the process of individuation within a heightened consciousness of dialogue. Their combined effort yields new insights on liberation and the imagination as it develops within the psychic space of rupture."

Aaron Kipnis' "Seeing Red: In a Dark Night of the American Soul," continues his research and thinking on America's violent youth. Arguing that violence can restore vitality to a deadening consumer culture, he explores the ways in which violence can redden psyche. He believes we have created an American Gulag where we warehouse violence through our male minority youth rather than having the courage to face violence head on to grasp what it is trying to tell us.

"The Lost Heritage" captures the sense of Nina Kelly's work with organ transplant patients and reveals that by assisting kidney transplant persons to imagine their new organ, they can heal more fully and embrace their bodily and psychological changes with a greater consciousness. She asks us to remember the holistic healing of the Greeks and to reclaim some of their wisdom in the process.

Suzan Still's essay, "Prison as Shadow," continues the process of finding and nurturing creativity where normally we do not think of its presence: the American prison system. She describes her use of writing in classes there and her astonishment at the sophisticated level of creativity among inmates. Dionysus, she suggests, may be the most appropriate god present in this world of violence and imaginal richness.

Jennifer Freed's "Roots of Eros: Wings of Desire," ends the volume. In it she recounts her work with adults and youth in creative work together in her Academy of Healing Arts for Teenagers (AHA!) co-founded and co-directed by Rendy Freedman. The aim of this program is to raise in the participants a communal and civic conscience. To that end, during the first series of classes an authentic community of youth and adults formed and congealed. Her description of what is possible might be a model for other cities to engage.

Edward Casey's "Taking a Glance at the Place of Soul in the Environment" combines phenomenology and depth psychology to imagine what we see when we glance at the landscape. Casey reveals that the glance is a form of soul-making that can lead to actively healing our polluted landscapes.

The Artist's Work, Imagining Community by William G. Doty, Ph.D.

> We need—perhaps desperately need—a reassessment of the role we have given to imagination and the arts, retrieving them from unreality and marginality to honor them in our psychology and our educational policy as treasured belongings, real worlds in their own rights. (Noel 1999)

> It is, I think, an act of real arrogance to think of ourselves and our civilization as anything but rough first drafts, with the real flowering of the human race yet to come. (Silverberg 1999: 4)

1. Introduction: Imagination, Temporality, Knowledge

The ancient Roman deity Ianus (the name means "gate" or "bridge") lent his name to Ianuarius/January, but his were also the repeated calends—the times of the new moon and the first of every month. Famously represented with two faces, one pointing backward and the other forward, Ianus was often besought for protection and help at *beginnings* of all kinds. We do well to pay homage to such a being during the transitional years of 2000 and 2001, ending one and beginning another millennium—regardless of how you reckon on the actual chronology. I invoke and praise him here by exploring some aspects of the human imagination and praxis.

It seems to me important to remain conscious of the three faces (or phases) of temporal duration, to locate meanings for the *future* in the *past* and the *present*. I attempt here something of *an exercise in the trans-temporal socio-historical, artistic, and scientific imagination*. The interactions of the human soul or psyche and the realm of experience known as art and symbol are located in the human imagination—it is responsible for insight, perception, and creativity; it is the realm of thinking as well as of graphic imagery in symbols and art. Hence "the artist" of my title is not just the painter, sculptor, or poet, but any of us, as we imagine the past, forecast the future, and attempt to live artistically in the present.

Insofar as the human imagination is shaped by the socio-historical frameworks wherein it appears, we need to explore questions such as: Does being human necessarily enfold consciousness of temporality? How does time/temporality relate to *trans*-temporality, archetypal or universal realities? And we must address epistemological questions: How is temporality related to gnosis/knowing? How ought we to differentiate gnosis—a religious claim to immediate knowledge—from analytical scientific knowing (words built from *ana-lysis*: taking apart, and *scientia*/science, from *scire*, separating)? (See the overview of positions on the dichotomy in Brockelman, *Cosmology and Creation*.)

So long dominant across any of our epistemologies (our various modes of knowing—in conversation, Dan Noel has called them *epistemythologies*), the eighteenth-century Enlightenment project of absolute knowledge has now been transformed into the postmodernist recognition of its limitations, so that we must inquire about what new contours epistemological knowing now follows because of our most contemporary worldviews.

2. Epistemological Revisionism; the Body, Nature, and Lived Life; Communitas for the Polis

It is always tempting to claim that the most recent perspective is the best (especially if it is one's own!) but it is important to recognize how modernism's "Make It New!" slogan operates behind so much of the trivializing of the past that permeates our culture. Charlene Spretnak's book <u>The Resurgence of the Real: Body, Nature, and Place in a Hypermodern World</u> very effectively illustrates how modernist platforms still drive our epistemologies, shunting aside as inferior, for instance, the human body, nature, the very physical life on our planet that is more immediate to any one of us than our abstract gray-matter ideas and ideals. It is important to reiterate that the natural is the imaginal, the imagined, insofar as everything experienced gets imaged within our physical sensorium (see Avens 1980). Think Hudson River school or Taos art colony, and you recognize right away how strongly nature is *shaped* by a priori esthetic perspectives.

Scientific positivism, widely adapted in every sphere of twentieth-century consciousness, tracks right back to the Platonic and Aristotelian split between the body and the mind, the dichotomy that enfranchised the entire Enlightenment project. And it is no wonder we have had to endure postmodernist, deconstructive, and now postcolonialist critiques that have broken the back of the notion that the sciences and technology are neutral and "natural" products of a unbiased and unallied academe and business. Already Thomas Kuhn's <u>The</u>

Structure of Scientific Revolutions (1970), and later such books as Women's Ways of Knowing

(Belenky, et al., 1986) and Sandra Harding's, The Science Question in Feminism, clarified just

how politically mired in centuries of sexism, racism, and politics the formal production of

academic knowledge has always been.

Neo-Enlightenment epistemology claimed to produce "god's-truth knowledge," but

then ignored the fact that, for example, Coca-Cola's money brought Emory University out of

small-school inferiority, and that post-WW2 military spending and oil corporations rescued

physics, geography, and biological sciences departments across our continents, even as the

humanities lost their former elevated status in academe because they didn't "contribute to the

economy." I find myself reminding audiences all the time that any esthetics, epistemology, or

mythology, is driven by features of its socio-historical settings and their ideological infections

(see Lease 2000). We declare knowledge important to consume when we see its political,

technological, or commercial markets blossom in the stock exchange, but in academic art or

humanities departments produce few wealthy alums.

And indeed it has been these sorts of ritualizations of contemporary existence rather

than any religious or ecological rituals, that have captured modern attention. Psychologist Erik

Eriksen (211), at the conclusion of a conference (apparently in 1968) on ethology, spoke about

the importance of appropriate ritualization in the developmental life cycle. It must be

determined "in line with a new world image. This new cosmos is held together by (1) the

scientific ethos, (2) the methods of mass communication, and (3) the replacement of 'ordained'

authorities by an indefinite sequence of experts correcting and complementing each other."

But unfortunately many if not most of us no longer share Eriksen's trust in any one of

these three communal values, let alone their holistic co-ordination. For instance, Joseph

Campbell emphasizes the need for a whole new cosmic imagery in our scientific world; and

reflections in Approaching Earth, Noel's postmodernist reflections upon our mythological self-

images after viewing the earth from the moon drive home how un-realized Eriksen's "new

world image" remains.

Certainly the human body, nature, and the very physical life upon our planet that were trivialized in the earlier modernist climate across the first half of the twentieth century have returned to the center of writings in cultural studies and philosophy. When I reached to my bookshelves to add some bibliographic references with respect to recent studies of the body alone, I decided that there were too many to list except in a mini-bibliography of its own (I'll let one example suffice: Lakoff and Johnson, <u>Philosophy in the Flesh: The Embodied Mind and Its Challenge to Western Thought</u>).

And by my phrase "the very physical life upon our planet" I am thinking about the psycho-political problems we all face as we look at polis-life, city-life across the globe. Negative surveys abound, but few positive imaginings of how to recover a public atmosphere that will bring us back into civil civic discourse.

Thurston Clarke's review in the <u>New York Times</u> Book Review (6 September 1998: 4) of Robert Kaplan's book, <u>An Empire Wilderness: Travels into America's Future</u>, summarizes Kaplan's projected future in the city of Omaha, Nebraska, and in California's Orange County: "Standardized corporate fortresses, privately guarded housing developments, Disneyfied tourist bubbles"; "isolated suburban pods and enclaves of races and classes unrelated to each other"; an automobile-oriented city where "you will be even less comfortable outside of your car in the future than you are now"; a business elite with its own foreign policy "dominated by the concerns of trade and *Realpolitik* rather than by human rights and spreading democracy"; a politically apathetic populace more interested in health clubs and the Internet than in community life; and a society where the poor are left to fend for themselves

Spretnak's own analysis of worldwide breakdown in <u>The Resurgence of the Real</u> conveys her feeling that the radical break effected by modernity in the fifteenth to the eighteenth centuries was not nearly radical enough, but actually inflated certain harmful propensities in Western thought. She proposes that only a profoundly *ecological postmodernism* can help our situation—in the sense not just of a passive "environmentalism," but of an ecological epistemology:

Instead of perceiving ourselves as social "atoms" colliding and combining with other discrete "atoms" in a human society that uses and projects concepts onto its background matter (nature), we perceive an unbroken continuity of cosmos/Earth/continent/nation/bioregion/community/neighborhood/family/person. These are the extended boundaries of the self [*instead of*, I insert, the limited soul-boundaries of ego-psychology]. Our field, our grounding, and our being is the cosmos. Moreover, we finally slough off the modern obsession with escaping from nature and realize that all human endeavor is derivative of the Earth community, not the other way around.

"Ecological postmodernism [. . .] replaces groundlessness with groundedness, supplanting freedom *from* nature with freedom *in* nature" (72).

And clearly it would support freedom *for communitas*, a medieval term for ideal communal existence that anthropologist Victor Turner stressed in several of his publications. To mix the Latin and the Greek, a strong sense of communitas across the future polis would not—à la Republican bills denying HMO patients adequate coverage—have approved my coworker's being sent home the same day she had back surgery last summer. Incredibly advanced medicine will make my colleague's or my own recent laser surgery seem rather primitive, but the plot of the example still turns around the classic Aristotelian values of caring for all of humankind.

Echoes of the recently-released prequel episode of <u>Star Wars</u>, of course—but if you think about the plots of nearly every such fiction, you'll recognize how frequently they puzzle the construction and maintenance of community. The search for an adequate "yoga" (a Hindi term from Sanskrit *yogah*: union, joining, yoking), the "ligaturing" of religion (from the Latin *religare*) that is the affectively-effective enabling of *Mitmenschlichkeit*. And of the elemental sounding-together of the humane, both symbol and myth (from Greek *mythos*, the root *mu-* having produced both myth and mystery, each a mothering muttering).

3. Re-employments of the Artistic

In this third segment I want to give a rather extended and specific example of societal movement from the ideal of the isolated Romantic individual artist to corporate involvement with the community. Hence I hop from modernist perspectives such as Dubuffet's *l'art brut* (art in the raw) and the more generalized attitude of *l'art pour l'art* (aesthetic commitment stuff) to something like <u>Art on the Edge</u>, a contemporary anthology of the way-out (edited by Weintraub, Danto, and McEvilley), and including several other contemporary perspectives such as Suzi Gablik's <u>The Reenchantment of Art</u> (1991) and politics/performance emphasis.

I can only touch upon a couple of the sea changes that recent decades have brought to the international art scene. Here I highlight only recovery of the social and experiential aspects and the consequent proactive attitudes of what is called New Genre Public Art (abbreviated NGPA, often more simply referred to as "Public Art," although that earlier term has complicating inferences that will be explored below).

3.a. Recovering Social and Experiential Aspects of the Arts

An originary and influential essay by Richard Bolton, "How Can Art Become Relevant Again?" argues strongly for recovering now, after the modernist emphasis upon the transcendental aesthetic-formal aspects of art, *its social and experiential aspects*. Otherwise, Bolton, and Gablik (1995a: 75) note, it remains only *narcissistic*.

Bolton hopes we can move from *deconstructive* to *socially-reconstructive* positions, and get beyond the traditional dichotomy between status-quo "formal" practices and oppositional "political" ones such as form./.content; beauty./.politics; and subjective experience./.objective fact: they all reduce art to poverty. The problem is that "Recent art has provided *but a partial hermeneutics*, striving in every way imaginable to *take meaning apart* but ignoring the task of *putting it back together*" (22, my emphasis) a judgment easily applied to most critical theory or deconstructive projects. While Bolton suggests that "The goal of all art is the development of *critical* consciousness [. . . ,] '*political art*' builds correspondences with the social world beyond the art object. Both strive to instill an ever finer consideration of what it means to be *a human being*" (my emphasis).

3.b. Shifting from Artist to Audience; Art (or Religion) as a Making Special for the Community

Even much recent political art has been problematic because of its claim that meaning is impossible, that institutions are all hopelessly corrupt. But from a radically new direction, New Genre Public Art (NGPA) practitioners stress the importance of recovering a sense of *an individual audience's experience* rather than *an artist's individual performance*. Already, John Dewey's aesthetics related artistic to social relations, yet many polemical approaches of art have merely alienated everyone and silenced possible conversations.

Hence Bolton wants us to work on "discursive and collaborative social meaning—[. . .] at heart a *pedagogical model of art-making*" (23, my emphasis): artistic "[b]eauty does not reside in any object but in the experience one has with that object. Beauty is a quality of a social interaction," a definition I like because it highlights the very extremely close connection between esthetics and ethics.

Gablik (1995b: 38) repeats art historian Ellen Dissanayake's claim that art first got split off from communal values when the very idea of "art" came about in the eighteenth century: subsequently it was treated as essentially superfluous, hardly a necessity of daily life for society or individual. Art for art's sake suggested that art is simultaneously sanctified and dismissed as rubbish. But we get a very different orientation if we regard art (or religion) as *a making special* (41-43,45), as *raising elements of our existence to a level that transcends ourselves* (166; see especially Lynda Sexson's <u>Ordinarily Sacred</u> and Crispin Sartwell's <u>The Art of Living,</u> and on making art "spiritual," that is, value-based and committed to changing the reigning paradigms, Gablik <u>Reenchantment</u> 143, 181-83.).

The ideal of communitas is at the heart of the matter. Lippard writes (1995: 127-28) that:

> Community doesn't mean understanding everything about everybody and resolving all the differences; it means knowing how to work within differences as they change and evolve. Critical consciousness [the critical activity we have seen Bolton supporting] is a process of recognizing both limitations and possibilities. We need to collaborate with small and large social, political, specialized groups of people already informed and immersed in the issues. And we need to teach them to welcome artists, to understand how art can concretize and envision their goals. At the same time we need to collaborate with those whose backgrounds and maybe foregrounds are unfamiliar to us, rejecting the insidious notions of "diversity" that simply neutralize difference.

3.c. A Participatory Esthetics

Gablik's own art led her to activism, "not political activism in the sense of demonstrations in the street, but an activism where the artist is engaging actively with, or intervening in, particular situations, and using his or her creativity to create a space for some kind of healing to occur" (1995b: 141). Thanks to her experiences, she now anticipates a future art that is essentially social and purposeful, *art that rejects the myths of neutrality and autonomy* (1991:4). It will have "a new connective, participatory aesthetics," it will "speak for a value-based art that is able to transcend the modernist opposition between the aesthetic and the social" (9).

What Gablik calls "bad modernism" with its "whole cultural ethos of alienation" (78) rested upon a Romantic "model of the artist as a lone genius struggling against society," a model that "does not allow us to focus on the beneficial and healing role of social interaction" (80).

Across the period from about 1975 to the present, it became increasingly clear in New Genre Public Art, and indeed in many contemporary artists' practices generally, that *art does have consequences;* Gablik establishes the crucial question, "whether art can build community" (1995a: 81). And she cites one example where such community-building does happen: "In Suzanne Lacy's The Crystal Quilt, performed in Minneapolis on Mother's Day in 1987, a procession of 430 older women, all dressed in black, sat down together at tables in groups of four, to discuss with each other their accomplishments and disappointments, their hopes and fears about aging, in a ceremonially orchestrated artwork."

Much of what came forth derived from the power of empathic listening to one another, a growth of critical understanding and appreciation that began not in theory or form, but in the embodied experience of ritual, a sort of "connective aesthetics" (84) where "the boundary between self and Other is fluid rather than fixed: the Other is included within the boundary of selfhood. We are talking about a more intersubjective version of the self that is attuned to the interrelational, ecological, and interactive character of reality. 'Myself now includes the rainforest,' writes Australian deep ecologist John Seed. 'It includes clean air and water.'"

3.d. Reclamation Art

Moving away from the dominance of the eye in modernism, a new field-like conception of the self brings into perspective more of the environment and community. It is no accident that much NGPA is referred to as "reclamation art," since these are largely projects that seek

> to restore landscape trashed by private use to the public domain. Landfills are turned into giant art parks that are actually waste processing centers by American artist Viet Ngo. A nature corridor is designed by Newton and Helen Harrison to surround and protect the Sava River Valley. A manmade mountain is erected in Finland by artist Agnes Denes on which 10,000 trees planted by 10,000 people from across the globe will grow undisturbed for 400 years. With his project Ocean Earth, Peter Fend has conceived a plan for reconfiguring the contours of coastlines [on] a global scale to promote better waste assimilation and redress erosional damage. (SCCA Discussion, accessed 5/18/00; see also the detailed interviews in Finkelpearl 2000)

The perspective we are describing dismantles the long-held Western dualism of perspective, and it would simultaneously indicate that a mythological gran recít (master narrative/scripture) *is* operative still, one that Gablik (1991: 26, in conscious opposition to postmodernists Lyotard and Jameson) entitles *saving the planet*.

This is something of a relief, even if it requires overturning much of what postmodernist thought has assumed, because cultures, communities, neighborhoods that survive and flourish are those that can tell their own stories and honor them, whereas "[w]hat happens to a culture *without* a living mythology is that it gets addicted to whatever numbs the pain of archetypal starvation and the vacuum of meaning. Opening one's vision [. . .] to a greater transpersonal realm, which defies control and rational description, is to see beyond the regarded boundaries and destitution of our present system" (Gablik 1991: 51, my emphasis).

3.e. Compassionate Action Art

Gablik has in mind combating the currently dominant cultural mythologies, which traditional artistic conventions have merely replicated, by actual interventions. In one chapter subtitled "Art as Compassionate Action," she refers especially to an artwork entitled The Great Cleansing of the Rio Grande begun in 1987 by Dominique Mazeaud. "Once a month, ritually on the same day each month, armed with garbage bags donated by the city, she, and a few friends who sometimes accompany her, meet to clean pollution out of the river" (1991: 119).

She keeps a diary (extracts from it are quoted in The Enchantment of Art), where her

meditations on the symbolism of water, and her prayers are shared—yes, she sees her actions

as prayers—as well as her rages against the people who persist in throwing bottles and trash

into the Rio Grande.

What impresses Gablik is that, unlike modernist practice by figures such as Marcel

Duchamp and Pablo Picasso), Mazeaud's "isn't based on a transgression of the aesthetic codes

at all. It comes from another integrating myth entirely: compassion" (121)—a compassion that

calls our explicit self-consciousness to precisely the nitty-gritty of the jejune against which

modernist art privileged abstraction and pure form. "What Mazeaud's project forces us to see

is the *power* operating in our cognitive and institutional structures. [. . .] Mazeaud isn't

competing in the patriarchal system at all, but stands true to her own feminine nature. By

returning to the river every month on the same date to resume her task once again, she makes

the ritual process into a redemptive act of healing" (122), noting that a friend of her sees the

project as a variation on the ancient myth of Isis and Osiris.

"The human debris she gathers are the dismembered parts of the murdered Osiris

(garbage being a wonderful cipher for how we are dismembered by our technologies).

Through her worry and care, Mazeaud resurrects Osiris's body, ensuring the renewed fertility

of the vegetable kingdom in the crescent of the river" (122). Gablik suggests that Mazeaud's

ritual raises "a useful action to the level of the spiritual (thus making it resonant and catalytic)"

(143). She also notes that "the sacredness of both life and art does not have to mean something

cosmic or otherworldly—it emerges quite naturally when we cultivate compassionate,

responsive modes of relating to the world and to each other" (181).

3.f. Out of the Gallery into the World: Public Art

Gablik sees strong justification for alternate art forms such as Mazeaud's in Arthur

Danto's argument that "the whole philosophy of modern aesthetics is under pressure of

redefinition. Traditional myths such as the masterpiece, the individual genius, the museum, and the gallery are being deconstructed by feminists and postmodernists alike" (123; see also Gablik's interview with Danto in her <u>Conversations before the End of Time</u>). And of course much of that deconstruction involved a much wider panoply of artists according to race, gender and class, as markedly the 1993 Whitney Biennial, which Gablik refers to as "an institutional melt-down" because it gave "others a voice and an opportunity to impose other standards for evaluation than the attribution of [the modernist standard] of 'quality,' taken as a definable, transhistorical [essentialist—WGD] measure of value applicable for all time and for a universal model of history" (1995b: 294-95).

Among the consequences: artists everywhere have begun to locate primary significance in the real world rather than the museum. I recently attended a conference at Land's End in Cornwall, where artist Sue Bleakley noted that hers is an art that can find inspiration in steel wool pot scrubbers or a stained ladies crocheted glove she found on a garbage heap and subsequently stuffed with coins and jewels. Such practices go beyond Cubist and other modernist appropriations from popular culture, and represent new aesthetic perspectives for both individual and community: they highlight artistic perspectives within quintessential everyday objects.

Lucy Lippard defines NGPA as "accessible work of any kind that cares about, challenges, involves, and consults the audience for or with whom it is made, respecting community and environment," and she identifies nine varieties, ranging from "works prepared for conventional indoor exhibition [. . .] that refer to local communities, history, or environmental issues [. . .]; traditional outdoor public art [. . .]; site-specific outdoor artworks [. . .] that significantly involve the community"; and other types (1995: 121).

Instead of supporting the art industry's "business as usual," NGPA projects (such as those treated by Finkelpearl, <u>Dialogues in Public Art</u>) often demand extensive revisions of what has come to be expected of the art world, especially as the artworks are themselves often transformative of spaces and "natural" situations that we usually prefer to ignore. Lippard indicates that: "As 'envisionaries,' artists should be able to provide a way to work against the dominant culture's rapacious view of nature [. . .], to reinstate the mythical and cultural dimensions to 'public' experience and at the same time to become conscious of the ideological relationships and historical constructions of place" (128).

3.g. A Politics of Reconceptualization

In her own career, Suzi Gablik has come to recognize that such relationships and constructions affect the traditionally removed praxis of the art historian and critic: "As a critic in the nineties, I am not really interested in writing catalog essays or art reviews. What I am concerned with is understanding the nature of our cultural myths and how they evolve—the institutional framework we take for granted but which nevertheless determines our lives."

This is not necessarily a "new subjectivism," but movement toward appreciative ritualizations and especially toward greatly heightened interactions between commercial and residential communities, and the providers of new artworks, and it foretells a focus upon art for social creativity that stands in sharp contrast to the self-expression motif that trashes the traditional (76). The modernist ideal was to "Make it New!" in a way no one else had ever done before—and the resultant shattering of the traditional was one of the primary influences upon the postmodern conclusion and attitude that the past is only the dead past, that the age of privileged metanarratives could only be ironically revisited.

3.h. The Artistic Creativity of Community Life

In the new frames we are exploring here, creativity itself is reconceived as communally configured and ethically driven. Just think how seldom we have sought to envision ways *community life* might be revivified! Or what little input has been sought from the "public" in Public Art. NGPA is opening the doors, recognizing how much of "art" has existed outside the realm of the public.

The spaces of Public Art entail various and usually rather-elitist assumptions, as noted by Finkelpearl (2000: x-xi): Public Art, as it is often sponsored by public agencies, usually exists outside museums and galleries, and addresses audiences outside the confines of the art world.

But the term "public" is often associated with the lower classes (public school, public assistance) as opposed to the term private—associated with privilege (private school, private estate). On the other hand, "Art is generally associated with the upper classes, at least in terms of those who consume it—collectors and museum audiences. Many of the projects in this book explicitly or implicitly address the class contradictions inherent in the term "public art" by bringing different sorts of people into contact in creative ways" (xi).

Even the concept and term of "community" can also have classist or racial overtones, so that, as Finkelpearl stresses: "art created for insiders in the art world is never referred to as community art. So, when one refers to community-oriented public art, the terms are loaded, but the usage is fairly clear: it is art that includes people from the lower classes in its creation, consumption, or both. This does not mean that the upper classes are excluded from participating in the projects as well, only that they are no longer the exclusive audience" (xi).

What is so remarkable about the work of the NGPA artists and cultural critics is their willingness to cross borders, to invent new forms of representation, and at the same time to interrogate the quality of social life by addressing the language of sexuality, social exclusion, identity, and power, while avoiding a doctrinaire politics or narrow critique of the sites in which art is produced. Committed to a vision of art that encourages participatory democracy, new genre public artists emphasize public art that privileges community involvement rather than the traditional art school esthetic emphasis upon individual creation/authorship. Refusing to take honored places in either the academic disciplines or the museum, many of these artists and critics—as public intellectuals—do not isolate themselves from the larger society, from the stories, experiences, and histories of those others who inhabit less privileged spaces and sites of learning while struggling to survive.

3.i. The Artist as Envisionary Pedagogue of the Imagination

Much of what I have been charting here has to do with the very redefinition of the artwork, and of the artist's role within her/his society, and in her/his role as the "envisionary"

(Lippard's term we met earlier), the pedagogue of the imaginary/imagination. Carol Becker

recognizes that with respect to the politico-ideological issues named above:

> [A]rt has become the focus of a much larger debate over who gets to write, to speak, to
> visualize, to tell their story; who gets to frame and interpret reality, to position their
> text, as part of the cultural master text.

The problems of this country are staggering, in part because there has never a more

racially, ethnically, sexually diverse population, divided along so many class lines, living in

such close proximity, pretending not to understand each other and yet so implicated in each

other's lives.

Imagine that such a complex, heterogeneous society is represented by George Bush [pere,

not George W., but see if it makes any difference!—WGD], a one-dimensional, white, male

anti-intellectual who is both monolingual and monosyllabic. Something needs to change. This

country is desperate for a new mythology, a new imagery, a new leadership, a new vision of

itself, one that presents a future based on the concept of multiple cultural centers,

collaboration, and cultural integration" (22-23).

That desperation is the underwater current that leads seekers of every generation to press for

better imaginings, *sharper* prognostications, and *more creative* communal experiences.

4. Imaginally Creative Education/Therapy

As I've proposed in an essay entitled "Imagining the Future-Possible," I think one of

our most important individual and social activities to be *imaginal education,* the development of

the creative imagination. I consider this to be a moral issue involving the focusing of the potent

resources of our culture toward fresher and more holistic visions. In referring to the imaginal,

my interest is not merely something like "We need better art appreciation classes in high

school," for all the relevance and appropriateness of that claim.

As throughout this presentation, I focus here not upon the appreciation and cherishing

of humankind's imaginal *past,* so much as upon the ways we imagine *now,* and the ways we can learn to imagine *prospectively*, as important components within our own era, of the significantly-imaginal metaphors through which succeeding generations will experience the planet's history.

Thoreau's journal entry for 6 August 1841 reflects his own understanding of the interlocking of past, present, and future, and I find it a helpful model: "Critical acumen is exerted in vain to uncover the past; the *past* cannot be *presented*; we cannot know what we are not. But one veil hangs over past, present, and future, and it is the province of the historian to find out, not what was, but what is."

Imaginal education must focus upon the quality of the various primal myths, must teach us to recognize how some of them—such as the Bereshith/Genesis version of human/male dominance over nature—are dangerously restrictive and shortsighted with respect to possible futures (Doty 1998: 116-17). Imaginal education, by teaching comparative analysis and evaluation, might instruct us in ways of finding the models of the self that will permit more comprehensive and equitable modes of interaction than those presently active in our social structures. James Hillman's "The Bad Seed," chapter ten of The Soul's Code (1996), on the pathological demonism of Adolf Hitler or more recent figures such as Charles Manson and Jeffrey Dahmer, is one of the most helpful lessons our culture has produced, with respect to determining where/how/when mythic impulses go evil.

Further, we certainly need to move beyond the purely personal autobiography or biostory to the cultural mythostories that both place the individual self within a meaningful social framework and emphasize the responsibilities we carry toward one another—the corporate social responsibilities that have vanished from the careers of heroes and heroines in much of our pop culture, yet are seldom lacking in utopian fictions (cf. Gearhard's Herland).

If we want more rational behavior, we cannot just sit around and wait for it to happen, nor is there any guarantee that evolutionary behavior will be more rational; Mihaly Csikszentmihalyi proposes in The Evolving Self that "The future is not constrained by rules and predictable outcomes. We need to cultivate more than logic if we want to thrive in [the future]. We must foster intuition to anticipate changes before they occur; empathy to understand that which cannot be clearly expressed; wisdom to see the connection between apparently unrelated events; and creativity to discover new ways of defining problems, new rules that will make it possible to adapt to the unexpected" (41-42; see also my second epigraph from Silverberg). I agree strongly with Robert Bosnak that "the training of the imagination is a discipline, just as important as the training of the mind" (1988: 71).

Yet the arts are the venue in which both the end of god's-truth epistemologies *and* reenchantment are experienced. It seems to me that the imagination is our species' greatest contribution to the future of planetary existence. I propose that imagination—especially artistic imagination—is *creativity projected onto reality*, both social and individual. Not unreality, because images always derive from experience—they may in fact be super-real or hyper-real, intensifying or revisioning reality.

Imagination may be projected into the future: speculative ("science") fiction, utopian visions, stock market trends; or the past: when Rosetta stones unlock whole realms of formerly unsignified images, or long-puzzling artifacts (a loom or banner weights and atlatls) are at last found in situ, and suddenly an ancient scene can be "read"—that is to say, comprehended as our imaginations mesh with those of the artifact-users.

The imaginal is the métier of daydreams and think tanks and research physicists . . . of meditation as well as sleep-dreaming: you'll note different levels of discipline and experience in these activities. I consider *the artist to be simply one of the most disciplined imaginers*, one who sees a bit further. Like the sage (often called a *seer*), the artist is able to squeeze more communication out of the ordinary, to make the banal extraordinary. The artistic imagination can demonize (propaganda) as well as divinize—hence the long tradition of iconographic practice and training and repetition represented by any atelier or "school" of art.

One way the imaginal sees through and extends the ordinary is *metaphor*, that is to say, an image or expression that does not just repeat, but enlarges with a broader/deeper meaning, some subtlety "carried alongside" (*meta-phorein*) the original. Roberts Avens writes (1980: 22):

"Poetic or true or creative imagination, in its most sharpened Western form, is a noetic vision; it is cognitively meaningful, requiring the maintenance and not the sacrifice, of ordinary consciousness."

Such noetic vision is imaginative vision, yet why do we so frequently denigrate future-thinking? The phrase "merely utopian" is a hang-up of our society, which deeply needs something like the *imaginal-soul training* of a James Hillman (cf. also Hill 1994), a training that is scarcely related to the Romantic notion of the isolated individual writing or painting in "his" cold garret. It has much more to do with supportive caring for the *anima mundi* (soul of the world) in its worldliness, its practical, political, and ecological dimensions. The artist's work is to imagine human continuance upon this planet in a soulful manner. Let us up the voltage on creative imagining!

How can we possibly imagine the future except in terms of the present and the past, and their unlimited possibilities? January-all questions have little temporality, remain essential every month of any year. And they are the sort of civilizational questions and projects that enable creativity at the most basic fundament. Who but ourselves as community artists will engage the creative fostering of the anima mundi? Not the traditional "artist"'s assignment, but that of all of us polis-dwellers: recreatively imagining community where I—and you—are at home.

References

Avens, R. (1980). Imagination is reality: Western nirvana in Jung, Hillman, Barfield, and Cassirer. Dallas: Spring.

Becker, C. (1996). Zones of contention: Essays on art, institutions, gender, and anxiety. Albany: SUNY UP.

Belenky, M.F., McVicker Clincy, B., Rule Goldberger, N., & Mattuck Tarule, J. (1986). Women's ways of knowing: The development of self, voice, and mind. New York: Basic.

Bolton, R. (1995). How can art become relevant again? Sculpture 14/3:20-23.

Bosnak, R. (1988). A little course on dreams. Boston: Shambhala.

Brockelman, P. (1999). Cosmology and creation: The spiritual significance of contemporary cosmology. New York: Oxford UP.

Clarke, T. (1998). "The Wasteland" [review of Robert D. Kaplan, An Empire Wilderness: Travels into America's Future (New York: Random, 1998)]. New York Times Book Review 6 September 1998: 4.

Csikszentmihalyi, M. 1993. The evolving self: A psychology for the third millennium. New York: HarperPerennial-HarperCollins.

Doty, W. G. (1998). Imagining the future-possible. In T. Pippin and G. Aichele (Eds.), Violence, Utopia, and the Kingdom of God: Fantasy and Ideology in the Bible (pp. 104-121). New York: Routledge.

Eriksen, E. (1996). The development of ritualization. In D.R. Cutler (Ed.), The religious situation (pp. 201-211). Upper Saddle River, NJ: Prentice Hall-Simon and Schuster/Viacom.

Finkelpearl, T. (2000). Dialogues in public art: Interviews. Cambridge: MIT P.

Gablik, S. (1991). The reenchantment of art. New York: Thames and Hudson.

Gablik, S. (1995a). Connective aesthetics: Art after individualism. In S. Lacy (Ed.), Mapping the terrain: New genre public art (pp. 74-87). Seattle: Bay P.

Gablik, S. (1995b). Conversations before the end of time. New York: Thames and Hudson.

Gearhart, S.M. (1978). The wanderground: Stories of the hill women. Watertown MA: Persephone.

Harding, S. (1986). The science question in feminism. Ithaca: Cornell UP.

Hill, M.O. (1994). Dreaming the end of the world: Apocalypse as a rite of passage. Dallas: Spring.

Hillman, J. (1996). The soul's code: In search of character and calling. New York: Random House.

Kuhn, T.S. (1970). The structure of scientific revolutions (2nd ed., enlarged). Chicago: U of Chicago P.

Lakoff, G., & Johnson, M. (1999). Philosophy in the flesh: The embodied mind and its challenge to Western thought. New York: Basic-Perseus.

Lease, G. (2000). Ideology. In W. Braun & R.T. McCutcheon (Eds.), Guide to the Study of Religion, (pp. 438-447). New York: Cassell.

Lippard, L.R. (1983). Overlay: Contemporary art and the art of prehistory. New York: Pantheon.

Lippard, L.R. (1990). Mixed blessings: New art in a multicultural America. New York: Pantheon.

Lippard, L.R. (1995). Looking around: Where we are, where we could be. In S. Lacy (Ed.), Mapping the terrain: New genre public art (pp. 114-130). Seattle: Bay P.

Noel, D.C. (1999). Epidemic of violence perhaps due to stifling of imagination. Barre/Montpelier Times-Argus 17 June.

Noel, D.C. (1986). Approaching Earth: A search for the mythic significance of the space age. Amity, NY: Amity House.

Sartwell, C. (1995). The art of living: The aesthetics of the ordinary in world spiritual traditions. Albany: SUNY UP.

SCCA [Soros Center for Contemporary Arts, Prague] Discussion. <http://www.ecn.cz/osf/scaa/eng/talk.htm>, accessed 5/18/00.

Sexson, L. (1991 [1982]). Ordinarily sacred. Charlottesville: UP of Virginia.

Silverberg, R. (1999). The best is yet to be . . . Right? Asimov's Science Fiction 23/5: 4-7.

Spretnak, C. (1997). The resurgence of the real: Body, nature, and place in a hypermodern world. Reading MA: Addison-Wesley.

Strozier, C.B., & Flynn, M. (Eds.). (1997). The year 2000: Essays on the end. New York: New York UP.

Weintraub, L., Danto, A., & McEvilley, T. (1996). Art on the edge and over: Searching for art's meaning in contemporary society 1970s-1990s. Litchfield CT: Art Insights.

Depth Psychology and Colonialism: Individuation, Seeing Through, and Liberation[1] by

Helene Shulman Lorenz, Ph.D. and Mary Watkins, Ph.D.

The Face of a Bird of Prey

> What we from our point of view call colonization, missions to the heathen, spread of civilization, etc., has another face--the face of a bird of prey seeking with cruel intentness for distant quarry--a face worthy of a race of pirates and highwaymen. All the eagles and other predatory creatures that adorn our coats of arms seem to me apt psychological representatives of our true nature.
> Jung, 1961, pp. 248-249

In 1925, at the age of 50, Jung visited the Taos Pueblo in New Mexico. According to

Jung(1961), Ochwiay Biano, the chief, shared that his Pueblo people felt whites were "mad,"

"uneasy and restless," always wanting something. Jung inquired further about why he

thought they were mad. The chief replied that white people say they think with their heads - a

sign of illness in his tribe. "Why of course," said Jung, "what do you think with?" Ochwiay

Biano indicated his heart.

Jung reported falling into a "long meditation," in which he grasped for the first time

how deeply colonialism had effected his character and psyche.

> ...someone had drawn for me a picture of the real white man. It was as though until now I had seen nothing but sentimental, prettified color prints. This Indian had struck our vulnerable spot, unveiled a truth to which we are blind. I felt rising within me like a shapeless mist something unknown and yet deeply familiar. And out of this mist, image upon image detached itself: first Roman legions smashing into the cities of Gaul, and the keenly incised features of Julius Caesar, Scipio Africanus, and Pompey. I saw the Roman eagle on the North Sea and on the banks of the White Nile. Then I saw St. Augustine transmitting the Christian creed to the Britons on the tips of Roman lances, and Charlemagne's most glorious forced conversion of the heathen; then the pillaging and murdering bands of the Crusading armies. With a secret stab I realized the hollowness of that old romanticism about the Crusades. Then followed Columbus, Cortes, and the other conquistadors who with fire, sword, torture, and Christianity came down upon even these remote pueblos dreaming peacefully in the Sun, their Father. I saw, too, the people of the Pacific islands decimated by firewater, syphilis, and scarlet fever carried in the clothes the missionaries forced on them.
> Jung, 1961, p. 248

Jung did not access these insights into the cultural unconscious while alone at his tower

in Bollingen. This meditation required his presence at Taos, a place which holds these

tragedies in its own history and countenance. It necessitated his being in deep enough relationship and dialogue with Ochwiay Biano that he was able to glance at himself briefly through the chief's eyes, to see his own shadow as a European for the first time. In his autobiography, he said, "That was enough."

In our view, it was not enough, but only a beginning. We need to sustain and deepen this glance in ways that Jung was unable to do in 1925. Our psyches and societies have been forged on the anvil of colonialism. As depth psychology was being born a hundred years ago, colonialism was stretching to its fullest reach. Depth psychology's development coincides with the rise of national liberation movements and the ending of the colonial era. To the degree that depth psychology is a social critique of the narrowed vision of the dominant aspects of Euro-American culture, it considers problematic many of the same dichotomizing and hierarchizing structures that are critiqued in post-colonial theory. We would not see this as accidental if we understood that the psychic structures and contents that depth psychologists describe reflect the psychic corollaries of colonialism, despite the fact that the context of colonialism is hardly ever named (e.g., you will not find "colonialism" in the index to Jung's collected works, his biographies or his autobiography.[2]

Re-membering the Context of Colonialism for Depth Psychology

> We live in a land where the past is always erased and America is the innocent future in which immigrants can come and start over, where the slate is clean. The past is absent, or it's romanticized. This culture doesn't encourage dwelling on the past, let alone coming to terms with, the truth about the past.
>
> Toni Morrison, in Gilroy,1993, p.180

All practices of healing - such as depth psychology - reflect their own cultural context, while also struggling to address and transcend those aspects of culture that give rise to suffering. Depth psychology can easily be studied to point out how its language and methods reflect a colonial mindset. Various writers have (rightly, in our view) critiqued aspects of depth psychology for being racist, antisemitic, sexist, and Eurocentric (Samuels, 1993). At the same time, depth psychology gives us a methodology with which we can creatively and imaginatively rework current assumptions, biases, or limitations in our ways of seeing the world. This is the aspect of depth psychology which we want to place in dialogue with post-colonial theory. In this paper, we would like to outline how depth psychology, particularly

Jungian and archetypal psychology, attempt to heal the psychic sequelae of colonialism.

From this vantage point, we can place depth psychology's restoratory methodologies alongside those of post-colonial theorists such as Freire (1989), Anzaldua (1990), hooks (1992), Belenky (1997), Griffin (1992), Sulak Sivaraksa(1992), Martin-Baro (1994), Thich Nhat Hanh (1987), and Aung San Suu Kyi (1997) who work with restorative methodologies of "liberation." Holding together Jung's process of individuation and Hillman's process of "seeing through" with processes and goals of liberation largely generated from the South, we can begin to chart paths to a post-colonial consciousness that can be regenerative for both cultures and individuals.

Colonialism, which created the material basis and wealth that gave rise to the technologies of the twentieth century, is based on two kinds of power. The first is the power of one group or individual to appropriate the resources, labor, and territory of another group or individual, creating hierarchy and inequality. The second power is the capacity to deny responsibility for having done so, to silence resistance and opposition, and to normalize the outcome. By normalization we mean that the resultant inequities and suffering are made to appear as if they are completely natural through mythologies of scientific racism, gender role, ethnic identity, national destiny, and social Darwinism. In "official culture," the supposed superiority of some is taken as fate, while the imagined inferiority of others is taken as fact. Beneath this tear in the social and psychic fabric, we each carry the uneasy feeling-sense that there is much about our experience of self, other, and community that can not be said, indeed, even formulated into thoughts.

Further, research into extremely repressive situations show that when people perceive atrocities and injustices, often they must actually renounce their own perception to avoid danger to themselves. In her study of the fourteen years of military dictatorship (1976-1983) in Argentina, which unfortunately was supported and financed by the U.S. government, Diana Taylor calls this "percepticide" According to Taylor, this renunciation "turns the violence on oneself. Percepticide blinds, maims, kills through the senses" (Taylor, 1997, p.124).[3] When whole populations are forced to not-know what is going on around them, when the media choose to not-name injustice, watching-without-seeing becomes "the most dehumanizing of acts." This kind of renunciation establishes a split within the self, where certain knowings are exiled and unavailable for the negotiation of one's life. Robert J. Lifton (1986), in his study of Nazi doctors, described this as a doubling of the self, where one self is condemned to numbness regarding what the other self knows and understands.

The fictitious "rational consumer" self in a homogeneous nation, mythologized in the official history of the modernist era, has been created by a long practice of percepticide. For how many years did history books portray the genocide caused by colonial expansion as a triumph of civilization, the tragedy of slavery and the plantation system as unrelated to the wealth amassed for industrialization, the exclusion of women, Native Americans and African Americans from the political process as the rise of democracy? Educated in this paradigm, how much have we learned to deny? How have we been maimed and blinded by the thousands of media images that allow us to normalize violence, stereotypes, and passivity? In order to see ourselves more fully, the pictures we paint of ourselves and our theories of psychology must also include the likelihood that our perspectives are limited by our situated histories; that what we can see is steeped in collusion with the paradigms that shape our consciousness.

As carriers of internal colonization, we may have developed the habit of silencing our own and other's suffering, resistances, and creativity when these come into contact with the official mythologies of normalized culture. Many of us have learned all too well what not to say and when not to speak. Carried too far, this split may produce in some persons a dissociated sense of a magic interior world where everything is possible, which lives alongside a harsh outer world where nothing can be altered. Interior journeys and aesthetic adventures may be chosen as preferred modes of being, protecting one from exterior realities that seem immutable and fixed. For others, sustained dissociation can create a sense of an impoverished and empty interior, yielding a sense of inferiority and alienation. Feelings of impotence and fatalism become linked with despair, addictions, and violence.

While many cultural groups continue to have public rituals where what has not yet been spoken can be aired communally, the fragmentation of modern urban environments and the dissociation of the individual from the group that is part of the myth of individualism sends others to small dialogue groups or therapy. Private therapy provides a safe space for some people to begin to listen to the silenced voices at the margins of their consciousness. What is known, but not yet said, is invited into the reality of the therapeutic relationship, where there is support for exploring, experimenting, resisting, and seeking alternatives through creativity and conversations with others. When people enter therapy or dialogue groups aimed at consciousness-raising, feelings silenced by shame, fear, and self-hatred emerge along the way to imaging new possibilities.

Individuation

> How old is the habit of denial? We keep secrets from ourselves that all along we know....For perhaps we are like stones; our own history and the history of the world embedded in us, we hold a sorrow deep within and cannot weep until that history is sung.
>
> Susan Griffin, 1992, pp. 4, 8

In addressing the restoration of a torn soul, Jung described the normative psyche he found in the first half of last century: a hierarchically organized psyche, dominated by a one-sided ego and collectively identified persona. Such a hierarchy pushes into the margins all that is inferiorized by the culture (the shadow), and sustains a sense of power through identification with collective norms. Dissociation, denial, repression, projection were the defenses to be studied and confronted - each a psychological variant of a cultural process that maintains the status quo balance of power in colonialism.

In depth psychological methodology, this psychic configuration necessitates a move away from a hierarchy wherein the ego and the persona control the construction and representation of identity. Through attention to dream, image, spontaneous thought, feeling and intuition, previously unrecognized knowings and points of view emerge, which supplant controlling monological thought with a vibrant, multi-layered complexity of dialogue among many.

Jung's hope for this kind of process was that one could begin to differentiate from mindless adherence to collective norms. With this differentiation would come a possible creative participation with culture, imagining and enacting alternatives to the status quo. When therapy is seen as only a retreat to an individual, interior, private space, cut off from culture, this hope becomes short-circuited. The American consumerist ethos too often allows us to see psyche or soul as a privatized possession of the individual, which makes it impossible to grasp the permeability of psyche and culture and the possibility that one's individuation may fuse with liberatory movements within one's culture.

Jungian work begins with "pathologizing" official stories of "normal" and "healthy" adjustment to taken-for-granted social values, and it invites dialogue with all that has been cast into the shadows. Jung's notion that we are surrounded by a collective consciousness that frames our ways of knowing ourselves and others means that to push outside of this frame leads to a "defeat of the ego" and the gradual creation of a new form of subjectivity that is, in its own way, also a defection.

The goal of Jungian work is "individuation," a differentiation of subjectivity away from the fixed and narrow conceptions of personhood which are given by a collective culture. This process could be described as a form of decolonization, a revalorization of those values cast aside by the technologization, industrialization, and rationalism of the modernist era. Jung was clear that this kind of psychic differentiation should not entail a literal isolation.

> Individuation is only possible with people, through people. You must realize that you are a link in a chain, that you are not an electron suspended somewhere in space or aimlessly drifting through the cosmos. You are part of an atomic structure, and that atomic structure is part of a molecule which, with others, builds up a body.
> Jung, 1988, p. 103

Creating community and dialogue was part of individuation.

> Since the individual is not only a single entity, but also by his very existence, presupposes a collective relationship, the process of individuation does not lead to isolation, but to an intenser and more universal collective solidarity.
> Jung 1966, p.155

Having lived through both World Wars as well as the rise of fascism in Europe, Jung believed that the only hope for peace and freedom lay in the ability of individuals to break away from repressive social agendas. Individuation always involves a rupture of the normalized roles of the surrounding social collective.

With this rupture we become capable of new ideas, utopian dreams, and healing insights. Apparently, we have a deep archetypal need to create spaces in our worlds where older, fixed complexes can be metabolized so that spontaneous creativity can emerge. Jungian analysis can be imagined as just such a space. Within the temenos of regular dialogue with a mentor in what Dora Kalff has named "a free and protected space" (Kalff, 1980), an analysand learns a method of self-witnessing, a kind of autoethnography and autoarcheology shared with an educator committed to participatory research. In the form proposed by Jung, Jungian analysis does not diagnose or reduce the images of the analysand to already-known reductive categories. Rather, the encounter is seen as one that involves and changes both in the dialogue, as the analysand practices remembrance in order to regenerate utopian potentials still outside literal everyday routines.

Jung developed the notion of a "transcendent function" as both the medium for, and the outcome of, individuation. A transcendent function involves the creation of practices of dialogue with whatever new images and events emerge spontaneously in our inner and outer worlds. In developing such a function, we work at critical reflection and imaginative interpretation, a hermeneutics that brings the already known into contact with the new. We gain different perspectives from this work, which leads us to understand what we are and what we can become from multiple points of view. Through such a practice we learn to bear the anxieties of disidentification with surrounding cultural constructs and old patterns of thought. We become less defensive and more open to the experimental, unknown, and synchronistic, more aware of unconscious potentials that are still preverbal. As a result, such work often involves the arts - writing, storytelling, painting, movement - in imaginative symbolizations of the dialogue process; and it often involves conversation with others. Jung claimed that the process of developing a transcendent function would lead to "a considerable widening of the horizon" and "a deepened self-knowledge" which might also "humanize" us and "make us more modest" (1966, p.137). He believed that the more we engage in this work, the more fully we can be with others in the world. Finally, there would be, Jung wrote, "no distance, but immediate presence" (Jung, 1973, p.298).

Seeing Through

> ...I do not ever truly have ideas; they have, hold, contain, govern me. Our wrestling with ideas is a sacred struggle, as with an angel; our attempts to formulate, a ritual activity to propitiate the angel. The emotions that ideas arouse are appropriate, and

authentic, too, is our sense of being a victim of ideas, humiliated before their grand vision, our lifetime devotion to them, and the battles we must fight on their behalf.
Hillman, 1975, p. 130

In archetypal psychology we direct our attention to the voices and images of pathology, to that which suffers, often in exile from heroic consciousness. But it is not only to the margins we turn. Indeed, much listening is done to the heroic ego itself, attempting to discern which ideas it has identified with, literalized, and taken for granted. These identifications have exiled other points of view, laying claim on reality and truth. When ideas remain unworked, the reality they spawn is experienced as natural and inevitable, something to be suffered or enjoyed, but not questioned. When ideas are seen through and worked with, they become "the nodes that make possible our ability to see through events into their patterns" (Hillman,1975).

> Listening to the truth through the perspective of the many at the margins, while practicing seeing what one holds most dear and true as a perspective are movements that support each other. They work to free us from false certitude and our easy dismissal of otherness. For Hillman, seeing through or deconstructing ideas is an ongoing process of liberation which allows us to create with ideas, rather than remain enslaved by them. "Ideas are ways of seeing and knowing, or knowing by means of insighting. Ideas allow us to envision and by means of vision we can know" (Hillman, 1975, p. 121).

Many depth psychologists are tempted to split ideas from action, psyche from culture, psychological work from cultural work. Indeed, it is difficult to hold psyche and culture together, to witness pain as it issues from both quarters, and to enter the mess and fray of participation, solidarity, and *respons*ibility. However, in Hillman's archetypal psychology, these separations are seen as false. Ideas and action are "not inherent enemies, and they should not be paired as a contrast" (Hillman, 1975, p.116). Reflection is an activity and action always enacts an idea. "[When] an insight or idea has sunk in, practice visibly changes... By seeing differently, we do differently" (Hillman, 1975, p. 122). Ideas such as "manifest destiny," "growth," "development," "racial superiority," "primitivity," "white supremacy," "noblesse oblige," "individualism" fueled colonialism, shaped psychological theory and research, and mapped themselves onto intrapsychic and interpersonal relationships. Seeing through them is no small matter, and it is a work that affects culture and psyche at the same moment. As in Jung's case, it requires dialogue with or among others who have carried the burden of these ideas.

Liberation

> For me education is simultaneously an act of knowing, a political act, and an artistic event. I no longer speak about a political dimension of education. I no longer speak about a knowing dimension of education. As well, I don't speak about education through art. On the contrary, I say education *is* politics, art, and knowing.
>
> Freire, 1985, p.17

In the year that Jung died (1961) a young teacher in Brazil named Paulo Freire was asked to initiate a literacy program that would involve teaching 5 million people previously denied education by institutions of neo-colonialism that had survived slavery. As in the United States, where also it was forbidden to teach slaves how to read and write, such deprivation was used in Northeast Brazil to disempower the masses and make claims of their inferiority easier. Such claims would then rationalize an abuse of labor, and the consignment of the masses to conditions of poverty, malnutrition and illness in order that others in power could profit. Freire deeply believed that the power to read and write should be linked with developing a capacity to decode the reality in which one lives. In literacy groups, a leader, or "animator," helped people engage in a process of questioning, of seeing through, their circumstances. Such questioning led to naming "generative" words and themes for one's writing and one's living.

As in psychotherapy, these groups directed participants' attention to what they were suffering. Unlike individual therapy, participants easily saw that their individual suffering was shared by others in the group. As the origins of suffering were interrogated, group members began to see that their personal difficulties were grounded in the arrangement of power and resources which they had largely taken-for-granted. Psychological change and cultural change were understood to be indissolubly linked.

Freire reasoned that everyone would discover obstacles as each began to examine the "limit situations" which restricted their freedom, obstacles which prevented further growth and in many cases made survival difficult. Some people would accept these limit situations as inevitable; whereas others would begin to perform what Freire called "limit acts." Limit acts are strategies that allow us to detach from seeing limit situations as unchangeable givens - a refusal and problematizing of what is normalized by those in power. The question then becomes how to break through the barrier by reflection, witnessing, acting, and reimagining.

By first seeing through arrangements one has taken as god-given, one emerges into a field of creativity and imagination that Freire named "annunciation." The goal is to uncover some "untested feasability": "something the utopian dreamer knows exists, but knows that it will be attained only through a practice of liberation" (Freire, 1989, p. 206). It is "an untested thing, an unprecedented thing, something not yet clearly known and experienced, but dreamed of."

Like Jung, Freire thought that his method of dialogical action would not provide a blueprint for an outcome. Only out of local dialogue could alternative futures be imagined by those who had the courage to refuse "being-in-a-lesser-way." No one can do this for another, because to think for others simply recolonizes them. To be free involves becoming an active participant in one's own context and history, to become *consciente* or aware and in dialogue with others. This is the prerequisite of humanization, becoming what Freire called *o ser-mais* - "being-in-a-larger-way" or being more-so.

The short-lived populist government of Goulart which created the National Literacy Program or Programa Nacional de Alphabetizacao, ended abruptly with the military coup of April 1, 1964 that was assisted by the US government and the CIA. The literacy movement was viewed as subversive to the status quo, which indeed it was. During the fifteen years of military rule which followed, Freire was forced to go into exile and many of the people with whom he worked were tortured and killed. His book, The Pedagogy of the Oppressed, became world famous, was translated into dozens of languages, but was banned in most Latin American countries as well as the Iberian Peninsula during the years of his exile.

In the Space of Rupture, Imagination

> The critical ontology of ourselves has to be considered not, certainly as a theory, a doctrine, nor even as a permanent body of knowledge that is accumulating; it has to be conceived as an attitude, an ethos, a philosophical life in which the critique of what we are is at one and the same time the historical analysis of the limits that are imposed on us and an experiment with the possibility of going beyond them.
> Michel Foucault, 1986, p.50

In the long development of modernist Eurocentric discourse, an image of the completed rational subject who ruled the psyche paralleled the notion of the nation-state which ruled the political-economic sphere. History was seen as a progressive evolution, blessed by God or at least "manifest destiny," from the "primitive" irrational to the "civilized" rational of contemporary Euro-American culture. In this fantasy, much was silenced that has begun to be spoken of today. In an era of globalization, difference, not consensus, multiplicity, not unity, conflict, not repression and disidentification rather than identity, is all too apparent.

In the second half of the twentieth century, numerous writers on every continent - including many depth psychologists - have begun to deconstruct modernist fantasies about unified selves evolving in a progressively developing world. The voices of communities and environments that have suffered as a result of the hymn to progress have found an audience, complicating the story and making it difficult to view the march of development as an unqualified success. As a result of this eruption of multiple points of view, much current research focuses on the local, the idiosyncratic, the forgotten, the denied, and the crossroads of influences and intentions that make up both psychological states as well as regional history.

Contemporary post-colonial studies posit rupture, disequilibrium, the witnessing of ones own conflicts and contradictions, and the imagination and creation of utopian dreams for alternative futures and experiences as central to our lived experience in globalized environments. What is most apparent in this discourse is the difficult, almost alchemical work involved in imagining a coherent self or a functional community in solidarity, no longer seen as given, but, at best, utopian goals. The norm has become denial, fragmentation, dissociation, and contradiction--states of being which Jung suggests points to a type of personality more like an archipelago than a continent. As depth psychologists, we must listen to dreamers who dare to imagine in the spaces created by these ruptures, dreamers who bring to us possibilities for post-colonial consciousness. Here, we have chosen as examples Ignacio Martin-Baro and Gloria Anzaldua.

Ignacio Martin-Baro, a Jesuit psychologist from El Salvador who was murdered for his alliance with the poor by "security " forces funded by the United States, wrote about the revolutionary ideal of community (*el pueblo* or *el pueblo unido)* linked to a process of liberation similar to what Freire described. He said that *el pueblo* is: "an opening - an opening against all closure, flexibility against everything fixed, elasticity against all rigidity, a readiness to act against all stagnation." It is "a hunger for change, affirmation of what is new; life in hope" (1994, p.183). In order to exist as a community or *el pueblo* a group of people must necessarily move beyond the current literal state of their relationships to imagine a "negation of non-solidarity." A "dis-associating and egoistic individualism," which denies the connection between self and culture, must be abandoned to forge this new consciousness "that does not involve the non-being of others, and that comes about through a *having* that is communitarian and united" (1994, p.183).

Martin-Baro's utopian vision of community involves a changed notion of self. "The self is open to becoming different, on a plane of equality with neither privileges nor oppressive mechanisms." It implies "an opening toward the other, a readiness to let oneself be questioned by the other, as a separate being, to listen to his or her words, in dialogue; to confront reality in relationship to and with (but not over) him or her, to unite in solidarity in a struggle in which both will be transformed" (1994, p. 183).

For Chicana activist Gloria Anzaldua(1990), a new way of being in the world emerges when one "has gone from being the sacrificial goat to becoming the officiating priestess at the crossroads" (p. 380), where "*mestiza* consciousness" can develope. With the notion of *la Mestiza*, Anzaldua is describing the development of a new type of subjectivity. "In perceiving conflicting information and points of view, [*la Mestiza*] is subjected to a swamping of her psychological borders. She has discovered that she can't hold concepts or ideas in rigid boundaries. The borders and walls that are supposed to keep the undesirable ideas out are entrenched habits and patterns of behavior; these habits and patterns are the enemy within. Rigidity means death. Only by remaining flexible can she stretch the psyche horizontally and vertically. *La Mestiza* constantly has to shift out of habitual formations; from convergent thinking, analytical reasoning that tends to use rationality to move toward a single goal (a Western mode), to divergent thinking, characterized by movement away from set patterns and goals and toward a more whole perspective, one that includes rather than excludes" (p. 379).

When we begin to live out of this open awareness, it changes the way we see the world, the way we understand ourselves, and the way we behave. By gathering up many lost and excluded parts of ourselves and our communities, we begin the process of giving voice to strengths, wounds, and needs as we "seek to recover and reshape" what Anzaldua(1990) calls our "spiritual identities" (p. 386).

Psychological and Cultural Restoration

> If we do not fashion for ourselves a picture of the world, we do not see ourselves either, who are the faithful reflections of that world. Only when mirrored in our picture of the world can we see ourselves in the round. Only in our creative acts do we step forth into the light and see ourselves whole and complete. Never shall we put any face on the world other than our own, and we have to do this precisely in order to find ourselves.
>
> Jung, 1960, p. 379

What can we contribute to a "picture of the world" from this holding together of depth psychology with post-colonial theory and practice? Can we begin to imagine the norm of both individual and community life as evolving interconnected systems of multiple elements that potentially are chaotic and discordant, that is, not necessarily moving toward order, unity, reason, progress, or enlightenment? Can we envision the alternating rhythms of seeing through and utopic imagining as liberating to both psyche and culture? Can we take the process of moving attention to the margin, of listening into the multiple voices that have been exiled from consciousness, as foundational to both depth psychology and post-colonial cultural work? What if, as depth psychologically-minded cultural workers, we labor against falsely separating the processes of individuation from those of liberation? Can we bear to acknowledge the complete interdependence of psyche and culture, while working to differentiate ourselves from identifications with collective norms and ideas?

Healing arts develop because every cultural environment evolves routines of normalization that are ruptured regularly by life circumstances. Chosen or unchosen transitions and circumstances - the death of a loved one, illness, growing into adolescence, new or ending relationships - break apart old ways of thinking and being everywhere. With the development of colonialism, whole populations began to suffer previously unknown types of rupture - genocide on a massive, unthinkable scale, slavery involving tens of millions of people, colonial conquest, world war, massive migrations due to the disruption of self-sufficient local economies. These ruptured conditions are documented contexts for the increased incidence of mental illness and experiences of suffering (Kleinman, 1988). The process of rupture is further intensified by globalization. In contemporary neo-colonial and hierarchical environments, the oppressed feel a constant assault on, and rupture of, their dignity, humanity, and dreams for happiness. Those privileged to live comfortable lives in the midst of human misery, must perform ever more complete percepticide within their own psyches if they are to sustain a sense of comfort.

In all of these forms of rupture, whatever structures of self-identity have existed up until that point may prove insufficient to navigate the new situation. At such a moment, we can imagine that a deep human need for meaning, coherence, community, and hope may reassert itself, attempting to create processes of restoration through the cultural work that arises from alternating waves of seeing through and utopian imagining. Such imagining necessarily reaches into the past for images of recollection which are capable of contextualizing, narrating, and mythologizing the current situation.

In what we call "creative restoration," restoration to an idealized past - a golden age - is neither sought nor possible. By creative restoration we mean psychologically-minded cultural work and culturally-minded psychological work that crafts psyche and world in the image of the deeply desired; that provides a healing context where what has been torn can be reimagined and sutured in concert with others. Such restorative work consists of acts of love and care that have both human and spiritual dimensions. While certain restorative work can be suffused with wrong turns and misreadings, sometimes it breaks into moments of grace and communitas that allow desired transformations.

However, the drag and weight of our historical, cultural, and personal complexes are forceful, and there is also a type of "normative restoration" that is constantly available in times of rupture. Here, ways of the past are anxiously referenced and rehearsed. Jung raised the possibility that when confronted with new potentials which needed to be assimilated to consciousness, his patients might instead move toward what he called "the retrogressive restoration of the persona" (Jung, p. 163). This can happen with communities and nations as well. In normative restoration, we cling rigidly to the constructs of the past, ceremonializing them and rejecting all new elements as polluting. Facing an unwanted rupture or rapid social change, fascist violence or personal crisis, we can use the arts of restoration - performance, storytelling, ceremony - to reify mythic figures and historical ideas, to defend against what is new and nearby, to create compassion fatigue and numbness toward current suffering.

Both agendas for social and cultural liberation as well as psychological individuation can yield a type of normative restoration. In many liberation movements, leaders have failed to realize that new societies would require new subjectivities - people who were critical, imaginative, and free to voice oppositional strategies and points of view. History yields many sad examples of movements that began as liberatory and ended as controlling and repressive. At the same time, many schools of psychology, intending to assist individuals in finding new potentials, stop short of critiquing and engaging the social limitations which make transformation impossible. Thus, often the mental health establishment helps to personalize, marginalize, and medicate what is essentially a protest against a dehumanizing and repressive social milieu.

If projects of social liberation and personal individuation are to become processes of creative restoration, each requires completion in the other. Anyone involved in the differentiation from collective consciousness for which individuation calls will soon find social situations where new images and behaviors are necessary. Jungian analyst Adolf Guggenbuhl-Craig hoped that depth psychologists would be thorns in the side of their communities. On the other hand, anyone who truly wishes for liberation for the marginalized and oppressed will soon discover their needs for individual experience and support in reimagining alternative identities and futures and in voicing their own, personal, critical and dissenting perspectives

Liberation and individuation projects that aspire to creative restoration require the capacity to question the status quo and work with imaginal scripts. bell hooks (1994) speaks of the kind of education that is needed to support such transgressing of boundaries, an education that whets the appetite and creates the capacity for the practice of freedom. She says, "It is also about transforming the image, creating alternatives, asking ourselves questions about what kinds of images subvert, pose critical alternatives, and transform our worldviews and move us away from dualistic thinking about good and bad. Making a space for the transgressive image, the outlaw rebel vision, is essential to any effort to create a context for transformation" (1992, p. 4).

In our analysis, the Jungian work of individuation, the archetypal work of seeing through, and the practices of liberation and conscienticization, are each instances of the arts of cultural and psychological restoration that have been practiced by healers all over the world for centuries in various local forms. Yet leaving behind the triumphalist and modernist fantasies of progress toward perfection, in a post-colonial discourse we are left with projects that are always provisional and incomplete. In a world desperate for new understandings that will mitigate suffering and inspire creation, we need to be clear that both liberation movements and individuation processes can also be retrogressive and support neo-colonial hierarchies. We need to learn how to distinguish creative restorations that bring together complex and multiple dissonant experiences through dialogue, from normative restorations that force our experience apart into oppositional and dissociative binary oppositions: pure vs. polluted, insider vs. outsider, sacred vs. profane, us and them.

Neither depth psychology nor post-colonial consciousness promises a safe distance in which we can stand free of the cultural constructs that form us and with which we constantly collude. Instead, both require a complex, ongoing and situated engagement that necessitates bearing suffering, witnessing our own involvement in neo-colonial relationships, and bending in toward the world to accept the responsibilities of attending to what has been experienced and understood. We need to reach for creative restoration cautiously, in dialogue with others who challenge us, knowing that we bring the past with us partly unconsciously. Yet we can be drawn forward by a paradoxical joy of vulnerability, which allows what has been suffered to be known, bringing with it potential relief from the dissociations of both self and community. If, as healers skilled in the arts of creative restoration, we are successful , we may find a sweet liberation from imprisoning ideas and cultural arrangements, and the pleasure which comes from working together towards a deeply -desired, just and peaceful world.

References

Anzaldua, G. (1990). Making face, making soul: *Haciendo* caras. San Francisco: aunt lute Foundation Books.

Aung San Suu Kyi (1997). The voice of hope. New York: Seven Stories Press.

Belenky, M., Bond, L., Weinstock, J. (1997). A tradition that has no name: Nurturing the development of people, families, and communities. New York: Basic Books.

Foucault, M. (1986). What is Enlightenment? In P. Rabinow (Ed.), The Foucault Reader. Harmondsworth: Peregrine.

Freire, P. (1985). Reading the World and Reading the Word: An Interview with Paulo Freire. Language Arts, 62, 1, 15-21,

Freire, P. (1989). Pedagogy of the oppressed. New York: Continuum.

Gilroy, P. (1993). Small acts. London: Serpent's Tail.

Glendinning, C.(1999). Off the map (An expedition deep into imperialism, the global economy and other earthly whereabouts). Boston: Shambhala.

Griffin, S. (1992). A chorus of stones. New York: Anchor Books.

Hillman, J. (1975). Re-visioning psychology. New York: Harper & Row.

Homi Bhabba. (1994). The location of culture. London and New York: Routledge.

hooks, b. (1992). Black looks: Race and representation. Boston: South End Press.

hooks, B. (1994). Teaching to transgress: Education as the practice of freedom. New York: Routledge.

Jaffe, A. (1977). Remembering Jung: Conversations about C. G. Jung and his work. Video produced by George Wagner, directed by Suzanne Wagner. Los Angeles: C. G. Jung Institute of Los Angeles.

Jung, C.G. (1960). The structure and dynamics of the psyche. CW Vol. 8. Princeton: Princeton University Press.

Jung, C. G. (1961). Memories, dreams, reflections. New York: Random House.

Jung, C. G. (1953/1966). Two essays on analytical psychology. CW Vol. VII. Princeton: Princeton University Press.

Jung, C. G. (1973/1975). Letters. G. Adler, A. Jaffe (Eds.). Princeton: Princeton University Press.

Kalff, D. (1980). Sandplay: A psychotherapeutic approach to the psyche. Boston: Sigo Press.

Kleinman, A. (1988). Re-thinking psychiatry. New York: Free Press.

Lifton, R. J. (1986). Nazi doctors: Medical killing and the psychology of genocide. New York: Basic Books.

[Lorenz], H. Shulman (1997). Living at the edge of chaos. Einsiedeln: Daimon Verlag.

Lorenz, H. Shulman (2000). The presence of absence: Mapping post-colonial spaces. In D. Slattery & L. Corbett (Eds.), Depth psychology: Meditations in the field. Einsiedeln: Daimon Verlag.

Martin-Baro, I. (1994). Writings for a liberation psychology. Cambridge: Harvard University Press.

Odajynk, V. W. (1976). Jung and politics: The political and social ideas of C. G. Jung. New York: Harper.

Samuels, A.(1993). The political psyche. New York: Routledge.

Sulak Sivaraksa (1992). Seeds of peace: A Buddhist vision for renewing society. Berkeley: Parallax Press.

Taylor, D. (1997) Disappearing acts. Durham and London: Duke University Press.

Thich Nhat Hanh (1987). Being peace. Berkeley: Parallax Press.

Turner, V. (1969). The ritual process. Ithaca, NY: Cornell University Press.

Watkins, M. (1992). From individualism to the interdependent self: Changing paradigms in psychotherapy. Psychological perspectives, 27, 52-69.

Watkins, M. (2000). Depth psychology and the liberation of being. In R. Brooke (Ed.), Pathways into the Jungian world. London: Routledge.

Watkins, M. (2000). Seeding liberation: A dialogue between depth psychology and liberation psychology. In D. Slattery & L. Corbett (Eds.), Depth psychology: Meditations in the field. Einsiedeln: Daimon Verlag.

---

[1]We dedicate this paper to Aung San Su Kyi, the leader of the democracy movement in Burma, and a Nobel Peace Prize recipient. Her leadership exemplifies the deep linkage between individuation and liberation this paper speaks to. Unfortunately, her life is presently in grave danger from the military government of Burma, and we urge you to write them in support of her.

[2]Aniela Jaffe remarked that the part of Jung's Memories, Dreams, Reflections that was cut was the chapter on his travels. It seems Jung had gone on at great length about their significance. To Jaffe these pages seemed out of tune with the rest of the book, and so they were deleted (Jaffe, 1977).

[3]Taylor sees the performance of acts of terror on the part of the Argentine military government as primarily aimed at normalizing the collaboration of the population with repression. "The military violence could have been relatively invisible. The fact that it wasn't indicates that the population as a whole was the intended target, positioned by means of the spectacle. People had to deny what they saw, and by turning away collude with the violence around them. They knew people were 'disappearing.' Men in military attire, trucks, and helicopters surrounded the area, closed in on the hunted individuals, and 'sucked' them off the street, out of a movie theater, from a classroom or a workplace. And those in the vicinity were forced to notice, however much they pretended not to. Other spectators who have suffered similar violence - Elie Wiesel watching the Nazis exterminate the man who destroyed one of the chimneys at Auschwitz, Rigoberta Menchu watching her brother be tortured and burned alive - have judged this watching to be the most dehumanizing of acts" (Taylor, 1997, p.124).

Seeing Red: In A Dark Night of the American Soul by Aaron Kipnis, Ph.D.

Introduction

From 1971 to 2001, the prison population in America grew almost seven hundred percent. With roughly 2 million Americans behind bars, we now have the highest incarceration rate in the world. Four million more are under criminal justice supervision in some form (BJS, DOJ, 1999) A fear of violence, or perhaps even dread of civil disorder, appears to be feeding the rapid-cell-growth of what can accurately be called an American Gulag (Lait, 1998). This is not a global phenomenon. It is particular to post-modern America and historically unprecedented in a free nation (Walmsley, 1997).

The fantasy of equality, liberty and justice seems deeply etched into America's multifaceted psyche. The myth of a free nation, with a passion to build a true democracy, is still resonant in the imagination of many Americans. The brighter a light shines, however, the more distinct a shadow it casts. From the perspective of many living in the eclipse zones, a dark night of the American soul permeates and persists in the borderlands of the American dream. America's poor, uneducated, mentally ill, substance-addicted, and racial minorities are visibly over represented among the residents in the archipelago of despair now referred to as "the prison-industrial complex" by many human rights activists today (Zimmring & Hawkins, 1991; Torrey, 1995; Currie, 1998).

Little psychological, vocational, or educational assistance is offered most inmates. Widespread neglect and abuse of prisoners has created, by default, a pervasive clinical fallacy about rehabilitation. The nihilistic mantra of those who make the policies fueling the incarceration jihad is: Nothing Works.

The seeming irrationality of a society willing to spend more money to incarcerate than to educate the "criminal class" (Ambrosio & Schiraldi, 1997; Phinney, 1998) serves an unbroken continuum of ruthless labor commodification in America, from Colonial era African enslavement to prison labor contracts now sold on 21st century stock exchanges. Psychologically, when a dominant culture uses its full power to disenfranchise and dehumanize a minority culture, a scapegoat complex is often active in that nation's psyche. As with wars and other catastrophes, today's trauma in the heart of American justice may open vents into deeper strata of the cultural unconscious. In my experience, the degree of injustice, oppression and violence tolerated toward specific groups in the United States has some people "seeing red"—a condition of blind instinctual activation in which both extremely heroic and horrific transformative acts are known to occur.

Within psychology, the dialog on violence is quite disparate. Like the blind reporting on elephants, most schools investigate but one small slice of a complex phenomenon. Cognitive psychology reduces the etiology of violence to faulty thinking; developmental and dynamic theory see recapitulations of personal and familial history; sociology examines the impact of hierarchical structures on specific groups, ecological and social psychologies point to environmental degradation; humanism finds negative self regard, neuroscience spotlights organic deficits, behaviorism prescribes retraining, psychiatry cites brain chemistry; theology laments spiritual alienation, religion decries moral decay; and criminal justice blames deviance. This paper considers a few themes that depth psychology might contribute to the wide-ranging academic and social discourse on violence and intolerance in America.

Perspectives on Violence

Most disciplines concerned with human violence today are roughly situated within one of two large camps. One contemporary stream of thought emerges from the essentialist headwaters of biological predeterminism—Nature. This perspective sees human beings as still dancing an evolutionary two-step to old tunes sung by DNA. The belief that the predominate etiologies of behavior and identity develop out of biological structures, is the neo-Darwinian theoretical foundation for the bio-psychiatry movement widely dominating behavioral science today. This research has created powerful techniques and chemicals that change behavior. It has thus seduced many of psychology's wayward children back to the shelter of their more respectable parents in neuroscience.

On the other side of the theoretical spectrum is social constructivism–Nurture. Many of this camp's inhabitants pitch their tents at the confluence of post-modern political, philosophical and social science theory. This field asserts that self and action are largely of Procrustean origin—the product of ubiquitous social norming forces. Constructivist theory has raised important perspectives about how rigidly defined consensus realities imposed on human potential and diversity can induce distortions of self. It has also advanced methods for the situational liberation of psyche, person and culture embedded in psycho-social structures designed to channel human libido into serving a dominant group's designs.

The founders of depth psychology leaned somewhat toward the essentialist camp of science and many of the last generation's "postians" break post-modern bread with the constructivists. Despite its theorists' proclivities, however, depth psychology does not fully scale either evolutionary or social psychology's epistemological vistas. To do so would be to leave the province of the soul--the first and overriding concern of archetypal psychology. Just as bio-psychiatry can relegate soul to a ghost in the machine, constructivism often eschews essentialism, reducing soul to a pathological component of social ennui. The notion of an autonomous interior life—particularly as related to any sort of asocial telos—seems to be an anathema to both major behavioral science camps. While not inured to social and developmental theories, archetypal psychology also investigates imaginal structures in which the rough beasts of cultural entropy may slumber or emerge, aroused and ravenous into the world of the living.

Denial of the Imaginal

In his early study of self-inflicted violence—suicide—James Hillman observed: "An objective enquiry in this field somehow betrays the impulse of life itself" (1976, p.17). This being so, however, we can begin by simply acknowledging that violence is a pervasive social phenomenon in America. We are embedded in a cultural matrix, which has a known, quantifiable violent proclivity. The incidences of violent human behaviors inhabit actuarial displays with roughly predictable tolls that, in most categories, far exceed the rates of all other industrial democracies (CDC, 1999).

Denial and dread, whether of our counter-transference in the consulting room or revulsion toward the violence outside it, can keep us from investigating less visible recess of the cultural imagination. In the volume quoted below, Jung cautions that not knowing is potentially more dangerous than facing the cultural shadow. Archetypal psychology suggests we may risk literalization of, or possession by, the psychological complexes we fail to work through, as a person or as a nation (Zweig & Wolf, 1998). As we attempt to feel our way past the sharp edged empirical silhouettes cast by behavioral and social science, we proceed unscientifically, with "beginners mind," toward the faint shape of intolerable images in the gloom. We are not as certain in this place of the imagination. We experience more paradox and less authority here.

From a depth psychological perspective, cultures are embedded with archetypal themes. National and cultural identity can be seen as representing imaginal streams in the collective psyche. We look to the cultural imagination as a source code for behaviors that condition membership in specific social structures. Cultural identity is as defined by what we unconsciously resist as it is by the ideals we consciously affirm.

From this vantage, archetypal proclivities are at play in both overt and covert forms of violence that dominant groups perpetrate against others. Moreover, individual psychodynamic concepts such as: projection, idealization, devaluation, repression, compensation, regression, conversion and sublimation, may also describe interpersonal, social, national, and global constructs in cultural psychology. What then do we imagine is feeding our nation's attempt to isolate and contain its shadow? Upon what imaginal foundations does America continue sanctioning expansion of the world's largest penal system?

The global wars and genocides of the last century readily reveal the consequences that collective denial and archetypal possession may hold for any culture. Carl Jung's examination of WW II Germany noted that his patient's prewar dreams reflected their collective humiliation and downward mobility in the years following the Treaty of Versailles. Jung believed that National Socialism exploited the "unexamined" shadow of the collective unconscious through an archetypal personification of order (Nazism) and violent projection of the cultural shame outward onto a scapegoat (the racially impure). He wrote,

> We are living in times of great disruption: political passions are aflame, internal upheavals have brought nations to the brink of chaos. [The analyst] feels the violence of its impact even in the quiet of his consulting room [and] cannot avoid coming to grips with contemporary history, even if his very soul shrinks from the political uproar, the lying propaganda, and the jarring speeches of the demagogues. We need not mention his duties as a citizen, which confront him with a similar task. (*CW* 10, para.11)

Hillman furthered the concern raised in Jung's 1946 *Fight with the shadow* by charging contemporary psychology with actually drawing libido away from the polis. He believes that an over emphasis on childhood and interiority, "deprives the political world" of our legitimate anger about concrete social issues and that therapy by, "ignoring the outer soul, supports the decline of the actual world" (1992, p.5).

At the confluence of Liberation and Depth psychology some of us have begun to imagine soul work and social work as two wings of the same bird that must beat in synchrony for sustained or graceful flight to ensue. Elsewhere in this volume, Helene Shulman Lorenz and Mary Watkins note,

> Many schools of psychology, intending to assist individuals in finding new potentials, stop short of critiquing and engaging the social limitations, which make transformation impossible. Thus, it is often the case that the mental health establishment helps to personalize, marginalize, and medicate what is essentially a protest against dehumanizing and repressive social milieus. (2001)

Liberation psychology suggests that intentional engagement with the world holds opportunities for individuation that may not otherwise emerge from introspection or analysis alone. At the inception of psychology's second century, many of us feel called beyond the borders of the consulting room, to meet our "duties as citizens," as part and process of an in-the-world, soul-making. History begs the question: What socio-political forces exploit the "unexamined" national psyche of America today?

The Deep Psychology of Violence

If we consider human violence as a dis-ease of the imagination—even a virulent, potentially contagious one—then current violence epidemiology seems more rooted in the 19th century than the third millennium. Historically, for example, many perceived alcoholism as a moral defect. Now, most clinicians believe it is a treatable illness. Thanks, in part, to Jung's contribution to the early formation of A.A., much of the addiction field also understands alcoholism as a spiritual malaise, which can thus be remediated as such. I believe we can appropriately view much criminal behavior in a similar manner.

Violent acts readily confuse inner and outer life. Violence is iconoclastic. It shatters the rigid details of egoic life into disassociated fragments. Violence, like Eros, can draw us out of a diminished self into greater complexity. In nature, an ecology of violence fosters its endless transformation. The cracked shell surrenders to the chick; seedpods burst and spew new life, a snake grows out through splits of skin and the winter fire's ash feeds the spring's wild flowers.

Violence is rarely "senseless." There is often a raison d'être behind violent acts. People employ violence as a tool to produce specific external and internal reactions. It has a function. People may act violently as an attempt to create more homeostasis in an unbalanced system. Violence is readily provoked by the intense emotions generated in people subjected to tyranny and injustice—the American Revolution was one such example.

Not unlike various drugs, violence has quasi-biological and psychological aspects that can catalylize alerted states of awareness. Some sociopaths, for example, actually become calmer when witnessing violent acts. Violence is energetic. It has force, direction, and flow. Violence has numinous, intoxicating, and archetypal dimensions. Perpetrators of violent acts frequently report feeling powerful, even godlike during their commission. Paradoxically, however, violent behavior is most often an expression of weakness and failure. And, as is often the case with all but the truly psychopathic, tremendous shame and grief arise about the wide range of loss that can follow their violent acts. The unbearable weight of shame, paradoxically, can then provoke more violent behavior in a self-propagating cycle of violence.

Violent acts are often symptomatic of a disintegrative, addictive system. Like most addictions, when left untreated, frequency and intensity of use tend to increase. Many hide violent fantasy just as they closet denigrated drug or sexual appetites, AIDS, poverty, ethnicity or other characteristics that may be deemed indicative of deviance by holders of dominant social norms. We may fear reprisal for openly acknowledging experience with violence or interest in it.

Varied historical events demonstrate that the more inhumane a culture becomes, the more violence it generates, internally or externally. Violent behavior is thus sometimes a completely normal response to an abnormal situation (Kipnis, 1999). Though some may be born that way, many theorists believe sociopathy is predominately learned behavior. With the highest rates of child poverty, abuse, and neglect in the industrial world, American children also have the highest violence and violent death rates (NCANDS, 1999). Abuse inculcates shame. Shame induces pain. Pain can be masked by: drugs, alcohol, sex, over-work, and other compulsions. Psychic pain can also be ameliorated by the cold, narcissistic deadness of sociopathy. But the psychic numbing of a libido wrapped up in a quasi-biological state of narcissistic stasis can be experienced as more disturbing to the psyche than pain itself.

Some sociopaths become vampiric in a desperate quest to draw red heat to a soul in ice. Violence then becomes the predominate way such an emotionally numbed person knows how to feel fully alive or powerful. Jungian Psychiatrist Adolf Guggenbuhl-Craig cautions that, "If we entirely repress the demonic side we become bloodless, empty, not connected to any sort of Eros" (1996, p. viii). Violence is vivid. It engages intense emotions. Violence, for a moment, can return vitality to an imaginal life desiccated by the vapid badlands of American consumer culture or pummeled into quiescence by brutality and indifference. Behaviorally speaking, violence can produce a range of secondary gains that promote rather than restrain the repetition of such acts.

Reddening the Work

Violence "reddens" psyche. Perpetrators of violent acts speak of: "seeing red; reaching a breaking, bursting, or flash point; exploding with rage." Criminals get caught red handed (with blood on their hands). Red permeates the lexicon of emotional intensity. Intense passions are not mauve, fuchsia, taupe or tangerine. They are crimson, scarlet, incarnadine, florid. Desire and hate smolder. Love becomes inflamed. Anger turns red hot.

Reddening reveals the flush of: desire, fever, excitement, estrus, embarrassment, pride, frustration, or rage. Dionysian revelry paints the town red. The mid-life crisis abandons the beige sedan to drive a red sports car. Women don red "power" suits for executive suites and redden their lips in other pursuits. Sun, irritation and spanking all redden the hide. Simply viewing red can speed a person's pulse, increase respiration rates and raise blood pressure.

Red is primary. It vibrates at the lower end of the visible spectrum. When recovering from temporary color-blindness induced by brain injury, patients begin to see red before any other color returns (Ensenberger, 1997).

Red tape infuriates. Red ink bankrupts. Red lining isolates. Red lights demand we: Stop! They also signal: ambulance, fire truck, police car coming; sex sold here; heavy equipment on the move, out of gas, oil pressure low, live wire, system failure, melt down, radiation leak, explosion eminent. Red alert! Red flag! Red Zone! Code Red! The president' red phone is a "Hot Line" to a finger poised upon a Red Button. The matador's red cape captivates the bull's red eye. Ole!

America was forged in a red-hot crucible of war. Thomas Jefferson's tree of liberty is steeped in the blood of tyrants and patriots, none less red than the other. America fought the Red Coats, the Redskins, the Red Guard and the Red Brigade. The English projected power toward the colonies under banners of the British Red Ensign (Union Jack). Hitler's Nazi banner was literally dipped in martyr's blood. Japan's flag is still emblazoned with the red solar disk of the Shinto War Goddess, Amataratsu, to whom Japanese emperors have always traced their divine lineage. The blood of slaves, indigenous people, immigrants, prisoners and the poor upon whose backs the few built wealth and power here, permeates the mortar holding together the bricks of our nation. No attempts to whiten history have successfully washed their reddened imprints away.

Reddening confers life and takes it. Violent death is as red as Birth. Seeing red signals that a moment of great transformation is about to occur. Reddening empowers a mother to lift a car off her child, a soldier to rush a machine gun, or a culture to throw off oppression through becoming "mad as Hell" (where a very red Devil lives). In alchemy, reddening (rubedo) denotes the last stage of the "work" before base material turns, at last, into gold. This is a reason why the alchemist's prime object of desire, the Philosopher Stone, was also named "Red Lion" or "Great Red Water" (Edinger, 1985, pp. 72, 148, 154). The Hebraic God of the Old Testament worked his own divine alchemy to create Adam out of red earth.

Hawaiian volcano goddess, Peli, embodies the paradox of red's equally destructive and generative power. An erupting volcano spews red rivers of molten rock. Everything in her path vaporizes into flame. Yet, new soil and fertile ash follow in her wake. Hawaii is the only place in the world where land mass is continually growing. As incandescent lava pours into the sea, one can actually witness the roiling birth of new earth.

Hephestus inhabits the volcanoes of European mythic landscapes. He is a lame but fecund figure who works the blazing heart of magma as a forge to make wondrous objects for the gods. Hephestus is Aphrodite's lover. She also mates with Aries, War God of the red planet--Mars. These archetypal personifications present two faces of the masculine soul, one reddened by generative power, the other by destruction. Beauty loves them both.

Tempering

Many indigenous cultures understand the reddening of psyche as a post-latency phenomenon that calls for the concerted focus of the entire adult population. In Africa they call this adolescent libido surge Latima. Various tribal traditions hold that if the wild red horse of Latima is not harnessed to the cart of community, the uninitiated young men will run wild and literally set fire to the village (Somé, 1994). With more young men dying from gunshots in American cites than in civil wars around the world, this metaphor of burning down the house does not feel so distant from our contemporary experience in the New West. Robert Bly contends that those who fail to build initiation huts for young men will have to build more prisons (1998).

Through studies in nuclear physics, Western science learned how to contain, transform and intentionally release elemental energy. But America has largely lost the sacred technologies which sustained social homeostasis for thousands of years in other cultures. Instead of hosting the alchemical process by which adolescent soulfire is directed into the engine of culture, advocates for social order increasingly embrace methods that attempt instead to turn down the heat of youth, contain their passions, and even extinguish their sacred fire altogether.

The U.S. now consumes over 90 percent of the world's Ritalin, up over 700 percent from a decade ago (Breggin, 1998). As diagnostic criteria for conduct and attention "disorders" increasingly pathologize the reddening of adolescence, roughly one in ten American schoolboys is being prescribed Latima quenching chemicals. From a depth perspective, this practice is dangerous. Archetypal forces do not simply submit to egoic will or neurological flattening; Latima will seek expression.

A person without fire has no will. They do not possess the power to actualize their dreams, protect the boundaries of others, or even defend their own. Passion, creativity and fire are intimately linked. When our talents are engaged we get "fired up." When suppressed, Latima smolders, like a coal fire that secretly burns underground for decades, until it finds a new vent to the surface and erupts. Poet Langston Hughes asks,

> What happens to a dream deferred?
> Does it dry up like a raisin in the sun?
> Or fester like a sore—and then run?
> Does it stink like rotten meat?
> Or crust and sugar over—like a syrupy sweet?
> Maybe it just sags like a heavy load.
> Or does it explode? (1951)

The Criminalization of Despair

Facing violence can be a step toward self-knowledge. But the province of Violence is not hospitable to tourists, nor does it readily issue exit visas. Like a rapacious Hades reaching for his lush Persephone, Violence is more likely to abduct than invite. Those previously held for ransom in its underworld enter our offices as trauma survivors and lost souls. For psychologists, the threat of violence can present the most difficult challenge of their professional life. One reason for this is the degree of liability and personal risk that accompanies such patients. His or her violent act can readily appear to nullify our therapeutic value. Moreover, society increasingly holds us accountable for our clients' behavior.

In our professional capacities, we are often on the front lines of domestic, work place, school and institutional violence. Violence is also the portal through which the state penetrates psychology's domain and stakes increasingly larger claims within it. Ever-widening mandates require clinicians to report any "reasonable suspicion" of potential assault, homicide or suicide, child, elder, or dependent adult abuse, neglect or fraud, and even threats against property As psychology is conscripted by the state to aid its containment efforts, legislative directives to forcibly medicate psychotic patients and calls for increased involuntary hospitalization powers are also on the rise (AB 1800, 2000).

In eras past, lepers were confined to colonies set apart from the rest of society. There was no cure for their disturbing illness. In a similar manner today, we shun and confine troubled minds in penal colonies. The most shameful chapter in the annals of psychiatric history is that of clinicians' willing presence on the leading edge of the Holocaust. It began with their rounding up of mental patients for the good of the community, then sterilization and eventually . . . extermination. And, as we know, one scapegoat then led to another. This is one reason that our drift toward law enforcement as the primary solution for our social ills is one that bears closer examination. I believe every clinician must ask himself or herself at some time: To whom do I owe my first allegiance—the state or the soul?

While the American Gulag impacts the lives of many citizens, its primary targets today are boys and young men of color at the lowest levels of the socioeconomic hierarchy (Breggin & Breggin, 1998). A significant contingent of lawmakers today appear to perceive this group as representing the greatest threat to their vision of social order. The incarceration frenzy that now has one in three young African American men in its thrall defies rational explanation. The disproportionality of racial criminalization (black men are 6 percent of the general population and 48 percent of inmates) shares more features with patterns of genocide than with social justice (Staub, 1989; Miller, 1996; Mauer & Huling, 1997). I believe we are compelled by our knowledge of history to wrestle with the discomfort this eugenics-laced shadow may bring.

The severity of punishment and scale of imprisonment in the United States calls into question our continuing status as a civilized nation. We live in the only Western democracy ever censured by Amnesty International, the UN and other human rights organizations for failures to enforce minimal international standards for the humane treatment of prisoners. (UN, 1998; AI, 1998) Evidence of beatings, torture, medical neglect and rape of prisoners is widespread and well documented (Hornblum, 1998; Krupers, 1999). In various upwellings of dissent across the nation I hear reddened voices loudly chanting: "No Justice, No Peace, No Justice, No Peace . . ."

Exile to the American Gulag is tantamount to a death sentence for many low-level, non-violent offenders. One tool in the slow motion extermination of addicts, the underclass and the mentally ill is the administratively sanctioned rape of thousands of incarcerated young men. Many are forced to serve as wives, slaves and the prostitutes who are an integral part of the sexual culture and underground economy of some prisons. This unprotected, often violent sex contributes to AIDS and Hepatitis C transmission rates soaring far beyond those of even the greatest at-risk, populations who are free to choose their lifestyle (Hanlon, 1993; Rachel, 1998). Conservative estimates indicate that rates of male prisoner rape parallel those for non-incarcerated females (Dumond, 1992; Donaldson, 1995).

Dehumanization of any group can result when authorities regard certain cultural or behavioral markers as indicative of their moral inferiority. For example, crime classification manuals do not even regard the sexual assault of prisoners as rape (Douglas et al., 1992). To reduce a young man to "dope-dealer," "gang-banger," "felon," or "super predator" is to define the sum of his entire worth by his most intolerable acts. Such judgments of "less than fully human" can then be used to justify the abrogation of their human rights. Through their silence our policy makers passively sanction medical neglect, brutality, chemical immobilization, torture and even the murder of the American Gulag's inhabitants. This year, half a million inmates will be ejected from the bitter heart of this burgeoning prison industrial complex and shipped straight back into our communities. What then?

Conclusion

If we believe it possible that: 1) reciprocal links exist between interior and exterior life; 2) archetypal themes are expressed in cultural psychology and 3) that it is as possible that we exist in an inter-related, subjective web of psyche as it is that we possess autonomous egos, then we might wonder at the effect repression of collective rage on such a megalithic scale is having on the ecology of our cultural soul. One need not believe the premises of depth psychology, however, to ask: Does out of sight really assure out of mind?

Prisons contain dense psychological material—anger, despair, grief, revenge, and apocalyptic fantasy. The more a dream is deferred, the stronger the container required to keep it suppressed must become. This alchemical metaphor of psychological containment reflects a belief in the value of holding potentially volatile transformations well enough to allow base material to experience a range of transformative processes. The alchemist's goal is for the material to become ennobled with out exploding or converting into poison in the process. Some view depth-oriented psychotherapy as such a possible method for the transformation of psychological contents.

As a psychological axiom, this alchemical principle might help explain one aspect of why our prison system keeps growing unabated. Modern penology builds excellent crucibles but seldom turns leaden lives golden. I believe that is a compelling reason for psychology to take up the issue of torture and repression in the American Gulag, to help actualize its innate potential as a soul-making realm. This was, in fact, the original intention of the Quakers who introduced the idea of prisons into American society.

Prison was first imagined as a quiet place for solitude, deep thought and penance—a penitentiary--in which broken spirits could mend and impoverished imaginations could be refreshed through contemplation instead of violent action. From this sort of temenos they would then return to community life renewed. Today, they return more humiliated than humbled and more broken than healed. Understandably, many emerge enraged and vengeful. Psychologists glimpse first hand the powerful dynamics with which the return of the repressed can become imbued. From this point of view, just as the energy potential of uranium is enriched and converted to plutonium in nuclear reactors, violence may become more virulent in the very crucibles designed to contain it.

Resistance can make violence more fascinating, just as sexual repression drives some into deeper obsessions. The suppression of naturally occurring forest fires ultimately causes more danger when the repressed contents (underbrush) reach critical "fire storm" mass. From my tiny, fogged peephole into the cultural psyche, it appears we may be approaching that condition. Will the reddening of the American soul create new gold or will it just explode? The question is too large for any single perspective to address. Its very complexity calls for a diverse, creative community's full consideration. Meanwhile, some of us blindly feel around in the dark, vainly trying to describe this irritable, hungry, red-eyed, bull elephant fitfully sleeping in the middle of America's living room. Shhhh.

References

AB 1800, " Involuntary Outpatient Commitment" (IOC) bill in progress in the California legislature. Contact: California Network of Mental Health Clients (CNMHC) main@cnmhc.com

Ambrosio, T. J., & Schiraldi. V. (1997, February) Policy Report: From classrooms to cell blocks: A national perspective. Washington, DC: JPI.

Arax, M., Gladstone, M. (1998, July 6) Corcoran: Former guard tells of brutality at prison. The Los Angeles Times, pp. A 1, 14.

Bly, R. (1998) personal communication.

Breggin, P. R. (1994) Toxic psychiatry: Why therapy, empathy, and love must replace the drugs, electroshock, and biochemical theories of the new psychiatry. New York: St. Martin's Press.

Breggin, P. R. (1998) Talking back to Ritalin: What doctors aren't telling you about stimulants for children. Monroe, ME: Common Courage Press.

Breggin, P. R., & Breggin, G. R. (1998) The war against children of color: Psychiatry targets inner-city youth. Monroe, ME: Common Courage Press.

Connolly, K., McDermind, L., Schiraldi, V., & Macallair, D. (1996, October) From classrooms to cell blocks: How prison building affects higher education and African American enrollment. San Francisco, CA: CJCJ, 6.

Currie, E. (1998) Crime and punishment in America. New York: Metropolitan Books, Henry Holt and Co., p. 13.

Donaldson, S. (1995, July) Rape of incarcerated Americans: a preliminary statistical look. 7th edition, Adult Male Jails. Stop Prisoner Rape, Inc. online.

Douglas, J. E., Burgess, A. W., Burgess, A. G. Ressler, R. K. (1992) Crime classification manual: A standard system for investigating and classifying violent crimes. San Francisco: Jossey-Bass Publishers, pp.191-246.

Dumond, R. W. (1992) The sexual assault of male inmates in incarcerated settings. International Journal of the Sociology of Law, 20: 135-157, pp. 146-47.

Edinger, E. (1985) Anatomy of the psyche: Alchemical symbolism in psychotherapy. La Salle: Open Court Publishing Company.

Ensenberger, M. (1997, July) Universals in Colours. Faculdade de Letras Universidade Do Porto. http://www.letras.up.pt/translat/i_unicol.html.

Gilligan, J. (1996) Violence: Our deadly epidemic and its causes. New York: Grosset/Putnam.

Guggenbuhl-Craig, A. (1996). In Thomas Moore. Dark eros: The imagination of sadism. Woodstock: Spring, p. viii.

Hanlon, S. M. (1993, December 24). State prisons taking a hit from AIDS. Washington Times, Online.

Hillman, J. (1976) Suicide and the soul. Dallas: Spring Publications, Inc.

Hillman, J. & Ventura. M. (1992) We've had one hundred years of psychotherapy and the world is getting worse. HarperSanFrancisco.

Hornblum, A. M. (1998) Acres of skin: Human experiments at Holmesburg Prison: A true story of abuse and exploitation in the name of medical science. Danbury, CT: Rutledge Books, Inc.

Hughes, L. (1951) The Panther and the lash. NY: Alfred A Knopf, Inc.

Kipnis, A. (1999) Angry young men: How parents, teachers, and counselors can help " bad boys" become good men. S.F. Jossey-Bass Publishers.

Krupers, T. A. (1999) Prison madness: The mental health crisis behind bars and what we must do about it. San Francisco: Jossey Bass Publishers.

Lait, M. (1998, August 24) Public fear of crime proves elusive enemy for L.A.P.D. Crime reports steadily increase in news but crime is less. The Los Angeles Times, p.B1.

Lifton, R. (1986) The Nazi doctors: Medical killing and the psychology of genocide. NY: Basic Books.

Lowe, H. (1998, November 6) Former inmates protest: They say they still suffer from experiments performed on them in Philadelphia prisons. Philadelphia Inquirer. Online.

Mauer, M. (1997) Intended and unintended consequences: state racial disparities in imprisonment. Washington, D.C: The Sentencing Project.

Mauer, M. (1997) Losing the vote: The impact of felony disenfranchisement laws in the United States. Washington, D.C: The Sentencing Project, p. 4

Mauer, M., & Huling, T. (1997, January) Young Black Americans and the criminal justice system: Five years later. Washington, D.C: The Sentencing Project.

Meyer, J. (1998, September 5) [Sheriff] Block says 8 sheriff's employees were in jail vigilante group. The Los Angeles Times, p. B3.

Miller, J. (1996) <u>Search and destroy: African-American males in the criminal justice system.</u> New York: Cambridge University Press.

Oshinsky, D. M. (1997) <u>Worse than slavery: Parchman farm and the ordeal of Jim Crow justice.</u> New York: The Free Press.

AP (1998, Aug. 16) <u>Over 3.9 million Americans on probation or parole.</u> Washington. D.C. Online.

Phinney, D. (1998, July 9) <u>Colleges or prisons? The options pose a stark contrast.</u> New York: ABC NEWS.com/ Online.

Rachel, G. (1998, September 11) S.F. may sue state over HIV prison care. Leno contends The City covers care of ex-cons with AIDS. <u>San Francisco Chronicle</u>. Online.

<u>Rights for all: USA report.</u> (1998) Chapter 4. London: AI Publications, pp. 349-353.

<u>Rikers Island guards beat inmates for years: Details emerge from NYC court settlement; reforms reported.</u> (1998, August 16) New York: AP online.

Somé, M. (1994) <u>Of water and the spirit.</u> NY: Tarcher/Putnam.

Staub, E. (1989). <u>The roots of evil: The origins of genocide and other group violence</u>. New York: Cambridge University Press.

Tashjian, H. (1997) <u>Racism in the California prison system.</u> The Prison Activist Resource Center. Online.

Torrey, E. F. Jails and prisons: America's new mental hospitals. (1995, December) <u>American Journal of Public Health,</u> v. 85, n. 12: 1611-13.

United Nations special rapporteur on torture. (1998, April 17) New York: UN Document E/CN.

Walmsley, R. (1997) <u>Prison populations in Europe and North America.</u> Helsinki: HEUNI.

Zimmring, F. E., & Hawkins, G. (1991) <u>The scale of imprisonment.</u> The University of Chicago Press, p. 174.

Zweig, C & Wolf, S. (1998) <u>Romancing the Shadow. Illuminating the dark side of the soul.</u> New York: Ballantine Books.

Abbreviations for Statistical Sources Cited In This Paper:

BJS: Bureau of Justice Statistics/Sourcebook.

CDC: Centers for Disease Control and Prevention

DoJ: Department of Justice

NCANDS: National Child Abuse and Neglect Data System

Statistical Sources:

Statistical Abstract of the United States. (1999) The National Data Book. U.S. Department of
    Commerce. Bureau of the Census. Washington, DC: GPO.

U.S. Dept. of Commerce. (1999) Bureau of the Census. Current Population Reports, series P-
    60-193, Money Income and Poverty Status in the United States. Washington, D.C: GPO.

Maguire, K., & Pasore, A. L. (eds.) (1998) Sourcebook of Criminal Justice Statistics 1999 U.S.
    Department of Justice, Bureau of Justice Statistics. Washington D.C: USGPO.

Office of Juvenile Justice and Delinquency Prevention. (1996, February) Juvenile Offenders and
    Victims: Update on Violence: 24. Washington, D.C: DoJ.

National Center on Child Abuse and Neglect (1999) National child abuse and data system.
    Washington, D.C: DHHS

National Center for Health Statistics. (1999) Washington D.C: DHHS

The Lost Heritage by Nina Kelly, Ph.D.

Modern medicine has come far in caring for and curing the human body through scientific analysis, research, and practice. Yet contemporary medicine often ignores the traditional art of healing rituals developed prior to the rise of the scientific method. In the past, modern medicine generally avoided considering using the mind-body-spirit relationship in the healing process. Considering the overall well-being of a person may not have been recognized fully until recently. Modern medicine simply cannot ignore the upsurge in healing modalities since the incorporation of alternative – complementary methods.

In antiquity, for example, the Greeks recognized the physical component as one segment of the whole of a person. With the increase in spiritual counseling and psychotherapies, modern medical praxis now acknowledges the necessity to explore additional complementary methods of healing. The ancients certainly knew the necessity for ritual, but modern scientific technology has put aside these same rituals. Within a new paradigm we must recollect and gather what has been lost. Ritual without medical scientific application suffers maladies as acutely as the absence of technology without ritual.

Patients as a Whole

Medicine uses the ancient symbol of the caduceus (the wand or staff of Mercury, the messenger of the gods) as its icon. This symbol, in existence since the ancient Greeks, can be traced even further back to the Egyptian god Thoth. Just as in previous times, modern medicine evokes many of the principles of the healing arts of the ancients. Faced with the same dilemma, the ancient Greeks and present-day physicians address the problems of the necessary procedures to cure a patient. A psychophysiological relationship was the focus of ancient people. Hippocrates of Kos (c 400 BC) believed that body and mind were united; if one was affected, as W.A. Jayne notes, so was the other (19). Thus, it was important for the ancients to understand the connection between the two. More recently, modern medicine has

once again had to face the possibility of complementary therapies by returning to the ancients'
philosophy of a mind-body correlation. Therefore, studying ancient healing practices will
enrich both the physician and the patient.

Connecting mind, body, and spirit may become a new paradigm in the forefront of
medicine. But the question remains: why are modern therapeutic modalities moving so slowly
toward implementing a method that at one time addressed the entirety of the individual?
Dianne Skafte, a Jungian psychotherapist and professor of psychology, notes in Listening to
the Oracle (1997) that "In all native cultures, ritual is seen as a force that influences events and
corrects things that have gone wrong" (164). It is currently thought that in the realm of ancient
medicine, illness and disease were viewed as something that had "gone wrong" in nature
and/or the persons afflicted.

The Greeks strongly associated healing with spiritual practices. They gave ample
consideration to the values of the divine, mental, and material healing practices. What
remains significant is the degree to which the Greeks honored the relationship of all three:
divine inspiration, emotional exploration, and the material component of ritual healing.
Prayer, sacrifice, and rituals were routine practices that people offered to the healing gods.
The ancients believed that such routines helped to protect them within the culture, thus
reinforcing the blessings of the future. Depending upon their gods to provide for the well-
being of the community, the Greeks expected their gods to protect them. Traditional folktales
and myths from many sources in Greek culture kept the gods real and powerful in the minds
of the people. These stories establish gods who, although invisible to men, appeared to them
in many and varied disguises, such as a swan or a bull and even as a cloud or a shower of
golden rain. When the Greeks were plagued by disease, they offered sacrifices and prayers as
atonement, seeking help from their gods. To combat illness and disease, ancient medicine men
used charms, spells, amulets, music, dancing, prayers, and sacrifices, to try to cure patients. In
the time of Hippocrates, according to Henry Sigerist, the physician could "fill in the gaps in
the account [or story of the illness] given by the sick" (114). In the Iliad, Homer (850 BC)

describes an important element of the treatment of the Machaon, Asclepius' own son, as "lots of storytelling" (qtd. In Majno: 142).

The Lost Past

This paper acknowledges those healing methods utilized by the ancient Greeks, with emphasis on their ritual myth and storytelling. These techniques were once actively used by those medical practitioners who first swore the same oath of allegiance to Hippocratic as physicians swear today. I hope to illustrate that organ donation and transplantation is not far removed from ancient ritualistic practices, and ultimately, that ancient ritual myth making, images, and storytelling may prove beneficial, specifically in the reduction of kidney organ transplantation rejection episodes.

Although the Egyptians were among the first to document medical practices, the Greeks significantly influenced modern scientific therapies. Ritual storytelling and, more specifically, the relationship between ancient Greek medical practices and healing rituals, were practiced in Epidauros, Greece. Ritual healing in the modern world can be a topic of controversy, and, as such, it is one that could benefit from scientific investigation. One particular area in which ritual healing was tested focused on the renal (kidney) transplant population. Kidney transplantation is one of the more common types of vascular organ replacement.

A pilot study was conducted at Louisiana State University Health Sciences Medical Center (LSUHSMC), in New Orleans, Louisiana, on the relationship between ritual healing, storytelling or storysharing, and the success of kidney transplantation. A qualitative research design was employed, using personal interviews between patients, and the organ procurement transplant coordinator who served as the research investigator, both before and after such kidney transplants, to solicit descriptions and answers relating to the research topic. A questionnaire focusing primarily on the patient's experience with the acceptance of a gift was developed and used, with an experimental group of renal transplant candidates. The interview/questionnaire was implemented on a regular and uniform basis with the transplant candidates and continued when they became patients. A control group was established to compare to the experimental group's responses and recovery history.

The main issue in this research is to assess the value of the ancient healing art of medical practice as a complement to modern medical therapies. The basis for the hypothesis was the difficulty in a patient's acceptance of what in affect is a "foreign body." This challenge for the patient became the vessel of storytelling, images, and healing as they pertain to alternative medical therapies in organ transplantation.

In the study patients told individual accounts of their life stories during several interviews that seemed to create a more accepting and peaceful attitude toward their illnesses over a period of time. Spending time alone with a critically ill patient opens the space for the listener to be acutely present in the moment. What occurs when two people engage in the ritual of storytelling is remarkable. The patients invite the presence of an "unknown" and through the telling of their personal story it awakens a place that has been closed. This element of exchange occurs in numerous ways. Of course, there is the regular exchange of information, but this opens to an even deeper level of emotional sharing once the researcher listens to the experiences the patients have to offer.

The Greeks originally helped to establish the significance of storytelling, storysharing, and physical healing practices. A resurgence of ancient healing practices through alternative therapies such as health gymnasiums, hydro-therapy, physical-massage therapies, aromatherapy, music therapy, and other alternative forms shared by the Greeks may continue to influence modern medical praxis. The pilot study conducted as an experimental research project at LSUHSMC demonstrates that ancient Greek tradition and cultural attitudes continue to flow into current cultural practices.

Just what were the healing rituals and miracles that took place during antiquity? Two methods of religious healing were used during the Greek period: the direct and the indirect. The direct method of divine healing power involved the laying-on of hands, the use of a sacred object or relic, the intervention of a priest or priestess, or the use of a sacred animal, such as a snake or a dog. The indirect method of healing came through dreams, visions, and oracles, in which the divine deity communicated remedies "for cures, such as baths, change of diet, herbs, ointments, or exercise" (Jayne, 1962: 228-32).

The Birth of the Physician

Asclepius, the "blameless physician" first mentioned by Homer in the Iliad, was celebrated by early Greek poets and writers, including Pindar and Hesiod. Myth has it that he was given some plant remedies by the centaur Chiron, known as the wounded healer. There are many different but detailed versions of the myth of Asclepius. The Edelsteins offer Pindar's version as the "earliest testimony preserved in which all these data [his ancestry, the tale of his birth and education, his deeds and death] are set forth coherently and in detail" (Edelstein and Edelstein 22).

According to Pindar, Asclepius was the son of Apollo and Coronis. While still pregnant with Apollo's child, Coronis was unfaithful to her mate by engaging in sex with a mortal. Apollo, discovering this infidelity sent his sister, Artemis, to kill Coronis. Apollo saved the child, a son, and placed him under the care of Chiron, the centaur who lived on Mount Pelion and who was renowned for his knowledge, especially of botany and the medicinal properties of plants and herbs. Asclepius became a prominent physician, but Zeus slew him with a thunderbolt when Asclepius "For money's sake...dared to heal those who were doomed to die." (Edelstein and Edelstein 23).

The growth of the healing cult of Asclepius shrines located at Kos and Rhodes even included medical schools. The most famous shrine to Asclepius, however, was at Epidauros and contained many temples and other religious buildings including baths, a library, gymnasiums, a stadium, a theater, and the abaton or sacred temple where sleeping patients made contact with the gods (Jayne 240-303 and Skafte 116-23).

Healing Process: Isolation or Community Support

Those who were sick or diseased flocked to the sites sacred to Asclepius because of the stories of miraculous cures originating there. Once there, the patients practiced incubation, i.e., sleeping in the abaton, or dormitory. During incubation, the god appeared in a dream and effected a cure or prescribed a treatment by either the direct or indirect method already described.

For the sick, the process of undergoing a cure took the form of a religious ritual. The process began with bathing to signify a cleansing or purification ritual and then the offering of a sacrifice. The poor were allowed to offer honey cakes, while others who were wealthier were expected to provide an animal for sacrifice. The most memorable was the cock made famous by Socrates' last words as reported in the Phaedo by Plato: "Crito, I owe a cock to Asclepius; will you remember to pay the debt?" (Kaplan. 160). Legend states that Socrates enjoyed good health all of his life; he therefore felt the need to sacrifice to Asclepius.

On their way to the shrine abaton for incubation, patients and supplicants were led through the antechamber heiron, the sacred enclosure or precinct of the god. During this process, priest-attendants told stories of the cult and recounted the narratives of the cures documented by the inscriptions on steles, tablets, columns, and walls.

Once in the shrine abaton the sick prepared for incubation by offering a final prayer before entering a sleep, during which they would be visited by the god. Some believed that Asclepius would appear in a dream to his worshippers and tell them how to care for their illnesses. After a night of incubation, the patients told the stories of their dreams to the priests or therapeutae. Therapeut, a term which Galen, the physician of late antiquity, applied to himself, was "a name originally given to those who were the attendants of the cult and who served the gods by carrying out the prescribed ritual" (Meier. 55-56). The priests or therapeuts recorded the dreams of the patients and gave directions for practical external treatment, which could include the use of salves, ointments, or lotions made from plants or roots, baths, diets, exercise, and the like. Internal remedies, such as potions and elixirs, were also recommended.

Sacrificial Offerings

Grateful patients left testimonials, thank offerings, and gifts, as well as payment for services received and cures effected by the god. Art in the form of statuary, murals, mosaics, vase paintings, jewelry, and bas-relief all honored Asclepius. Although Asclepius was preeminent as both a physician and a god of healing, other deities and mortals of this era earned a place in the history of healing and medicine. Asclepius' "gifts" of ancient healing practices offer a pathway to the forefront of modern scientific medicine.

According to tradition, Cosmas and Damian, appearing posthumously in a dream, miraculously replaced the gangrenous leg of the sacristan of a church "with the leg of a Negro who had died of old age" (Lyons and Petrucelli 291). Literally dozens of paintings from the beginning of the Middle Ages with these figures occur until as late as the sixteenth century.

The Giving and Receiving the "Gift of Life"

Unlike the ancients, contemporary physicians have sought to cure disorders and diseases by using surgery and prescribed medications and have lost or put aside the essential ingredient of "sharing story," a model of treatment that served the Greeks in alternative methods of healing. A critical factor in the process of kidney transplantation is the role of the organ donor. This person truly provides a "gift of life" to the recipient. The theme of giving and receiving is one that is woven through the myths and legends of ancient Greek culture, and the attitudes developed by mankind over time about giving and receiving a gift are most certainly important. If positive and negative attitudes about the consequences of giving and receiving a gift are rooted in man's earliest civilizations, such as that of Ancient Greece, it is possible that these attitudes could prove foundational to the problem in medical transplantation of accepting or rejecting another's organ as a gift of life.

Other questions to consider include whether the art of storytelling can help with gift receiving and whether the art of storysharing can help with the psychological problem of gift receiving. The pilot research study's hypothesis addressed this question: does storysharing and storytelling contain a critical element in the psychological and pathophysiological healing process?

The first experimental session was scheduled one week after the initial interview. Pictures of healthy kidneys as well as a reinforcement of positive statements were stressed to the patients about to undergo organ transplantation. The purpose of this visualization was to encourage the patient to accept the "gift of life" from someone else. The researcher also engaged the patient in a story of preparation and positive reinforcement for his or her relationship to the transplanted kidney. The purpose of this exercise was to reinforce acceptance of the newly-transplanted kidney. The researcher repeated and reinforced the procedures used in the first experimental session.

Offering encouragement to embrace the "gift of life" from the donor was the main priority. Subsequent visits were then made to see the experimental group every week for the first month, then monthly for three months.

The visual aids consisted of photographs of viable kidneys, pictures of viable kidneys, and a plastic model of a kidney used to demonstrate the anatomy of the actual transplanted organ. Positive terminology such as "acceptance" or "gift of life" was used, and negative terms such as "graft failure" were avoided. "Gift of life" was a key phrase used repeatedly, as the main focal point to promote positive healing thoughts. It was important to stress the significance of the word "gift." The word "acceptance" was also stressed because the patient is receiving a "gift."

Listening was the most important tool employed by the researcher, a vital element necessary to hear and understand the patient's concerns and apprehensions concerning the transplanted kidney. The researcher intended to acknowledge the patient's experience of illness and fear. Since the researcher understood that the essential element in this particular study was listening, the patient was given the opportunity to express fears, concerns, and anxieties related to accepting a gift that would offer a renewed life.

Modern Parallel "Understanding"

Using the model of the kidney, the researcher first described the function and operative placement of the newly-transplanted kidney to the patient. Second, the researcher asked the patient to observe a pink, healthy kidney. The researcher emphasized pink, instructing the patient to "think pink." Once the patient had been shown the artery and vein of the kidney model, the researcher explained how these vessels are connected to the life support system, the "heart." Finally, the researcher had the patient hold and feel the model of the kidney while asking the patient questions concerning the sense of touch and allowing the patient to feel the size of the modeled kidney. This procedure was carried out prior to surgery in order to inaugurate a relationship between the patient and the transplanted kidney.

Healing Affects of the Senses

The researcher used the phrase, "think pink," to allude to the appearance of healthy organs. Pink is a color that the patient can relate to because it gives a sense of connection to the heart. Everyone associates red with the heart; pink is a softer and more comforting color. Part of the reception of this gift rests on one's ability to relate to the new kidney in a relaxed and accepting manner.

The use of a plastic kidney model provided the visual image, which allowed the patient to touch, to sense, and to realize the size and shape of the newly-transplanted kidney. By encouraging the patient to handle the model, the researcher was able to engage the patient in a stronger connection between the gift and the receiver. Deep breathing is also critical to the postoperative patient, since it will increase blood and respiratory circulation, both essential to the vital organs and a most successful recovery.

The ritual of listening, however, appears to be the most significant common denominator between the studies. The three most critical elements in the ritual of story healing are storytelling, storysharing, and story listening. The physician, as previously noted carries the role of the active participant. He shares the story of the process of renal transplantation, but due to the very nature of his profession, he does not have the time to assume the role of the story listener, which seems to be critical in the ritual healing process. Such was the case in the Greek healing rituals, where the patient told the story of the disease, slept, dreamed, and shared the story of the dream with the physician the next morning. The physician then gave the patient the remedy for the cure.

Give Back to the Community:

The most significant finding, in addition to the degree of reduced rejection episodes and lower creatinine levels, was that each participant in the study group verbally expressed a desire to give service back to the community. The researcher was deeply impressed that the patients' recovery extended beyond their individual medical scope. Patients requested the opportunity to share or "give back" to the community what each had experienced during her individual process. One speculates that this gesture could very well signal the soul's desire to participate in a more kind of global thinking because it was a universal response from each of the patients involved in the study.

Final Analysis:

The focus of this study was ritual and storytelling. It investigated the relationship between story, images, and healing in the context of kidney transplantation. The question addressed was: would story decrease the amount of rejection episodes post-transplant? The experimental research tested the relationship between ritual, healing, storytelling, and storysharing, and the success of kidney transplantation. The results demonstrated that traditional kidney transplant success rate measures, including normal creatinine clearances, normal serum creatinine level, and decreased or reversible rejection episodes are worth an investigation that implements the use of story and physical images. Patients in the study group, using storytelling to enhance the healthy image of their new, vital kidney, exhibited higher average transplant success rates, than those in the control group [including fewer rejection episodes, along with lower serum creatinine levels] a determinate factor in the function of the kidney.

All eight patients in the experimental group expressed their appreciation of the phrase, "think pink." The researcher instructed the patients to use the term "think pink" in connection with the gift of their transplanted kidney. The patients were to imagine that their kidneys were healthy and vibrant and just beautifully pink. In addition, they were encouraged to imagine the life force flowing from their own heart to welcome this newly-transplanted kidney. The patients responded positively to this suggestion. They moved from acknowledging what was foreign to their native physiology, to incorporating positively this "gift of life." Again, in moments of fear and doubt, they were advised to reflect upon their individual stories of receiving a gift that they accepted unconditionally. Last, and extremely important to recovery, patients were instructed to deep-breathe, increase their fluid intake, and begin to walk as soon as possible after surgery. Similar to the ancient Greek healing rituals where exercising in the gymnasium was a necessary part of healing, patients were advised to concentrate on connecting the body and mind functions. The aim challenged the patients to discover how both the mind and body create the space to potentially unite in the mutual goal of returning the patient to a productive, healthy life.

A critical component in this study was to focus on the ability of the patients to create their individual story of receiving a gift of love. The story came from each patient and was one that each used to associate during periods of anxiety and fear.

The researcher noted the fact that each of the individual experimental patients actually requested an opportunity to give service back to the community. In Greek antiquity, once healing took place, the recipient was requested to give a gift of acknowledgment for the healing process. One of the experimental patients wrote a short story about the importance of the experiences that occurred with the relationship of "think pink." Still another patient requested a plastic model of a kidney to allow her to teach little children at school about kidney failure. Then several of the patients wanted to teach their grandchildren and other small children the importance of good health. Still another patient who worked for an insurance company felt she had the potential to educate the insurance world about her healing progress. One of the male patients requested to return to the dialysis clinics to encourage patients to take responsibility of their overall healthy physical condition . Another patient began to draw and to express himself through art. He wanted to share his personal experiences with children at his church. The researcher was impressed by the active voice of the participants of this study group.

With each step implemented, the strongest component of the healing ritual was the patients' ability to focus on the role of the heart. Anatomically, the vessels from the transplanted kidney's artery and vein were surgically anastomosed to the artery and vein of the heart. Once the patient visually saw the diagram, there seemed to be a stronger connection between the individual's story of receiving a gift that he could freely and unconditionally accept as well as relating the entire process to his heart. Visualizing a healthy, vibrant, and pink kidney seemed natural once patients were able to touch the model, see the actual size of the kidney, and comprehend that their newly-transplanted kidney was indirectly connected to their heart. The patients' relating to their heart, and personal stories of accepting a gift, gave more sense to this frightening and often overwhelming experience. This nonscientific method offered meaning, purpose, and vision to people afflicted with what often seems to them a meaningless illness. Once they accepted their condition and gave it the safe container of a story, it appears, as the ancients seemed to know, that a successful recovery could be achieved.

References

Edelstein, E. J. & Edelstein, L. (1945). Asclepius: A collection and interpretation of the testimonies. Baltimore: The John Hopkins University Press.

Edelstein, L. (1967). Ancient medicine. Baltimore: The John Hopkins University Press.

Jayne, W. A. (1962). The healing gods of ancient civilizations. New Hyde Park, CA: University Books, Inc.

Kaplan, J.D. (1971). Dialogues of Plato. New York: Washington Square Press.

Lyons, A.S. & Petrucelli, II, R.J. (1978). Medicine, an illustrated history. New York: Harry N. Abrams Inc., Publishers.

Majno, G. (1967). The healing hand: Man and woman in the ancient world. Baltimore: The John Hopkins Press.

Meier, C. A. (1989). Healing dream and ritual, ancient incubation and modern psychotherapy. Einsiedeln, Switzerland: Daimon Verlag.

Sigerist, H. (1941). Medicine and human welfare. New Haven, CT: Yale University Press.

Skafte, D. (1997). Listening to the oracle. San Francisco: Harper Collins.

Prison as Shadow by Suzan Still, M.A.

I bring you greetings from a handful of inmates in a northern California prison, who are standing invisibly with me, sending support, as I give voice to our communal concerns. In fact, the men of my creative writing classes are deeply honored - - and more than a little amazed - - that space is being allotted in such an important international collection of papers, to discuss their plight, and they want me to convey their heartfelt thanks for your interest.

In preparing this paper, an image came to me: it was the yellow wood, from Robert Frost's "The Road Not Taken":

> Two roads diverged in a yellow wood,
> And sorry I could not travel both
> and be one traveler, long I stood
> And looked down one as far as I could
> To where it bent in the undergrowth (1965)

. . . but I'm getting ahead of myself. Before I tell you what I see, down each fork, let me first explain what the road I have been traveling looks like.

I teach creative writing in a medium-to-high security men's prison. Through my classes, over the years, have passed hundreds of men of all races, educational and socioeconomic levels. Yet commonality is easy to pinpoint: almost to a man, they have suffered early childhood physical, emotional or sexual abuse - - many of them, all three.

This leads me to conclude that those whom we incarcerate - - now nearly 2 million strong - - are among the most severely psychologically wounded citizens of our nation. It's not without reason that one of my favorite students, a black man whose mother was a prostitute, who never knew a father, and who was born addicted to crack cocaine, has said, "The Department of Corrections says my name is Michael David Adams, but I'm here to tell you, my *real* name is *Madniz!*"

As a class warm-up, we often do a 15-minute writing exercise, and then read them aloud to one another. I assign topics that are familiar in order to overcome the enormous sense of failure most students have about their abilities. What was your home like, when you were five? Tell us about the first time you were busted. That kind of thing.

Through sharing these pieces, an intimacy grows which transcends race, class and gang barriers. Black, white and Hispanic men listen in deep empathy, as terrible tales begin to tumble out: a man who calls himself Enigma tells how he and his twin sister starved, while their crack addict mother spent the welfare check on dope, and how , abandoned, they lived on the street from the age of ten. Another relates how, from the age of eight, his uncle would shoot him up with cocaine so that his mother could rape him. Bruce, child of migrant workers, stutteringly reads the magazine article he has painstakingly copied verbatim, in order to teach himself spelling and syntax. Sibrian, from Guatemala, tells of seeing his mother attacked and hacked with a machete during political unrest, when he was four. Madniz hints at the scenes he witnessed and the sounds he heard, as the young son of a prostitute. Slowly, we learn to give voice to the unspeakable, to conditions that, in the words of my poet friend, Roxanne Williams, "hone an immaculate child into a knife" (2000 "The Arrowhead," unpublished).

One evening's class stands out particularly in memory. It was Saturday, and the next day was Father's Day. Why not, I suggested brightly, write about our fathers? The class, which is usually electric with the energy of anticipation, suddenly went dead, as if a collective plug had been pulled. I urged and cajoled, and finally insisted: "Just *try* it. Write what you can."

The writing was over in a couple of minutes.

"Who wants to read?"

Silence.

Finally, Phil, usually the jolly Trickster of the class, started. His piece was one sentence long: "My father called me once, in 1984."

One by one came the briefest, most sobering accounts of beatings, verbal and sexual abuses, violence toward mother and siblings, alcoholism, drug addiction, and desertion. There wasn't a Hallmark father in the bunch. The failure and loss of the father constituted a truly unspeakable wound.

These are the people we incarcerate in increasing numbers in what is now being called the prison-industrial complex. With this trend, a new and insidious threat has arisen, which strikes at the heart of the democratic process, of Constitutional guarantees, and of the moral and ethical underpinnings of our nation. Masquerading as a virtuous, conservative anti-crime movement is a plan to reinstitute what virtually amounts to slavery.

This might sound preposterous, but consider the facts: prison industries showed a 40-billion dollar profit last year, yet inmates at our prison are paid between 6 and 65 cents an hour. They have no benefits, no union, and no vacations. Their work hours are not necessarily limited to 8 per day, nor are they compensated for overtime or hazardous duty. They live in quarters designed to hold 12, which now house 36 - - with two toilets and one shower. In the summer, they swelter without air conditioning, and in the winter, they shiver, fully clothed, under thin blankets. They are overseen by supervisors who are also correctional officers, and who have ultimate power over their lives.

Consider further that 3-Strikes laws and mandatory minimum sentencing nationwide, have filled prisons to overflowing with non-violent offenders, many of whom will be incarcerated for life, three out of four of whom are people of color. Behind conservative political hyperbole about "making our streets safe" lurks the specter of greed, and a deliberate economic policy geared to compete with third world countries in the labor market - - with the added element of gratifying racist agendas.

To recapitulate for emphasis: despite its name, the Department of Corrections is much more involved in warehousing and commodifying than in redeeming human lives. Therefore, one finds a situation in which those who are among the most severely-traumatized individuals of our society are shut away in subhuman conditions which both recapitulate and exacerbate the original trauma. Here they are targeted as a virtual slave labor force in the prison industries. That a nation which thinks of itself as among the most civilized in the world could treat its wounded so abysmally is a shocking thing and speaks to our collective, medieval notions about criminality.

Such is the road I have been traveling. Now, I come again to the fork in the road. As recently as last Saturday, I was unsure which fork to take. We discussed this juncture long and earnestly, in my prison classes, and the final decision was unanimous - - I was to take you down the road less traveled.

Down the road *more* traveled - - and that only slightly so - - is the political agenda of prison activists, and the horrific litany of statistics which support their cause:

    * 6 and a half million citizens are under some form of correctional supervision.

    * "supermax" prisons house 20,000 mostly minority inmates, some of them underground, where they are never exposed to sunlight, in engineered solitary confinement and sensory deprivation.

    * blacks are imprisoned for drug offenses at 14 times the rate of whites.

    * 1 in every 3 adult black men in the nation can anticipate being sentenced to prison sometime during his life.

    * women constitute the fastest-growing prison population.

    * 75% of women in prison today are there for nonviolent crimes - - many taking the rap for sons and partners, to protect them from a third strike.

    * Penalties for drug convictions now sometimes exceed those for violent crimes like rape and murder.

    *At a time when Civil Rights are once again in jeopardy, 1.4 million black males - - 13 % - - can no longer vote as a result of felony disenfranchisement laws (Miller, 2000)

. . . and so it goes. These aren't numbers of a civilized society; these are statistics from Hell: we're looking at our national shame. This is the shadow of America, lurking in the undergrowth, there, where this line of inquiry bends out of sight.

Around that bend? Unless we *free* citizens speak out and persist in seeing justice done, we will find the institutionalization of slavery becoming so embedded in the economic structure of this nation, that it will seem impossible to maintain the economy without it. It will become ineradicable.

Now - - what of that other fork, the road *less* traveled, which my students have urged me to take? This is less a road, really, than a trail, or a slight crimping of the grasses, where Coyote has passed through on Trickster feet.

Because this is where our prison road deposits us in the wild lands of the archetypes. Going is rough, the path easy to lose. If I falter here, please forgive me. This is new territory, and I'm casting back and forth, like an animal, myself, for an elusive scent, a faint imprint, that will lead us forward.

Jason, a talented musician and songwriter, down for several years on drug charges, has an I.Q. of 164. He asked me, recently, "Why don't people of my type *fit*?"

What type was Jason referring to? What he was intuiting, I think, echoes my own suspicions: in a society which runs on Apollonian rationality, within a system that encodes the dreary control issues of the Senex, are entrapped the passionate, irrational, ragtag armies of the likes of Eros, Dionysus, Hermes, and Wotan. What looks like a 21st-century phenomenon of social malaise, is really a dilemma as old as humankind. Euripides wrote about it 2500 years ago, in his play, The Bacchae (405BCE/1974), in which Dionysus and his maenads confront and utterly confound the patriarchal structure of a city.

The dilemma is this: how does society, with its need for order based in consensual reality, incorporate the irrational, disruptive, but life-bringing forces of Eros? Because deep in the core of these "true-life, street-life warriors", as Madniz calls them, burns an unquenchable - -often misdirected - - frequently Tricksterish - - *joie de vivre*.

For me, this is one of the stunning discoveries about prison. In the very place where I expected a dull thug-like energy to pervade, I find instead a crackling intelligence and explosive creative urge.

There is statistical evidence indicating that as many as 25 to 30 % of those incarcerated may be Gifted! A little quick mathematics tells us that if 2 million people are presently incarcerated, then there's a good possibility that around 500,000 of them are Gifted. That's an army! And because we have failed as a society to protect, love, guide, feed, educate and inspire them, they have gone their own wild ways - - as maenads, bacchantes, mercenary warriors, Berserkers and coyotes are wont to do.

In some ways, after having endured many of the abuses that life can deal the human psyche, they are indestructible. So it's appropriate that Dionysus, as an archetypal image of indestructible Life, be called forth to elucidate our problem.

Dionysus is sensual, less involved with intoxication than with the eternal, quiet but aggressive, vegetative aspect of Nature, symbolized by the vine. As such, he carries a strong erotic charge. Indeed, the phallic element of Dionysus gave rise to early comedy. He has also been viewed as an aspect of creative madness and the irrational ground of being.

But where the Greeks knew Dionysus through myth and image, through theater, and the visionary experiences of their rituals - - in an holistic manner, that is to say - - we of the 21st century know him scarcely at all from personal experience. We have become voyeuristic, just like young king Pentheus, in <u>The Bacchae</u>. We would rather *spy upon* the rites of Dionysus than *partake of* them. And as a result, our society is being ripped to shreds by the god's followers, just as Pentheus and his city were rent by the maenads.

It is one of the dubious gifts of Columbine High School, and other places like it, to represent for us in a manner we cannot avoid or deny, the unrestraint of irrational thoughts, winged by desire, and breaking through all civilized barriers. Although statistics show that this is massively projected onto people of color, the young, white, middle-class shootists of Columbine have shown us the truth: we have met the submerged irrationality of America - - and we of all colors, and our children, are it.

How much more so, then, for people whose psychic twig is bent toward the Dionysian, whose inclinations are less of the head, and more of the heart: those people, in other words, *born* to be artists and poets, craftsmen, dancers and gypsies?; those who in other, more traditional societies, would have been priests and priestesses, shamans and medicine men, oracles and witches and warlocks? What place does America offer those who would follow in Dionysus' train, in maenadic reverence for earth and uninhibited sexual naturalness? Where do we invest the fierce energies of the Berserkers, whose warriors, possessed of battle frenzy, careless of their own safety, and unable to feel fear, now cruise our streets, as rapists, drive-by shootists and home invasion robbers?

The story of one of my students, Mickey, is allegorical:

Mickey is over 6 feet tall, brown-haired, blue-eyed, and as handsome as a movie star. He moves with the unconscious elegance of command. If you saw him on the street, you might imagine him as the son of wealthy, doting parents, who had carefully groomed him in the best schools. Maybe he rows for Harvard or plays tennis at Stanford.

In reality, both of Mickey's parents are drug addicts. Mickey robbed his first liquor store at the age of 8 to feed his parents and younger siblings, and he took up car theft at 9.

Mickey's is an archetypal tale, demonstrating what is lost when such a brave spirit is not nurtured: during class one night, Mickey was aloof, because he was pouring over my copy of Sister Wendy's *Story of Painting* (Beckett, 1994), a book on art history. He said he never missed one of Sister Wendy's programs on PBS. Suddenly, mid-session, Mickey erupted from the back of the class shouting, *"Oh my God . . . !!!"* We all turned to him, startled. He had leapt to his feet, book in hand, and an enraptured look on his face.

"It's the Madonna of the Rocks! It's right here! " And then, stammering with excitement, his gaze never leaving the image in the book, Mickey told us the history of Leonardo. The entire class sat, transfixed, as Mickey's passion swept the room. His eyes glowed and his voice was powerful with warmth and fervor. Then, as suddenly as he had erupted, he stopped, looked embarrassed, and sat down.

Mickey is only 25 years old. If he were my son, or your's, he would probably be in the university right now, getting his Masters degree in Art History, maybe spending a year studying in Rome or Florence. But Mickey's story doesn't end happily ever after. Shortly after that incident, Mickey's visits to class became fewer and further between. He'd been marked by the white supremacist Aryan Brotherhood for inclusion in its ranks, a summons one disregards at his peril.

The last time he came to class, he brought me a sheet of beautifully-executed calligraphy: MERRY CHRISTMAS, SUZAN. LOVE MICKEY, and he thanked me. Then he disappeared into the black rat hole of prison hate groups, and I've never seen him again.

To lose one such soul is a grievous thing. To lose 500,000 is a Holocaust.

Rico and Lonnie and Russell and Henry also have stories. As do Ron and Richard, Rodney and Supreme. Aldo and Alejandro and Raymond and Michael.

Jeremy, Ricardo, Bruce and Jagindar. Anthony, Jason, June Bug, and Larry. Danny, Brian, Shermon and Billie. Rajil, Madniz, Cleve and Enigma: to the world, they're just criminals - - dangerous, expendable and richly deserving of punishment. To me, they are my brothers and sons, who fell through a crack in an inner city sidewalk one day, into a world so dark, so terrible, so brutal, so grotesquely depraved, that, in truth, I cannot bear to think of them there.

Violence is not so much an act as a language, spoken by the psychologically wounded to recount their wounding. To the perpetrator, the legality or illegality of an act is not the point. It is, rather, a healing rite, performed in ritual space. It is a story, recounted within the *temenos* of the crime scene, and its object is cleansing.

These acts are performed by the ones whom depth psychology does not address: the disempowered, the seasoned in Hell, the broken on the social wheel, and the desperately soul-hungry. Those, in other words, already living in the depths. Ironic, *non* ?

The more we defile their ceremonies of healing by pathologizing them, the deeper their faith in them will be. The more we attempt to suppress their voices, the louder they will shout.

If we expended even half the energy used in capturing, trying and incarcerating these people on getting to know and coming to encourage them instead, we would be living in a different society today. Unless we find a way legitimately to incorporate these archetypal energies, so at odds with the prevailing ones, they will continue to tear apart our world.

As wise old blind Tiresius says in <u>The Bacchae</u>, commenting on the futile attempts of the king to repress the followers of Dionysus: "You are a fanatic, sir. A sick fanatic. There is no cure for madness, when the cure itself is mad" (p.89). As Hermann Hesse once warned, chaos demands to be recognized and experienced before letting itself be converted into a new order.

Let me tell you what new order I see, beyond the bend in this road less traveled. Somewhere, out there beyond the brush and wild grass we've been hacking through, the trail widens and the prospect opens. I don't see an end to prisons - - not in this lifetime, anyway. But I can clearly imagine prisons as leadership academies, as institutions of education, and particularly as places where wild, irrational energies meet the kinds of activities which suit them.

In fact, my students and I have already imagined the site of the first such institution. We call it USQ - - University of San Quentin. There, in the stone fortress of one of California's oldest prisons, we envision a situation in which the cultural resources of the San Francisco Bay Area could flood in: dancers, singers, magicians, musicians, actors, story tellers, painters, sculptors and writers. Where civic leaders from black, white, Asian, Native American and Hispanic communities could come to instill new ideas and values, and to challenge inmates to take up responsible positions of leadership within their communities, upon parole. Where inmates could complete their education to the highest degree to which they aspire. Where, as in the monasteries of the Middle Ages, an aging prison population could find hospice for their dying, and hardened hearts could turn to tending. Where gardens could flourish, and food be prepared from them, that nourishes body and soul. Where labor unions could set up apprentice programs, and outreach programs to disadvantaged youth could find their most street-wise, compassionate and empathetic volunteers.

Pie in the sky? No. Already there is a California prison which has a full time curriculum of religious and basic education, and which features a vegetarian diet (UPMI, 1999). In San Francisco, the Garden Project feeds the poor while employing parolees (Sneed, 2000). In Pennsylvania, a federal prison operates more like a college and vocational school and it costs 25% *less* than other prisons (*Yes!* staff, 2000).

USQ is possible. Investing the Dionysian energies of prison inmates and their giftedness back into our culture **is** possible. Maybe we can't see just how, yet. That part is hidden around the next bend. But unless we investigate this road, in spite of its fearful inconsistencies, its lack of a map, and its wildness, passing as it does through territory claimed by highwaymen and coyotes, we will have missed an opportunity, the one "that has made all the difference" (Frost, p. 131).

There is a type of pine that only casts its seeds after the tree has been severely burned in fire. My students are like that. Scorched. Rage bubbling like pitch. But they are so willing to throw open the armored cones of their hearts, and eject new life into receptive earth.

Madniz is my favorite example because for weeks he came to class apologizing: "I'm sorry, but I'm *still* down in the darkness, lookin' for a light." And then he would read a poem filled with the violent conflagration of the streets that have been his home all his life.

Then, one day, he came to class with a poem he was very excited to read, in honor of the class, and of poetry, and the courage of poets to speak out. In it, a new kind of fire burned, a fiery dawn.

"Words are like gems," he said passionately, in preamble, "they glow with color." This is the last stanza of the poem he read that day:

>All wordz aren't wordz anymore. . .

they . . . soulfully dance . . .
out of the face of truth
eternally spitting
sparkz out of the
very pit of
foreverz never-ending
immaculate
creative
flame
with each living syllable uttered.

I want to leave you with the suggestion that each one of these people is such a spark from the never-ending, immaculate creative flame. Our job, as depth psychologists, as archetypal activists, as citizens, and as souls, is to fan the flame!

References

Beckett, Sister W. (1994). <u>Story of painting</u>. New York: DK Publishing, Inc.

Euripides. (1974). The bacchae. In P. Roche (Trans.), <u>Three plays of Euripides: Alcestis, Medea, the Bacchae</u> (pp.78-126). New York: W.W. Norton & Co.

Frost, Robert. (1965). <u>Complete poems of Robert Frost.</u> New York: Holt, Rinehart and Winston, 131. (Original work published in 1949)

Miller, J. G. (2000). The American gulag. <u>Yes! A Journal of Positive Futures, 15</u>, 11-17.

Sneed, C. (2000). Seeds of change. <u>Yes! A Journal of Positive Futures, 15</u>, 26-27.

UPMI (United Prison Ministries, Inc.) (Producer). (1999). <u>Changed by choice, not chance: Breaking out of a life of crime!</u> [Film]. (Available from UPMI, PO Box 8, Verbena, AL 36091).

Williams, R. (2000). "The arrowhead". Unpublished poem.

Yes! staff writers. (2000). Prisons that work. <u>Yes! A Journal of Positive Futures, 15</u>, 28. (Adapted from "A Model Prison", by Robert Worth, from Atlantic Monthly, November, 1995; "Prison without walls", by Jim Merkel, from In Context, Spring, 1994; and "Politically correct punishment", by Jeffrey Banner, Mother Jones' MoJo Wire, March 2000.)

Roots of Eros: Wings of Desire by Jennifer Freed, M.A.

At one time I had planned this paper to be about something I call, "The Coupling Conspiracy", and how our psychological field needs to expand its notion of Eros and desire, a theme which has preoccupied my observations and thinking for years. This essay will actually focus on the teen program I have been co-directing this last year which developed out of years of creative angst in our field of depth psychology. How do the two topics relate?

I believe our dominant culture and our psychological field overvalue personal love, "soulmate love," at the expense of a love for humanity. We highlight the singular other, locating intimacy largely *between* self and other instead of *among* others. Analysis and psychotherapy in their basic dyadic modes teach us about pairing and reinforce the proliferation of binary images.

The United States suffers from some of the highest rates of civic apathy. Our national psyche is obsessed with privacy, ownership, exclusivity, and their shadow--sex scandals. We have a great zeal for that Platonic notion of the spheres and for finding our other half. The Gore kiss satisfies our need to see Eros between Man and Wife. He received much less press for his actual policies.

In Depth Psychology, we too often look at the psyche of the individual and couple instead of the psyche of our communities. As Aaron Kipnis points out, we have the largest and fastest growing prison industry in the "free world" and 25% of our African Americans are serving prison time. We are the only country to have our prison business listed on the New York stock exchange (American Gulag lecture, 2000). We may have been so focused on going deeper into our psychological methods that we have not noticed the plight of those people left out of our inquiry. I believe our civic selves have atrophied in the process, causing a cavernous loss to our collective psyche.

In twenty years of seeing primarily upwardly mobile clients, the search for personal love as salvation has been a dominant theme. Our largely Caucasian upper middle class field suffers directly and indirectly from what I call the "Coupling Commandments"; these commandments are unconscious dominant culture dictates which emphasize the attainment of the personal other at the expense of the polysemous relational field. This narrowing of vision threatens the safety and health of the democratic psyche . How many of our private clients come to us in despair because their neighbors are being oppressed? Instead, we so often hear complaints regarding our clients' performance or experience of intimacy . It is as if a repetitive personalized consciousness possesses the upwardly mobile psyche while it marginalizes the potential to serve the collective and be nourished by it.

The following is a partial list of the most obvious coupling commandments :

1. You shall have one mate for life.

2. You shall be consistently and eternally happy with your mate.

3. You shall bear children.

4. You shall have frequent and exciting sex.

5. You shall live with your mate.

6. You shall spend most of your social time with your mate.

7 . You shall be in a same race, same class, marriage.

8. You shall be heterosexual.

9. You shall be romantic at all times.

10. You shall be fulfilled by your "soulmate."

No matter who you are, you cannot live up to these commandments which fuel the obsession to achieve them and leave many people empty and ashamed. My contention is that we need to relocate Eros as the center of community instead of the couple. Doing so will inherently provide more balance to our personal relationships which cannot bear the burden of carrying the Self archetype or godhead. The image I see is the windmill whose form honors a more plural nature and produces energy through the many interdependent paths of motion. The sails of the windmill connect internally and externally to provide life for the community. This is why my focus for the remainder of this essay will be on the community project my partner, Rendy Freedman and I , along with fourteen other professionals, created called The Academy of Healing Arts for Teenagers (AHA!).

This program sprang from frustration with the overly-individualistic psychotherapeutic model and the dream of many sails guiding the wounded adolescent psyche within a vital web. Our program invites teenagers to develop their imagination, emotional intelligence, and their civic conscience within a community model. This summer we started with nineteen youths ages 12-19. The program met for four hours a day during the entire month of July. The teens represented diverse racial, age, and economic backgrounds. The program consisted of poetry, acting improvisation, body intelligence, yoga, Chi Gong, deep listening council, dreamwork, visualization, Mexican shamanism, mythic symbols and most importantly-- Eracism--a class designed to challenge our fear of others and otherness.

We found all our participants through community referral and provided thirteen full scholarships through business sponsorship. We were amazed when the first ten voluntary sign-ups were male. People thought our curriculum might be too touchy-feely to appeal to young men; instead we found young men hungering for a climate in which they could receive and express their deeply relational and imaginative sides.

We designed the program so at least two adults would facilitate each class; often there were more than four adults present. We believe that youth need elders. We also discovered through this project that adults need youth to become elders. Mentorship is a key to generational wisdom flowing in both directions simultaneously. One of our facilitators shared with us that it was through his immersion in the teen culture of AHA! that he came to realize how badly his fatherless nephew needed him. He was moved to tell his nephew that he was now making it official that he would serve as that boy's father figure, and also what he now expected of him. His nephew was thrilled and immediately requested that they get him his real ID because for years he had been using a fake. We also believe that segregating youth from adults and from youth of different ages in our learning environments is a huge loss and contributes to an artificially-constructed generation gap. We consistently found that the older kids liked helping and learning from the younger ones and vice versa.

We also found that when adults and young people are dreaming, acting, writing poetry together, and holding intentional listening, there is no gap. Most importantly, we found that if we created a small village which more accurately reflects a diversity of race and ethnicity in both the adults and youth, then the so-called barriers of prejudice begin to erase. Bigotry needs a rigid routine and a lack of curiosity to exist. Once typical place and affiliation were disrupted we found that our racial, gender, and status identities started to dissolve.

Our youth population consisted of 10 young men and 9 young women. There were 9 Caucasians, 5 Latinos, 2 African Americans, 2 Brazilians, and 1 Hawaiian. In our Eracism class we worked with experience and exercises instead of lectures. One exercise which melted the room occurred when each of us wrote down names and words we would never want to be called, even if they would not typically apply to us. We then read them aloud. After twenty minutes of having obscenities, insults, and racial slurs read aloud, we asked ourselves, "What has happened to this room?" "What is the effect on our bodies?" "Our relationships to one another?" The teens remarked on how badly they felt and never realized the power of expression and the spoken word. We then had each person make a list of names, identities, and adjectives he/she would want to be called, and the room flowered with possibility. The teenagers volunteered to refrain from their negative word slinging for the rest of the month in an act of protest against cultural splitting.

There was one boy who I will call Bobby who proclaimed himself to be a Neo-Nazi at the beginning of the program and had the necessary skin head to enforce that persona. The group struggled with him to understand his hatred of the other. Bobby would often say "I don't really know, I just hate coloreds and faggots." Members of the group would let him know how offended they were but still kept a space for Bobby's anger and confusion. One day another boy was sharing how he used to get beaten up in school because he dressed differently. All of a sudden Bobby burst out and said he had been too. He then described how he was a dreamy and artistic boy when he was young and when he went to the big junior high he liked to dress in bright colors and costumes. Over time he became the target of vicious remarks and was attacked on three different occasions, simply because he did not wear the conforming drab colors of the social dress code. Now we understood how Bobby had developed the dominator persona and the accompanying bigotry. Bobby never wanted to be the "sissy" again. Without directly confronting Bobby on this point, we recognized from that day forward that his rigid stance eased up. He even let his hair grow some in response to positive female comments from the group.

These kids stated from the beginning that they would not normally hang out together. By the end they referred to themselves as a family and acted that way in the positive sense of loyalty, protection, and appreciation for different roles. The faculty also was colorful and included seven men and seven women, different sexual orientations, and a healthy mix of racial and economic differences. The adults had as many barriers to overcome and the teens were often the centrifugal force which enabled the adults to cross previous affiliation lines.

The program focused on living *with* each other instead of on the pursuit of the "other." Our small community of nineteen youth and fourteen adults experienced a container much larger than romantic love or personal transference. We had the numinous experience of the plurality of Eros. Our curriculum included a strong emphasis on the body and instinct and how our bodies move and sense in community. Will Gale worked with the teens on a process he originated called "Body Intelligence." Teens were taught how to utilize their senses in setting and releasing boundaries. Will helped them tune into their subtle bodies and guided them in how to use their imaginations to create the weight and density of their interaction and touch. Too many teens are being raised on screens, both computer and television, where the body no longer exists in its fleshy wisdom. In this project, kids that were labeled ADD had no problem doing highly focused Yoga and Chi Gong because they were among others who cared about them, valued their physical presence, and gave their bodies outlets for intense curiosity and their desire for responsiveness.

We also were able to take the entire project to a modern dance concert through the donation of an arts agency. Right before the show started the rep from the company informed us that there would be partial nudity and homosexual inferences. Some of the youth left at intermission uncomfortable with the content, whereas others became inflamed with humor and inspiration. To our surprise, the next day many of the teens planned to perform their satire of the dance for our small community. They turned on the music, shut the curtains all around the room and proceeded to perform a bacchanal rendition of the dance, dressed in their skimpiest clothes and some impressive lingerie. The room exploded with laughter and release. Nearly all the teens and adults joined in a jubilant dance maintaining appropriate boundaries and celebrating the sheer explosion of libido. This was an enactment of adolescent lust in a fully contained and ritualized space. The room was electrified in pure rapture and the tribal archetype was deeply felt.

AHA! also made room for dreams and silence. In our world so manic with activity and expectation, it is rare for young and old to gather in circle to listen for oracles, dreams, and the invisibles impregnating the silence. Each week we held the dreamstar which was constructed by all of us laying with our heads towards the center in a cozy circle. We allowed the dreams to drift up through the silence and be shared as collective images. The sharing of the dream was followed by long silence until the next reflection was organically shared.

Themes of destruction and primal fear were shared as well as vivid images from the animal and natural world. No one commented on the dreams or interpreted them into something else. The dreams filled the room with their own voice and animation, and soaked into the collective body and drawing the circle closer through unseen threads.

We held AHA! at the Boys and Girls Club right in the center of Santa Barbara because we wanted our program to be in the middle of the polis instead of at a sanitized therapy institute which has no true texture for the adolescent life. Our program had to be limited to nineteen youth; however, many younger children from the club would visit. Without direction from the adults the older kids graciously hosted our little visitors. Sometimes younger brothers and sisters of the participants would spend a day with AHA!. It was phenomenal how six and seven year olds would participate in challenging emotional exercises with no difficulty in concentration. It seemed that the circle itself became a carrier of stewardship and maturity. In fact, a number of the parents and participants commented at the end of the month that AHA! had helped participants relate much better to their siblings.

The last day of the summer project we all caravanned down to a local beach for a picnic. Coming from such a colorful array of backgrounds and experience, we had surfers, fully dressed non-beach goers, loners, and mystic poets trucking across the hot sand towards the misty blue. Within seconds of our arrival we spotted a pod of dolphins just beyond the small waves. In a blur of frenzy the gaggle found its way into the water, clothes and all. Surfers helped weak swimmers, elders guided the younger, and the social ones brought in the shy ones. For the next hour the small community was surrounded by playful dolphins leaping in and out of the surrounding water . This was magic. And yet, by now it seemed to be the norm for this group.

In saying goodbye to the summer, it was clear that the community we created would be fragmented as the school year began, and many of our pod would be lost in the institutionalized numbness of modern education. We have continued with a weekly afterschool group, yet over half the summer participants could not attend. It is clear that a month of windmilling cannot sustain the psychological benefits and burdens of an ongoing community. We have continued our efforts to raise money for a year long program and curriculum which can be implemented in the schools. Fortunately at the time of this writing we have sustained a small grant which will allow AHA! to conduct a pilot program in a local high school and continue on with the summer program.

For all the great efforts we make on behalf of our individual clients in private therapy, there is a desperate need for a gathering of sensitive souls in an environment of exchange, equality, and possibility. We need a form which allows the adult healers the same healing as the clients in order to create a more solid ground for authentic modeling, development, and the transmission of wisdom from both directions. When Eros is reinstated as the God among us, instead of the God between us, we can find ties which resuscitate a genuine interest in community life and enrich the tribe a thousand fold. As C. Turnbull reminds us,

> In adolescence we are in many ways like empty but organic receptacles fully formed though still growing, waiting to be filled. And like receptacles we are capable at that stage of life of receiving with all our being, becoming one with what is within us. Sexual and spiritual awareness as modes of experience are just as valid as physical and intellectual awareness; and like those other modes of apprehension they can be turned in any direction, inward or outward, restricted to the individual self or encouraged to expand and encompass the infinitely greater social self....Education and socialization can be accomplished in the solitude of the rational domain, but it is the intensity that these other modes of perception can bring to each and ever experience that gives such education an inner significance, endowing it with a vital force. It is this intensity of perception, together with the integrity of being, that can make of human society a living, thriving, truly loving, joyously full and exuberant organism, rather than a cold, mechanical, empty theoretical concept. That is the magic of transformation, and that is the potential of **adolescence.** (Turnbull, 1983, p. 83)

References

Kipnis, A. (2000, December). American Gulag. Unpublished Pacifica Graduate Institute lecture, Carpinteria, CA.

Turnbull, C. (1983). The human cycle. New York: Simon and Schuster.

Taking a Glance at the Place of Soul in the Environment by Edward S. Casey, Ph.D.

> Everything that happens and everything that is said happens or is said at the surface.
> -- Gilles Deleuze, <u>The Logic of Sense</u>

> The surface is where most of the action is.
> -- J.J. Gibson, <u>The Ecological Approach to Visual Perception</u>

> Can things have a face?
> -- Emmanuel Levinas, "Is Ontology Fundamental?"

> All things show faces, the world [is] not only a coded signature to be read for meaning, but a physiognomy to be faced...
> -- James Hillman, "Anima Mundi"

> Everything is brought back to... fluctuations of intensity.
> -- Pierre Klossowski, "Oubli et anamnèse"

I

In this essay I want to take a new look at the glance. The glance -- not the gaze or the regard or studied scrutiny (the prescribed attitude of so much of Western philosophy and psychology) or even bare contemplation (an ascetic ideal). The glance has none of the gravity of these more austere and traditionally sanctioned kinds of looking. It is a mere featherweight by comparison. Instead of bogging down, the glance alleviates. Rather than petrifying things -- as does the stare -- the glance graces what it looks at, enhancing and expanding it. The glance does not make entities more entitative; rather than ballasting them with Being, it endows them with the lightness of Becoming. The spirit of gravity, which seeks to fixate and to identify, is dissipated in the mereness of a glance.

Apophansis, that urge to predicate and judge which has held some two millennia of Western thought in thrall, is suspended in the glance. Instead of a logic of statement -- of affirmation and confirmation -- the glance returns us to the original and literal meaning of the Greek: "apo-phansis": to <u>show</u> something <u>from</u> itself. From off its very surface. Which is precisely what the glance is uniquely capable of doing. Even the most penetrating glance stays on the surface rather than piercing it all the way through or going behind it. This is not to say, however, that the glance lingers on the surface. It would not be a glance if it did. From one surface -- of one thing or group of things -- it is deflected to another. The glance moves on. Contrary to what Husserl said, The look does not abide.[1] Not if the look is a glance.

But what is the glance? What happens in it? (What happens to it is all too clear; it is bypassed, outright neglected in almost all of Western philosophy and psychology, which assume that the glance can only be concerned with trivialities. But to be concerned with the surface is not to be concerned with what is superficial.) What happens in the glance is this. A glance takes in -- it takes a lot in, namely, all kinds of surface. In so doing, it takes us places, all kinds of places. For places are what hold surfaces together in more or less coherent clusters, giving them a habitation if not a (local) name: giving them a "layout."[2] If we can say of surfaces what Socrates says of shapes -- namely, that they are "the limits of solids"[3] -- they are not only the surfaces of things but of places as well. The world at which we glance is a layout of surfaces.

In these two regards, that is, by taking in surfaces and taking us places, a glance takes us out of ourselves, out of our customary egoic identity. It suspends this identity as surely as it dissolves the apophantic obsession with identification. In its egoless ecstasis, the glance refuses to succumb to the grasping that is so endemic to any settled sense of self and that is the essence of samsara, the state of suffering. By effecting this release, the glance can take us virtually anywhere -- to almost any surface and place of the world. Indeed, it brings us to the world itself. The world at a glance: the world in a glance.

I said that the glance "takes in." The glance not only goes out; it comes (back) in. It is informative. As performative of perspectives, it is informative of the world. For it is by glancing, just glimpsing, that we learn a great deal of what we know about the world. Perhaps finally everything. Not merely in the sense of many items of knowledge, much less an itemized sum of things. A glance reveals an entire situation, a whole scene of action. And it does so with surprising comprehensiveness and scope. Let me give some examples:

(i) in being in a big city such as New York, I learn much by just glancing around at my surroundings: the glance suffices to tell me that 'now I am in mid-town', 'I must be on the

West Side', 'Soho should be coming up', etc. I need not scrutinize the situation to pick these things up; they arise within my mere glance. (New York cabbies, it has been shown, often know where they are by the mere momentary feeling of wind currents as they drive about: here is the kinesthetic equivalent of the glance.) It doesn't matter that the City is a very complex entity; the more complex, the better suited to being known at a glance;

(ii) or take the very different circumstance of traveling in Montana, where the landscape may be as complex as the New York cityscape; yet, just by glancing about me as I hike in the woods or (for that matter) drive on Highway 90, I find that I take in an enormous amount: "amount" not as additive sum but as an amassed body of knowledge; I perceive six or seven different types of weather in different parts of the sky; I see the Crazy mountains suddenly rising from the plain on my right and the Absaroka on my left; having climbed twice before in the Crazies, I recognize them instantly; but even if I do not recognize the Absaroka, I take them in as south-central Montana mountains without pausing to scrutinize them one by one and without having to check my map. These outsize momentous Things, like the diverse weather hanging over them, are <u>all there in the glance</u> -- in one or two quick looks on my part;

(iii) or take the case of sexual identity: someone is walking toward me and I glance in that direction; usually, in most cases I know instantly that this is a man or a woman; even in cases of cross-dressing I can tell fairly soon if this is a male who is dressing as a woman, or vice versa; only if I cannot tell do I pause -- if I am interested in this question -- and examine the content of my perception; and even then the examination will tend to consist in nothing but a set of further glances, now from closer up and with a more particular disambiguating purpose than before;

(iv) finally, ponder the circumstance of "sizing up a situation"; this happens all the time among human beings (as well as between human beings and animals, and among animals themselves); but it is effective and informative -- often being all we need to understand what is going on, even if the circumstance is complicated (she is angry at how he treats her friend, who, however, has in certain ways provoked him); this is not to deny that some are more adept than others at quickly taking in a social situation; but virtually everyone possesses a modicum of such a skill -- a skill that requires no more than a glance for its enactment.

Thus, in four different circumstances -- two of them bearing on perceived "scapes" and two on social settings -- the power of the glance is strikingly evident. In all four cases we witness the primary paradox of the glance: namely, the fact that something so diminutive in extent and bearing can provide such far-ranging and subtle insight. What the glance takes in greatly exceeds its meager means, whether these means be gestural or physiological (the glance is only one among many micro-movements of which human beings and other animals are capable), spatial or temporal (the motion of the glancing eye is a matter of centimeters at best; and it lasts only for the very briefest moment). It is as if the glance were a fulcrum, an Archimedean point of leverage, for quite massive being-in-the-world. The glance is, as it were, the perceptual analogue of our instantaneous emotional insertion into the world. (The cognitive counterpart would be short-term memory, which within micro-seconds takes in an enormous amount of sophisticated data.)

Let us say, then, that the glance is the most poignant point of access, of immediate intromission, into the surrounding world. It is an incisive inroad into this world; it gets us there, and it keeps us there by repeated relooking. It gets us to the surface of things, as many surfaces as we can bear -- thus as many places as we can go. These surfaces and places are not bare or brute; they are telling; they say themselves, they show themselves, to the glance that takes them in.

II

In the rest of this paper, I shall focus on how the glance figures into a new way of looking at environmental ethics -- no longer regarded as a matter of principles alone (such as not doing harm to others, or stewardship, or other like conceptions) and as independently of any humanism as we can get. If we can rethink the moment of initial encounter with the natural world, perhaps we can gain a different understanding of where the imperative to do something about a damaged or threatened environment stems from. Perhaps as well, we can open a new space for soul within this same environment.

I shall begin with a basic consideration of how the glance intersects with the environment, grasping its imperativity, before I consider the place of soul in all this.

An ethics of the environment must begin with the facticity of being struck by something wrong happening in the environment. It is by noticing that something is out of joint -- does not fit or function well -- that a response is elicited and an action induced. Unless the environment is apprehended in its very problematicity, it will remain noxious, troublesome, harmful. Deadly chemicals will circulate freely in the air and food will be poisoned -- unless attention is given to what is awry in these circumstances. Not that notice is enough; the full force of ethical action requires reflection and consultation: in a word, follow-through. But the first moment of noticing is indispensable: without this, nothing will happen, nothing will follow.

This first moment of ethical responsiveness is the moment of the glance. The glance, meager as it seems to be, is indispensable for all ethical action of any consequence. This is so despite the fact of its almost complete neglect by ethical theorists, who tend to find in it something merely trivial, perhaps a predecessor to significant action but in any case beneath theoretical dignity. And yet it is of enormous significance, both in interhuman ethical action and in the broader field of so-called "environmental ethics." For it is by the glance that we can first tell that something is going wrong in the world round us -- those shore birds unable to fly because of the oil on their feathers, the smog that settles over the Grand Canyon, the trees in Appalachia dying from acid rain. By the bare encounter with these distressed phenomena, we know that all is not well with the natural environment and we find ourselves wanting to do something about it -- yet frustrated b y the fact that the causes of these environmental disasters are so remote from where we stand: the oil pipelines in Alaska, the pollution of Los Angeles, the Midwestern power plants that generate the acid rain.

But the where that matters even more than these particular locations is the where of the imperative to rectify these distraught circumstances. From where does the urgent sense that something must be done to change the course of things come? Certainly not just from ourselves -- from our private interiority in reason or even in the heart. Nor is it to be found in others -- in what others tell us to do. But where then?

In pursuing an ethics of the environment, the Where precedes the What of determinate content -- i.e., what one should do in order to be ethical -- as well as the How of how to apply the What: how to make it work or stick in a given circumstance. Even if it is true that the What and the How come first in the order of ethical <u>conduct</u> -- we must know what to do and how to do it if we are to get anywhere at all in the moral life -- an environmental ethics must first ask where the source of the compelling power of the ethical is to be found.

In the history of Western ethics, there have been at least four major answers to the Where question. The sanction or source of the ethical has been located in the Good, in God, in the spiritual Self, and in the Face. Either the source of the ethical lies in something transcendent to the human -- in the Good, as the final object of knowledge, or in God as the ultimate metaphysical or theological force -- or in something intrinsically human: whether this be the deep self (as in Kant's view of the noumenal or spiritual self) or the face (as in Emmanual Levinas's ethics of the human Other). I set aside here the ancient and medieval moves to locate the seat of the ethical in the supra-human: as also in Kantian ethics, they ask us to accept a totalizing metaphysical system which is inimical to the particularity and poignancy that must be part of a truly compelling ethics, including an ethics of the environment.[4]

Levinas, reflecting the demand of twentieth-century thinkers in the wake of Husserl and Heidegger and Sartre, argues that the compellingness of the ethical be available to every human subject in a non-totalizing form. This is why he makes the move to the face, which in its idiosyncratic tellingness fiercely resists any totalization. In his pathbreaking essay of 1951, "Is Ontology Fundamental?" Levinas asserts that:

> It is above all a question of finding the place from where human beings cease to concern us exclusively on the basis of the horizon of being [as in Heidegger]. The human existent (l'étant) as such (and not as an incarnation of universal being) can only exist in a relation where it is invoked [as such]. The human existent is the human being, and it is as a fellow being (prochain) that human being is accessible. [And it is accessible] as a face.[5]

Significant here is Levinas's express effort to find a "place from where" (la place d'où) ethics takes its origin as "accessible" to human beings in their particularity. The point of access is found in the face -- the face of the other, my "fellow being." What matters in ethics is the relation to the face, its acknowledgement as the source of ethical imperativity, beginning with the command not to murder the other with whom we are face-to-face. not the face as such: Levinas says expressly that "To be in relation with the Other face to face -- this is not to be able to kill [that Other]."[6] The face has the requisite particularity and weight for ethics to find its fulcrum in something compelling about the other person.[7]

Levinas's achievement is that he has located the force of the ethical in a feature of the actuality of the subject, the face of the Other in its presence here and now to me as its witness and fellow sufferer.

III

Let us grant the promise and power in Levinas's model of the source of ethical imperatives -- a source, a where, straight in the face of the Other. But where are we to find the equivalent of the face in the environing natural world? Where is there in this world a comparably compelling source for ethical comportment? Without this source, we would not be drawn to do anything ethically pertinent. Human beings rarely if ever act from abstract principles, not from the Kantian categorical imperative in its three formulations and not even from the Ten Commandments! (Which themselves, let us remember, were revealed to Moses at a particular place in the wilderness!) Where can we find in the other-than-human world the imperativity that being ethical requires? More particularly, is there anything like a face that commands us in the presence of nature?

It is remarkable that Levinas, who says very little about an ethics of the environment at any point, raises this very question: "Can things [the things of nature] assume a face?"[8] Such a face must be grasped as something distinctive, not just another feature in a surrounding context. Yet the very word "environment" emphasizes precisely the idea of something surrounding us, thanks to the meaning of the prefix environ-. In any given natural scene, it is difficult to locate anything with the force, much less the authority, of a human face. It seems that either there is nothing like a face in the environment -- as Levinas himself would doubtless conclude, given his stringent conditions of selfhood -- or the face is all over the place: in which case, its meaning will be so diluted as to lose its ethical urgency. This is the kind of dilemma into which Levinas, no less than Kant before him, puts us: either the face is strictly human (and then no ethics of the other-than-human environment is possible) or it is merely part of a decidedly non-ethical totality called "life" or "nature."[9] Ethics is human or does not exist at all. But this rigid choice gets us nowhere when we want to consider right and good action in the non-human world.

What to do, then, in the face of this dilemma? One tempting move is to give up any search for a human face but still look for something human or humanlike in the environment as the hook on which to place the hat of ethics. Levinas would be only too happy to comply with this search insofar as he rejects the literal face to start with: other parts of the body, a shoulder or hand, can play the role of the face in the ethical relation.[10]

Could we not say that the whole natural world is like a body, the "world's body," and that it is therefore capable of presenting a face to us? Suggestive as it is, the idea of the world's body remains parasitic on the human body: what other kind of body could be invoked as a paradigm in the circumstance, hence what other kind of face? To generalize the human body, starting with its peculiar face, over the entire environment is only to indulge in an unremitting extension of humanism, making man indeed "the measure of all things."

Could it be that soul, and not body, is a better basis for finding face in nature -- given that soul is not merely or originally personal but belongs to the larger world, the cosmos, of which the natural world is one major expression?

IV

We need to make a new start to find if not an actual face at least its equivalent in the environment. Instead of trying to locate this source of imperativity in a particular feature of that environment -- its body or its mind, its sentience or its feeling (as in Buddhism or Whitehead), much less its literal face -- we should look to a more compassing framework that does not borrow any of its basic traits from human beings. I refer to what I like to call the "place-world." Every entity of the environment, both human and non-human, belongs to a place-world by virtue of the habitat in which it resides. Thinking this way avoids invidious ranking of species in the ethical realm; it focuses on what all natural entities, including unspeciated ones, share: belongingness to the place-world. All things, living or not, are part of this world, and therefore one ultimate ground of ethical force is to be found in the environment regarded as a coherent set of places.

A simple thought-experiment points to the rightness of this line of thought. Faced with the choice as to whether we would destroy a given member of a species or its habitat, we would surely prefer to save the habitat even if it meant sacrificing the animal. The value accrues not just to the larger whole but to the place-world in which any given animal flourishes. Or to put the same point somewhat differently: whereas we value human animals primarily for what they are in each individual case (we can be face-to-face with only one Other at a time; we can substitute ourselves only for one other at a time), we value animals not only for themselves (this we certainly do as well, as we know from the case of favorite pets) but also and ultimately for their belonging to the place-world which they co-inhabit. The source of the ethical commitment they inspire in us stems in good measure from our appreciation of the places to which they belong as co-ordinate members of the same habitat or territory.

Another clue, this time from the history of language: ethos, the Greek word that lies at the origin of "ethics" and that meant 'character' in Attic Greek, first meant (in Homer's time) 'animal habitat', for example, the place where wild horses go when they settle down at night. There is, then, a long line of thought that ties together ethics and place in the West.

Even if you will grant me that place-worlds are an ultimate source of ethical force in the environmental field, you will rightly want something more specific to anchor the imperative to undo or at least diminish damage to the environment. If we meditate upon the place-world, we find that its two primary characteristics are "layout" and "surface." Layout is J.J. Gibson's term for "the persisting arrangement of surfaces relative to one another and to the ground."[11] It is the manner in which various visual, kinesthetic, auditory, and other phenomena co-constitute an environment, its very extendedness. Layout also refers to how a given environment offers relevant "affordances" to its inhabitants: opportunities to act in certain ways.[12]

Still more specifically the layout of the place-world is composed of <u>surfaces</u>. Not only is layout a matter of the arrangement of surfaces in relation to each other, but the very ground to which each of these surfaces relate is "the basic persisting surface of the environment."[13] In other words: the earth. Indeed, "environment" itself, the single most encompassing term of all, is in effect a concatenation of surfaces since the "substances" of which it is composed present themselves only through surfaces, and the environment is imperceptible except in terms of particular surfaces such as the edge of the wind or the ripple on a lake. Since a surface can be regarded as "the interface between a substance and [a] medium,"[14] it is the indispensable mediatrix between everything of import in the environment; everywhere we feel and sense, we are confronted by surfaces: by their phenomenal properties (such as their shape, color, size, texture, etc.), their intersection, and finally their layout. They are the constituent units of every environment, starting with the worlds of animals: "Animals," observes Gibson, "perceive surfaces and their properties, since animal behavior must be controlled by what the surfaces and their substances afford."[15] All the more is this true of plants and stones, which are even more fully affected, indeed dominated, by the surfaces around them.

Suddenly we realize that the very word "surface" <u>includes</u> the face: it is the <u>on-the-face</u> of the environment, that which the environment presents <u>as its face</u> -- and <u>puts in our face</u>, letting us <u>face it</u>. Facing the environment, putting our face to its face, being face-to-face with it -- this is granting it the full force of its very sur-face.

V

Although we are surrounded by surfaces -- "animals [including human animals]," says Gibson, "see their environment chiefly [as] illuminated surfaces"[16] -- we rarely pause to take note of what is special about them, especially not with regard to their role in ethical life. Yet if the glance indeed plays a central role in ethics, then the perception of surfaces will be essential to this life. For surfaces are precisely where glances alight: we pick up environmental distress directly from the surface. But what it is about surfaces that makes them so well suited for presenting ethical imperatives that command us to remedy this distress?

At one level of analysis, surfaces show themselves to be eminently capable of expressivity, thanks to variations in pliability, elasticity, edgedness, extendedness, coloration, texture, and doubtless others: all of which, once co-ordinated, bring about the expressive form of a given layout of surfaces.[17] It is just because of this multiplicity of co-variant factors that the full range of expressivity is possible, whether it is displayed in a face or a landscape.

At a second level, a surface is able to hold together and present these diverse parameters precisely because of its own comparative simplicity. Consider the surface of a mirror or that of a window pane. It is its very smoothness, its lack of qualitative complication, its transparency or its sheer reflecting power, that allows it to hold within its frame very complex objects and scenes. It is virtually a law of "ecological optics" that the simpler the surface, the more complex the contents it can set forth, on the surface in the case of the mirror, through the surface in the case of the window pane.[18]

Given that surfaces facilitate expressiveness and that their very simplicity allows for the conveyance of environmental complexity, we have at hand a ready basis for their presentation of what can spur an ethics of the environment. This is the direct presentation of environmental disturbance. When I glimpse the dumping of waste in a swamp, I am witnessing disorder in the environment -- in its expressive and reflective surfaces.[19]

In such directly grasped environmental disruption, I find myself in the presence of a veritable corpus contra naturem, a work against nature. By this, I do not mean merely a "freak of nature" -- though this can be environmentally telling too, as in the case of birth defects caused by chemical pollution of underground water -- but any feature of the layout that goes contrary to the natural order. Then, instead of an optical array that is well-ordered with regard to being and well-being, we are confronted with manifest disarray. What I have been calling "distress" or "disturbance" refers to any kind of environmental turpitude that is registered -- expressively -- in the surfaces of the layout occupied by a given group of natural entities. The signs of such disorder are telling something to us; they are expressing a wound to the ecosystem, a tear in its fabric, an illness in the landscape. To those who had eyes to see, the early effects of nineteenth-century industrialism in England and America were manifest in the country as well as in the city -- as acute observers from Blake and Dickens, Thomas Cole and Thoreau all saw so poignantly.

Or let us say that these ecologists of perception, before there was any science of the subject, grasped at a glance the destruction that was billowing in the air and poisoning the ground. So we, today, can apperceive the initial effects of global warming in such expressive elemental phenomena as changing weather patterns, whose persistently hotter surfaces we sense in our skins, and whose deadly effects are visible in the massive losses of sea otters and seals in the Pacific Ocean. "Apperception" is the specific perceptual mode by which the glance takes in the folds, the creases and crevices, of a single surface or set of surfaces. All of this in a single place: when I apperceive dis-ease in the environment, I attend to where it is located, in what place, and especially on which surfaces of that place. This is why the glance is so integral to this circumstance: its pointed penetrating power allows it to go straight to where the problem is, like a hawk zeroing in on its prey. The glance, like a lance, is typically thrown at its target (as the French say, when we glance we 'throw a blow of the eye': jeter un coup d'oeil). The target in landscape apperception takes the form of a given place in the environment, a set of surfaces that betrays instantly the state of its health.

Analogues to this situation abound: the practiced medical doctor knows by a mere glance what her patient is suffering from, the painter knows by the briefest of looks what has to be added or subtracted from the work, the cook to the dish being prepared, the poet to her text. But in the case of the environment, the glance is cast wide: it is literally a "sweeping glance." In such a literally com-prehensive look, the place-world is seen as existing within its own normative parameters, geomorphic or evolutionary, agricultural or wild -- or else as exceeding or undermining these parameters, as ill at ease with itself. The glance takes all this in suddenly, without needing judgment or reflection. A bare apperception, a mere moment of attention, is enough: a glance suffices.[20]

VI

And where is the place of soul in all this? Where is its face, its intensity?

If the environing place-world is not just the physical world -- the world of extended substance, of obdurate and atomically structured matter (though it is somehow this, too) -- but a world enlivened by psychical forces, a panpsychical whole that exudes soul at every moment, then it will be all the more expressive and intensive in its bearing. Such expressivity and intensity are not the outpouring of subjective spirits transplanted to the cosmic realm -- that way lies displaced humanism and anthropocentrism, between which I have been trying to steer a not-so-delicate course throughout this essay. Instead of pursuing any such misguided Romanticism, let us regard the existing place-world as the very articulation of what Jung called "objective psyche." This is psyche fully invested in the surrounding world, at one with it -- psyche out there, in the environment. This means that the psychical is found in every natural thing -- in rocks and trees, animals and mountains, and not just in human beings. It inhabits each of these denizens of the earth differently, in accordance with an "eachness" that is distinctive in every case.

I would also maintain that the psychical infuses what we call "landscape" as well, that is, the detotalized totality of earthly things that constitutes the scene of any coherent perception (and not just ours, either: that of animals and plants and stones as well).

If the psychical is truly everywhere -- wherever there is not just a person or a god but a place -- then we are confronted with nothing less than a cosmic spectacle, a theater of ensouled places: we encounter what James Hillman, with an eye on Renaissance Neoplatonism, calls "anima mundi":

> Let us imagine the anima mundi as that particular soul spark, that seminal image, which offers itself through each thing in its visible form. Then anima mundi indicates the animated possibilities presented by each event as it is, its sensuous presentation as a face bespeaking its interior image -- in short, its availability to imagination, its presence as a psychic reality. Not only animals and plants ensouled as in the Romantic vision, but soul is given with each thing, God-given things of nature and man-made things of the street.[21]

This passage is remarkably suggestive. First of all, it reconceives environment -- the totality of God-given and man-made things -- as a scene of soul, each kind of thing involving its own unique mode of animation. Then, it moves us to the very brink of the glance by speaking of "visible form" and of "soul spark": the glance, after all, is the sparking event of perception which takes in at an instant the form of things it sees so suddenly. Third, it recognizes the signal importance of the face, which we have seen in the wake of Levinas to be indispensable to any ethics that has compelling force. Hillman adds this crucial claim:

> All things show faces, the world not only a coded signature to be read for meaning, but a physiognomy to be faced... psychic reality appears in the expressive form or physiognomic quality of images.[22]

The world as a "physiognomy to be faced," and one that "appears" (i.e., is apperceived) in an explicitly "expressive form"! Here we have already on hand a compelling list of ingredients for a renewed sense of environmental ethics -- a sense for which I have been arguing on independent phenomenological grounds. (This is not the first time, nor will it be the last, in which phenomenology and archetypal psychology have joined forces across an ostensibly unbridgeable abyss.)

But we need to take another basic step. This is to recognize the deep and lasting link between soul and place: "There could be a profound shift in therapy of soul," says Hillman: "Soul could be reclaimed from soulful places out there filled with God-given beauty."[23] It is hardly accidental that Hillman here invokes the natural realm as a place, a place-world, in which to find soul. And he invokes the same realm when its beauty is marred -- when it is wounded in a manner not unlike that which I have called the "symptom" resulting from an injury to the environment:

> The gaping red construction site [becomes] the new operatio going on in my Adamic body... The great wound in the red earth, whether in my dream or in my neighborhood, is still a site of wrenching upheaval, appealing for an aesthetic as much as a hermeneutic response. To interpret the world's things as if they were our dreams deprives the [natural] world of its dream, its complaint.[24]

Not only an aesthetic and hermeneutic response is called for by such earth wounds but also, and especially, an ethical response. A call to change our practices in relation to the earth, to begin to care for it as a matter of soul and not only as a matter of matter.

Such a response begins with the glance that picks up, in one alarmed look, the wound to the earth politic -- that sees this wound festering at and in the surface of the earth. "The great wound in the red earth" is a trauma to the earth's surface, a trauma that sports symptoms which we can see immediately and which are capable of moving us to action.

We can see these symptoms -- these contorted expressions of nature turned against itself in an action that goes contrary to its inherent beauty -- in a glance. Here, too, Hillman is prescient. He speaks of a special form of attention, notitia, acute noticing: "In depth psychology, notitia has been limited by our subjective view of psychic reality so that attention is defined mainly in regard to subjective states."[25] To this I would add that such noticing is accomplished in the glance: a glance that is trained on the surfaces of the environing world, "as this thing or that spontaneously comes alive, arrests our attention, draws us to it."[26] This glanceful attending is drawn to the animated world in its "self-display," the Portmannian concept so central to Hillman's notion of anima mundi. Such self-display is a manifestation of surfaces, whether of the earth or sky; or of the denizens of the earth, organic or inorganic. The depths, the distinctively psychical depths, are indeed on these surfaces -- there to be noted, there to solicit our glance, there to be impelling, there to act upon: if only we are able and willing to take in what we see in a glance. The world at a glance, the world in a glance.

Here we come full cycle from our beginning. The glance takes in the world it sees; it has cosmic scope: not by way of cogitation or judgment, but by way of its instantaneous comprehension of the landscape world that is its proper object. But this phenomenological truth gains ground and scope from the Neo-platonic cosmology of anima mundi. It takes an animated world, scintillating with sparks of soul, to draw out the glance into the depths of its own surface. The alacrity and acuteness of the glance answers to the "particular soul spark[s]" emitted by a fulgurating panpsychic world that "indicates the animated possibilities presented by each event as it is, its sensuous presentation as a face." Plato, in his celebrated Seventh Letter, spoke of the "spark" by which the knowing soul leaps out to the intelligible Forms. So too the spark of the glance leaps out into the expressive forms of an animated cosmos, filled with the soul "given with each thing."

When these soul-ful things are things of nature, natural things, they constellate into an environment of concatenated places -- as they always do in any given natural setting, no matter how wild, no matter how violent. When violence is done to them, when they are wounded and traumatized, they emit symptomatic sparks, telling tribulations that bespeak the pain of soul murder in the earth. It is to these expressive sparks, these intensive protests, that our glance turns when it has the requisite <u>notitia</u>, when it attends to what has become damaged and distressed in the environment. The disarray of the phenomenal surfaces of this environment, so evident in its many disturbed places, tells those who have eyes to see -- looks to glance -- that a massive metastasis has occurred. The meltdown at the North Pole is one such telling symptom among many that things are awry in the natural environment: to see a single photograph of this <u>corpus contra naturem</u> is to realize suddenly that the natural world is calling out to be seen in its distress.

Only the glance can notice such unnatural nature with the requisite alarm and recoil: for its genius is the sudden apperception. In this quick apprehension of how things are -- especially how they are not going right, how they are ill -- we have the beginning of practical wisdom. For the glance, directed at the suffering surfaces of the world, goes under the surface of our own sensitive skin: it affects us at once and so deeply that we have no time to invoke the high horse of principle, the false balm of meliorism, the safe distance of skepticism. We are moved, immediately and altogether. Moved to care; moved to act; moved to make a difference to the fate of the earth we share with all other natural beings. Moved to be ethical in a new way, a way that responds to the animated state of the world soul with the concerted activism of our own soul. Between the two kinds of soul, sparking their difference and revealing their relation, is the glance that leaps from one to the other and then back again.

Glance out, glance back; take it in; act on it. But above all, let the glance connect, in one outlandish leap, your soul with the soul of the world -- a cosmic soul whose natural surfaces are troubled today in expressive and intensive ways never before imaginable in the known history of this planet. Then perhaps healing action can begin, ethical conduct may start, and the collective political force that will make a genuine difference can finally get under way. Finally and for the first time -- the time of the glance. The world at a glance: grasping this world, in all its tribulations and terrible beauty, in a glance. Improbable perhaps; but necessary definitely. Only the acumen of the sudden searing insight accomplished by the glance can save us -- or begin to do so. The longest journey, in the natural as in the cultural world, starts with the smallest step, the least leap, the minimal action, the merest look: it starts with the glance. Where else could it begin?

References

Hillman, J. (1989). Anima mundi. In T. Moore, (Ed.), A blue fire (pp. 99). New York: Harper.

Gibson, J.J. (1986). The ecological approach to visual perception. Hillsdale, NJ: Erlbaum.

E. Levinas, E. (1991). Entre nous: Essais sur le penser--à-l'autre. Paris: Grasset.

---

[1] "Contrary to the assurance that Husserl gives us a little further on, 'the look' cannot 'abide'" (Jacques Derrida, Speech and Phenomena, tr. D. Allison [Evanston: Northwestern University Press, 1973], p. 104).

[2] I borrow "layout" from J.J. Gibson, The Ecological Approach to Visual Perception (Mahwah, N.J.: Erlbaum, 1987).

[3] "Shape is that in which a solid terminates, or, more briefly, it is the limit of a solid" (Plato, Meno 76 a).

[4] If Plato calls for a dialectical metaphysics of the Good and Aristotle (and his Christian legatees) for a cosmological metaphysics of God, Kant demands a "metaphysics of morals" as the sole basis for any adequate ethics. To his credit -- credit explicitly accorded to him by Levinas, who acknowledges that his own ethics was "suggested by the practical philosophy of Kant, to whom [I] feel particularly close"("L'Ontologie est-elle fondamentale?" in E. Levinas, Entre Nous: Essais sur le penser--à-l'autre [Paris: Grasset, 1991], p. 22) -- Kant locates the imperativity of the ethical, literally the source of the categorial imperative itself, within the legislative powers of the human person, that is to say, in pure practical reason, the deepest level of the rational subject. But this level is so deep indeed -- so spiritually Other -- that it is altogether unavailable in ordinary human discourse and action, where only its effects show up (e.g., as the rational incentive to be good, etc.). There is at last the location of the ethical imperative in the person -- in keeping with the Enlightenment's implantation of human freedom and rights within the rational subject -- but this location is itself barred from direct access. It can only be posited within a metaphysics of morals; even if it is concretized in the discrete free acts, it does not deliver itself as such to untutored perception. It remains a creature of pure rational will (Wille), which is noumenal in status. Looking straight at the Kantian subject, I could not say where the locus of the moral might be; it forms no part of the phenomenality of this subject, even though it subtends and legitimates her ethical actions.

[5] "L'Ontologie est-elle fondamentale?", p. 20.

[6] Ibid., p. 21. Levinas equates outright "the encounter with the face" with "moral conscience"(p. 22).

[7] Ibid., p. 22.

[8] "L'Ontologie est-elle Fundamentale?", p. 22. But Levinas immediately diverts this question into whether the question of whether "art is an activity that lends faces to things," perhaps through "the impersonal allure of rhythm"(ibid.).

[9] "The living being (le vivant) in totality exists as a totality, as if he occupied the center of being and were its source..."(E. Levinas, "Le Moi et la totalité," in Entre Nous, cit. supra, p. 23)

[10] As Levinas remarks in passing to Nemo: "I analyze the inter-human relation as if, in proximity to the Other -- beyond the image I make of the other person [i.e., in perception] -- his face, that which is expressive in the Other (and the whole human body is, in this sense, more or less, face), were that which orders me to serve him." (EI, 104. My italics; Levinas underlines "orders.")

[11] J.J. Gibson, The Ecological Approach to Visual Perception (Hillsdale, N.J.: Erlbaum, 1986), p. 307.

[12] "Different layouts have different affordances for animals"(ibid.).

[13] Ibid. Cf. p. 10: "The literal basis of the terrestrial environment is the ground, the underlying surface of support that tends to be on the average flat -- that is to say, a plane -- and also level, or perpendicular to gravity." (My italics; Gibson underlines "basis.")

[14] J.J. Gibson, "What is Involved in Surface Perception?" in J.J. Gibson, Reasons for Realism: Selected Essays of James J. Gibson, ed. E. Reed & R. Jones (Hillsdale, N.J.: Erlbaum, 1982), p. 111.

[15] Ibid., p. 112.

[16] "Ecological Optics," in Reasons for Realism, p. 75. He adds: "The perception [of the environment] is of one surface behind another... What we see is not a projection, an image, or a picture, but a layout of surfaces." (Ibid., p. 75; his italics)

[17] Conditions for being indicative are characteristically both more austere -- e.g., a bare sign -- and more sophisticated: to grasp an indicative sign is to have to understand the larger context within which it functions.

[18] This has special relevance to ecological optics, if it is truly the case that the elemental is "non-possessable" in Levinas's word; if the various elements cannot be possessed as objects, they can at least be held as images in mirrors, framed for view in windows, and depicted on photographs: all of these being surfaces that gather the elemental for display. As Levinas says, "Every relation or possession is situated within the non-possessable which envelops or contains without being able to be contained or enveloped. We shall call it the elemental"(TI, 131). Levinas also emphasizes the indeterminate character of the elemental: TI, 132.

[19] The disorder may be more subtle, of course -- in which case, however, a trained ecologist will then be able to detect it in a glance. This is especially important in the case of early warning signs of environmental distress, say, the perception of the larvae of what will become an insect destructive of trees once it is fully developed.

[20] Here the glance is strangely the counterpart of the earth, which as Levinas says also suffices in its own way: "The earth upon which I find myself and from which I welcome sensible objects or make my way to them suffices for me. The earth which upholds me does so without my troubling myself about knowing what upholds the earth." (TI, 137) This last sentence could well be a statement about surfaces, about whose support we also do not concern ourselves; even the ground to which they ultimately relate is itself, as Gibson avers, a surface of its own.

[21] "Anima Mundi," Spring 1982; reprinted in James Hillman, A Blue Fire, ed. Thomas Moore (New York: Harper, 1989), p. 99; his italics).

[22] Ibid., p. 99; his italics.

[23] "Natural Beauty," in ibid., p. 104.

[24] "Anima Mundi," in ibid., p. 101.

[25] Ibid., p. 101.

[26] Ibid., p. 99.

Contributors

BARBARA ANNAN, Ph.D., holds two degrees in religion as well as a Ph.D. in Clinical Psychology from Pacifica Graduate Institute. She recently presented a paper in Turkish Cyprus titled "Subjectivity and the Other: Khidr and Transformative Encounter in Liminality," which will be published in 2001 by Peter Lang Publishing. She lives in Alaska where she has a private practice, and travels frequently for research on strange encounters.

GUSTAVO BARCELLOS, Ph.D., is a Jungian analyst in São Paulo, Brazil, and a member of the Associação Junguiana do Brasil and the International Association for Analytical Psychology-IAAP. He writes and teaches in the field of Archetypal Psychology.

ALAN BLEAKLEY, M.D., is a Senior Lecturer in Medical Education, University of Plymouth Postgraduate Medical School, and convener of Psychoanalytic Studies for the Doctoral program in Clinical Psychology, University of Exeter. He is currently researching situated learning in communities of practice within hospitals, and clinical decision-making. His background is in both the biological sciences and the humanities, and he has been central in developing the study of Archetypal Psychology in Britain. His most recent publication is The Animalizing Imagination (St Martins Press, 2000).

ROBERT BOSNAK, Ph.D., a Jungian analyst, is the author of A Little Course in Dreams and Tracks in the Wilderness of Dreaming. He is director of a website that facilitates online dreamwork, developing emotion recognition technology for computers, and providing a forum for reflection on the location of the Web in the imaginal.

EDWARD S. CASEY, Ph.D., is Leading Professor at the State University of New York at Stony Brook, where he was chairman of the department of philosophy from 1991-2001. He has recently extended his exploration of place to the area of environmental philosophy. His essay here is part of that exploration, which will culminate in The World at a Glance, currently under completion. His other books include Imagining; Spirit and Soul; Getting Back into Place; The Fate of Place; and Representing Places in Landscape Paintings and Maps.

JOSEPH COPPIN, Ph.D., is chair of the Depth Psychology Program at Pacifica Graduate Institute. He teaches courses in archetypal psychology, culture, clinical practice, and research from a depth perspective. Dr. Coppin is a Marriage and Family Therapist and has been in practice for 25 years.

LIONEL CORBETT, M.D., a British-trained psychiatrist and Jungian analyst, is a core faculty member at Pacifica. He is author of The Religious Function of the Psyche.

WILLIAM DOTY, Ph.D., is professor and chair emeritus of religious studies at the University of Alabama/Tuscaloosa. He is editor of Mythosphere: A Journal for Image, Myth, and Symbol, and most recently author of the second, fully-revised, edition of Mythography: The Study of Myths and Rituals. He has been the Goodwin-Philpott Eminent Scholar at Auburn University, and has taught or lectured at a number of other colleges and universities here and in Europe.

CHRISTINE DOWNING, Ph.D., for almost twenty years chair of the Department of Religious Studies at San Diego State University, returned from what she thought was retirement to join the Core Faculty at Pacifica when it introduced its doctoral program in Mythological Studies. Author of nine books, including The Goddess and Myths and Mysteries of Same-Sex Love, she continues to be fascinated by the connections and fissures between the perspectives of depth psychology, Greek mythology, and feminism. When not in Santa Barbara, she lies amidst the quiet beauty if Orcas Island with her partner, poet and therapist River Malcolm, and their two dogs and two cats.

JENNIFER FREED, M.A., M.F.T., served as core faculty for Pacifica Graduate Institute for twelve years. She has over twenty years experience working with teens and their families as a private practice clinician. Jennifer was statewide director for a Youthworks project focusing on preventing high school drop outs, and she also directed the statewide Media Project for youth which focused on drug and crime prevention. Both projects received awards, and the Media Project appeared on Good Morning America and Hour Magazine. Jennifer is the Co-Director of The Academy of Healing Arts for teens (AHA!) and Executive Director of Astrological Counseling Seminars. She is also co- author of The Ultimate Personality Guide, a Putnam Tarcher release.

ROBERTO GAMBINI, Ph.D., is a Zurich-trained Jungian analyst in São Paulo, Brazil and the author of, most recently, Indian Mirror -- The Making of the Brazilian Soul.

HONOR GRIFFITH, Ph.D., is a Jungian-based psychotherapist in private practice in British Columbia. She also conducts workshops based on the principles of archetypal psychology for the general public. She has a Ph.D. in clinical psychology from Pacifica Graduate Institute, and has recently completed a fellowship at the University of Victoria's Centre for Studies in Religion and Society. Her review of Robert Romanyshyn's book, The Soul in Grief, has appeared in The San Francisco Jung Institute Library Journal.

JAMES HILLMAN, Ph.D., renowned author and psychoanalyst, is a leading scholar of Jungian and archetypal psychology. An innovative clinician and an inspiring teacher, James Hillman has led the movement in psychology which aims to broaden the focus of therapy to include in its care disorders of the world soul. Having retired from analytic practice after 40 years, Hillman now devotes his critical attention to concerns of contemporary culture. He is the author of the bestseller, The Soul's Code: In Search of Character and Calling and, more recently, The Force of Character and the Lasting Life.

NINA KELLY, Ph.D., received her Ph.D. in Mythological Studies from Pacifica Graduate Institute. She presently holds a clinical instructor position with Louisiana State University Health Sciences Medical School in New Orleans, Louisiana. Currently she is creating a course curriculum on the spiritual aspects of the terminally-ill patient.

AARON KIPNIS, Ph.D., is on the core faculty of Pacifica Graduate Institute. He is the author of Knights Without Armor, co-author of What Women and Men Really Want, and has written dozens of book chapters and articles on the psychology of men and boys. He is an international speaker and consultant who is currently aiding the development of boy-sensitive curricula and pedagogies at the Harvard School of Education and the California Youth Authority. His most recent book is: Angry Young Men: How Parents, Teachers, and Counselors can Help "Bad Boys" become Good Men (1999, Jossey-Bass).

HELENE SHULMAN LORENZ, Ph.D., is a core faculty member in the Depth Psychology Program at Pacifica Graduate Institute. She has a Ph.D. in philosophy from Tulane University and completed training as a Jungian analyst at the C.G. Jung Institute in Zurich. She is the author of Living at the Edge of Chaos: Complex Systems in Culture and Psyche, and has published several articles linking depth psychology with cultural studies. She has been active for many years in cultural movements for social justice and community development in Latin America and the United States, lecturing and giving workshops on the contributions depth psychology might make to understanding and transforming social conflict.

DAVID MILLER, Ph.D., is a faculty member at Pacifica and is the Watson-Ledden Professor of Religion at Syracuse University. His books include The New Polytheism: Rebirth of the Gods and Goddesses and Gods and Games: Toward a Theology of Play.

GINETTE PARIS, Ph.D., is the author of Pagan Meditations and Pagan Grace. She is a core faculty at Pacifica Graduate Institute and the Research Coordinator for the Mythological Studies Program.

ROBERT ROMANYSHYN, Ph.D., is a writer, teacher, and former psychotherapist. He is the author of three books and numerous articles in edited volumes, professional and literary journals and magazines. He has done television and radio work and is a featured speaker at various societies in the U.S. and abroad. His latest book is The Soul in Grief: Love, Death and Transformation. Currently he is learning magic and is at work on a book of poems called "Dark Light."

SHANTENA AUGUSTO SABBADINI, Ph.D., was a researcher in physics from 1968 to 1976, first in Milano, Italy, where he studied problems involved in the theoretical foundations of quantum mechanics, then in Santa Barbara, California, where he worked on the first identification of a black hole. In later years he founded a spiritual community and organic farm in Tuscany, Italy, traveled extensively and held various jobs. In the last ten years he has been a member of the staff of the Eranos Foundation, Ascona, Switzerland. Together with Dr. Rudolf Ritsema, he has produced the first Italian translation of the I Ching directly from the Chinese original.

BENJAMIN SELLS, Ph.D., is a psychoanalyst, syndicated columnist, lawyer and sailing captain. He is the author of The Soul of Law and Order in the Court. He has also edited and contributed to a new collection of essays entitled Working with Images: The Theoretical Base of Archetypal Psychology (Spring, 2000). He is owner/operator of Fairwind Sail Charters outside Chicago, Illinois. This article is part of a forthcoming book, The Essentials of Style.

BARBARA SHORE, Ph.D., is a depth psychologist practicing in Santa Monica, California whose work blends backgrounds of teaching, art, counseling, and mythology. She is a doctoral graduate of Pacifica's Mythology Program where she is currently teaching as an adjunct faculty member. Additionally, she is working on a book, tentatively titled Pseudoinnocence: An Invitation to Murder.

GLEN SLATER, PhD, is a member of the core faculty at Pacifica Graduate Institute. He has published articles in the Spring and Salt journals and is a regular essayist on psyche and film for Zion's Herald.

DENNIS PATRICK SLATTERY, Ph.D., is a core faculty member at Pacifica Graduate Institute. He is the author of over 150 articles and book reviews as well as The Idiot: Dostoevsky's Fantastic Prince (Peter Lang, 1984); editor and contributor of a collection of essays on William Faulkner and Modern Critical Theory (New Orleans Review, 1983); The Wounded Body: Remembering the Markings of Flesh (SUNY Press, 2000), editor with Lionel Corbett of Depth Psychology: Meditations in the Field (Daimon-Verlag, 2001); Casting the Shadows: Selected Poems (Morris Publishing, 2001). He has with Charles Asher, written a novel, Simon's Crossing. Currently he is writing The World is Too Much With Us: Memoirs of a Monastic Pilgrimage on his experiences staying at 12 retreat centers and monasteries in the western half of the United States.

SUZAN STILL, M.A., is a painter, sculptor, poet, and performing artist. As an instructor of creative writing at a California men's prison, she has brought her interest in depth psychology to bear both on prison reform and on the effects of creativity upon criminality.

JOANNE H. STROUD, Ph.D., a Founding Fellow of the Dallas Institute of Humanities and Culture, is presently Director of Publications and faculty member there. She is Editor of the Gaston Bachelard translations on imagination. Her latest book, The Bonding of Will and Desire, was published by Continuum Press in 1994.

ORION TATE is an artist and award winning graphic designer living in New York City. He holds a BA from Vassar College in Film Studies. He is currently employed as Art Director for the New York creative studio, Heavy Industry.

MARY WATKINS, Ph.D., is the Coordinator of Community and Ecological Fieldwork and Research in the Depth Psychology Doctoral Program at Pacifica Graduate Institute. She is the author of Waking Dreams, Invisible Guests: The Development of Imaginal Dialogues, the co-author of Talking With Young Children About Adoption, a co-editor of "Psychology and the Promotion of Peace" (Journal of Social Issues, 44, 2), and essays on the confluence of liberation psychology and depth psychology. She has worked as a clinical psychologist with adults and children, and has also worked with small and large groups around issues of peace, envisioning the future, diversity, vocation, and social justice.

Index